Karl Barth
and the Theology
of the Lord's Supper

Issues in Systematic Theology

Paul D. Molnar
General Editor

Vol. 1

PETER LANG
New York • Washington, D.C./Baltimore
Bern • Frankfurt am Main • Berlin • Vienna • Paris

Paul D. Molnar

Karl Barth and the Theology of the Lord's Supper

A Systematic Investigation

PETER LANG
New York • Washington, D.C./Baltimore
Bern • Frankfurt am Main • Berlin • Vienna • Paris

Library of Congress Cataloging-in-Publication Data

Molnar, Paul D.
Karl Barth and the theology of the Lord's Supper:
a systematic investigation/Paul D. Molnar.
p. cm. — (Issues in systematic theology; vol. 1)
Includes bibliographical references and index.
1. Lord's Supper—History—20th century. 2. Sacraments—History of
doctrines—20th century. 3. Barth, Karl, 1886–1968—Contributions in
doctrine of the Lord's Supper. 4. Barth, Karl, 1886–1968—Contributions in
doctrine of the sacraments. 5. Reformed Church—Doctrines—History—
20th century. I. Title. II. Series.
BV823.M58   234'.163'092—dc20   95-13780
ISBN 0-8204-2825-6
ISSN 1081-9479

Die Deutsche Bibliothek-CIP-Einheitsaufnahme

Molnar, Paul D.:
Karl Barth and the theology of the Lord's supper: a systematic investigation/
Paul D. Molnar. –New York; Washington, D.C./Baltimore; Bern; Frankfurt am
Main; Berlin; Vienna; Paris: Lang.
(Issues in systematic theology; Vol. 1)
ISBN 0-8204-2825-6
NE: GT

Cover design by James F. Brisson.

The paper in this book meets the guidelines for permanence and durability
of the Committee on Production Guidelines for Book Longevity
of the Council of Library Resources.

© 1996 Peter Lang Publishing, Inc., New York

Printed in the United States of America.

Contents

Preface ix

Acknowledgments xi

Part One: The Lord's Supper as the Work of the Holy Spirit 1

I The Analogy of Faith: Sacraments and the Doctrine of God 3
   Analogy 5
   God and Creatures: Essentially Distinct in Communion 7
   Parity 7
   Disparity 8
   Synthesis 11

II Grace and the Knowledge of God: Phenomenological
    and Christological Implications For the Sacrament 20
    Grace 20
    Symbol and Mediated Knowledge: Implications for
    Phenomenology and Christology 27
    Implications for Grace and Sacrament 35

III Transcendence and Immanence: Christological
     and Sacramental Applications 51
     Divine/Human Possibility 51
     Christ and Christians: Eucharistic Implications 52
     Ebionite—Docetic Christology 53
     Secularization and Sacralization 58
     Christomonism and Anthropomonism 71

IV Resurrection, The Trinity, Barth and More Recent Theology 87
    Resurrection—God's Act as Self-Grounded 87
    Implications for Phenomenology of Personal Presence:
    Symbolic Views 88
    Barth's view of God's Action 93
    Moltmann's View 94
    Pannenberg's View 96
    Küng's View 97
    Rahner's View 98
    Implications of Barth's View of the Power of the Resurrection as
    God's Act 100
    Pledge and Promise 105
    Implications for Revelation 106
    Action of the Triune God/Event 109
    Holy Spirit 111

**V The Relationship Between the Doctrine of God
and the Lord's Supper** 129
Prayer 130
Relation of Immanent and Economic Trinity 130
Rahner's Axiom of Identity 131
Implications For Understanding the Lord's Supper 136
Divine/Human Freedom 146

Part Two: The Lord's Supper as the Work of Creatures 153

VI The Basis of the Lord's Supper as the Work of Creatures 155
Possibility and Limitation of the Lord's Supper 157
Role of the Created Elements 158
Analogia Fidei—Christology 160
Promise/Command 165
Sacramental Implications of Oneness with Christ 166
Lex Orandi/Lex Credendi 168
Sin 171
Rejection of Ex Opere Operato 173

VII The Goal of the Lord's Supper as the Work of Creatures 185
Obedience, Human Freedom, and More Recent Theology 186
Pentecost and Human Action 193

VIII The Meaning of the Lord's Supper as the Work of Creatures 210
Union of the *Analogia Fidei* and the Event of the Lord's Supper 213
Absolute Basis and Goal of the Lord's Supper 215
Incarnation 215
Experience and the Knowledge of God 217
Meaning of the Lord's Supper as a Human Act 222
Holiness 222
Sacrament 225
Event 226
Rejection of Term Sacrament 227
Rejection of Monism, Dualism, Synthesis 231
Assessment of Barth's View of Sacrament 233

**IX The Significance of the Lord's Supper as the Work of
Creatures** 249
Valid Sacrament 250
Divine/Human Action—*Analogia Fidei* 251
Resurrection and Knowledge of Christ 252
Real Presence 255

Doctrine of God (*Analogia Fidei*)/ Eucharistic Event   257
Necessity of Faith   259
Omnipresence/Real Presence   261
Christ and Church   262
"At the Right Hand of the Father"   263
Eschatology   266

X   **Transubstantiation: Occasion for Unity and/or Dialogue?**   278
Necessity of Faith   285
Eucharistia   287
Prospects for Rapprochement   289
Critical Discussions   292
   Rahner, Barth, and Unity   292
   Docetic Concerns   295
   Zwinglianism   299
   Water Baptism—Baptism in the Spirit: Gnostic Dualism?   303

Selected Bibliography   314

Index of Subjects   325

Index of Names   332

Preface

The purpose of this book is to present the implications of Karl Barth's doctrine of God for his view of the sacrament by analyzing the Lord's Supper. By exploring his Christology and ecclesiology we hope to show that sacramental theology can be properly evaluated only within the context of a clear doctrine of God. Hence, this systematic theology seeks to illustrate what can and cannot be said about sacraments and sacramental action if faith and Christ's uniqueness are taken into account. It is hoped that this will provide a foundation for discussing such traditional notions as transubstantiation, *ex opere operato*, and *ex opere operantis* which Barth rejected. By demonstrating systematically how Barth's insights concerning sacraments developed from his views about the possibilities and limitations of human knowledge of God, we hope to trace the disagreements between Reformed and Roman Catholic theology to trinitarian and christological questions and ultimately to their foundation in the biblical revelation itself. It is hoped that this will enable us to evaluate Barth's "later" view of the sacrament.

In order to accomplish this we shall analyze Barth's conceptions of God, revelation, grace, and sacramental causality showing how these various elements cohere in Barth's theology; i.e., a perception of the God of the Bible necessitates a very definite possibility and limitation when describing the God who is present at the celebration of the Eucharist. To clarify his views it will be necessary at times to compare them with the convictions of other contemporary and more classical theologians. It will be suggested that Barth's conception of God's freedom, when rightly understood, might advance ecumenically a theological understanding of the problems involved in explaining eucharistic real presence today together with possible solutions; this may well prove to be agreeable in this age when trinitarian theology has received the attention it deserves as pointing to the foundation of both theology and practice within the church. Barth, of course, is famous for having re-orientated twentieth-century theology on this dogmatic foundation, and it has clear implications for his understanding of the sacrament. While this is principally a presentation and development of Barth's understanding of the Lord's Supper, which he did not live to write but which he suggested could be gleaned from his previous work, it is also a systematic attempt to see that precise thinking about God and sacramental signs go together. Thus, while many modern sacramental theologians feel very comfortable with a *symbolic* explanation of the working of the sacraments, it is important for scholars to see why Barth's thinking would lead him to say that such a view compromises God's freedom in himself and in relation to history. The deeper question then as to which idea of God's freedom is more adequate to the biblical revelation, would also have to be addressed in this context.

It is my intention to show that if there is to be serious dialogue about sacramental practice today, scholars must realize that the problem here stems from the way the possibilities and limitations of human knowledge of God are conceived. This is often misunderstood or ignored by contemporary theologians. Hence, Barth's insights and those of others at times are arbitrarily harmonized (obscuring the real problems which must be faced) or it may be assumed that theologians cannot agree simply because they are being faithful to their heritage. Both of these alternatives fail to address the problem of how we know the ultimate norm for understanding God, revelation, faith, and grace. This is what I hope to point out and to develop systematically in this work. If successful then a foundation shall have been set for discussion that would go beyond partisanship and press on toward the heart of the question of how and why Protestant (especially Reformed) and Catholic theologians understand the relationship between the doctrine of God and the Eucharist as they do.

Protestants and Catholics in particular have shown a renewed interest in Barth's theology in recent years, though this has not been and should not be an uncritical concern. It is hoped that this work, which will develop Barth's view of the role of the Holy Spirit, the elements (bread and wine) and the role of the creature in connection with the sacrament of the Lord's Supper, will have historical and systematic appeal on a scholarly level. Since much material that has been written on liturgy and sacraments lacks an objective systematic theological foundation, this book will be useful in providing such a foundation. Further, it may have ecumenical significance and could perhaps advance the contemporary theologian's understanding of how God relates with us in ways that do not destroy his being as God or our being as sinful creatures, who are really related to God by God's own action.

The argument presented here follows the structure of Barth's own approach since it moves from God to the human action in the sacrament instead of the other way around. One could of course begin with what Barth would have considered to be good eucharistic practice and then show why that practice actually presumes his trinitarian and christological position. But my goal here is to emphasize that the Lord's Supper derives its meaning from God himself through the analogy of faith. This necessarily involves only a limited discussion of eucharistic practice.

Also, just as Barth clarified his theology by contrasting it with opposing views, this book explores what other theologians say about the possibilities and limitations of our knowledge of God and of sacramental practice toward that same end. Hence, this is not an exhaustive study of these other theological views but an attempt to clarify some important implications of Barth's theology today.

ACKNOWLEDGMENTS

I would like to thank the late Rev. George Litch Knight, who was pastor of the Lafayette Avenue Presbyterian Church in Brooklyn, New York, for thirty one years, for his consistent support and encouragement. I am also grateful to James O. Duke for reading an earlier version of this manuscript and for offering encouragement and advice along the way. In addition, I am indebted to James J. Buckley for reading the manuscript and offering valuable and important advice. I also wish to thank St. John's University for providing me with a semester's research leave and with a summer grant in order to finish this project. Another thank you is due to John J. McCormick who read the work through several redactions and made important suggestions at each stage. A special thank you is reserved for Heidi Burns for her extra attention to detail, for going beyond what would normally be expected of an editor, and for her assistance and support. But, of course, the sole responsibility for any errors resides with the author.

Also, I am grateful for permission to reprint material previously published by Darton, Longman & Todd Ltd. (*Theological Investigations, Vol. IV: More Recent Writings* by Karl Rahner, translated by Kevin Smith. A translation of *Schriften zur Theologie, IV,* published by Verlagsanstalt. Benziger & Co. A.G., Einsiedeln. Translation © Darton, Longmann & Todd Ltd. (London) 1966 and 1974. Reprinted by permission of The CROSSROAD Publishing Co., New York.); Epworth Press (Geoffrey Wainwright, *Doxology: The Praise of God in Worship, Doctrine and Life.* New York: Oxford University Press, 1980. Reprinted by permission of the publishers. All rights reserved); Wm. B. Eerdmans Publishing Co. (Karl Barth, *The Christian Life, C.D. 4, 4, Lecture Fragments.* Translated by Geoffrey W. Bromiley. Grand Rapids: Wm. B. Eerdmans Publishing Company, 1981. Reprinted by permission of the publishers. All rights reserved.); Wm. B. Eerdmans Publishing Company. (*Karl Barth Letters 1961-1968.* Edited by Jürgen Fangemeier and Hinrich Stoevesandt. Translated and edited by Geoffrey W. Bromiley. Grand Rapids: Wm. B. Eerdmans Publishing Company, 1981. Reprinted by permission of the publisher. All rights reserved); SCM Press, Ltd (EXCERPTS from *THE WAY OF JESUS CHRIST: CHRISTOLOGY IN MESSIANIC DIMENSIONS* by JÜRGEN MOLTMANN. English translation copyright © 1990 by Margaret Kohl. Reprinted by permission of HarperCollins Publishers, Inc.); T & T Clark Ltd (Karl Barth, *Church Dogmatics*, 4 vols. in 13 pts. Edinburgh: T & T Clark Ltd Publishers, 1958-81. Reprinted by permission of the publisher. All rights reserved); T & T Clark Ltd (Paul D. Molnar, *The Function of the Immanent Trinity in the Theology of Karl Barth: Implications for Today,* in *Scottish Journal of Theology,* vol. 42, 1989. Reprinted by permission of the publisher. All rights reserved); The Thomist, (*Christology from Above and Below,* by Edward Krasevac, O.P., vol. 51, 1987. Reprinted by permission of the publisher. All rights reserved); Westminster John Knox Press (From *REDISCOVERING THE LORD'S SUPPER* by Markus Barth. Used by permission of Westminster John Knox Press.)

Part One

The Lord's Supper as the Work
of the Holy Spirit

I

The Analogy of Faith: Sacraments and the Doctrine of God

Although Barth never lived to complete his intended treatment of the Lord's Supper as part of the doctrine of reconciliation, there is enough material in the rest of the *Church Dogmatics* from which to grasp his position on the subject. Indeed Barth's "radically new" view of the concept sacrament proposed in Volume 4, Part 4 (Fragment) of the *Church Dogmatics*, according to his own estimation, formed the basis upon which " . . . intelligent readers may deduce . . . how I would finally have presented the doctrine of the Lord's Supper."[1]

It would be misleading, to say the least, to ignore Barth's prior treatment of sacrament, especially in the doctrine of the Word of God, at the beginning of the *Church Dogmatics*, and in his doctrine of God where the notion of "sacramental reality" played an important role in his view of analogy. Although his view of the term sacrament certainly did change, the reason for the change itself was dictated by his basic theological presuppositions which prevailed throughout the *Church Dogmatics*.[2] In other words, Barth later rejected the term sacrament in favor of his theological understanding of the relationship between divine and human being and action. He believed the term historically came to mean that divinity was either noetically or ontically inherent in the human activity of the church.

Barth's primary theological concern always was to demonstrate God's freedom from and freedom for his creatures. Unless God could be distinguished clearly from the visible church in its sacramental action, the Holy Spirit could be confused with and controlled by the church's sacramental or moral actions. Therefore, Barth rejected two parallel expressions of this thinking in his ecclesiology, i.e., *sacramentalism* and *moralism* in order to advance his grasp of the *union* and *distinction* between the triune God and us. Since this rejection is ultimately shaped by Barth's *analogia fidei*, it is hoped that an understanding of what he means here will lead to a better preliminary understanding of his view of the analogy of faith.

To comprehend the nature of the church's holiness without identifying, separating, or synthesizing the church's historical existence with the grace of God, Barth consistently sought to show that the community could only depend continually upon the *miracle* of God's free intervention into human history for its infallibility. This in itself means there is no facile solution to the questions of where the true church is to be found and who actually is saved. Indeed for Barth these questions continuously confront Christians pointing them to their total dependence on God.

Sacramentalism tries to solve this need for dependence on God by identifying true holiness with the church's sacramental action. Thus, for example, in Barth's view of baptism, sacramentalism "points to baptism as the factor by which a man is placed in the *communio sanctorum* and on the basis of which he is a true member of it."[3] Accordingly, one receives the Holy Spirit, becomes holy, and is a true believer by the "fact that he is baptised . . . The number of true Christians is therefore the number of the baptised. How can it be otherwise when baptism has this power *ex opere operato*?"[4] Barth continued, "We are not concerned for the moment whether this is good baptismal teaching. Nor are we considering the absurd result that in this way (*via* infant baptism) whole populations of whole countries have automatically been made and can automatically be made the holy community."[5] Rather, the key problem with this idea is that "the question of the gathering of the community by the Lord himself is mischievously evaded"[6] because the spiritual mystery of the community's existence as the body of Christ is "replaced and crowded out by an arrogantly invented sacramental mystery."[7] Hence, Barth identified and rejected as sacramentalism any suggestion at all that the community (church) can *make itself* holy or augment itself by means of this or any other human action. This kind of implication and the consequent attempts to describe and to build community actually obscure the real action of the Holy Spirit which is the true source and power of the upbuilding of the community as the body of Christ.[8] Of course we shall ask at the proper place whether or not it is really necessary to hold Barth's radically new view of the term sacrament in order to avoid sacramentalism. We shall also have to explore some contemporary criticisms of Barth's theology of ministry and of other aspects of his theology later in this book.[9]

But now it is important to note that Barth also believed that it was a constant temptation on the part of theologians to correct this sacramentalism with what he called moralism. Moralism attempts to solve the problem of how to define the church's holiness by ascribing the holiness of Christians to certain attitudes and actions which distinguish them from others. Examples of such distinguishing actions might be the regularity of attendance at Sunday worship, a conversion experience, a certain usual or unusual life style or a habit of Christian living.[10] But this solution presumes that in order to know of this holiness "some law or standard by which the presence of these distinguishing marks of Christianity can be established."[11] If, however, it is really the Holy Spirit who decides in this matter, then there actually is no law by which we can decide who has or has not the Holy Spirit—who is a believer or an unbeliever. We have no law by which we can determine who belongs to the *communio sanctorum*. Therefore, for Barth, the deciding factor in the church's authenticity is God alone in the action of his Spirit. This is why the church's truth and holiness cannot be ascribed either to a sacramental *opus operatum*, to a moral or religious *opus operantis,* or to a combination of the two. In Barth's eyes all of these explanations evade the fact that the church is constantly dependent upon the action of the Holy Spirit for its existence. Accordingly, the church cannot control either its being in Christ or the action of the Holy Spirit.

Barth's rejection of this thinking coincided with his objections to Schleiermacher and Ritschl. Both theologians believed that they could think theologically by using a Cartesian method, i.e., by assuming that revelation was somehow grounded in one's experience. Barth rejected Cartesian thinking and moralism because he believed that any kind of identification of Creator and creature denies both God's transcendence and his real presence in history in his Word and Spirit.[12] The reason why Barth took this position stems from his definition of the *analogia fidei.*

It is by now apparent that our primary concern in this work is not to trace the development of the *term* sacrament in Barth's theology. Instead we intend to explore Barth's theological presentation of the relationship between divine and human being as revealed in Christ in order to see what this means for understanding the Lord's Supper. Later we shall ask and answer the question: to what extent is Barth's theology of the Lord's Supper the same as in his previous writings? For now, it is important to see that his view of analogy and his rejection of sacramentalism and moralism follow from his own theological method of moving from faith to understanding rather than vice versa. This method itself is dictated by the unique object of inquiry, i.e., the mystery of Christ himself.

Analogy

A brief introductory outline of Barth's view of analogy will illustrate how theological certainty can be achieved to the extent that revelation is and remains the starting point and norm for one's definition of God and creatures; only such an approach can avoid the pitfalls of sacramentalism and moralism. In a way, this discussion centers on the general relation between philosophy and theology. All attempts by natural theology to know God actually create uncertainty here by grounding their knowledge of God in something other than God's own action *ad extra*; in that way they demonstrate the need for faith, grace, and revelation in order to see the true similarity between divine and human reality established and maintained with unshakable certitude by God alone.

Barth's view of the *analogia fidei*, which held that there were no analogies which were true in themselves—since their truth is grounded in God's own action *ad extra*—led him to reject three views of analogy in his doctrine of God, i.e., analogy based on parity, disparity, and synthesis. In his Christology, ecclesiology, and in relation to the sacrament Barth applied his insight that analogies could become true only as God himself acted in specific historical events to disclose himself.

For Barth any question as to the nature and meaning of analogy or of the sacrament of the Lord's Supper could not be posed independently of the question of God. To do so, by pursuing a phenomenology of being or symbols for instance, would be to call God's existence into question by a reality distinct from him and dependent upon him. This very procedure abstracts from faith which, as knowledge of the truth, realizes that only God himself can raise questions in this vein. In Barth's eyes, the error of natural theology, and of all analogies based upon a general concept of being consists in this "independent" investigation of truth.[13] Any such conviction fails to take into account the fact that the reality of God itself is the answer to the question of God; it does not allow the reality of God, which transcends all human ideas and experiences, to precede and determine its truth character.[14] Once this reversal occurs, Barth's entire theology, which always intended to move from faith to understanding and never from understanding to faith, is misunderstood. It is this primacy of divine in relation to human being and activity which is the determining factor in Barth's view of sacrament, of Christ, of the church, and of human knowledge of God. And it is precisely this point which is most criticized and least understood not only in the discussion between Reformed and Roman Catholic theology[15] but also, in varying degrees, among some of Barth's avowed supporters such as Jürgen Moltmann, Wolfhart Pannenberg, and Eberhard Jüngel.

Colin Gunton calls attention to this difficulty by noting that Barth's understanding of God's relation with the world was "based on his doctrine of the Trinity," and was not, as von Balthasar supposed "brought to it in order to support it."[16] In Gunton's eyes, the consequences of this kind of thinking "have contributed to what has now become a received opinion about Barth."[17] In the view of John Bowden the "treacherous character of Barth's theological edifice" consists in the fact that his "analogy of faith" has "no obvious building controls."[18] In fact the building control for his doctrine is the trinitarian self-revelation.

Therefore, Barth's concept of analogy sets the possibilities and limitations which govern both human knowing enclosed in the mystery of the Trinity,[19] and human knowledge of and action in the Lord's Supper. In this way faith (more accurately, the object of faith) determines the relationship between Barth's

doctrine of God and his theology of the Lord's Supper. We hope to clarify this
in connection with the sacrament by showing how this relates to Barth's doctrine
of God. His concept of analogy leads to his definition of the sacrament as an
event in which human action corresponds faithfully to God's prior action in his
Word and Spirit.

God and Creatures: Essentially Distinct in Communion

In his doctrine of God, Barth's concept of analogy stressed that human
knowledge can be nothing more or less than a consistent representation of the
being and activity of God.[20] Only in that way can we know the real possibility
and limitation of human knowledge of God. This means that in order to speak
clearly of communion between God and creatures established by God *alone*,
creatures can neither be merged essentially into God nor God into creatures. This
is why analogies which intend to describe God on the basis of parity, disparity,
or synthesis are impossible. We cannot speak intelligibly of God, who by nature
is inaccessible to human insight, by examining human insight or the products of
human insight, i.e., the world of metaphysical ideas. Any such attempt would
assume that it could establish the possibility of God's revelation by grounding
God's existence in its ontology, whether conceived on the basis of parity between
divine and human being, disparity, or synthesis. The basic error here consists in
the fact that the creature—a reality distinct from God—is thought to be able to
reveal what only God can reveal, i.e., the being and nature of the one who exists
independently as the creator and Lord. In this way the creature becomes Lord,
in the sense that he or she can disclose what, according to faith only God can
unveil. The key error of this reasoning, in Barth's eyes, consists in its abstraction
from faith at the outset; in this way both grace and revelation are overlooked as
well. We must give precision to Barth's *analogia fidei* here.

Parity

According to his theory of knowledge, the metaphysical concept of parity
between divine and human being mistakenly presumes that creator and creatures
arise out of a common metaphysical essence. But if this is the case there is no
way to avoid explaining the relationship between God and creatures monistically.
Consequently, creation would be conceived as essential to and necessary for God
as would the incarnation and the existence of the church; thus conceived, the
relationship between God and creatures is reversible. As creatures, Christ, and
the church arise out of the essence of God, so too would the sacrament. This
kind of thinking would lead to a very different understanding of the Lord's

Supper than one which is dictated by the object of faith; it could of course lead quite logically to a form of sacramentalism or of moralism as defined above.

In expounding the content of faith, in this case, the *creatio ex nihilo*, Barth decisively rejected monism as a viable way of knowing God; it fails to note God's sovereign existence in relation to what God is *not* and confuses creator and creature. We shall see that Barth consistently maintained an anti-monistic position in his theology by insisting, in his doctrine of God, that the immanent and economic Trinity is not identical and in his Christology that the divinity and humanity of Christ could not be confused. In his ecclesiology Barth maintained this same position by insisting that the church is not identical with Christ and his Spirit but can only attest his presence in its obedient human actions.

His theology reflects this insight theoretically and practically by not reversing creator and creature, the Logos and the man Jesus, and by not reversing the body of Christ with its heavenly head. Barth based this insight on faith, grace, and revelation and not on understanding, nature, and reason. Similarly, as we shall see, Barth defined the sacrament, seeking to avoid a monistic explanation of the Lord's Supper. For that reason there is no reversing human and divine action. In faith, this simple fact is seen as both the possibility and limitation of the church's sacramental action. Indeed thinking which does not respect this fact may lead to the idea that, since God transcends all our language, we can freely invent analogies based upon a variety of experiences rather than just one particular experience or set of experiences.[21] In Barth's mind G. W. Leibniz personified the attempt to speak about the relationship between divinity and humanity on the basis of a concept of parity.[22]

Disparity

In his theory of knowledge Barth also maintained that analogies which claim to recognize the disparity between divine and human being apart from revelation cannot truly describe God. Since the possibility of God's revelation cannot be grounded in an ontology conceived on the basis of parity, it cannot be grounded in an ontology conceived on the basis of disparity. Such an assumption mistakenly presumes that God and creatures arise out of disproportionate metaphysical essences, conceivable to creatures, apart from revelation. But if this is the case there is no way to avoid explaining the relationship between God and creatures dualistically. This means that God and creatures are and remain totally apart and that communion between them can never mean anything more than stating the infinite distance between human conceptuality and the divine being. Thus, no human view or action corresponds to the reality of God since that reality exists far beyond the sphere of human views and concepts possible to creatures. At best, God might be considered the highest conceivable idea possible to creatures. Even then, we have no way of knowing God's actual being;[23] if conceived in this way, the relationship between creator and creatures is, at best, a superfluous metaphor since there is no real and actual communion between God *in se* and humanity *in se*. They are infinitely disparate entities. Nominalism exemplified this kind of thinking for Barth.

Barth therefore argued for the fact that the multiplicity of the divine perfections (attributes) which we experience in revelation are not merely assumed by God for the sake of revelation (as a modalism might assume) but actually "constitute His own eternal glory."[24] God is neither simply three gods nor is God one without his three modes of being in and through which we know God's oneness and his perfections. Hence God's simplicity is not in conflict with the multiplicity of his perfections but rather confirms his unique being as the one who loves in freedom precisely in and through them. This thinking is contradicted by nominalism in its extreme and moderate forms.

> The extreme expression of it is seen in the strict nominalistic thesis as represented by Eunomius in antiquity and William of Occam and Gabriel Biel in the Middle Ages. According to this all individual and distinct statements about the being of God have no other value than that of purely subjective ideas and descriptions (*conceptus, nomina*) to which there is no corresponding reality in God, who is pure simplicity. According to Eunomius God is in fact to be characterised only as *nuda essentia*. Schleiermacher too is probably to be understood in the sense of this extreme opposition . . .[25]

For Barth there have been many representatives of the more moderate form of nominalism which is traceable to the view of John of Damascus that "God is nameless, but in His mercy allows Himself to be named, as befits our need."[26] These include Calvin, Thomas Aquinas, C. I. Nitzsch, and others. According to Barth there is a "nominalistic background and tendency" to their opinions insofar as each theologian leaves open the possibility that God's simplicity exists first as a *nuda essentia* which is and remains unknowable and that all other knowledge of God follows from this. This allowed the idea of the divine simplicity to be defined by the general idea of "pure being" taken from Stoicism or Neo-Platonism rather than from the doctrine of the Trinity.[27] This very fact represented the dualism Barth was seeking to overcome by understanding God as simultaneously one and three.

In opposing nominalism Barth consistently rejected this kind of dualism. Thomas Torrance has traced dualisms of this kind to what he calls "the

Augustinian, Cartesian and Newtonian dualism built into the general framework
of Western thought" which tends to damage and even to sever "the ontological
bond between Jesus Christ and God the Father."[28] Thinking in *abstractive formal
relations* and in *external relations* has led to what Torrance calls the Latin Heresy
or the attempt to think about the reality of God in abstraction from God's own act
of reconciliation and redemption in Christ and the Spirit. Its roots can be traced
"to a form of linguistic and conceptual dualism that prevailed in Patristic and
Mediaeval Latin theology."[29] Thus, for example, Arius operated with an
epistemological and cosmological dualism which kept God from any direct
interaction with the world because he conceived Christ's sonship as external to
God by arguing that Jesus participated in the Godhead only by grace and not by
nature.

As Torrance makes clear and as we shall see in his own writing, Barth
rejected any dualistic understanding of God and creatures for the same reason that
he rejected a monistic understanding. From faith, by grace, and through
revelation we know that, although God was not merged essentially into creatures,
he nevertheless willed to have communion with them, and in fact did so and does
so in Christ himself.

> The choice or election of God is basically and properly God's decision that
> as described in Jn. 1:1-2 the Word which is 'the same,' and is called
> Jesus, should really be in the beginning, with Himself like Himself, one
> with Himself in His deity. And for this reason it is *per se* an election of
> grace . . . God would not be God . . . if this had to be so. The eternal
> God was not under an obligation to man to be in Himself the God whose
> nature and property it is to bear this name. That He is, in fact, such a
> God is grace, something which is not merited by man but can only be
> given to him. And that God is gracious, that in assuming this name He
> gives Himself to the man who has not merited it, is His election, His free
> decree. It is the divine election of grace . . . Without any obligation, God
> has put Himself under an obligation to man, willing that that should be so
> which according to Jn. 1:1-2 actually is so.[30]

The fact of Christ then is the repudiation of all dualistic, monistic, and synthetic
understandings of the creator and creature relationship. Barth consistently
maintained this anti-dualistic position in his doctrine of God, Christology, and
ecclesiology by insisting that, although the immanent and economic Trinity on the
one hand and the divinity and humanity of Christ on the other are not identical,
they cannot be separated either. We cannot know the inner divine *esse* without
the *oikonomia*. God, however, remains *freely* bound to the *oikonomia*. For that

reason, Barth maintained that the immanent Trinity and the eternal Logos absolutely precede and never follow human being and action (including the action of understanding). In his ecclesiology Barth maintained this position by insisting that, although the church, as the body of Christ, is not identical with its head, Christ himself, it cannot be understood without its head or apart from its head. Its *esse* is completely dependent upon God in his revelation and to that extent is grounded, not in itself but outside itself, in God. It is this precedence of divine in relation to human sacramental action, known in faith, which we shall use to explain Barth's view of the Lord's Supper.

Synthesis

Finally, in his theory of knowledge, Barth maintained that analogies developed on the basis of synthesis were wrong. Any such analogous attempt to know God would suppose that it could establish the *possibility* of God's revelation by grounding the existence of God in its ontology conceived on the basis of a synthesis of divine and human being. The error here is that a metaphysical concept of synthesis presupposes that God and creatures can be combined into a common metaphysical essence. Such a view is unable to distinguish between God and creatures because it has combined them either with each other or into some third thing, namely its synthesis. Thus conceived, the relationship between God and creatures is not only reversible as in a concept of parity, but is actually one and the same in the *form* of the synthesis.

Synthesis presumes that God can be identified with a reality other than himself; this would make Christ, the church, and the sacrament nothing more than the products of such a human synthesis. Then, the human action of the church becomes indistinguishable from God in his action in Christ or the church. Understanding the synthetic construct is all that is demanded to comprehend revelation in this context.

In this respect Barth likened Paul Tillich to Schleiermacher in his attempt to understand God's act of revelation as part of the general expression of human life as illustrated in the history of religions.[31] Paul F. Knitter, in part following Tillich's history of religion approach, carries this thinking to its logical conclusion by arguing for his "non-dualism" which is a form of panentheism which he claims can be understood under the synonym: incarnation.[32] Thus, for Knitter, the incarnation is a myth expressing the universal truth of a non-dualist identity between God and creatures.[33] In essence, Paul Knitter has reconstructed Christianity on the basis of the mysticism of Frithjof Shuon.[34] Christ therefore cannot be viewed as the only norm for theological truth; that norm is the God who can be discerned in the universal experience of religion which he presumes is embodied in and accurately represented by the non-dualist experience that "the soul *is* God, but at the same time one must also say that it is not."[35]

In a more serious vein, Jürgen Moltmann's attempt to reconceive the doctrines of the Trinity and of creation "panentheistically" ultimately leads him to a synthesis of reason and revelation, nature and grace, and creation and redemption.[36] Indeed he finally argues that "The trinitarian concept of creation integrates the elements of truth in monotheism and pantheism" by enabling us to "find an integrating view of God and nature which will draw them both into the same vista."[37] The very idea that God and nature can be viewed from within the same vista epitomizes the synthesis beyond the distinction between creator and creatures which Barth rejected.

In explaining the content of faith Barth decisively rejected synthesis (pantheism or panentheism) as a possible answer to the question of God.[38] Once, again, synthesis fails to note the fact that creator and creatures cannot be synthesized together, or under some higher, or third reality. God remains God and humans remain human in a relationship between God and creatures established by God. God is not synthesized with any reality distinct from himself. Barth consistently sought to avoid pantheism by insisting, in his doctrine of God and Christology, respectively, that the immanent and economic Trinity is distinct even in its union, and that the divinity and humanity of Christ are distinct even in their union. In his ecclesiology, Barth maintained this position by insisting that the church is distinct from Christ and his Spirit, even though it is in closest union with him by the power of his Word and Spirit.

Barth's theology reflects this insight by neither synthesizing creator and creatures nor synthesizing the Logos and the man Jesus into each other or some third reality (an incarnational principle perhaps) in his Christology. His ecclesiology does not combine the body of Christ with its heavenly head, or into some *tertium quid*. Barth asserted all of this on the basis of faith, grace, and revelation insisting he did not discover this for himself or from his metaphysics, but from God himself in his action *ad extra*. As this particular knowledge is in no way innate to creatures, even Christians, it cannot be known by general metaphysical analysis. That is why Barth's presentation of the sacrament reflects the absolute priority of divine in relation to human action. Only on the basis of the particular knowledge of God perceived in faith, by grace, and from God's own self-revelation is the actual relationship between Barth's doctrine of God and the sacrament of the Lord's Supper comprehensible.

As we consider the Lord's Supper, we shall see how Barth applied the *analogia fidei* developed in his doctrine of God. By maintaining that the basis, goal, and source of meaning of the church's sacramental action lie outside itself and in God alone, Barth sought to remain faithful to the insights developed in his doctrine of God, Christology, and ecclesiology. This particular basis and goal gives the church's action a very definite and limited meaning which neither confuses, separates, nor synthesizes divine and human activity.

One further preliminary remark is necessary. It is ironical to note that when theology is thought possible outside of scriptural faith as defined above, i.e., on the basis of analogies of parity, disparity, or synthesis, not only is the independent existence of God obscured, but so also is our distinctive human existence. The very phenomenon that is sought, namely, the rightful self-determination of creatures, literally cannot be found unless it is perceived as enclosed in the mystery of the Trinity. Even this cannot be known without faith. No general philosophy will keep to this possibility and limitation. As we shall see, this causes problems both in the doctrine of God and in sacramental theology.

This treatment of the Lord's Supper, while not exhaustive, will attempt to see how Barth worked out his view of the sacrament in *Church Dogmatics*, 4, 4, using the presuppositions developed in his doctrine of God. It is hoped that the systematic coherence of Barth's thought might provide useful insights toward a better understanding of eucharistic real presence. It is impossible to cross-reference every idea with those expressed in previous volumes of the *Church Dogmatics* since it would involve a needless rewriting of the *Church Dogmatics*. We shall therefore cross-reference where it appears necessary to see how Barth's view of the sacrament actually developed from his conception of analogy.

This analysis will begin by paralleling Barth's understanding of baptism as a work of God in his Spirit. It is on that basis and for that reason that baptism is a divine work which includes rather than excludes creatures in their self-determination.[39] Working in this fashion should clarify how Barth maintained the positive and negative aspects of the divine freedom which he initially developed in his doctrine of God.[40] Barth's method does not result from some abstract theoretical presupposition. Nor is it arbitrary and uncritical as some have suggested.[41] His purpose was to define clearly the relationship, fellowship, and communion *actually* established by God himself with us.[42] This is neither an idea nor an experience of communion; it is a genuine relationship established, maintained, and brought to completion by God himself—not the idea or experience of God, but the reality of the triune God.[43] Only in this way will the analogy of faith lead to a clear and consistent escape from the false solution to this problem offered by sacramentalism and moralism.

Notes

1. Karl Barth, *Church Dogmatics*, 4 vols. in 13 pts. Vol. 4, Pt. 4: *The Doctrine of Reconciliation. Fragment*, ed. G. W. Bromiley and T. F. Torrance, trans. G. W. Bromiley (Edinburgh: T. & T. Clark, 1969, hereafter abbreviated: C.D.), p. ix.

2. This is particularly important in connection with his analysis of human knowing in C.D. 2, 1, chapter five, pp. 3–254. Our analysis of the concepts of parity, disparity, and synthesis is based upon Barth's investigation in this chapter. This is especially pertinent to Barth's definition of analogy. As will be seen, this will serve as a basis for evaluating Barth's own "new view" later on. In Part Two we shall address T. F. Torrance's question of whether Barth had returned to an earlier dualism with this view, *Karl Barth: Biblical and Evangelical Theologian*, (Edinburgh: T. & T. Clark, 1990, hereafter abbreviated: *Karl Barth*), pp. 134f. and 138.

3. C.D. 4, 1, p. 695

4. Ibid., p. 695f. Barth considered the problems involved with this view in connection with infant baptism in C.D. 4, 4, pp. 169ff.

5. Ibid., p. 696. This thinking is a development of his position expressed in C.D. 1, 2, pp. 146ff. and 247ff.

6. Ibid.

7. Ibid. It is interesting to note that Markus Barth, *Rediscovering the Lord's Supper*, (Atlanta: John Knox Press, 1988), pp. 36ff., 69 and 99 takes a similar view by tying it to Paul's rejection of idolatry in 1 Cor. 11. Also interesting is Barth's own argument in *The Christian Life*, *Lecture Fragments* C.D. 4, 4, (Grand Rapids: William B. Eerdmans, 1981, hereafter abbreviated: *The Christian Life*), that thanksgiving (eucharistein) means giving thanks to God for his benefits. Thus it cannot focus on the benefits but "must also be an honoring of God for his own sake," (p. 87).

8. It may be noted in this context that Barth's rejection of this manner of thinking initially took shape in C.D. 1, 2, pp. 525ff. where he rejected a false supranaturalistic explanation of scriptural inspiration, i.e., one which identified the sovereign action of the Holy Spirit with the human action of the biblical authors. Here Barth could maintain that the human authors were fallible by insisting on God's sovereignty.

9. For example S. W. Sykes, editor, *Karl Barth: Centenary Essays*, (New York: Cambridge University Press, 1989), wonders whether Barth's theology "*concretely* acknowledges the sovereignty of Christ," p. 76. And Colin Gunton thinks that his "theology can take on a docetic air," p. 60.

10. C.D. 4, 1, p. 696.

11. Ibid.

12. See, e.g., C.D. 1, 1, pp. 195f. and C.D. 3, 1, pp. 350–63.

13. See, e.g., C.D. 2, 1, pp. 224–254.

14. On the importance of allowing God to *precede* and determine the truth here, see C.D. 2, 1, pp. 25, 27, 29f. Barth maintained this point throughout this volume. See also pp. 215 and esp. 305ff.

15. Cf., e.g., Grover Foley, "The Catholic Critics of Karl Barth In Outline and Analysis," in *Scottish Journal of Theology* 14, (1961): 136–55, hereafter abbreviated: *SJT*. Hans Urs von Balthasar, *The Theology of Karl Barth*, trans. John Drury (Garden City: Doubleday & Co., Inc., 1972), pp. 226 and 265 believed that the theologian could move from faith to understanding and from understanding back to faith without compromising the priority of faith, grace, and revelation and also saw harmony between his view and Barth's where there really was conflict (cf. Foley, p. 152).

16. Colin E. Gunton, *Becoming and Being: The Doctrine of God in Charles Hartshorne and Karl Barth*, (Oxford: Oxford University Press, 1978), p. 174.

17. Ibid., p. 175.

18. Ibid. Bowden cited in Gunton.

19. Because Barth maintained that the *terminus a quo* and the *terminus ad quem* of human knowledge and of sacramental action is God alone, he defined true knowledge as follows: "Knowledge of God is then an event enclosed in the bosom of the divine Trinity," C.D. 2, 1, p. 205. Therefore only God is the guarantee both here and in connection with the sacrament.

20. C.D. 2, 1, p. 32. It is important to note that this very insight leads to Barth's definition of revelation as a sacrament. "Revelation means the giving of signs. We can say quite simply that revelation means sacrament, i.e., the self–witness of God, the representation of His truth, and therefore of the truth in which He knows Himself, in the form of creaturely objectivity and therefore in a form which is adapted to our creaturely knowledge," C.D. 2, 1, p. 52. The substance of "sacramental reality" for Barth is "the existence of the human nature of Jesus Christ. *Gratia unionis*, i.e., on the ground of and through its union with the eternal Word of God, this creature is the supreme and outstanding work and sign of God," Ibid., p. 53. "Yet the sacramental reality . . . is not itself and as such identical either with revelation or with the real knowledge of God. It serves it, because God reveals Himself and is known. But it can also not serve it; it can even hinder and prevent it," Ibid., p. 55.

21. Paul F. Knitter basically takes this position in his book *No Other Name? A Critical Survey of Christian Attitudes Toward the World Religions* (New York: Orbis, 1985, hereafter abbreviated: *No Other Name?)* Cf. Paul D. Molnar "Some Dogmatic Consequences of Paul F. Knitter's Unitarian Theocentrism" in *The Thomist* 55 (1991): 449–95 for more on this. This is Anne Carr's solution to the problem of finding analogies for God in *Transforming Grace* (San Francisco: Harper and Row, 1988), p. 143. She writes: "The use of many images more clearly affirms the fully transcendent and incomprehensible reality of God while natural and cosmic images work to subvert not only sexism but the related homocentrism of the Christian attitudes that have supported technological exploitation of earth, land, sea and air." The problem with this reasoning is that the source for our knowledge of God and of our revision of the concept of God is not God's self-revelation but the multiplicity of images which can be used to make people feel included. Hence the concept of God "must be relativized by the use of many other images for God. These would include female symbols . . . " p. 141. Gordon D. Kaufman, e.g., explicitly rejects starting theology with revelation as authoritarian in *Theology For a Nuclear Age* (Philadelphia: The Westminster Press, 1985, hereafter abbreviated: *TNA*), p. 18. In *God, The Problem* (Cambridge: Harvard University Press, 1972) Kaufman writes: "theological method can no longer be formulated on the *basis* of God's revelation as the entire neo-orthodox generation had supposed: it must now explore, criticize, and reconstruct or reconfirm that basis itself . . . theology . . . must be able to justify what it does and how it does it before the bar of ordinary human reason," p. 24. For similar ideas see Gordon D. Kaufman *The Theological Imagination* (Philadelphia: The Westminster Press, 1981, hereafter abbreviated: *T.I.*), pp. 46 and 32. In spite of his rejection of God as an unknowable X (*T.I.*, p. 45) this leads Kaufman to make various theological perspectives and frameworks his norm for truth insofar as they enable human beings to relativize and humanize society. This reflects Kaufman's complete reduction of theological truth to the social functioning of ideas (e.g., *TNA*, p. 57). Among other things, and in spite of his theoretical rejection of pantheism, this leads him to the basic pantheism intrinsic to all views of emergent evolution (e.g., *TNA*, pp. 42–4) and to a denial of Christ's actual uniqueness by insisting that "in the biological and historico-cultural terms with which we now conceive human existence, no individual person can have this sort of absolute significance (i.e., as savior)," p. 56.

22. C.D. 1, 2, pp. 6–7. Cf. also Karl Barth, *Protestant Theology in the Nineteenth Century: Its Background and History* (Valley Forge: Judson Press, 1973, hereafter abbreviated: *Protestant Theology*). Barth had Leibniz in mind when he accurately depicted eighteenth century thinking as the human attempt to

absolutize the human spirit by raising and answering all questions, including the Christian question: "This was the absolutism also inherent in his inner attitude to life; he assumed it to be self-evident that in taking himself to account, and himself answering the account and then acting in obedience to it he was also showing the existence of God . . ." (Ibid., p. 76). "The purest form to which this new humanism rose already is in the early eighteenth century—its transfigured form, so to speak—was embodied in the personality and philosophy of Gottfried Wilhelm Leibnitz [*sic*]," Ibid., p. 77. Barth wondered whether Leibniz' notion of the monad and the emanationism implied therein did not "represent Stoicism in its most sublime form . . . a Stoicism which is a triumph of humanism . . . which . . . seems not to know of a question which might be posed to it?" Ibid., p. 79. Cf. also C.D. 2, 1, p. 538 and 3, 1, pp. 388ff. and 406ff.

23. Sallie McFague "Imaging a Theology of Nature," *Liberating Life: Contemporary Approaches to Ecological Theology* (New York: Orbis Books, 1990), p. 208 attempts to find "models" for God in exactly this way and reaches the following conclusion: "A praxis orientation . . . acknowledges with the apophatic tradition that we really do not *know* the inner being of divine reality . . ." This very thinking leads to the dualism McFague and others seek to avoid. We are left to use Christian and other images to construct our own image of God as we think this should enable us to help society and to preserve the environment. There can be no real relationship with a real God independent of this humanly constructed image, simply because God's inner being remains ultimately unknown and unknowable. This is the dualism Barth actually was trying to overcome by arguing that we really know God's inner being through the Son and in the Spirit in a way appropriate to us, i.e., through the historical revelation.

24. C.D. 2, 1, p. 327.

25. Ibid.

26. Ibid., p. 328.

27. Ibid., p. 329.

28. Thomas F. Torrance, "Karl Barth and the Latin Heresy," *SJT* 39 (1986): 463. Cf. also T. F. Torrance, *Karl Barth*, chapter eight.

29. Ibid.

30. C.D. 2, 2, p. 101.

31. C.D. 1, 1, pp. 48ff., 54ff., 62ff. 138ff. and 152ff.

32. Paul F. Knitter, *No Other Name?*, p. 189.

33. Ibid., p. 191.

34. Ibid., pp. 48-9.

35. Ibid. See also Molnar "Some Dogmatic Consequences . . ." for more on this.

36. For more on this see Paul D. Molnar, "The Function of the Trinity in Moltmann's Ecological Doctrine of Creation," *Theological Studies* 51 (1990): 673–697, hereafter abbreviated: *TS*.

37. Jürgen Moltmann, *God in Creation: A New Theology of Creation and the Spirit of God*, trans. Margaret Kohl (New York: Harper and Row, 1985, hereafter abbreviated: *Creation*), p. 98. See Molnar, *TS* (1990), for how this leads him into modalism and tritheism.

38. C.D. 2, 1, pp. 312–313. For more on how this relates to Moltmann's theology see Paul D. Molnar, "The Function of the Immanent Trinity in the Theology of Karl Barth: Implications for Today," *SJT* 42 (1989): 367–399.

39. Naturally baptism is the beginning of the Christian life and as such precedes entry into the community which celebrates the Lord's Supper as its renewal.

40. See, e.g., C.D. 2, 1, p. 301. "God's being as He who lives and loves is being in freedom. In this way, freely, He lives and loves. And in this way, and in the fact that He lives and loves in freedom, He is God, and distinguishes Himself from everything else that lives and loves . . . Freedom is, of course, more than the absence of limits, restrictions, or conditions. This is only its negative and to that extent improper aspect—improper to the extent that from this point of view it requires another, at least in so far [*sic*] as its freedom lies in its independence of this other. But freedom in its positive and proper qualities means to be grounded in one's own being, to be determined and moved by oneself. This is the freedom of the divine life and love." Both the positive and negative aspects of the divine freedom must be in evidence for a correct description of God's freedom. This insight applies both to Barth's concept of analogy and to his view of the sacrament. See also C.D. 2, 1, pp. 302ff. What Barth meant by divine freedom is what the early church meant by the aseity of God, C.D. 2, 1, p. 302. Unfortunately later in church history God's freedom was considered in a largely negative way using terms such as *independentia*, *infinitas*, and still later, the unconditioned absolute, C.D. 2, 1, p. 303. These negative conceptions have historically tended to overshadow the important scriptural idea that God's freedom is the freedom of his self-determination. (Cf. Ex. 3:14). Conceived as the unmoved mover of Aristotle, God could be viewed at best as partially self-moved, *but* certainly not as *continually* self-motivated prior to, during, and after creation. Everything, then, depends upon the fact that in speaking of God's revelation, we realize that it is free. Otherwise it is not recognizable as God's self-sufficient action *ad extra* and it might be confused with the processes of creation.

41. Bruce L. McCormack, "Divine Revelation and Human Imagination: Must We Choose Between the Two?," *SJT* 37 (1984): 431–455 presents an excellent analysis and critique of Gordon Kaufman's criticisms of Barth in this regard.

42. This is why Barth defined God as the One who loves in freedom (C.D. 2, 1, pp. 257–321). We shall consider Moltmann's belief that Barth's view of God's freedom included "a nominalist fringe" in a later chapter. But problems can be seen already in the way Moltmann conceives that nominalist fringe. Moltmann refers to Barth: "He [God] could have remained satisfied with Himself and with the impassible glory and blessedness of His own inner life. But he did not do so. He elected man as a covenant-partner," (Jürgen Moltmann, *The Trinity and the Kingdom, The Doctrine of God*, trans. Margaret Kohl (New York: Harper & Row, 1981, hereafter abbreviated: *Trinity*, p. 52). "This God has no need of us. This God is self-sufficient. This God knows perfect beatitude in Himself. He is not under any need of constraint. It takes place in an inconceivably free overflowing of His goodness if he determines to co-exist with a reality distinct from Himself, the world of creatures, ourselves," (*Trinity*, p. 53 and *Creation*, p. 82). But Moltmann asks: "Does God really not need those whom in the suffering of his love he loves unendingly?" As God's suffering love is God's nature, Moltmann argues that if God did not reveal himself and actually could be contented with his glory, he would be contradicting his own nature; any reasoning that God could or could not have when applied to the being of God who is glorified in the cross of his Son is inappropriate, because here we meet a God who cannot possess an untouched glory at all.

43. This is the reality of God as defined in C.D. 2, 1, chapter six.

II

Grace and the Knowledge of God: Phenomenological and Christological Implications For the Sacrament

How can a human person, who is unable to be faithful to God by his or her own noetic or ontic possibilities, nevertheless become faithful by the divine judgment? How can a creature, who is unable by his or her own power to perform any holy action, believe and know that it is a fact that such action may become holy by the divine judgment? Observing how Barth answers these questions will illustrate how he would develop and maintain divine and human freedom in connection with the Lord's Supper.

Grace

A correct answer to these questions, in Barth's eyes, must resist three mistaken views of grace. Barth identified the first as the popular Roman Catholic view; this would include any opinion that conceives God's action toward and for creatures as an "infusion of supernatural powers by whose proper use man can do what he cannot do in his own strength, namely, be faithful again to the faithful God."[1]

Here it is important to note that while some of Barth's opinions about Roman Catholic theology (e.g., that preaching was utterly unimportant compared to the sacrament) simply became outdated by changes that took place at Vatican II, this particular view still finds expression in contemporary Catholic theology. Thus, for example, the eminent theologian Karl Rahner who is at pains to distinguish our obediential potency and supernatural existential from grace still holds a view of grace which Barth would reject: Rahner writes, "grace pervades the essence of man from his very roots with divine influence, and thereby gives him the possibility of acting positively for his own salvation, and so implants in him a free and active tendency towards his own consummation."[2] In order to avoid this conclusion Barth argued, from the very outset, that a genuine recognition of grace means that, because of the Fall, we have no obediential potency for grace and that the action of the Holy Spirit cannot be synthesized with any human existential (conceived as supernatural or not) without falling into Pelagianism.

The second view Barth identified with a revival of Pelagianism and with what he had previously called Protestant Modernism or Neo-Protestantism.[3] This would include any idea that "locates the possibility in God's power to be gracious to man by summoning and spurring him on to the fulfilment of his natural religious and moral impulses."[4] The chief figure in Barth's mind here certainly was Schleiermacher, who sought to understand Christian revelation as a particular instance within the general feeling of religious self-consciousness; this, for Barth, makes one's general ontology the norm for truth and, to that extent, revelation can have no independent significance. Barth held that this was exactly the difficulty in Bultmann's application of existential philosophy to theology. Barth consistently sought to avoid nominalism; hence, in his view of the divine perfections he rejected any notion that attempts to "define and order the perfections of God as though they were the various predicates of a kind of general being presupposed as known already."[5] This led him to reject what he viewed as the sincere attempts by Schleiermacher and his student Alexander Schweizer to get beyond a merely formal concept of God by relating his attributes to the way pious feeling finds God in nature, ethics, and in the Christian life. Even though theologians as different as Gordon Kaufman and Jürgen Moltmann also criticize Schleiermacher's approach, it is important to realize that Kaufman's theology is overtly nominalist while Moltmann's theology vacillates between nominalism and his own distinct anthropological theology. Kaufman actually insists that the symbol God can be no more than a regulative idea[6] while Moltmann leaves us with no real immanent Trinity.[7]

Barth associated the third view with the Reformation interpretation of justification as held by Melanchthon and later by Lutheran orthodoxy. This view includes any attempt to restrict God's gracious power in relation to one who has been "judged afresh and with grace" by implying that this divine action actually leaves humans in themselves unaltered. We have an indication of Barth's criticism of Melanchthon at the beginning of his treatment of the Reality of God in his doctrine of God. Barth wished to stress that revelation is an act of God in Christ which alone actually discloses to us the true being of God as well as the actual benefits that are ours in Christ. This is not the content of a general statement constructed from an experience of the benefits received from Christ. Hence, speaking of the "first dogmatician of the Evangelical Church" Barth indicated that in his *Loci* of 1521 Melanchthon wanted to "suppress the special doctrine of God" in order to proceed to a study of the *"beneficia Christi."* But Barth's contention was that while the benefits are important and need investigation they could not be understood correctly unless one first grasped the divine mystery in its proper place and then understood the *beneficia* from revelation rather than from reason and experience. That was Melanchthon's first mistake. His second mistake, in Barth's view, was worse; i.e., when he then took up the doctrine of God in his *Loci* "he began to create it from another source than from the revelation of God, namely, from an independently formed and general idea of

God."[8] Here he fell into the danger that he had originally attempted to avoid, namely, he allowed the general doctrine of being to determine the content of both the doctrine of God and of the *beneficia Christi*.

The error can develop in two ways. On the one hand God might be characterized as a being hidden behind his revelation. This is why Barth refers to Melanchthon's example as "disastrous" for "the whole of Protestant orthodoxy." For if God remains hidden behind his actions *ad extra* then we have no true and certain knowledge of God or of our justification even through our faith in Christ and the Spirit. In Barth's words:

> In a less happy moment Melanchthon (*Loci communes*, 1521) emphasized the benefits of Christ instead of Christ himself as the incarnate Logos of the eternal Father. Various movements in modern Protestant theology have praised him for this. But it has had the result that in Protestantism praise of the divine Benefactor has become a very feeble matter, relevant at most only in poetry.[9]

On the other hand the being of God might be deduced from formal logic rather than from the Father through the Son in his action *ad extra*. And the danger here is that a general doctrine of being then would define God; this would make his unique trinitarian being, which was revealed in his action *ad extra,* a particular instance to be defined within a general doctrine of being. Then anthropology and theology would have been reversed and the danger of philosophy defining God rather than God disclosing himself in and through the concepts of philosophy would have taken place. In spite of these dangers, however, Barth insisted that what ought to be learned from Melanchthon's predicament is that

> When we ask questions about God's being, we cannot in fact leave the sphere of His action and working as it is revealed to us in His Word. God is who He is in His works. He is the same even in Himself, even before and after and over His works, and without them. They are bound to Him, but He is not bound to them. They are nothing without Him. But He is who He is without them. He is not, therefore, who He is only in His works. Yet in Himself He is not another than He is in His works.[10]

This kind of distinction between the immanent and economic Trinity takes account of the fact that while God really encounters us as God within the history of the world he is "not swallowed up in the relation and attitude of Himself to the world;" thus, "while He reveals Himself in them [his works *ad extra*], He remains at the same time superior to them."[11] As I have indicated elsewhere, those students of Barth who fail to take account of this point in their own theologies really tend to compromise the traditional trinitarian and christological safeguards against monism and dualism.[12]

According to Barth, then, none of these explanations makes it clear how a specifically Christian action, namely, a fully human action of faithfulness to God's faithfulness comes into existence. Barth avers,

> The three views were from the very first no more than complementary to one another. Each in its particular over-emphasis bore some responsibility for producing and hardening the other two. Hence one can hardly award the palm to any of them. Different though they were and are, they share the common feature that from the standpoint which we have here adopted they are all deficient, since none of them makes it clear how . . . the man who as a free subject is God's true partner in the covenant of grace.[13]

Rejecting these three viewpoints it is incumbent on Barth to state clearly what the proper notion is supposed to be; and he does not disappoint.

According to Barth, a fitting view of grace is one which recognizes that the human ability to be faithful to the covenant of grace (i.e., the fellowship established between God and creatures by God alone) is a divinely created possibility.[14] Hence, the beginning and *continuation* of one's life as a Christian are and remain grounded in God *alone* and his *direct* action in and through creation.[15] The key point here is that this divinely created possibility occurs *in* and *through* the creature's own free decision and not without it; though not identical with the human action, it *freely* includes it. This simple insight might slip by unnoticed. It is, however, so important that a pause to trace the implications of this definition of grace is necessary.

In his doctrine of the *Word of God*[16] Barth carried through his distinction between God *in se* and God for us in order to demonstrate that the Word of God is completely self-grounded and that we may know this particular Word indirectly in and through the form of human words and actions as in revelation, scripture, and preaching. For Barth, the antecedent existence of the Word in the triune being of God is decisive here.[17] It is this distinction between God *in se* and God for us that is determinative for Barth's doctrines of the Trinity (as we have already begun to see above in connection with Melanchthon), of the Word of God, of analogy, of election, and of his view of the sacrament.

For Barth, creatures can participate in the fulfilled covenant of grace, but not by their own power; human participation does not take place in *identity* with grace but in obedient hearing and response to grace. Any notion of identity in this context would dissolve both divinity and humanity. To avoid this error Barth insisted that only God could reveal God; only God could make himself present to us. That the creature is opened to God by God himself from within, as well as from without, means that we are speaking of an operation of grace and not of nature.[18] Thus, as Jesus Christ is true God and true man, there takes place God's freedom for us and our freedom for God. "This was Agape, which descends from above, and by the power of this descent simultaneously ascends from below. Agape is both movements in equal sovereignty, or, rather, this *single* movement."[19] This aspect of Barth's thought, as we shall see later, could be exploited to overcome the problem in Calvin's theology which makes it appear that we merely respond to Christ's sacrifice rather than also share with him in his offering to the Father.[20] Great care must be exercised at this point. For much contemporary theology which ignores the fact that *only* God can reveal God more or less overtly solves this problem by making experience a source for theology.[21]

The connection between this thinking and Barth's concept of analogy is decisive. For example, Barth began his consideration of the problem of knowledge of God by noting that it is important to know whether what is presupposed as God is really God and not just an idea of God.[22] He argued that the problem of knowledge is solved by the Word of God, namely, the object of the scriptural testimonies, i.e., the one God who discloses himself to creatures in the form of human words and works, and supremely, in the incarnation.[23] This means that human knowledge of God is mediated knowledge. But what Barth meant by mediated knowledge and what is meant by mediated knowledge in a general phenomenology differ significantly. Barth meant that only God can reveal God. Thus, mediated knowledge can *never* mean that some reality other than God has the capability of revealing him. As there can be no confusion of nature and grace, there can be no mixture of medium and divine reality in Barth's theology. Rather, although we know God only through the medium of his word and work, it is God *alone* who makes himself known. The truth and certainty of human knowledge of God therefore rest solely on the fact that God has made himself known and will do so again. Therefore true human knowledge of God cannot in any sense rest on an epistemological or phenomenological analysis; this would compromise God's grace revealed in Christ by denying Barth's major premise that theology takes place as a *miracle*—an act begun, upheld, and completed by the triune God.

Barth reinforced this insight throughout the *C.D.* by describing the human apprehension of the event of revelation as one of *recollection* and *expectation* of the Christ event.[24] He argued that in particular historical circumstances we today *recall* definite *historical* interventions by God such as in the Exodus, in the apostolic community, or in Christ himself and *expect* (hope) that this same God will uphold us and will intervene again and again according to his promise. We live, therefore, by this promise of God and not by direct sight. Hence, human knowledge of revelation is never direct, but indirect; that is why faith is always necessary. This is precisely how Barth excluded identity between nature and grace from his theology. In his view, any idea that one could discern revelation in its uniqueness by investigating history or nature from the general view of religion, sociology, philosophy, or psychology would represent an attempt to know revelation directly and without faith. Indeed for Barth the prophetic testimonies themselves are a time of expectation which is fulfilled in Christ, while the time of the apostolic testimonies recollects that particular fulfilled time.

Here Barth neither means that Christians can activate faith using their memory of Christ via scripture nor that they do not have an actual and fully human participation in revelation. In fact he wished to stress the *historical* nature of human participation by emphasizing that we are directed in very human ways back to the man Jesus who, as the One Mediator, can alone guide us to the truth and certainty of God himself.

With the broad outline of the *analogia fidei* presented in chapter one we can see that Barth's notion of *grace* negatively resists any identity between nature and grace but positively stresses that by grace we have true and certain knowledge which comes from God and never comes under our control. The striking consistency of Barth's thought here is clear: Grace means God's act of justification and sanctification in his Word and Spirit. Thus, it cannot mean that we ever have the inherent strength to be faithful to God even in the midst of our actual human acts of faithfulness. One example should clarify this difficult point.

Speaking of the limits of our human knowledge of God, Barth argued that we have no power over God even as God gives himself to be known by us in revelation; our only power is "the power to be His child, trusting and obedient to Him."[25] God's continued hiddenness even in revelation is the mark of his grace, i.e., of the fact that we are not in control here, but he is. Yet, there is no hidden God beyond his Word and Spirit acting *ad extra* "at the back of his revelation." While Barth noted that it "may often look like this in certain contexts in Luther" the proper way of seeing this according to scripture is to see that God, in the mystery of his incomprehensibility, "encounters and gives Himself to man without reservation."[26] Nevertheless, while God encounters us through the "world-reality distinct from Him . . . which in His revelation necessarily becomes his witness [the world-reality] is certainly never identical with Himself." Our views and concepts, Barth argued, can only grasp world-reality and not God's reality; while they are powerless to grasp God, they are not therefore a hindrance to God in his revelation, i.e., their inherent impotence cannot keep God from enabling us to know him using our views and concepts. God makes himself known in his Word and Spirit not by annulling our human situation but by enabling us to do that which we, of ourselves cannot do, namely, to speak with our limited views and concepts of the transcendent God.

> What we of ourselves cannot do, He can do through us. If our views and concepts and words are of themselves too narrow to apprehend God, it does not follow that this sets a limit to God Himself, that it is impossible for God to take up His dwelling in this narrowness . . . why should our views and concepts and words be too small for God to be in them in all His glory?[27]

At this point Barth clearly maintains the force of his argument by stressing that our concepts do not have the inherent capacity for God (thus confusing nature and grace) while at the same time our concepts can neither be eliminated nor stand in the way of God's granting us the capacity to actually know him. And here is where Barth's careful distinction has a consequence. For at this crucial point his refusal to identify nature and grace led him to argue that

> It is not a question of a power to receive this guest [God] being secretly inherent in these works of ours. They have no power to do this . . . But there is a power of the divine indwelling in both the broad and the narrow which our works cannot withstand for all their impotence. This indwelling does not involve a magical transformation of man, or a supernatural enlargement of his capacity, so that he can do what before he could not do. He cannot do it afterwards any more than he could do before. But he is taken up by the grace of God and determined to participation in the veracity of the revelation of God . . . As a sinner he is justified.[28]

It is God's own truth which judges human concepts, showing their actual impotence, while at the same time it makes us really responsible to God himself and to others on the basis of the divine claim. Sanctification comes to us through this claim. Sin is therefore not ignored, excused, or set aside. But it is forgiven. While we still remain incapable of speaking of God on our own, we can, by the grace of God actually speak of God.

> The veracity of the revelation of God, which justifies the sinner in His Word by His Spirit, makes his knowledge of God true without him, against him—and yet as his own knowledge, and to that extent through him. By the grace of God we may view and conceive God and speak of God in our incapacity.[29]

This, of course, calls for humility which acknowledges that God's judgment and grace are really effective here. It does not call for resignation which would represent another human attempt at self-justification. It is in this precise way, in relation to our knowledge of God, that Barth avoided the three notions of grace which he rejected above.

Symbol and Mediated Knowledge: Implications for Phenomenology and Christology

Having said this, it is important to realize that neither Barth's concept of analogy nor his view of the sacrament can be understood correctly if it is thought that he is offering a phenomenological explanation of the problem here as a preparation for his theology. To show what Barth is *not* saying we shall briefly contrast what he means when he calls human knowledge mediated knowledge and what, for example, Karl Rahner means when he speaks of mediated knowledge. Such a contrast, of course, opens many theological doors. But the primary concern here is to see more clearly how and why Barth's theological method is shaped by the trinitarian self-revelation; it is because theology can only begin and end with the Word heard and believed, that it cannot be based on any set of experiences or ideas.

We begin by noting that Barth's concept cannot be equated with the modern phenomenological conception of the symbol.[30] According to this theory, it is commonly assumed that since persons participate in their symbols and since symbols embody the personality of the persons who use them, therefore symbols give people the possibility of extending their presence beyond the limits of space and time.[31] A common foundation for this reasoning is Rahner's distinction between "arbitrary signs" which have a merely representative function and symbols which have the "function of expressiveness."[32] Applying this thinking to the Eucharist, it may be said that the priest both takes the place of Christ and at the same time Christ is the one who is acting in the sacrament.[33] Explained symbolically one may say that the symbol (appearance) "is the reality, constituted by the thing symbolized as an inner moment of moment itself [*sic*], which reveals and proclaims the thing symbolized, and is itself *full of the thing symbolized*, being its concrete form of existence."[34] As a symbol, then, the humanity of Christ is the "appearance" which allows God to be present to that which he is not. Since it is full of what is symbolized it has the ability to render present God himself.[35] Thus, for Rahner, both Christ in his humanity as such and the visible church do not simply designate God's grace but are themselves *full of the reality symbolized*;[36] not only are they mutually and necessarily related to the divine reality and being but they are *extensions* or *continuations* of it in time and space.[37] Accordingly, because all beings are symbolic they must "'express' themselves in order to attain their own nature,"[38] and "The symbol strictly speaking (symbolic reality) is the self-realization of a being in the other, which is constitutive of its essence."[39] The key point here is that the historical manifestation is seen as the condition for the possibility of the reality itself since sign and thing signified are mutually and necessarily related.

It is this thinking which led Rahner, in his Christology, to argue that "This man, is as such the self-utterance of God in its self-emptying, because God expresses *himself* when he empties himself." Hence the human nature shared by all persons comes to be when God utters himself into the "void." What differentiates Christ from the rest of us is the fact that "in his case the 'what' is uttered as his self-expression, which it is not in our case." Still, we must say, according to Rahner, that "If God wills to become non-God, man comes to be, that and nothing else, we might say . . . And if God himself is man and remains so for ever, if all theology is therefore eternally an anthropology . . . man is for ever the articulate mystery of God." Since "God's expression of himself outside himself" is man Rahner believed that "Christology is the end and beginning of anthropology. And this anthropology, when most thoroughly realized in Christology, is eternally theology."[40] Carried to its logical conclusion this thinking actually led Rahner to assert both that "philosophy is an inner moment of theology" and that "grace, understood as the absolute self-communication of God himself, must always presuppose as a condition of its own possibility (in order to be itself) someone to whom it can address itself . . . since revelation is a moment in this free self-opening-out by gratuitous grace, it presupposes as a condition of its own possibility the one to whom this revelation remains unowed."[41]

The related problems of identity and necessity are clearly apparent in this reasoning and the point to be noted in this context is that they can hardly be avoided since it is intrinsic to the nature of "symbolic reality" as Rahner defines it that it must express itself in another, that the other must be full of the reality expressed, and that the other has the capacity to render present the reality. This is why, in his sacramental theology, Rahner argued that there is an "effectiveness *inherent* in the sign precisely *as* such"[42] and that the church as the basic sacrament does not just point to the "res" but participates in it quasi-formally and thus can actually render it present.[43] The fundamental difficulty here is that Rahner believed that God, as the highest instance of symbolic reality, must express himself *ad intra* and that his action *ad extra* is a *continuation* of that immanent expression into the void. As that is true, it was literally impossible for Rahner to preserve the freedom of God which he himself believed must be maintained.[44]

Another of the so-called phenomenological approaches to the sacraments is employed by G. van der Leeuw,[45] who begins by analyzing the human phenomena and in that way attempts to fathom the meaning of the sacraments. It begins therefore with the human structures such as the meal when examining the Eucharist, or water and initiation when investigating baptism. The phenomenological method also seeks the meaning of the sacraments through analysis of interpersonal dynamics or interpersonal relations.[46]

Although this approach has the distinct advantage of focusing on the genuine personal relationship of the church (as the community of believers) with Christ, there are at least three problems which emerge when this sacramental method is compared with that of Barth as it is dictated by his definition of grace and faith. *First*, it assumes that the phenomena can explain a meaning that by definition transcends the very attempt; in that way the method abstracts from the knowledge of faith by which we know that the phenomena do not set the meaning for revelation but that revelation occurs in and through the phenomena. This is a continual problem in Rahner's thinking.[47] The next step is to reduce the church to a sociological phenomenon while adding, of course, that all this takes place through Jesus Christ, our Lord. But, on this view, there is no credible or compelling reason why we would *need* Jesus except as that historical figure who validates our own previously held viewpoints. Karl Barth actually wrote to Rahner about this problem in 1968, after hearing Rahner preach on the radio.

Last Sunday I heard you on radio Beromünster, at first with pleasure . . . In the end and on the whole, however, I was completely stunned. You spoke much and very well about the 'little flock,' but I did not hear a single 'Baa' which was in fact authentically and dominatingly the voice of one of the little sheep of this flock, let alone could I hear the voice of the shepherd of this flock. *Instead, the basic note was that of a religious sociology and the other favorite songs of what is supposed to be the world of modern culture.* In the way you are speaking now, so some fifty years ago Troeltsch was speaking of the future of the church and theology . . . our Neo-Protestants were and are in their own way pious and even churchly people . . .[48]

This reasoning led Rahner to believe that Christ is supreme as the irrevocable or irreversible stage in humanity's self-transcending movements; but he did not actually hold that in Jesus something completely new happened which would make the movement directly from anthropology to Christology impossible. Nor did he admit that what Christ is and what he brings us actually transcends all our acts of self-transcendence; rather Christ is simply the irreversibility of that for which we all inherently strive. Similarly Rahner did not believe that grace means that particular unmerited act of good pleasure on God's part which actually transcends all the ideas of grace and mystery which we might formulate based on our variously perceived "orientations."[49] While grace does transcend all our ideas in Rahner's thought, it cannot be essentially different from the reality we already glimpse in our basic human orientations toward the absolute. In that sense, its meaning cannot really transcend an idea of grace or mystery drawn from our experience of the "whither."[50]

Second, it can describe the relation between Christ acting in the sacraments and creatures in terms of mutual conditioning. This clearly compromises the sovereignty of God's action in Christ and the Spirit; something which Christian theologians have always tried to avoid. John McKenna, e.g., is concerned to maintain Christ's sovereignty when speaking of his real presence in the Eucharist in personalist terms. But because, in a personal encounter, we do not have a full relationship without the other's response he concludes that

> the personal presence of Christ offering himself to his Father and to his faithful does not constitute presence in the fullest sense since . . . presence to be fully personal must be mutual, reciprocal. In the Eucharist, then, the Church must also respond by opening up to Christ's gift of himself; otherwise we do not have presence in its fullest sense.[51]

It should be noted that the underlying reasoning which gives weight to this thinking is Rahner's belief that symbols are intrinsically related to that reality which they symbolize. Hence, between the symbol and the reality we have "a case of an *intrinsic* and *mutual causal* relationship. What is manifesting itself posits its own identity and existence by manifesting itself in this manifestation which is distinct from itself . . . The sign is therefore a cause of what it signifies by being the way in which what is signified effects itself."[52]

Third, it usually builds its understanding on a Christology from below which misconstrues the scriptural and traditional comprehension of the person and working of Christ. Here we must move from a discussion of phenomenology in general to see the implications when Christology merely becomes a specific instance within a general phenomenology. Thus, for example, one contemporary sacramental theologian writes:

> Phenomenologists can be of the greatest service to theology, since what these men are studying is basically the human phenomenon. If we cannot come to some insight of Jesus as man, then Jesus is not a sacrament to us; he is not revelatory of the good news. The humanness of Jesus—or, more

abstractly, the incarnation—is the key to the Christian understanding of both God and our world, but the humanity of Jesus remains just another phrase until we are in a position to appreciate the very phenomenon of the human . . . This understanding of the human phenomenon leads us to appreciate the humanness of Jesus and only on that basis can Jesus become a sacrament for us.[53]

Yet within traditional Christology, the incarnation refers to the fact that the Word became flesh (Jn. 1:14) and dwelt among us. And if this is true (and no Christian theologian wishes to deny this) then a study of the human phenomenon of Jesus is not in the least likely to disclose this particular truth to us. Indeed a study of the human phenomenon will lead to a confusion or separation of the two natures but not to a clear grasp of Jesus' uniqueness. To underscore the importance of this point and to illustrate the significance of a clear Christology as a foundation for understanding the sacraments I believe one more example will be practical.

Edward Krasevac, O.P. speaks for many today when he analyzes Christology from above and writes: "Although God's action in the Incarnation preceded in absolute priority the public ministry of the Lord . . . that action was only fully understood in all of its implications in a gradual historical process that took place over many years." Here it would seem that the mystery of God's action in Christ is unequivocally the foundation for all true understanding (Christology) both in the early church and today. But, unfortunately, within the context of the rest of this article it is clear that that is not what is being stated here. The author explains, "In a real sense, the foundation or proximate source of Christian faith is the apostolic witness to God's salvific actions, rather than those actions themselves . . . Christological faith is an apostolic faith that has its origins in a historical process which began with the public ministry of Jesus . . ." Hence Christology from above refers to God's act of incarnation and to the hypostatic union while Christology from below refers "to the gradual process by which the apostolic understanding of that action developed. As a process, 'Christology from above' holds absolute priority over 'Christology from below.'" Because Krasevac really believes that Christology from below can legitimately take Jesus' history in itself as a starting point for understanding the mystery of the Christian faith, he here uncritically substitutes what he sees as the development of the church's christological understanding for the reality of Christ himself.[54]

While, in the Gospels, Christ himself is the salvific act of God which alone validates the apostolic witness as well as Christology itself, according to Krasevac this cannot be the case. Thus, instead of arguing that Jesus himself, the Lord Incarnate, is and remains the sole foundation for the truth of the apostolic faith and for ours, it is argued that Christology from below refers to a *process* of understanding while Christology from above refers to a divine action. In fact, though we today are dependent upon the apostolic witness to know the truth of Christology, Christ is not. The process of understanding therefore must be distinguished clearly from Jesus, the man who was and is the Lord and Christ. This means that if we try to move from below to above as Krasevac thinks we can, we shall invariably deny the central assertion he evidently wished to maintain, i.e., that God's action from above precedes absolutely all further christological reflection. This cannot happen if we substitute a process of reflection for the humanity of Jesus in its union with the Word for the foundation of Christology.

And this precisely is the problem with contemporary Christologies from below. They begin with the historical phenomena and reconstruct the truth of the Christian faith in light of what the phenomena seem to be saying. But according to this view the norm for truth clearly is history and experience and not Christ himself. To that extent theology is not faith in him, true God and true man, seeking understanding (as it was for the early and later New Testament testimonies). Rather faith means faith in the historical process which we are told begins "with no Christology at all" and ends with the idea that when Jesus first walked the earth he was not seen as messiah, savior, and Lord and that high Christology is grounded in the "impression" Jesus made on his followers.[55] In point of fact, however, we must admit that to the extent that Jesus' uniqueness is grounded in the impression he made on his followers, it can have no absolute priority in itself as such. His very divinity will not be seen as self-grounded in a sovereign action *ad extra* of the triune God but as grounded in and discernable through the impressions made on his followers. Such a divinity can have no independent significance and to that extent will always be contestable by other teachers or lords who may evoke similar or more profound impressions from us. As J. N. D. Kelly notes, this is precisely the thinking of Ebionism.[56]

We may note here that it is to avoid this very problem that Barth wrote to Pannenberg questioning his Christology:

My first reaction on reading your book was one of horror when . . . I found you rejecting M. Kähler in a way which led me to suspect that, like others, you . . . intended to pursue a path from below to above . . . Is not this to build a house on the sand—the shifting sand of historical probabilities . . . *In its positive content is your christology—after the practice of so many modern fathers—anything other than the outstanding example and symbol of a presupposed general anthropology, cosmology, and ontology?*[57]

Indeed a study of Pannenberg's method discloses that his starting point cannot be the mystery of Jesus *as* God and man. Rather his Christology begins from "below" because he believes Christology today cannot presuppose the divinity of Jesus. Thus, the incarnation cannot be its own validation or starting point for this Christology. "Instead of presupposing it [Christ's divinity], we must first inquire about how Jesus' appearance in history led to the recognition of his divinity."[58] This eliminates any real immanent Trinity existing before, during, and after the incarnation and resurrection of Jesus: "How the divine Logos, the Second Person of the Trinity, would be thought of apart from the incarnation and thus apart from the man Jesus completely escapes our imagination."[59] To this extent the immanent Trinity can become little more than a metaphor signifying the universal religious attempt to distinguish reality from myth (pre-existence);[60] it is deprived of a genuinely determinative significance here.[61]

This method reverses faith and understanding and leads to mutual conditioning which Barth believed expressed some form of identification of God's action with the historical process; this invariably leads to some form of adoptionism. Indeed as Pannenberg assumes that "the maker himself is changed *by* the production and shaping of another being" an adoptionist implication follows:

> Thus, Jesus' unity with God—and thus the *truth* of the incarnation—is also decided *only* retroactively from the perspective of Jesus' resurrection for the whole of Jesus' human existence on the one hand . . . and thus also for God's eternity, on the other. Apart from Jesus' resurrection, it would not be true that from the very beginning of his earthly way God was one with this man. That is true from all eternity *because* of Jesus' resurrection.[62]

While the resurrection certainly revealed the eternal truth of who Jesus was before Easter and in eternity as the pre-existent Word, the truth of this eternal existence cannot possibly be identified with the resurrection event in this way without confusing the development of thinking on the part of the disciples with a corresponding development in the being of God himself. This would have to end in adoptionism. Of course the reason Pannenberg thinks this way is because he believes Christology today cannot presuppose the divinity of Jesus. And that is precisely the problem involved in all Christologies from below.

As the resurrection and revelation are, for Pannenberg, principles which dictate the true meaning of the historical events of incarnation and resurrection, analogies are clearly considered to be true in themselves. With Rahner, Pannenberg believes the incarnation is a doctrinally certain instance verifying the axiom of the identity of the immanent and economic Trinity.[63] Yet Pannenberg explains that datum of faith quite differently from Barth. Pannenberg's "idea of revelation" seems to be the determinative principle of his Christology rather than the person and work of Christ. Thus, he writes, "Today the *idea of revelation* must take the place of the Logos concept as the point of departure for Christology."[64]   This explanation however will never work, since it is conceivable that the "problem of Christology" may never be recognized from the "idea" of revelation. Unless that idea is determined by and subordinate to the reality of Jesus, true God and true man, it cannot have a true meaning. Indeed when *any idea* at all is the point of departure for Christology, Barth correctly insisted that it had to lead to Docetism.[65]

How does all of this relate to Rahner's theory of knowledge and to his theology of the symbol? An analysis of Rahner's method reveals that he began thinking about God, Christ, the church, and the sacraments from an experience of one's horizon. From this experience he made his "transcendental deductions." This very method follows the pattern of the phenomenologist. It begins from human experience and from there seeks to understand Christian doctrine. The problem with this method is that it assumes both a direct and indirect knowledge of the trinitarian God.   The direct knowledge is what Rahner called "transcendental revelation."   The indirect knowledge is what he called "categorical revelation." His theory of "mediated immediacy," which we shall discuss in chapter four, attempts to distinguish God from creatures while describing their union according to a notion of quasi-formal causality which cannot but assimilate creatures to the creator. This left him in the unfortunate position of maintaining the traditional distinctions implied in the *creatio ex nihilo* while at the same time never fully escaping the pantheist dilemma.[66] The ultimate form of this problem is expressed in the fact that Rahner's description of the God-world relation, as well as his description of sacramental causality, involve the kind of mutual conditioning between subject and object which one inevitably finds at the heart of symbolic ontology.

As it relates to Christology, the problem can be illustrated by noting that he really believed that "it is possible to say very much with regard to the most central reality of the Christian faith without doing this directly from the point of view of Jesus Christ." Thus, there may be "different fundamental statements of the faith which 'quoad nos' can initially be made without any explicit reference to Jesus Christ," for example, the "first article of the Apostles' Creed."[67]

How is Christ's uniqueness maintained according to this perspective? According to Rahner, "any explicit Christianity must explicitly contain the reference of what is expressed elsewhere to Christ or the reference of Jesus to *this other truth* which is expressed, and this means that it must have the structure of an affirmation of faith that is christological."[68]   Each problem inherent in Rahner's theological method is here in a nutshell. For if we can say or imply, even for a moment, that knowledge of the creator God and Father of all is a different truth than confession of Christ's Lordship and of his divinity as the Word or Son in relation to the Father, then we have in fact divided what cannot be divided. Once this happens, christological thinking is factually detached from the truth that God's oneness cannot be recognized or confessed unless the Father and Son are seen as consubstantial in their being and in their creative and reconciling functions. What follows is an attempt to think christologically which makes Christ the highest symbolic expression of God in the world, but not the only possible expression *ad extra*.[69] And that is the problem in Rahner's Christology. It is not christological at the outset and simply makes Christ a principle for ordering his interpretation of the transcendental experience of absolute being. We have explored something of Rahner's view of symbolic mediation to see how a symbolic view of grace compares to Barth's view of mediation which does not allow the necessities of symbolic ontology to dictate the meaning of nature and grace. Let us now return to Barth's view of mediation to see more clearly his positive point.

Implications For Grace and Sacrament

For Barth, the medium or sign never ceases to be a fully human action and neither is nor becomes mingled with the action of God in Christ which is always the reality to which it refers.[70] Not only does the medium *not* give him the possibility of extending his presence beyond the limits of space and time as the phenomenologist would hold (this is comparable to Rahner's statement that Jesus' "materiality expresses *him,* the Logos himself, and lets him be present in his world")[71] but that possibility, for Barth, is grounded solely in God and certainly not partially in God and partially in the medium. The phenomenologist's thinking is simply a variation on the theme that the relationship between creator and creature can be seen and understood on the basis of analogies of parity. As there is a similarity between symbol and reality symbolized (an *analogia entis)* in the created realm, so this same relation exists in God in an absolute sense.

What follows is an assumption of mutual reciprocity between God and creatures which compromises God's freedom in the encounter. In Barth's theology of the Word, he repeatedly and emphatically asserted that we know only the medium and can never know God *directly*.[72] For that reason media, which *may* serve as analogies in faith are *never* reversible with the object to which they are determined to refer, namely, God himself. By contrast, this reversibility is necessary to phenomenology because it must assume that somehow grace inheres in human experience and can be known by directly analyzing the nature of symbols. To assume any sort of direct knowledge of God by his creation is to dissolve revelation into nothing more or less than the created medium or sign. In this case both the realities of God and creatures are compromised. Grace and the related concepts of divine sovereignty and faith become meaningless in such a setting.

In his *analogia fidei* Barth's entire emphasis was on showing that true analogies can only be analogies which point to the mysterious presence of God's Word in history without becoming confused with it. Thus, there are no analogies which are *true in themselves* and there can be no concept of mutual reciprocity between the Word of God and the views and concepts of creatures.[73] This does not mean that there is no reciprocal relationship between God and creatures; it means instead that such a relation is grounded in grace and cannot be explained from the phenomena themselves. However interesting phenomenological thinking may be, it cannot be applied to knowledge of God's presence without denying its freedom and self-sufficiency and implying that there are analogies which are true in themselves.

The fact that this inclusion of creatures in the covenant of grace is a *free* divine action means that persons have no claim here.[74] It means that this power is never "given over" to us so that we can now control it at will in our human actions as such. This divine decision and action does not depend upon the creature's decision of faithfulness to be effective to and for us.[75] The divine action calls for a corresponding human act of faithfulness but does not depend on it. Because this is a free divine action to and for creatures, human participation in the covenant is a *limited* participation, i.e., limited by the preceding and determinative divine action. But how can creatures recognize this free divine action as something real and not just another profound idea or experience? Certainly not by attempting to define "the human" apart from Christ. Again, it is crucial to realize the difference between Barth's method and the phenomenological method here. For instance, while Rahner began each major doctrinal consideration with an analysis of the creature's self-transcending acts and their implications, Barth refused to do this. Indeed Barth's opposition to the approaches of both Moltmann and Pannenberg rested on his rejection of this kind of method.[76]

Barth's extensive analysis and criticism of various theories of self-transcendence illustrate both the problem and his proposed solution.[77] He noted that it has always been an observably human phenomenon that creatures repudiate their present being and work, and that there is always a final anxiety and dissatisfaction with current situations. There have always been discernible situations which Jaspers called "frontier situations."[78] But the theological question at stake here concerns the *basis* for true and certain knowledge of God. Is it the Word of God acting *ad extra* or a principle derived from a supposed analysis of creaturely self-transcending actions? There are all kinds of general and phenomenologically observable ideas and experiences which seem to point to this same notion. Barth compared this kind of philosophy with Christian knowledge of God maintaining that anything which is directly observable to creatures as such (apart from faith), within or outside themselves, might just as easily be a demon as a god.[79] Therefore, it cannot be the basis for true and certain knowledge. In his definition of "real man" Barth's criterion was the man Jesus in his union with God. Apart from knowledge of this man we may not be describing our human relationship with God himself. We may be describing merely the phenomena of the human. Barth wrote:

> No definition of human nature can meet our present need if it is merely an assertion and description of immediately accessible and knowable characteristics of the nature which man thinks he can regard as that of his fellows and therefore of man in general. From the standpoint of all our criteria, human self-knowledge on this basis must be regarded as a vicious circle in which we can never attain to real man . . . Only a phantom man thinks that of himself he can know himself . . . We cannot and will not dispute that he sees and grasps something which perhaps indicates the nature of true man. Why should there not be certain phenomena in the picture of the cosmos in which he who knows real man can see symptoms of real man? But supposing he does not know real man at all? . . . In these circumstances he will co-ordinate these phenomena, perhaps combining them to form a system. He will think that in their sum, or in the system which they yield, he can form a picture of real man. But he will not succeed in doing so . . . We have first to see real man if we are to understand his symptoms, and are not to fall into the condemnation of being led astray by such phenomena as are accessible and transparent to us. For these phenomena as such are neutral, relative and ambiguous. They may point in various directions. They may or may not be symptoms of real man. They are so only for those who know him already and can therefore interpret them correctly. In themselves they convey no knowledge of real man.[80]

Part of what is natural to creatures, i.e., part of the phenomena of the human, includes our thinking, willing, behaving, and acting. "All this takes place as we will and do it, in the transcendent act of our existence." This activity, for Barth, is a "natural phenomenon occurring within the sphere of our perception." Even perceiving the creature who exists in freedom and decision (the ethical creature), is not yet to see "his uniqueness in creation."[81] Barth's criteria are not just formal but material. Thus,

> If they are right, in relation to real man we have to do with God and man,
> with God's action towards him, with the glory of God in his existence,
> with God's lordship over him, with man's action in relation to God, and
> with the service of God which man must accept in this relation. Even the
> new human phenomenon which we have just been considering does not
> satisfy any of these material criteria. Even this new phenomenon fails to
> tell us whether God even exists. It shows us man, and man alone. But
> man alone is certainly not real man, the being who as man is finally
> different from other beings. It shows us man's existence in freedom and
> decision, but in so doing only a form in which he exists if he really is and
> is really different from other beings. But his reality and his real difference
> from other beings does not consist in mere form. It consists in a specific
> decision, in a particular, true and exclusive freedom, in the existence
> which is thus filled with a rich content. The man who could decide
> otherwise, the man who has another freedom, is not real man, the man
> who as such is different from other beings . . . The phenomenon as such
> leaves this question open; it includes both possibilities. As a phenomenon
> it is neutral and indifferent; it forbids us to make the decisive statement.
> No doubt it speaks plainly of a certain possibility. But the possibility of
> which it speaks is also in the full sense the possibility of the man who fails
> to make the essential decision and thus forfeits his true nature. It is also
> the possibility of the sinner, of the man who alienates himself from God
> . . . It may also be the freedom of the man who in virtue of his
> disobedience is enslaved. Hence the ethical view of the phenomena of the
> human cannot and must not be equated with real man.[82]

To prove his point, Barth critically evaluates Johann Gottlieb Fichte's *Die Bestimmung des Menschen*, 1800.[83] Since Rahner and others see in Fichte a positive force for understanding Christianity I believe a brief summary of Barth's objections to Fichte would be instructive.

Barth appraises Fichte's "transcendental Idealism" by noting that in all of his analysis concerning human doubting, human knowledge, and faith, Fichte believes that he has discovered more than the phenomenon of the human, i.e., "real man."[84] Fichte thinks that in discovering our ethical capacity he has penetrated beyond the phenomena. Beginning and ending with our humanity, however, Fichte's inquiry has the creature as a self-enclosed system for its parameter. Barth concluded that Fichte believed that man is first to be examined in his "naive and yet uncritical self-knowledge." In this way he discovers and declares his own freedom. Next, the creature is seen as the measure of reality in his act of knowing so that "Man as Fichte understands him has no other source of knowledge. There can be no knowledge from without because there is no 'without' anyway."[85] Thus, Barth noted that Fichte spoke of a free man who really can know nothing about himself. Barth sums up Fichtean faith with the question:

> Does not this really bring us back to the point from which the whole essay started, to the vision, as it appears to uncritical knowledge, of the one in the all, of the all in the one, of the great life stream in which man is only a tiny drop? We do not overlook the fact that everything is now reversed. This is the triumph of Fichtean faith. Man as seen in the light of his practical reason, and therefore understood to be free, is himself the stream in the onward sweep of which all other things are only tiny drops . . . But is this reversal, this transition from bondage to freedom as important as it seems? . . . Is the unique reality of man assured by the fact that he understands himself to be free, to be the centre of all things . . . have we really made any progress when we consider everything from the standpoint of indeterminism rather than determinism, and set it under an optimistic rather than a pessimistic sign?—everything, i.e., the totality to which in either case man himself belongs. No, we must deny that the phenomenon of man proving his freedom in decision and action has been rightly interpreted even (and supremely) at this point where the concept of human freedom is filled out in this unprecedented fashion.[86]

Barth concluded:

> We have already said several times that Fichte had some reason for trying to work exclusively with this presupposed idea of the autarchy, the absolute subjectivity of man. The reason is quite simple. Fichte was determined to view man apart from God. We must not be deceived by the fact that he gave his third book the title 'Faith.' For even in this book there is not a single word about faith in God. The god in whom Fichtean man believes is himself, his own mind, the spirit of the protesting voice in which he puts his confidence and in the power of which he knows himself to be free. Nor must we be misled . . . where . . . he speaks of the one single and eternal will. For this Thou is not to be taken any more seriously than the midnight spirit at the beginning of the second book. A Fichtean dialogue can only be an alternative form of monologue . . . A God to whom man belongs as to another; a God who can act in relation to

man and become his Saviour; a God who has His own glory in which the essential concern of man is to be seen; a God who reigns; a God in relation to whom man gains his freedom and whom he must serve in his freedom; a God who confronts and limits man and is thus his true determination, is for Fichte non-existent. Fichte's god is Fichte's man, and Fichte's man is Fichte's god. And it is because God is non-existent that Fichte has had to conceive the idea of absolutely autarchic and subjective being, to ascribe this being to man, and to regard the resultant figure as real man. And it is for the same reason that he cannot even see and interpret correctly the phenomenon of the human. It is for this reason that here, too, the contours are all blurred. It is for this reason his philosophy is particularly unconvincing as a philosophy of freedom. If the aim was to provide a philosophy of freedom, it would have been better not to regard God as non-existent, and therefore to become blind even to the phenomenon of man. This is the warning which we are finally given by this stimulating example.[87]

Of course Barth's analysis would apply similarly to any attempt to know the truth about God and creatures by starting from a phenomenological analysis of the human. This includes the various examples discussed above including Rahner's transcendental method, and in Barth's mind it especially includes Tillich's idea that revelation is a symbol.[88] Barth's critique of Jaspers and Fichte raises significant questions for Rahner's transcendental method since it is so similar in orientation to both Jaspers and Fichte.[89] Obviously, however, Rahner differs from these philosophers to the extent that he explicitly wishes to be a Christian theologian.

Now that we have seen why it is a problem to begin to understand sacraments with a phenomenological analysis of the human, we can now show how exactly Barth's Christology shaped his view of the sacrament and how this contrasts with other more recent approaches which actually start from a phenomenological analysis of the human.

Notes

1. C.D. 4, 4, p. 4.

2. Karl Rahner, *Theological Investigations*, vol. 10, *Writings of 1965–67 2*, trans. David Bourke, (New York: Crossroad, 1977), "Immanent and Transcendent Consummation of The World," pp. 273–289, at p. 280. [This series which now includes 23 volumes, hereafter abbreviated: T.I.]. The idea that grace is "implanted" in us as "freedom in the mode of a formal object" is the

foundation for Rahner's theory of anonymous Christianity. Cf. T.I. 14:288.

3. Cf. C.D. 1, 1, pp. 34ff. et al. C.D. 1, 2, pp. 4ff., 56ff. and 546ff. et al. Barth says that this view is "not without parallels in the Roman Catholic world," C.D. 4, 4, p. 5.

4. C.D. 4, 4, p. 5.

5. C.D. 2, 1, p. 337.

6. Kaufman writes: "Kant saw that the central ideas with which metaphysics works—ideas like 'God' and 'world' and 'self'—function differently in our thinking from concepts dealing with objects of direct experience . . . the latter are used to organize and classify elements of experience directly . . . the former 'metaphysical' notions function at a remove from direct perception or experience: they are used for ordering and organizing our conceptions . . . and function, thus, principally as 'regulative ideas.' The 'world,' for example, is never an object of direct perception . . . The concept of God, also, can be properly understood only as a construct of the mind," *T.I.*, pp. 242-3. Since God can be no more than this regulative idea, God cannot be an object over against us which we can know. This nominalism leads Kaufman to conclude that we can use metaphors from our direct experience of objects in the world to name God as far as this does not lead us into the idolatry of believing that God is a particular object of experience. Cf. also *An Essay On Theological Method* (Atlanta: Scholars Press, 1990), pp. 44ff.

7. Cf. Molnar, *TS* (1990).

8. C.D. 2, 1, p. 259.

9. C.D. 4, 4, *The Christian Life*, p. 87.

10. C.D. 2, 1, p. 260.

11. Ibid.

12. See, e.g., Paul D. Molnar, "The Function of the Immanent Trinity in the Theology of Karl Barth . . ." *SJT* (1989), and "The Function of the Trinity in Moltmann's Ecological Doctrine of Creation" *TS* (1990). Part of Melanchthon's problem here might well be traceable to the fact that he "remained an ardent admirer of Erasmus all his life," *Erasmus—Luther Discourse On Free Will* trans. and ed. Ernst F. Winter, (New York: Continuum, 1990), p. viii.

13. C.D. 4, 4, p. 5. We must be able to maintain the humanity of the church's action in explaining the Lord's Supper. If the human action of the Lord's Supper is seen as more than human, it can no longer claim for its basis and goal the one who loves in freedom. If the human act is obscured in this way, so also is the divine act to which it must point. If the two are fused or confused, we have no way of knowing which is divine and which is human.

14. Ibid., pp. 6-10.

15. On this point see C.D. 4, 3: "The promise of the Spirit . . . is His [Jesus'] direct and immediate presence and action among and with and in us. In it He is the hope of us all," p. 350. See also C.D. 1, 1, p. 450.

16. C.D. 1, 1, pp. 125ff., esp. p. 132.

17. Ibid., pp. 321. and 414ff.

18. Ibid., pp. 75, 155, 451 and 468. Cf. also C.D. 2, 1, pp. 20ff., 69ff., 179ff., 204ff., and 353ff.

19. Karl Barth, *Evangelical Theology: An Introduction*, trans. Grover Foley (Grand Rapids: William B. Eerdmans, 1979, hereafter abbreviated: *Evangelical Theology*), p. 203.

20. Cf. Alasdair I. C. Heron, *Table and Tradition: Toward an Ecumenical Understanding of the Eucharist* (Philadelphia: The Westminster Press, 1983, hereafter abbreviated: *Table and Tradition*), p. 169.

21. Among many possible examples see the *Proceedings of the Forty-Third Annual Convention of The Catholic Theological Society of America* 43 (1988): 44–61"Experience as a Source for Theology," by Ellen Leonard, C.S.J. She actually believes that "It is the task of theology to revision God in the light of contemporary experience . . . ," p. 56. The result is her correction of the image of a "white male God" with female imagery drawn from women's experience and leading us to the idea that God shares responsibility with us. This thinking completely ignores the problem of theology which was so nicely captured by Roland Frye, i.e., that neither the Bible nor the tradition ever wished to ascribe maleness or femaleness to God. Instead, both attempted to understand God through God's own naming himself within the realm of experience. Cf. Roland M. Frye, "Language for God and Feminist Language: Problems and Principles," in *SJT*, 41, 4, (1988): 441–470, esp. 444ff. This is substantially re-presented in *Speaking the Christian God: The Holy Trinity and the Challenge of Feminism*, ed. Alvin F. Kimel, Jr. (Grand Rapids: William B. Eerdmans, 1992), pp. 17–43. With the same methodology Anne Carr argues that "Feminist theology turns to the experience of women in its quest today for fuller understanding of God . . . In exploring these experiences as a possible source for understanding God, theology is led to reflect on the hiddenness and mystery that is God . . . ," *Transforming Grace*, p. 145. Among the several images of God she discovers is the image of God as friend. Thus, God "desires relationship, even the relationship of equality," p. 150 and even needs creatures as well as redemption, pp. 150ff. Jürgen Moltmann begins his theology in the same way in *Trinity*, p. 4. Certainly Karl Rahner is famous for beginning his theology this way in *Foundations of Christian Faith: An Introduction to the Idea of Christianity*, trans. William V. Dych, (New York: The Seabury Press, 1978, hereafter abbreviated:

Foundations), pp. 43 and 53. See also T.I. 4:50ff.

22. C.D. 2, 1, pp. 3–4.

23. Ibid., pp. 13ff. and 52ff.

24. See for e.g. C.D. 1, 1, pp. 99ff. and C.D. 1, 2, pp. 481–92.

25. C.D. 2, 1, p. 210.

26. Ibid.

27. Ibid., p. 212.

28. Ibid., pp. 212–13.

29. Ibid., p. 213.

30. Many modern sacramental theologians base their views on Rahner's theology of the symbol. Cf., e.g., John H. McKenna, *Eucharist and Holy Spirit*, (London: Alcuin, 1975), chapters seven and eight. Gerald McCool, ed., *A Rahner Reader* (New York: Seabury, 1975) notes this connection pp. 120f. and 278f.

31. See, e.g., John H. McKenna, pp. 179ff.

32. Karl Rahner, T.I. 4:221–252 "Theology of the Symbol," pp. 224–25.

33. T.I. 10:79.

34. T.I. 4:251, emphasis mine.

35. Ibid., p. 239. Thus "the Logos, as Son of the Father, is truly, in his humanity as such, the revelatory symbol in which the Father enunciates himself, in his Son, to the world—revelatory, because the symbol renders present what is revealed."

36. Though not stating his indebtedness to Rahner, Eduard Schillebeeckx, *Christ the Sacrament of the Encounter with God*, trans. Paul Barrett, revised by Mark Schoof and Laurence Bright, (New York: Sheed and Ward, 1963), says the same thing, p.60 and draws the logical conclusions on pp. 89ff. and 99ff.

37. Rahner, *The Church and the Sacraments* Quaestiones disputatae, 9, trans. W. J. O'Hara, (New York: Herder, 1968, hereafter abbreviated: *C.S.*), p. 18. Cf. also "The Church as the Subject of the Sending of the Spirit" T.I. 7:188ff. Regarding Christ, cf. T.I. 4:115: "God's creative act always drafts the creature as the paradigm of a possible utterance of himself. And he cannot draft it otherwise, even if he remains silent . . . The immanent self-utterance of God in his eternal fullness is the condition of the self-utterance of God outside himself, and the latter continues the former."

38. T.I. 4:224.

39. Ibid., p. 234.

40. Ibid., pp. 116–17.

41. T.I. 6:72 and 75.

42. T.I. 14:177.

43. Ibid., p. 144.

44. Cf. Paul D. Molnar "Can We Know God Directly? Rahner's Solution From Experience" in *TS* 46 (1985): 228–261, at pp. 250ff. for more on this. See Paul D. Molnar "Toward a Contemporary Doctrine of the Immanent Trinity: Karl Barth and the Present Discussion," forthcoming in *SJT* for how this thinking relates to the doctrine of the Trinity.

45. Michael J. Taylor, S.J., Editor, *The Sacraments: Readings in Contemporary Sacramental Theology* (New York: Alba House, 1981), p. 46. See below (chapter four) for Barth's view of van der Leeuw.

46. See, e.g., Taylor, p. 51 and John H. McKenna, pp. 176ff. James White uses this same method in his book, *Sacraments as God's Self Giving: Sacramental Practice and Faith*, (Nashville: Abingdon Press, 1983), by beginning with the human experience of self-giving and assuming that God's self-giving can be understood as a deepening of that experience. His language incorporates biblical and reformed statements regarding the sacraments but simply ignores the serious theological questions being discussed here in the process.

47. See, e.g., "Is God Essentially Different From His Creatures? Rahner's Explanation From Revelation," in *The Thomist* 51 (1987): 575–631, at pp. 588ff. Rahner's method compelled him to include revelation and grace as elements within our experience and this makes it impossible to distinguish clearly between philosophy and theology, reason and revelation, and ultimately between nature and grace. Thus, while he insisted that grace is an act of the Holy Spirit, he also believed that grace refers to our orientation toward absolute being [mystery]. "We call this orientation grace and it is an inescapable existential of man's whole being," *Foundations*, p. 57. And revelation as the self-communication of God does not refer exclusively to God's act in his Word and Spirit but to "a modification of our transcendental consciousness produced permanently by God in grace." This is a "permanent element in our consciousness . . . And as an element in our transcendentality . . . it is already revelation in the proper sense," *Foundations*, p. 149. This identification of revelation with our transcendentality made it possible for Rahner to understand nature and grace both from human experience philosophically interpreted and at the same time claim that his initial insights came from revelation. But in effect this method amounts to a re-interpretation of revelation by his philosophical interpretation of experience. See also "Reflections on the Problems involved In Devising a Short Formula of the Faith," T.I. 11:243 where Rahner explained quite clearly that our inquiry into the "future in the absolute" is *eo ipso* and implicitly itself the foundation for what is

expressed in the doctrine of the Trinity and in Christology. In our experience of our transcendentality Rahner holds "God is experienced, and moreover, the God of the supernatural order of grace."

48. Karl Barth, *Letters 1961-1968*, ed. Jürgen Fangemeier and Hinrich Stoevesandt, trans. and ed. Geoffrey W. Bromiley, (Grand Rapids: William B. Eerdmans, 1981, hereafter abbreviated: *Letters*), pp. 287-8, emphasis mine.

49. Cf. T.I. 11:243 et al. on this.

50. Cf. T.I. 4:36-73, "The Concept of Mystery in Catholic Theology."

51. McKenna, p. 182.

52. Rahner *C.S.*, p. 38. Emphasis mine.

53. Kenan Osborne, "Methodology and Christian Sacraments" in Taylor, p. 51.

54. Edward Krasevac, O.P., "Christology from Above and Below," in *The Thomist* 51, (1987): 299-306, at pp. 299-301.

55. Ibid., pp. 302-3. Most theologians today begin their Christology from below. Hans Küng, e.g., *On Being a Christian*, trans. Edward Quinn, (New York: Doubleday, 1976), asks "Would it not perhaps correspond more to the New Testament evidence and to modern man's historical way of thinking if we started out like the first disciples from the real human being Jesus, his historical message and manifestation, his life and fate, his historical reality and historical activity, and then ask about the relationship of this human being Jesus to God, about his unity with the Father. In a word, therefore: can we have less of a Christology in the classical manner, speculatively or dogmatically 'from above,' but—without disputing the legitimacy of the older Christology—more of a historical Christology 'from below,' in light of the concrete Jesus, more suited to modern man?", p. 133. Küng believes he can "build up a minimum of authentic Jesus material" (p. 158) and then affirm who Jesus really was. While Küng believes Jesus is important because Christians *consider* "Jesus as ultimately decisive, definitive, *archetypal* for man . . . " (p. 123) and that we meet God the Father in Jesus, he never actually maintains that the man Jesus really is God. Hence when describing what is unique about Jesus, Küng argues that he is God's advocate and that "It is therefore in this ultimate reality—which he calls God, his Father and our Father—that his basic attitude is rooted . . . This question of Jesus' relationship to his Father brings us to the ultimate mystery of Jesus . . . although Jesus himself did not expressly claim the title 'Son' . . . the fact cannot be overlooked that the post-paschal designation of Jesus as 'Son of God' has a real foundation in the pre-paschal Jesus. In all his proclamation and behavior Jesus was interpreting *God*," pp. 317-18. Hence Jesus is important as the man

who unites Christians to God, but others may find God in some other way. Indeed "the decision of faith was centered, not on particular names and titles, but on this Jesus," (p. 318), i.e., the archetypal human Jesus who represented God to us. What is the function of the titles? For Küng they only "substantiate" the uniqueness of the "call, offer and claim *made known in and with Jesus*" p. 449. It was of "divine origin." Yet this analysis leaves out the main point, i.e., that Jesus *is* the only Son of the Father from the very beginning. He is the Word who was and is God who became man. Küng's basic adoptionism is confirmed by his belief that the New Testament statements about the Father, Son, and Spirit refer only to an economic Trinity (pp. 475-6) and that "*Christologically defined, 'truly God' means that the true man Jesus of Nazareth is the real revelation of the one true God,*" p. 477. Here Jesus is not the revealer because he alone is the Word of God. Here he is the revealer because Christians consider him a model of God, the ultimate reality.

56. J.N.D. Kelly, *Early Christian Doctrines*, (New York: Harper and Row, 1978), pp. 139ff.

57. Barth, *Letters*, p. 178, emphasis mine.

58. Wolfhart Pannenberg, *Jesus—God and Man*, trans. Lewis L. Wilkins and Duane A. Priebe (Philadelphia: The Westminster Press, 1977), p. 34.

59. Ibid., p. 35.

60. Ibid., pp. 151ff. and 319.

61. For more on this see ibid., p. 384. See also Paul D. Molnar, "Some Problems With Pannenberg's Solution to Barth's 'Faith Subjectivism'" in *SJT 48*, (1995): 315-339. For a more recent discussion of the method of Christology see Wolfhart Pannenberg *Systematic Theology Volume 2*, trans. Geoffrey W. Bromiley (Grand Rapids: William B. Eerdmans, 1994), pp. 277–97. Compare to pp. 345 and 365. While Pannenberg here attempts to clarify his position in *Jesus—God and Man*, ambiguities still remain. On the one hand, he explicitly rejects adoptionism: "We must see in the Lucan story testimony to the fact that Jesus was the Son of God from the very first and did not become so later, whether by his baptism or his resurrection," p. 302. On the other hand, refusing to equate incarnation with Jesus' birth, since "No one has full personal identity from the moment of birth," Pannenberg argues that Jesus' identity is not fully realized except in light of his end on the cross and in the resurrection. He thus appeals to his idea of a "retroactive force" and to the experience of "anticipation" and suggests that we ought not assume that at the very beginning of his history (Jesus' birth) "the incarnation of the Logos had taken place," pp. 302-3. When taken together with his belief that Jesus' claims needed confirmation to be true, Pannenberg's thinking clearly manifests an adoptionist perspective: "Confirmation

is more than disclosure of a meaning that the person and history of Jesus already had . . . so that it was his even without the Easter event, though in a hidden form . . . We depreciate the Easter event if we construe it only as a disclosure or revelation of the meaning that the crucifixion and the earthly history of Jesus already had in themselves. Only the Easter event determines what the meaning was of the pre-Easter history of Jesus and who he was in his relation to God," p. 345. Here the meaning we receive in light of Easter is confused with a corresponding development in Jesus himself and thus his unique identity before Easter, which is the mystery of his person and work, is compromised. For more on how this relates to the doctrine of the immanent Trinity cf. Paul D. Molnar, "Toward a Contemporary Doctrine of the Immanent Trinity . . . " *SJT*.

62. Ibid., pp. 320–321. Some emphases mine.

63. Cf. Karl Rahner, *The Trinity*, trans. Joseph Donceel (New York: Herder and Herder, 1970, hereafter abbreviated: *Trinity*) pp. 23 and 27. See Wolfhart Pannenberg, *Systematic Theology Volume I*, trans. Geoffrey W. Bromiley, (Grand Rapids: William B. Eerdmans, 1991, hereafter abbreviated: *Systematic Theology I*), chapter five, esp. pp. 327ff. for a more complete discussion of the relationship between the economic and immanent Trinity. (Cf. also Pannenberg, *Jesus—God and Man*, pp. 129–30, pp. 158–60 and p. 183.) See also Molnar "Reflections On Pannenberg's *Systematic Theology*," *The Thomist* 58, (1994): 501–12.

64. Pannenberg, *Jesus—God and Man*, p. 168. Emphasis mine. Compare this to how his idea of revelation functions, pp. 154–5ff.

65. The list of Christologies from below could be multiplied endlessly since, as noted above (n. 55), that is the preferred method today. Yet the same difficulties which we encounter here arise in all of them. Dermot Lane, *The Reality of Jesus: An essay in Christology*, (New York: Paulist Press, 1975) e.g., basically adopts Pannenberg's method in his "low ascending christology" (chapter one). And the result is that his own Christology issues in both docetism and adoptionism, although he thinks he has avoided both. On the one hand, he ignores the problem of sin and Jesus' uniqueness by arguing that between God and us there is "an underlying magnetism" which reaches its "definitive moment" in Jesus p. 128. On the other hand, he argues that the resurrection is not some "exception" or "isolated incident" but that it is "the realisation and crystallisation of man's deepest aspirations . . . the full realisation and actual fulfillment of those seeds of indestructibility which exist within the heart of every individual," p. 64. Finally, instead of beginning his thinking from the unique God-man Lane begins from an "intuitive grasp of a deeper dimension to life" and turns "to Jesus so as to enlarge our awareness and understanding of this abiding mystery in life [i.e., what we call God]," p. 142. Hence Jesus is the highest instance of the

incarnational principle and we do not need to begin our thinking about God or revelation with him. John Knox in his book, *The Humanity and Divinity of Christ: A Study of Pattern in Christology* (New York: The Cambridge University Press, 1967) falls into the same difficulty. While Knox makes every effort to maintain Christ's full humanity (p. 113) and insists upon his divinity (p. 114) his explanation cannot distinguish Jesus, true God and true man, from the community's response to him. Hence he writes, "It is the actual experienced reality of this communal existence to which every christological statement ultimately refers and by which its truth or adequacy must be tested," p. 114. Instead of allowing the truth of Christology to be gauged by its faithfulness to the risen Lord as attested in Scripture, Knox substitutes the community's experience of communal existence and thus detaches truth from God's own action *ad extra*. Rahner also begins from below (cf., e.g., T.I. 19:214-5 "Mary and the Christian Image of Christian Woman") arguing that "A dogmatic Christology today (notwithstanding the rights of an independent fundamental theology) must itself start with the historical Jesus . . . " p. 214. While none of these authors wishes to deny the truth of Christology from above and each wants to authenticate Christology for modern people, the fact remains that each *actually* does transform the essential starting point and content of Christology with his choice of starting points.

66. See, e.g., Paul D. Molnar, *The Thomist* (1987), p. 592.

67. T.I. 11:237.

68. Ibid., emphasis mine.   How can a theological statement have a "christological structure" without explicitly recognizing what is precisely recognized in the Apostles Creed, namely, that Jesus is the only Son of the Father? Any other christological structure will not reflect the truth that God was and is in Christ reconciling the world to himself. The problem here is that the object determining Rahner's thought is not Jesus, true God and true man, but Jesus as understood in light of our experienced need for a savior.

69. In T.I. 4:221-252, "The Theology of the Symbol," Rahner works out his basic principles of symbolic ontology in order to apply the resultant insight as "a general principle without restrictions," (p. 227) to Christology and to the Trinity (p. 228). Recognition of Christ's uniqueness precludes this very assumption as I have shown (*TS*, vol. 46, cited above). For Rahner, however, "the theology of the Logos is strictly a theology of the symbol, *and indeed the supreme form of it* . . ." p. 235, emphasis mine. Thus, Christ is the highest symbol. But it is this very thinking which leads Rahner to compromise Christ's unique mediation envisioned by scripture as in the following statement: "we shall try to understand the mediatorship of Christ as the eschatologically perfect and consequently the

highest, the unique 'case' of human intercommunication before God and of the solidarity in salvation of all men," (T.I. 9:169–84, "One Mediator and Many Mediations," at pp. 173–4). The rest of the article makes his general understanding of human intercommunication the norm for understanding Christ's mediation. Christ's mediation becomes an instance of his general ontology in such a way that all that is really necessary to know and to love God is an experience of intercommunication. No explicit recognition of Christ is necessary (p. 178) because he is the "highest and ultimate factor" in this history of salvation (p. 180) which everyone can know and experience without explicitly knowing Christ. Rahner concludes: "My sole intention was to say this: the saving intercommunication of all (justified) men is the existential ontological precondition for the mediatorship of Christ," p. 184. Christ cannot possibly be the sole mediator in the scriptural sense if there is any precondition for it at all.

70. Cf. C.D. 2, 1, pp. 17, 51, and 320; see also C.D. 1, 1, pp. 126–7 where Barth specifically states that one cannot ground the doctrine of the Word of God in existentialist philosophy because it is self-grounded. By contrast Rahner insisted that we must speak of the incarnation in "primarily existential categories" (T.I. 9:166) for the dogma to make sense. This means in order to understand the incarnation "in terms which express man's total spiritual and cognitive nature" (T.I. 9:166–7) we must describe the incarnation as follows: "This fact of issuing from an origin and proceeding to an end is the essence of the spiritual creature. The more radically this fact is realised in actuality, the more independent, i.e. the freer man is. Therefore the realisation of thus originating in a source and being bound for an end is to an increasing extent the gift of God *and* man's act. If a man receives this human essence from God in such absolute purity and integrity and so actualises this relationship with God that *he becomes God's self-expression* . . . we have what we call 'Incarnation' in a dogmatically orthodox sense" T.I. 9:167, emphasis mine.

71. Rahner, "Christology Within an Evolutionary View of The World" T.I. 5:177.

72. Cf. C.D. 2, 1, p. 18 and C.D. 1, 1, pp. 131ff. Rahner's view of transcendental revelation compromises this also. See Paul D. Molnar, "Can We Know God Directly?" and "Is God Essentially Different From His Creatures?" for more on this. While Gordon Kaufman makes much of the fact that we cannot know God directly (e.g., *T.I.*, p. 22) his argument that God cannot be a particular Being objectively known shows that the God he actually knows was directly described as a regulative idea whose reality could be equated with the historical process itself, if that would lead us to envision and then to create a better society (e.g., *T.I.*, pp. 46ff., esp., p. 54). In *TNA* Kaufman describes God as "an

ultimate tendency or power, which is working itself out in an evolutionary process," (p. 43) and as an "ecological reality behind and in and working through all of life and history," p. 45.

73. See also C.D. 1, 1, pp. 138ff. for Barth's critique of Paul Tillich on this same point.

74. The fact that this insight cannot be accepted by many theologians today simply represents the extent to which contemporary theology has moved toward synthesizing nature and grace. Thus, e.g., James A. Carpenter, *Nature and Grace: Toward An Integral Perspective*, (New York: Crossroad, 1988), p. 74 argues "If God owes us absolutely nothing, if we have no claim whatever on the divine grace, then by analogy at least there may be something deficient in the divine 'parenting'."

75. See C.D. 2, 1, pp. 569–71, C.D. 2, 1, pp. 69ff.

76. Cf. Paul D. Molnar, *SJT* 42, (1989): 367–399.

77. C.D. 3, 2, pp. 11–32.

78. Ibid., p. 117.

79. Ibid., pp. 116–21ff.

80. Ibid., pp. 75–76; also pp. 69–74. For Barth's criteria for determining "real man" see pp. 72–73.

81. Ibid., pp. 92–4.

82. Ibid., p. 95.

83. For the details of this critique see C.D. 3, 2, pp. 97–109.

84. Ibid., pp. 98–104.

85. Ibid., p. 106.

86. Ibid., pp. 107–108.

87. Ibid., pp. 108–109.

88. Cf. C.D. 1, 1, 132ff. for Barth's instructive critique of Tillich on this point. Even though Gordon D. Kaufman argues against Tillich that the religious experience of "depth" is not a raw given of experience itself (which can be directly experienced) and thus it cannot be a foundation for theology, his own solution is that it is "the structure of the idea of God" (*An Essay On Theological Method*, p. 69, n. 6) as used by us which validates the experience. In this sense his thinking is identical to Fichte's.

89. See, e.g., Karl Rahner T.I. 4:36–73, "The Concept of Mystery in Catholic Theology," and Karl Rahner T.I. 11:68–114, "Reflections on Methodology in Theology."

III

Transcendence and Immanence: Christological and Sacramental Applications

Divine/Human Possibility

How exactly, then, did Barth confront the problems he sought to avoid by refusing to adopt any sort of "transcendental method"? In Barth's eyes, human history is filled with profound and shallow ideas and experiences of transcendence which people can and do explore. There has always been

> a desire to strike out for new shores, to conquer self and leave it behind, not merely to become different but to become another, and to be able to make a highly serious beginning as such. Always and everywhere the inescapable vision of the finitude of all human striving and the imperfection and transience of all human achievement and accomplishment . . . inspiring him, impelling him, keeping him on the alert . . . this new beginning implies a possibility which is not at man's disposal, which has first to liberate him for freedom, which is thus higher, transcendental, and in some sense divine.[1]

Indeed, it is a tremendous temptation for the Christian to view the above mentioned divinely created possibility (the fellowship of grace) which enables her or him to be a Christian as

> a particular instance of the general search for, or experience of, this final deepening, exalting, transcending and at the same time realising of human existence on the basis of its radical transforming from without . . . Nothing is indeed more natural than that there should be a more or less considerable corner in its self-understanding where it, too, can regard itself as a participant in this general striving and experience, so that it hesitates to insist with final certainty that what it understands as the new beginning of human life is the only possible one, or even perhaps by far the best among many others.[2]

What is the answer to this truly vexing question? Among the many available philosophies such as process philosophy, classical philosophy, postmodern philosophy, transcendental Thomism, to name only a few, which philosophy should we choose as the foundation of our "new life" as a Christian and therefore of our specifically Christian ethical and eucharistic action? Barth put it this way:

> How is that which must be thought and said about the foundation of the Christian life to conduct itself at the annual fair of philosophies and panaceas, of disguised or undisguised religions, with the very different, yet confusingly similar, foundations of life which they espouse and proffer?[3]

His answer was really quite simple. All non-Christian views of this divine possibility regard it as a direct relation of the creature to a godhead, variously depicted, which is present and active generally, namely, outside time and space. It may even be restricted to the relation of only certain people to this godhead. The Christian does not dispute the existence of a power like this which may exist in direct relation to us. "On the contrary, the existence and work of a supposed deity of this kind, and hence the possibility and actuality of a direct relation between it and man, will be presupposed by the Christian as a foil to the foundation to his Christian life." This is the being which was in fact overcome in and by the divine possibility which the Christian confesses. The key question for the Christian consists in asking whether this supposed deity is identical with the "God whom he sees active and self-revealed in the origin of his Christian existence."[4] What then is this new possibility which eludes the creature as such, but nevertheless is possible for God?

Christ and Christians: Eucharistic Implications

For Barth, the answer was that true human freedom is grounded in the God of Abraham, Isaac, and Jacob. It is based in God who exercised his sovereignty in a very particular way, i.e., in the history of Jesus Christ. "This history is the change, impossible with men but possible with God . . ."[5] Commenting on the petition in the Lord's prayer "Thy Kingdom Come" Barth wrote:

> Jesus Christ is the new thing. *He* is the mystery that cannot be imprisoned in any system of human conceptuality . . . *He* is God acting concretely within human history . . . not, then an it, however lofty or profound; not a transcendent world of light . . . not a new philosophy . . . not a christology . . . Simply and solely *he himself*: accomplishing and completing God's work for the salvation of the world . . . [6]

For the Christian, the only divine possibility is the divine possibility actualized in Christ who was elected in eternity to be head and savior to all creatures.[7] In time, he responded to God's faithfulness with human faithfulness. In that way he obeyed his eternal election to fellowship with God. He died in accordance with that election. This death itself is the expiation of our enmity "in which man as such stands against grace, is expiated and abandoned before God by God Himself, before the Father by His only begotten Son, but by the incarnate Son of God and therefore in our place."[8]

Jesus Christ is the victory of grace over human enmity, i.e., the new man who suffered our punishment for us and is, as the incarnate Word, the "new man." His resurrection revealed the fact that he did for everyone what they in themselves could not do. The change which took place in this particular history actually took place for everyone. In the particular history of Jesus Christ a man was, for the first time, fully faithful to the covenant. He lived by grace and by faith alone. In this particular life, Christian living and acting became possible. It is this unique history of Christ, namely, his historical existence which Christians have in view in celebrating the Lord's Supper; they recognize this history as effective and saving history when they celebrate the Lord's Supper.

What is the difference between this unique history and the history of Christians? For Barth, "A Christian . . . is a man from whom it is not hidden that his own history took place along with the history of Jesus Christ."[9] The Christian is one who accepts the *de jure* fact of his or her representation once for all in the history of Christ. He or she accepts the fact that this particular history is the decisive event in his or her life. This is a word spoken to the Christian in the power of the Holy Spirit of the risen Lord. "He himself in the midst of all other men can see himself as one of those for whom and in whose place Jesus Christ did what He did."[10] It is the history of Jesus Christ alone then which is the beginning, middle, and end of Christian living and acting. Faithful recognition of this fact distinguishes Christian thinking and acting from all other thinking and acting. Barth maintained a distinction in union between Christ and the Christian here in order to avoid a monistic, dualistic, or synthetic view of the two; this particular distinction in union also eschews a docetic or an ebionite view of Christ's presence.[11]

Ebionite—Docetic Christology

Ebionite Christology assumes that Christ's divinity is grounded in the impression Christ made upon his followers. Thus, it rests not in Christ's existence as God and man but in the experiences of his followers. To that extent it is a denial of his actual uniqueness. For Barth, an ebionite view of the two natures tends toward identity. This would lead to identity in terms of analogy and thus to the idea of direct knowledge of the transcendent God. This is wrong for the same reasons that analogies of *parity* confuse divine and human being and action monistically. As seen above, the problem with more recent Christologies from below is that they do indeed start with the same presuppositions as ebionite Christology, i.e., they begin with our self-transcending experiences and analyze them in relation to the New Testament and traditional portraits of Jesus. While they may explicitly deny that they are grounding Christ's uniqueness in anything but his own mystery, the fact remains that it is human experience and interpretation of it that determines the content of those Christologies.

As seen above, that is precisely why Rahner could move both from anthropology as self-transcendence to Christology and from Christology back to anthropology. Not only did Rahner believe that Jesus' humanity *as such* can reveal his divinity but, in accordance with his theology of the symbol, he held that his humanity is the exteriorization of the Logos. The "incarnate word is . . . filled as nothing else can be with what is symbolized."[12] This led Rahner to believe that all reality now has this symbolic extension and therefore that a human experience of self-transcendence and of self-acceptance is in itself already an experience of Christ and of grace, at least anonymously.[13] Rahner himself completed the logical circle of this position arguing, e.g., that "one can speak of genuine faith on condition that a man freely accepts his own unlimited transcendence which is raised up by grace and directed to the immediate presence of God as its final goal."[14] Since the human spirit has an inner dynamism toward "absolute being," which Rahner equated with the Christian God, he concluded that "Without reflection he accepts God when he freely accepts himself in his own unlimited transcendence. He does this when he genuinely follows his conscience with free consent . . ."[15] While it is certainly true that one does not, in every instance, have to be consciously adverting to God in order to obey God morally and "existentially," Rahner's thinking went beyond this to argue from the universal experience of self-transcendence to the universal nature of God's salvific will. He thus equated self-acceptance with grace and salvation. Rahner argued in the same fashion with respect to revelation: since our orientation to absolute being (God) is a "grace-given" elevation of human nature Rahner actually equated self-knowledge with revelation. Hence Rahner wrote:

> And when man of his freedom accepts himself together with this *a priori* awareness which is already revelation, then that is present which can in the true and proper sense be called faith . . . Yet this *a priori* awareness of man (called revelation) is always accepted in faith wherever and whenever

an individual in unreserved faithfulness to his own moral conscience accepts himself in freedom as he is . . .[16]

In Barth's view, the equation of self-acceptance with acceptance of grace follows Rahner's re-definition of the Chalcedonian *unio* as a more intimate union so that all created reality can be described as tending toward grace. This thinking is the logical result of a Christology which began to analyze the union of natures from our experience of self-transcendence interpreted in symbolic terms. All creation is infinitely extended and altered in virtue of the incarnation and thus human experience becomes the source of the truth of Christology itself.[17]

Docetic Christology assumes that Christ's divinity is grounded in the timeless ideas of truth which Jesus' disciples had prior to and after their encounter with him. Thus, Jesus' uniqueness would be seen as an instance of a divinity which creatures perceive as true independent of Christ. This denies Christ's uniqueness by detaching Jesus' divinity from the historical Jesus and the historical teaching of the church. Docetic thinking assumes it can speak about the reality of God in abstraction from the historical Jesus and thus without recollecting this specific historical content. It thus grounds knowledge of God and of reconciliation in its ideas or experiences. As Barth noted, there are amazing similarities between this kind of christological interpretation and the nominalism of Eunomius, Occam, and Biel. In effect what this scheme represents is an attempt to speak about God on the basis of analogies of *disparity* between the general philosophical constructs and the reality of God. Nominalism of course assumes that the reality of God is a *nuda essentia* and to that extent, could be construed, when applied to Christology, as docetism. But if the triune God who loves in freedom is the norm here, this is precisely what he cannot be.[18]

Rahner explicitly rejected nominalism. But his notion of God as the nameless and wordless silence which we encounter as the term of our transcendental acts actually led him to *define* the immanent and economic Trinity according to the principles of his symbolic ontology. This method shows that Rahner understood truth first from within a general metaphysics and only then from revelation insofar as this is a particular instance of God's general engracing of the world.[19] Moltmann also explicitly rejects nominalism. But, as he develops his notion of God's relation with the world from mysticism, panentheism, and the experience of suffering, he himself forms God's revelation in Christ according to his own prior understanding obtained from his panentheistic ideal of mutual relationships. This is precisely why Moltmann cannot make any definite distinction between the immanent and economic Trinity.[20]

Barth's rejection of ebionite and docetic Christology forms the background for understanding how creatures participate in the holiness of God. Their actual participation in the Godhead will be misunderstood if it is described on the basis of analogies of parity, disparity, or synthesis. It will be misunderstood if one's picture of Christ results from an ebionite, docetic, or a synthetic construct. The creature's holiness is a holiness "hidden" with Christ in God. For that reason it is never a property of human experience (ebionitism), human thinking (docetism), or of creation in general (pantheism or panentheism).

In this context Moltmann presents a tantalizing view of the messianic secret in relation to Jesus' self-understanding. Nevertheless, while he theoretically rejects adoptionism, his own view of Jesus' uniqueness is based on the adoptionist view that "Jesus does not *possess* the messiahship; he grows into it."[21] In connection with the resurrection, Moltmann believes "Jesus *is* the Lord because God *has raised* him from the dead. His *existence* as the Lord is to be found in God's eschatological *act* in him, which we call raising from the dead . . . He is not the Christ apart from this act of God."[22] Consequently his thinking is not determined by the fact that Jesus *is* God's Son in time and eternity but rather by the fact that Jesus is "born of the Spirit and filled with the Spirit." Hence Jesus did not really pre-exist as the Son of the Father in eternity. Instead his Abba experience as a "child" of the Father, which clearly is an experience of the historical Jesus in time is, according to Moltmann, "constitutive" for the Father-Son relation itself. Only in that sense can we speak of pre-existence. But the problem is, if the *history* of Jesus constitutes the immanent life of the Trinity, then in fact theology has been defined by anthropology and actually has ceased; holiness then results from history rather than from God's act within history. God's action then would be that which comes to be in the mutual relationship of Jesus and God within his messianic history. For Barth our holiness can be seen and described in specific human actions corresponding to the divine action that took place in Jesus' own history. For Moltmann our holiness can be seen and described in human experiences of suffering and freedom. Thus, on the one hand

the history of the world is the history of God's suffering. At the moments of God's profoundest revelation there is always suffering: the cry of the captives in Egypt; Jesus' death cry on the cross; the sighing of the whole enslaved creation for liberty. *If a person once feels the infinite passion of God's love which finds expression here, then he understands the mystery of the triune God.* God suffers with us—God suffers from us—God suffers for us: *it is this experience of God that reveals the triune God . . .* Consequently fundamental theology's discussion about access to the doctrine of the Trinity is carried on today in the context of the question about God's capacity or incapacity for suffering.[23]

And "*Easter* determines the *form* of belief in Jesus Christ, but not its content. The *content* is determined by the *history of Jesus' life.*"[24] On the other hand Moltmann can say regarding miracles that "In the context of the new creation, these 'miracles' [of the kingdom] are not miracles at all,"[25] and that

> Jesus himself grows from the expectation and faith of these women. He surpasses himself, as we say—he grows beyond himself . . . he grows into the One whom he will be, God's messiah . . . [indeed] The divine power of healing does not come from his side alone . . . The healings are stories about faith just as much as they are stories about Jesus. They are stories about the reciprocal relationships between Jesus and the faith of men and women. *Jesus is dependent on this faith*, just as the sick are dependent on the power that emanates from Jesus.[26]

Of course Barth consistently rejected this kind of mutual conditioning arguing that the eucharistic action is holy, i.e., it participates in the holiness of God, as it recognizes and lives its new history in Christ. This the church attests in eating the bread of life and drinking the wine which is the cup of eternal life. To underscore this point in his ecclesiology Barth insisted that Christ is present to his community by his own transcendent power. This actual presence is what the church attests in its worship and its daily behavior. Christ is present to his body, and recognizably so, as the church is faithful to his command. According to this command the common eating and drinking of his disciples

> is no more and no less than His body and blood (the κοινωνία of His body and blood according to 1 Cor. 10:16). This action . . . is the direct proclamation of His death until He comes (1 Cor. 11:26). In this provisional form as the action of the community, it is His own action; the work of His real presence. Here and now He himself is for them—His offered body and His shed blood—the communion of saints thanking and confessing him in this action.[27]

Later we shall examine how Markus Barth's view of the Pauline *koinonia* enables him to affirm the unity of Israel and the church as well as Christ's real presence without falling into the pitfalls of an ebionite or docetic view. Here we simply note that he believes Paul's use of the word *koinonia* means that Paul had in view our fellowship with the risen Jesus rather than the idea of a change in the bread.[28] Further, he argues that Paul is not saying to the Corinthians that they are eating and drinking the Holy Spirit. Rather the rock from which the water flowed in the Old Testament typified Christ, the rock.

Abstraction from the *analogia fidei* (and thus also from grace and revelation) in analyzing the church's action in the Lord's Supper would mean that what is actually the case, namely, God's personal presence with his community in his Word and Spirit, would not be recognized. Not perceiving that its sole possibility and limitation is Christ, the church might then suppose that its mission and task were quite different from what they actually are. It might assume that God depends upon the church to "convert the heathen" in order to make his kingdom present on earth. The impossibility and foolishness of such an assumption could only be illustrated by such historical tragedies as the Inquisition and the Crusades. The point here is simply this. As Christ alone is the criterion of the church's being and action, there can be no thought of the church attempting to do what only God can do, namely, to convert others and to make himself known and present to others either sacramentally or morally. The church's task is no more and no less than to proclaim Christ's actual presence until he comes again. The church is therefore limited to faithful witness to God's ongoing action in and for the world; it cannot do this by confusing the two. When this truth is forgotten, the church may succumb either to secularization or sacralization[29] as alternative expressions of its failure to perceive that its sole norm is the living Christ present in the power of the Spirit.

Secularization and Sacralization

Its norm is neither its secular form nor its sacramental (sacred) form. An understanding of the church grounded in ebionite or docetic Christology will always begin thinking about Christ as a model construct whose foundation is in Christian experience or in a particular ideology. As long as this remains the starting point, however, the norm for truth will always be the sacred or secular form in which God actually encounters us in Christ. As the church tries to orientate its own life according to patterns of world history, it runs the risk of self-justification and of identifying its essence with that of the world. As the church tries to orientate its own life according to patterns of sacramental action, e.g., liturgy, it runs the risk of self-glorification and thus of self-justification once again. In either instance, Christ's role as the One Mediator is compromised; and so also is its true essence, i.e., its holiness. Clearly, Barth's model for the holiness of Christians is neither an experience, an idea, nor a general conception of the numinous. It is the holiness which, according to the divine freedom, remains "always a new thing, something that God actually brings into being in specific circumstances."[30]

Barth's view here is to be contrasted sharply with the views of Geoffrey Wainwright on secularization and sacralization. Wainwright correctly criticizes "the teilhardian vision" of G. Martelet whose "model of transubstantiation is projected from the liturgy onto the whole universe, so that the goal seems to be some kind of pantheistic identification between Christ and the 'transubstantiated' universe as his body." He also rightly rejects "liturgical escapism" and "sacralization" in the form of clericalism.[31]

But the problem in his reasoning is that the corrective to these distortions is not to be found exclusively in Christ as the unique mediator of revelation. Rather "sacralization may provoke a reaction in favour of the secular. Secularization can be a healthy corrective, but it runs the risk of . . . ideological secularism."[32] In this context Barth was directing theologians to the fact that the only "healthy" corrective of "sacralization" will be one grounded in the fact that the sacred and profane are held together in the history of Jesus Christ. Correcting clericalism with secularism then, already betrays an incorrect shift of norms from knowledge informed by revelation and faith to knowledge informed by secular sciences.

For Barth, the divine possibility actualized in Christians as they hear this particular Word and obey it, is and remains distinct from them. Its actuality can neither be found in Christians nor in non-Christians. It can only be seen in Christ himself who lives by the power of his Spirit. Only by hearing and following this Christ, who did what creatures as such could not and cannot do, is it possible for people to know with certainty of their new life and actually to live it. In this particular hearing and obeying, the creature as such is changed without being divinized.[33] Creatures literally cannot know this same truth by analyzing their ideas or experiences. Their ideas and experiences do not necessarily lead to this particular mystery of revelation in which the "totally other" acted to and for mankind in a very definite way which demands a very definite, but limited response. Because it is the "totally other" with whom we have to do here, even as the history of Christ is unveiled by the Holy Spirit, it remains veiled inasmuch as it remains a historical event.[34]

Barth's concept of veiling and unveiling was decisive in explaining the meaning of revelation without identifying, separating, or synthesizing divine and human being and action. What he meant in the doctrine of the Word of God and in the doctrine of God when he used this expression was that, because only God reveals God, it is factually impossible for us to integrate Christ into an anthropological or philosophical system. Human systems had their significance only as they allowed God's action in Christ to precede and determine their truth character normatively. Thus, Barth maintained consistently that human interpretation and the fact of Christ cannot be reversed.[35] He believed that Anselm was a historical example of someone whose interpretation of revelation did not make this reversal. For that reason, the substance of all that he says in developing his concept of analogy and in applying this notion to the sacrament, is lost if it is thought that theology might just as easily become understanding seeking faith as faith seeking understanding.[36] Barth also noted that the New Testament passages concerning death are often misconstrued as mystical or spiritual dying. He believed that the New Testament meant to convey the fact that death was actually a "sting." With that in mind, those who perceived their inclusion in the Christ event, knew that it was *only* the death and resurrection of Christ which had saving significance.[37]

This significant point is compromised by Geoffrey Wainwright's attempt to grasp Christ's uniqueness as implied in the Johannine claim that "no one comes to the Father but by me." Wrestling with Rahner's anonymous Christianity, Panikkar's "unknown Christ of Hinduism" and John Hick's view that this thinking of Rahner and Panikkar still represents "Christian Imperialism" [because he believes it is better to put God and not Christ at the center of the universe of faiths] Wainwright proposes that we may

> look upon Jesus as the *ultimate* revelation of God in the sense that Christ loved humanity 'to the end', that is, unto death . . . [Hence] *Wherever* self-giving love is shown by human beings in any degree at all, God must be said to be present in the transformation of human character into God's own moral and spiritual likeness . . . [human self-giving is a reflection of Christ] for it is in the case of Christ that they see this pattern [of self-giving love] displayed with such primordial clarity and such final intensity that this person becomes the focal point of reference for all other instances. This view of the matter would claim for Christ a uniqueness of the pattern-setting or criterio-logical kind, transcending the 'exclusive/inclusive' or 'culture-bound/imperialist' alternatives . . . It might be said that the function of Christian worship *within the world* is to bear symbolic witness to the Christ-pattern.[38]

The first problem with this solution is that it operates with the ebionite assumption that Christ's uniqueness can be seen as a quality ascribed to him so that he becomes the focal point of all other instances of self-sacrificing love. This thinking denies both the veiling and the unveiling described above. And the second problem with this solution is that it ends with the docetic idea that Jesus' uniqueness can be equated with the fact that he is not truly the only way to the Father because he *is* the Son beside whom there is no other, but that he is the pattern for all the self-giving love which we already know and experience within the world. Consequently, we already know the true meaning of who Christ is and what he brings simply by experiencing and knowing the meaning of self-giving love. Christ is the "most" primordial example of this for Christians. This position certainly makes sense in light of his proposal that some form of adoptionism in Christology today is necessary.[39] But it simply does not do justice to the issue which is here being discussed. For any hint of ebionite or docetic Christology means that human experience or human ideology are still the starting points and norms for our definition of theological truth. As that remains the case there is no way to speak about a "totally other" meeting all people in the history of Christ and realizing a genuinely effective salvation which can only be seen and understood by faith, i.e., through the Holy Spirit.

Wainwright's attempt to mediate between the "exclusive/inclusive" and "culture-bound/imperialist" alternatives neither begins nor ends with Jesus' actual uniqueness as the one Son of the Father. Hence, the fact that only God reveals God is compromised by incorporating Christ into an anthropological system which allows Christ a certain primordial and final intensity but does not admit of a genuine *need* for him *alone* as the source of our justification and sanctification. The result is that he can deduce the meaning of Christian worship *from the world* as well as from an analysis of Christian worship. As this is thought possible there is no *real* need for Christ except insofar as we need a pattern for what occurs in the secular sphere.

It is worth noting that Karl Rahner solved this particular problem in a similar way by arguing that the church's liturgy simply represents a particular instance of the "world's liturgy" since the world is already "engraced" in its very structure. Thus, speaking of the effectiveness inherent in sacramental signs Rahner wrote:

> This effectiveness of the sign as such (the sign of that grace of God which is already taking effect always and everywhere throughout the world right from its very roots!) can be explained in several stages . . . this concrete process of self-fulfillment is itself all along and in all cases a 'real symbol' under which the individual brings to fruition this basic attitude of his, his *option fundamentale.*[40]

What Rahner meant was that one's interior disposition, which may give rise to genuine human acts of freedom, is a sign and cause of "that which is promulgated." Thus, the free individual "brings himself to his fulness as an event of grace in this sense *in that* he expresses himself, and this expression is, in the sense explained, the cause of the act imbued with grace and of the grace itself."[41] The importance of this reasoning is that it yields a universal salvation identical with God's grace which in fact is indistinguishable from the world. The distinction between the church and the world is not between the sphere of the godless and the holy. Rather, what happens in the church is the realization of a hidden reality which is already taking place in the world, namely, our self-realization and self-acceptance. In actuality then God's grace which

> was already present in the world achieves its own fulness in history,
> expresses itself, and so enters upon that mode of existence towards which
> it has been orientated from the outset . . . [thus] sacraments designate and
> promulgate [in] society and history that grace which is designated . . . by
> the basic sacrament of the Church . . . they constitute signs of the grace
> of the *world*, that grace which is present and effective within the world
> constantly and from the first. That grace of God which is implanted in the
> world also sustains the Church and her sacraments . . . [sacraments are]
> pro-cesses (in the etymological sense!) of the grace of the world which
> even within the world is perceived by him who, through word and
> sacrament, has experienced the fact that the life of himself and of the
> world has all along been sanctified and opened up to the inconceivability
> of God . . .[42]

All of this follows from Rahner's natural theology which leads to the idea that sacraments are symbolic manifestations of the "liturgy of the world."[43] Men and women live in a "divine world." Hence "the liturgy which the Son has brought to its absolute fulness on his Cross belongs intrinsically to it, emerges from it, i.e. from the ultimate source of the grace of the world . . ."[44] Since the world is "permeated by the grace of God" everyone has a chance to accept his or her life as meaningful and thus accept God as the goal of that transcendental movement. This, because grace "proceeds from the innermost heart and centre of the world and of man: it takes place not as a special phenomenon, as one particular process *apart from* the rest of human life. Rather it is quite simply the ultimate depths and radical dimension of all that which the spiritual creature experiences . . ."[45]

Certainly, Rahner was attempting to make sense of the sacraments in a way that would not allow people simply to isolate their worship at Mass from the rest of their lives. In itself this intention is valid and ought not to be rejected.[46] What must be rejected however is the radical blurring of the distinction between nature and grace which has taken place in Rahner's thought. Instead of explaining the meaning of the liturgy from God's action in Christ by way of the church's worship and then in relation to the world and the life of Christians in the world, Rahner located grace within the transcendental orientations of everyone in the world and defined Christianity as the particular process by which people give expression to their experiences of mystery within history.

Thus, the world is not only divine, as in pantheism, but true liturgy celebrates more a person's experiences of depth than the fact that, by faith, that person turns from himself or herself to the Lord who promised and indeed effected salvation in his Son. Because Rahner did not clearly distinguish knowledge of God from knowledge of the nameless term of an individual's transcendence in his doctrine of God, he was led to a conclusion which is irreconcilable with his own belief that it is in Jesus alone that the world actually finds its true meaning. It is no accident then that Rahner saw a way from anthropology to Christology and vice versa. And it is just that reversibility which discloses that he has not actually described grace in its sovereignty but rather he has depicted the depths of human experience using the Christian ideas of grace and salvation as universals within everyone's experience.

Paul Tillich has essentially the same problem because he clearly confuses our experiences of depth with the experience of God. He could even say that

> The name of this infinite and inexhaustible depth and ground of all being is *God*. That depth is what the word *God* means. And if that word has not much meaning for you, translate it, and speak of the depths of your life, of the source of your being, of your ultimate concern, of what you take seriously without any reservation. Perhaps, in order to do so, you must forget everything traditional that you have learned about God, perhaps even that word itself. For if you know that God means depth, you know much about Him. You cannot then call yourself an atheist or unbeliever. For you cannot think or say: Life has no depth! Life itself is shallow. Being itself is surface only. If you could say this in complete seriousness, you would be an atheist; but otherwise you are not. He who knows about depth knows about God.[47]

This rather overt equation of a human experience of depth with knowledge of God has been exploited by various theologians to argue that God is not a *particular* being existing "out there" who enters into history from outside; rather "God" is simply "a name for the dimension of depth all of us experience . . . "[48]

It is easy to see that such a re-definition of the word God is not merely formal but material. The name God no longer refers exclusively to the Father, Son, and Holy Spirit uniting us with himself by acting within the secular sphere. Rather the name God refers to one's ultimate depths which can be described in sacred or secular terms as that which is divine. But the fact is that a theology of Christian worship has already ceased because an experience of depth is not in itself an experience of God and an experience of God would actually forbid this equation of self-experience with an experience of God! Such a method will lead to secularization (any word which is substituted for the Christian Word will do) and to sacralization (Christian sacraments express this divine depth in word and sign).

Rahner's well known belief that God can be known as the term of our transcendental acts led him to conclude that this *term* or goal [God] could have "a thousand other names." It could be "'absolute being' or 'being in an absolute sense'" or the "'ground of being' which establishes everything in original unity."[49] Rahner himself called it "the holy mystery."[50] A being which could have a thousand other names, however, cannot be the unique being of the Trinity, even if subsequently conceived as trinitarian; for once God is conceived in this way, it is clear that what is here described is nothing more than the experience of our own horizon which can be called by any one of a number of names. Once this door is opened, the possibilities are endless. God could be called an ecological reality with Kaufman, our motherly Father with Moltmann, or our ultimate concern with Tillich. But in each instance the idea of God is neither grounded in nor defined by God's trinitarian existence; it is rather a creation of creaturely experience and leads to secularization just because the ultimate norm for truth has become the creature instead of the creator. As seen above, in Rahner's description of the "divine world" which is celebrated in the liturgy, it can also lead to sacralization, i.e., the idea that the church's sacraments actualize and effect the world's divine depth in a special way.

Jürgen Moltmann reaches similar conclusions and thus has similar difficulties when he speaks of cosmic Christology.[51] While he correctly insists that Christ cannot be "fitted into the laws and rhythms of the cosmos as it is" as some "New Age" thinkers would have it, following Jung, he himself agrees with Teilhard de Chardin that Christ is not merely present in the world in a hidden way. Rather "He is also immanently efficacious in 'the heart of creation'."[52] Yet when Moltmann concludes that the risen Christ is efficacious "in the human victims of world history" as well as "in victimized nature too;"[53] that "the cosmic Wisdom-Christ will come forth from the heart of creation;"[54] that "She is therefore also *inexistant*, or inherent, in all things;"[55] that Christ is "the moving power in the evolution of creation"[56] and that "God is the innermost life of the world"[57] it is clear that instead of understanding the cosmic process in light of Christ as he believes he should,[58] Moltmann finds Christ directly within history and nature. To that extent he cannot distinguish the wisdom of God from the movements of the world and argues that the world is evolving toward God,[59] that "nature and grace are so closely interwoven that it is impossible to talk about the one without talking about the other," and that "the Spirit and the Word—wait and strive in all things for the liberation of them all."[60] While Barth decisively rejected Teilhard's Gnostic pantheism in order to avoid such conclusions,[61] Moltmann labels Teilhard a gnostic only because Teilhard overlooked the ambiguity inherent in evolution itself. He overlooked the fact that evolution could be cruel and was not simply something positive. Evolution had its victims too. One cannot therefore acquiesce "in evolution's victims, as the unavoidable fertilizers of that future—not even the Omega Point, with its divine fulness." Moltmann's solution is to see Christ as a victim among the other victims of nature and history and thereby to avoid gnostic conclusions which would make historical faith irrelevant. Hence "If Christ is to be thought of in conjunction with evolution, he must become evolution's redeemer." Yet, a Christ who is thought of in conjunction with evolution as Moltmann has, is in fact indistinguishable from the movements of creation itself. Hence for Moltmann, he must become evolution's redeemer; he cannot be the redeemer already. And he is already the power inherent in the suffering of evolution's victims; thus he cannot have been present among the inventors of the atomic bomb and no meaning can be given to the mass deaths of the world wars of this century.[62] Yet by conceiving of God's free act of redemption from within the perspective of suffering Moltmann concludes that "It is not through supernatural interventions that God guides creation . . . Seen in terms of world history, the transforming power of suffering is the *basis* for the liberating and consummating acts of God."[63] By this reasoning, which identifies the immanent and economic Trinity in light of the cross of Christ, God cannot overcome suffering since suffering itself is the *principle* which encompasses his very being and love.

In view of Christ, then, the New Testament unequivocally saw faithfulness to God as a free act of creatures that involved an inner change in which a person freely decided to think, act, and conduct himself or herself differently than before. This human action of obedience was itself that which was possible with God. Indeed, it took place *extra nos* in the history of Christ, very God and very man; but its *telos* was mankind and not some abstract idea of dying and becoming which supposedly explains how this event *extra nos* becomes an event *in nobis*. Its *telos* was the creature who in himself or herself is disobedient, and thus seeks himself or herself and not God. Human life in general is possible and actual only as it perceives its *actual* unity with Christ, i.e., only as it is obedient as he was obedient.[64] As Barth saw it: "Jesus Christ's obedience consists in the fact that He willed to be and was only this one thing with all its consequences, God in the flesh, the divine bearer of the burden which man as a sinner must bear."[65]

This is the meaning of *kenosis* for Barth and it has absolutely nothing to do with ethical heroism which is simply another intolerable attempt at self-justification. This must be contrasted sharply with Rahner's characterization of salvation as the acceptance of meaning in life in spite of being faced with egoism and despair in face of death and other threats. The pivotal point here is that for Rahner grace can be seen and experienced "whenever . . . life is lived as man would seek to live it, in such a way as to overcome his own egoism and despair of the heart which constantly assails him."[66] Thus, on the one hand, Rahner insisted that there are real differences between believers and unbelievers when their different views of life are consistently lived out. But, on the other hand, Rahner contended that if an unbeliever lived like a believer he could say "If this person angrily insists that he naturally respects the moral norms of life just as unconditionally as the first, then, on my terms, if his statement is true and radical in intention, he is a believer who is unable to analyse the implications of his own principles of conduct . . . "[67] For Barth grace may be seen for what it is only through an understanding of the particular act of justification which took place *extra nos* and *pro nobis* in the history of Jesus Christ. Hence it cannot be equated with the moral action of individuals at all without compromising the fact of our justification by faith and grace.

For this reason, Jesus was not presented as a great moral ideal in the New Testament. Such an assessment leaves us in the dilemma of having to choose between the synoptics and John and Paul. No such choice is required because both ebionite and docetic thinking are ruled out in advance by the simple fact that Jesus was and is unique. In his obedience to the will of the Father "God reconciled the world to himself."[68] Jesus lived by grace as no one else could, because he alone was and is the God-Man. He allowed God to precede and he simply followed. In this way the world was drawn out of its enmity with God. For Barth, our reconciliation is real, but it is so as a result of God's gracious action in Christ. In Christ God fulfilled the covenant. The offense offered to God by human unfaithfulness was removed in this way. In keeping the covenant himself, God keeps his own glory and in that way upholds creatures. Thus,

> It is apparent at once that the formula 'God everything and man nothing' as a description of grace is not merely a 'shocking simplification' but complete nonsense. Man is nothing, i.e., he has fallen prey to nothingness, without the grace of God . . . In the giving of His Son, however, in reconciling the world to himself in Christ, God is indeed everything but only in order that man may not be nothing, in order that he may be His man, in order that as such he, too, may be everything in his own place, on his own level and within his own limits.[69]

Everything, then, depends upon the fact that Christ is the same as other creatures but in quite a different way. It is as the eternal Word and only as the eternal Word that he is man. That is why his history is saving history and our history as such, apart from him, is not and cannot be saving history. Being a Christian means quite simply being *in* Christ in this manner. It means acknowledging his veiling and unveiling as an act of the triune God. It ought to be stressed that this particular feature of Barth's theology seems to cause the greatest difficulty today.

While Barth explicitly argued that Christ's *historical* uniqueness consists in his being the Incarnate Word, many more recent theologians insist on defining his uniqueness some other way first and only then explaining his actual uniqueness. Yet, to the extent that Barth's method was actually dictated by the uniqueness of Christ, this very procedure subverts the historicity of revelation. One brief example will serve to illustrate the point.

In his dialogue with Maurice Wiles and John Hick concerning the divinity of Christ, Geoffrey Wainwright thinks that there is a "measure of subordinationism" possible for Christian theology. Accordingly he writes: "To take the ontological risk: I myself go for 'subordinationism'. I understand that the Son is *God as self-given* (the divine self-giving takes incarnate form in Christ), while the Father is *God as inexhaustibly self-giving.*"[70] This Wainwright suggests may not be far removed from Athanasius' view that the Son is fully God except that he is not the Father. Yet it really is quite different. Athanasius admitted no subordination within the Godhead or in God's action *ad extra;* for Athanasius the Son was the Son "before all worlds." In Wainwright's thinking it appears that the Father is the only one who *really* exists before all worlds, while his eternal self-giving takes incarnate shape in the Son as self-giver.

This subordinationist grasp of Christ's deity is confirmed by Wainwright's conclusion that he can best understand Christ's humanity in terms of his call to communion with God and his "divinization" or "transformation" into

> self-giving love which is moral and spiritual likeness to God . . . [Thus] God has set the highest value upon him ('has super-exalted him', Philippians 2:9). If God might almost be said to 'worship' Jesus Christ as his life-companion, then it is hardly surprising that human beings should set such high value upon the one whose footsteps they hope to follow.[71]

Is Christ's Sonship the embodiment of our human need to value him and of God's own setting a value upon him? Or is he not the eternal Son of God whose being as the Incarnate Word does not rest upon any value we think ought to be placed on his human life whether by God or creatures?

In any case Wainwright's Christology falters at exactly the point that he is unwilling to allow his thinking to be dictated by Christ's actual uniqueness as God and man. As we have already seen, he redefines the incarnation in a more or less ebionite fashion, to mean that Christians value Jesus as the ultimate expression of God's self-giving love. Hence he equates self-giving love with God's presence and argues that God is present "in the transformation of human character into God's own moral and spiritual likeness."[72] Here ebionitism issues in a docetic definition of God's love and finally into the moralism which Wainwright really believes he avoids. And Jesus Christ, God and man, is not really the active mediator of all truth for Wainwright, though he states that Jesus actively mediates his presence to us since Protestant theology holds to this.[73] Rather, Christ is the "pattern" in which Christians recognize the focal point of all other instances of self-giving love, and as we saw above, his uniqueness is then reduced to a "pattern setting" kind of uniqueness.

It is important to state here clearly that we are confronted at this point with what often has been termed the "scandal of particularity" with the regard to the Gospel. For Barth Christian worship bears witness to Jesus Christ, God and man, who is as such the savior of all. For Wainwright Christian worship bears witness to a Christ pattern which is discernable quite apart from faith in the Son and Spirit in the patterns of self-giving love within and without Christianity. A discussion of some sacramental implications of this thinking will illustrate exactly how and why it is important to avoid both the ebionite and docetic starting points in order to grasp Christ's uniqueness.

When Wainwright explains the meaning of the Eucharist he seeks to deal with the "difficulties which many modern theologians find with an interventionist understanding of God's action." He indicates that the difficulty which many modern theologians have concerning "interventionism" is one of their own making. In somewhat deist fashion they first removed God from the world and then argued that we "are then obliged to see any alleged 'post-creational' action of God in respect to the world as 'intervention'." Wainwright says that Bultmann is typical of this view because he held that modern science does not admit of divine interventions and thus he tended to dismiss the sacraments as "magical forces . . . influences upon God . . . material means of feeding man's spiritual life."[74] The question as Wainwright sees it then is how to interpret Chalcedon in such a way that we have a credible "concursive operation between God and humanity?" He turns to Ninian Smart for linguistic assistance

> When you say that God is in all things and when you say that God is beyond or behind all things, you appear to be saying two different things; but how can you be, considering that 'in', 'behind' and 'beyond' are analogical, not literal? . . . Thus there is no strong reason to differentiate between transcendence and immanence. Indeed there are some reasons of a doctrinal sort to encourage the identification of the two locations of God.[75]

If we couple the idea that God may also be "multipresent" and "present in varying degrees" then we have a basis for learning "the lessons of the sacraments in order to avoid the kind of interventionism which has helped to render the notion of incarnation unacceptable to some modern theologians." What then is Wainwright's solution to this problem?

> If, then, God intervenes, he intervenes not as a stranger to his own creation, but 'from within'. [Hence] sacraments are *interpersonal events*, meetings between God and humanity for the purpose of advancing the communion with God to which humanity is called . . . [they] are thus not capricious interferences by divine powers, such as seem to be envisaged when Bultmann apparently rejects them as irretrievably mythological . . . They express the pattern of God's set purpose of communion between humanity and himself, and in so doing they promote its success . . . there is no need to understand the presence and action of God in a more crudely interventionist way in his [Jesus'] case than in the case of the sacraments . . . The action of God is, then, to be conceived *within* an existing relationship . . . [Hence sacraments] enable us to conceive of God's action less in spatial terms ('intervention') and more in terms of values. The definitive values are those of the divine kingdom, which is also human salvation: love, peace, justice, joy . . . In all sacramental action, God is present to transform into his own moral and spiritual likeness those who consent to the values of his kingdom. The sacraments are but focal instances within the continuing relationship between God and his creatures which is directed to God's kingdom. As effective displays of the ultimate values, neither they nor Jesus himself as the *Ursakrament* require a divine intervention 'from without'.[76]

Wainwright actually argues for a position which allows for a variety of accents between the extremes of "augustinianism" and "full pelagianism" as long as "God and humanity are all along kept in concursive play."[77]

This example shows that Barth's linking of worship with his rejection of ebionite and docetic Christology is no idle matter, even today. By grounding Christ's uniqueness in a human experience of ultimate values, Jesus' divinity can no longer be perceived as something utterly unique and inexplicable apart from faith; rather it is itself a particular instance of that which humans already value in the moral and spiritual sphere. We neither have to choose between grace and nature here; nor do we have to distinguish sharply between them. Instead, grace is to be seen as a deepening of our experience of ultimate value. We do not have to choose Christ in order to understand God's action which comes into the world from outside because God's transcendence, according to this schema, is already part of the realm of immanence in the form of our spiritual and moral life.

Sacraments symbolize this and Jesus is the ultimate symbol or image of this concurrence within history.

The problem with this analysis then consists in the fact that, while Bultmann's view is certainly mistaken, Wainwright overcame the problem by agreeing with Bultmann's own assessment of the modern situation, i.e., that God can only intervene from "within" his creation. Since that is the case, we no longer have the particular deist view which might have upheld Bultmann's interpretation but we do have its theological equivalent. We have a description of God's action within history, including the history of Jesus, which can be described as an interpersonal event embodying more intense patterns and values which we all experience within human life itself. According to this analysis there can be no real God actually intervening in human life from outside history since sacraments merely are focal instances of the "goal-directed personal relationship between God and humanity." But the word God has no more than a moral, spiritual, and social meaning in this context and when it is applied to Christ, as God and man, he is no more than the ultimate content of various human value orientations. He cannot be utterly unique, i.e., one and only. He cannot be needed absolutely. Similarly the sacraments cannot be actions of the church which stand in need of God acting in specific circumstances to speak his Word; rather they too are focal instances of the human quest for values with God as the ultimate value.

Karl Rahner was caught in this same conflict. While he argued that the conceptual model of God intervening from outside into human affairs cannot simply be rejected he believed that this idea "for people today somehow savours of the miraculous and mythological."[78] For this reason he regarded grace as something that occurs permanently "always and everywhere" within the world.

> When we say that we celebrate the death of the Lord until he returns, we are saying that we are giving space and time explicitly in our own life to the culmination of the history of the world liturgy which is present in the cross of Jesus . . . what happens in worship of this kind is not something that does not occur or has not permanently occurred elsewhere in the world, but something that occurs always and everywhere or has occurred for all time and for everywhere in the world . . . This ecclesial worship is important and significant, not because something happens in it that does not happen elsewhere, but because there is present and explicit in it that which makes the world important . . . To anyone who has (or might have had) absolutely no experience in his own life of this history of grace of the world, no experience of the cosmic liturgy, the Church's liturgy could only seem like a strange ritualism . . .[79]

From this Rahner concluded that "he whom we call God is always present from the very outset and even already accepted; as infinite offer, as silent love, as absolute future, wherever a person is faithful to his conscience and breaks out of the prison walls of his selfishness . . . [hence] worship is the explicit celebration of the divine depth of their ordinary life."[80] For Rahner, as for Wainwright, the mystery of revelation is the mystery of humanity faithfully becoming less selfish and thereby actualizing the grace that is already part of the depths of its ordinary life. Accordingly, one does not have to think of revelation as a particular miraculous action of God coming into history from outside or operating within history as the distinctive action of God's Word and Spirit. Instead God's Word and Spirit are here identified with self-transcendence and self-acceptance. Hence holiness can be equated with the ordinary and ritual actions of creatures who live morally acceptable lives.

For Barth, however, we must not attempt to dispel the mystery of revelation in attempting to explain the divine change which enables a creature to live as a saint (a *sancti*, one made holy by God). It is a great temptation to blunt the mystery or to evade it by reinterpretation as we have just seen. What Barth had in mind here is the same point he made in his Christology.[81] Creatures can do no more than recognize the mystery of revelation because revelation is a fact which we neither conjure nor control even after recognizing it. We cannot explain its *how* and consequently must not attempt to resolve what cannot be resolved.[82] This is the condition of the possibility of participating in the real mystery of revelation as opposed to an idea (docetism) or an experience (ebionitism) of the mystery of revelation.[83] For Barth, Christology is not identical with the mystery of revelation. Thus, its *how* is beyond human comprehension, while its facticity is true; "It [Christology] faces the mystery. It does not stand within the mystery."[84] That is why revelation and reconciliation can only be attested. They are divine actions which we cannot control either conceptually or existentially because they are in no way identical with any immanent process at all. Having analyzed the problems inherent in Geoffrey Wainwright's approach, it is best to show exactly how Barth maintained Christ's uniqueness against this train of thought, while at the same time he was able to speak of revelation as a miracle [against Bultmann] which yet includes creatures within a genuine relationship with God within history.

Christomonism and Anthropomonism

If we want to explain how this divine possibility affects one's inner life then two false interpretations of the Christ event which is itself the basis and goal of the church's celebration of the Lord's Supper must be avoided. The first false

understanding is a "christomonist" explanation. Christomonism attempts to solve
what cannot be solved, i.e., the mystery of revelation, the problem of
Christology; namely, the problem of *how* God can be revealed yet hidden, veiled
and unveiled.[85] On this view the contrast between Christ and us is denied in an
attempt to explain our union with Christ.[86] The contrast between Christ and
created reality (i.e., bread and wine) is just as certainly denied if our union with
Christ is depicted as a state in which the elements are extensions of his deity.[87]
This is exactly what Barth was denying here. And this is clearly the problem in
Wainwright's presentation discussed above.

   He denied it in his Christology by maintaining the irreversibility of the Logos
and Christ's humanity. That is why humanity as such, particularly the humanity
of the man Jesus, cannot be the subject of a theological inquiry. This evades the
divinity of the man Jesus and in that way blurs the contrast between Christ and
others. This is what Barth believed occurred in the quest of the historical Jesus
in Protestantism and in the Heart of Jesus cult in Roman Catholicism.[88] On this
view the *in nobis* is seen only as an appendage of Christ, and cannot decisively
involve creatures as such, since human action is nothing but an extension of
Christ's own activity. Therefore our human possibility must finally be viewed as
something *extra nos*. "It is itself a divine action, not a human action evoked by
God and responsible to him." Such a concept sees faithful humanity as a
manifestation of the act of God fulfilled in Christ.[89] It cannot, however, see a
creature as one who freely accepts the verdict of God actualized in Christ. From
this standpoint anthropology and soteriology are swallowed up in Christology.

   Christology is the unifying principle which explains our origin and goal which
is our indistinguishable oneness with Christ. This is wrong because the summons
of 2 Cor. 5:20 "Be ye reconciled to God" is rendered innocuous.[90] No real
human action is required. A *true* Christocentricity would forbid this viewpoint
for the same reasons that it would recognize and reject any docetic interpretation
of Christ or the church.[91] This interpretation cannot make sense of the fact that
the church's action of eating bread and drinking wine remains a fully human
action, achieved by human beings themselves, even though they are awakened
and empowered to do so by God's grace.[92] It cannot explain the fact that bread
remains bread and wine remains wine in the Lord's Supper. In this way the
question of a human activity corresponding to a divine activity is answered by
dismissing it as a possibility altogether.

   The second false interpretation of the mystery of revelation, which is just as
artificial as the first, consists in viewing Christ's history (*extra nos*) as a predicate
or instrument of what took place *in nobis*. On this view, the creature is the
subject of this happening. At best, Christ is an interesting example of what can
happen to and for a person who lives a generally demonstrable, "authentic"

existence. The human change, i.e., the creature's "resolving on faith and love and hope, his much-vaunted decision, is now as such the truly divine change."[93]

To avoid this notion in his theological anthropology Barth argued against any attempt to unite faith with a world-view[94] as Feuerbach, Schleiermacher, and all those who have sought to make humanity in general the theme of theological anthropology actually have done.[95] This fails to recognize that the theme of theological anthropology is the creature in his or her relation with God which has its foundation in the Word of God. Barth noted that "Theology itself has only to be unsure about its foundations and its truth, and this uncertainty has only to mount to a crisis like that which marked the age of Schleiermacher, and it is led at once to the discovery and assertion of L. Feuerbach, that at bottom it too is perhaps nothing but concealed anthropology."[96] Obviously the foundation that Barth was speaking of here, as elsewhere, is the truth which faith professes in its Christology. But a theological anthropology which is grounded in Christology could not attempt to equate its anthropological relationship with Christ with the divine action in Christ. This is precisely what is done when Christology is seen as a unifying principle which humanity can discover in an anthropology. Again, this is plainly what transpired above in connection with Wainwright's position. Indeed he sees no problem in equating Christianity with a world-view with universal claims which is then adjusted according to the demands posed by relativism.[97] At the same time, this discovery must deny the necessity of salvation as the form of one's relationship to Christ established by God himself. Barth absolutely refused to ground his anthropology in a speculative theory of humanity because faith knows it to be grounded already in God's action in Christ.[98] This is humanity's only true justification and possibility for salvation.

The secret of salvation history in the anthropomonist view is thus the creature himself or herself in his or her free act of obedience. But the question, of course, is obedience to what? Is it the creature's obedience to himself or herself or to a reality other than himself or herself? This interpretation cannot explain how and why the human action of eating and drinking has its origin in God's grace. Nor can it explain how its origin is transcendent, even though it is not itself transcendent. It cannot explain the fact that bread and wine remain bread and wine and do not become semi-divine or semi-created realities. From this point of view, Christology is "swallowed up by a self-sufficient anthropology and soteriology."[99] This comprehension of the Christ event is wrong for the same reasons as ebionite Christology is wrong and for the same reasons as Paul of Samosata's ebionite Christology was originally rejected.[100] Any assumption of identity as in ebionite thinking means that divine transcendence is thought to be grasped in the human action and in the phenomena of bread and wine as such. They are in fact indistinguishable. To the extent that this is thought to be the case, the divine freedom (grace) is compromised, and so also is the truth and certainty of the human knowledge and action. This, simply because as one reality is indistinguishable from another, consistency demands that we never really know for sure when we are speaking of human and/or divine action. Christology therefore really becomes superfluous because it can tell us nothing that cannot be known by a phenomenology of bread and wine and of human actions of eating and drinking in community. Faith, revelation, and grace are not necessary here. Phenomena supply what they claim to supply. To use Wainwright's analogy, Christology merely displays for us the pattern of our own desire for ultimate values such as peace and justice.

This reversal and confusion of divinity and humanity is precisely what is prohibited by the reality of God as known in Christ and according to the *analogia fidei*. Only a clear Christology and trinitarian theology can state the nature of God's freedom and the basis, possibility, and limitation of really knowing God, as well as the reality *distinct* from him and created by him. This response literally cannot have the character of gratitude because it was always something innate to the creature which could be produced out of one's experience. Here too the ethical side of Christian living is "solved by its dismissal as pointless."[101]

For Barth, the common misunderstanding of the christomonist and anthropomonist positions is that they both approach the New Testament data "from outside and with the aid of an alien concept of unity"; thus they do not let the matter in question speak for itself[102] and conjure away the mystery which confronts them. Unless one accepts this riddle by letting it interpret itself, the actual solution of this problem from within *will never be seen.*[103]

Barth's position here was based on his distinction between interpretation and illustration when speaking of scriptural exegesis. For Barth, theological language must say "the *same thing* in other words," i.e., it must be interpreted. It should not illustrate, i.e., say "the same thing in *other words.*" The emphasis here cannot be on the theological terminology as such but on the object to which it refers, namely, the object of faith. Scripture must be allowed to speak its own message without being transformed by an a priori or a posteriori principle. There is a practical implication to this reasoning. During the Enlightenment, criticism took what is natural or reasonable as its criterion for truth and then rejected what it considered unnatural and unreasonable. In the process, the doctrines of the Trinity and of the two natures became quite contestable since they were seen as impracticable to the life possible to creatures as it could be discovered apart from scripture and apart from faith.[104] For Barth a correct reading of scripture expounds the material only in light of its theme. That is why criticism is wrong in presuming an a priori definition of truth behind the statements it is dealing with. The truth of the scriptural witness depends upon its unique theme which is

Jesus himself. Any historical or methodological criticism must respect this particular truth. Because of this truth Barth rejected every historical attempt to claim that Christ can be understood "as the revelation of the deepest and final reality of man."[105] Barth perceived in the theology of A. E. Biedermann, R. A. Lipsius, H. Lüdemann, and A. Ritschl just this kind of denial of Christ's uniqueness. It is a denial of the fact that "Before Him and after Him there is no one to be compared to Him. He is utterly different from all others, the proper *Χριστός*, of whom they are but types."[106] Once this uniqueness is obscured by a historical methodology, however forceful the subsequent emphasis on the once-for-allness character of Christ's existence may be, it really becomes irrelevant. Between this opinion and the above mentioned "liberal" opinion "the only difference left concerned certain questions of judgment and taste."[107] But it could no longer be a question of truth.[108] Truly thinking christologically means beginning and ending one's thought with Christ himself. It means not substituting a historical process for that uniqueness. With this in mind Barth's words on this point are instructive:

> Luther and Calvin did not need to aim at a 'christocentric' theology, like Schleiermacher and later A. Ritschl and his pupils, because their theology was christocentric from the very outset, and without the singular attempt to make or call it so. It did not need to become christocentric. And how can theology or piety or church life become christocentric, if it is not so at the very outset? The strainings and the unhealthy zeal and historical and systematic devices by which the moderns have tried to become christocentric bear clear and eloquent testimony that they were not christocentric at the outset and therefore cannot be . . . they believe that this is something which we can choose for ourselves, though the actual choice is different. The belief that the name Jesus Christ is something we can choose is the radically unauthentic element in the Jesus-cult of Pietism and the revival movements of the period.[109]

It should be stressed at this point that Rahner's view of Jesus Christ within an evolutionary perspective is a very clear instance of the historical process rather than Jesus himself defining the truth. Thus "the Saviour is himself a historical moment in God's saving action exercised on the world . . . as the climax of the development in which the world comes absolutely into its own presence and into the direct presence of God."[110] Hence for Rahner, in virtue of human self-transcendence, the incarnation is seen as the point where "self-communication and acceptance attains an irrevocable and irreversible character in history—an event in which the history of this self-communication realizes its proper nature and in which it breaks through."[111] It is clear that for Rahner then the incarnation was the irrevocable attainment of oneness between divine and human being toward which *both* have always tended. "Consequently it is not pure fantasy (though the attempt must be made with caution) to conceive of the 'evolution' of the world *towards Christ*, and to show how there is a gradual ascent which reaches a peak in him. Only we must reject the idea that this 'evolution' could be a striving upward of what is below by its own powers."[112] Since Christ has always been involved in the historical process as its "prospective entelechy . . . it should then be possible . . . to learn from it [history] who the Christ is to whom it is orientated and whom it has brought forth from its womb."[113]

It is this thinking which leads directly to the moralism, which Rahner specifically wished to avoid,[114] yet which we find in Ritschl: Rahner saw Jesus as that irreversible occurrence of the tendencies inherent in history itself tending toward the absolute. Thus "The event of God's promise of himself in Jesus makes that deepest promise by God of himself to the world historically accessible and irreversible."[115] And "we may say . . . that wherever and whenever we experience the unshakeableness of our own hope of a final victory of our existence, there takes place, perhaps anonymously, that is without reference to the name of Jesus, an experience that he is risen."[116] Finally, Rahner believed that "wherever man posits a positively moral act in the full exercise of his free self-disposal, this act is a positive supernatural salvific act in the actual economy of salvation"[117] in virtue of God's universal salvific will and divinizing grace. Since a person's unconscious horizon is oriented toward the triune God, this is enough to show, in Rahner's view, that transcendental revelation and faith make such a moral act a salvific act as well.

What then is the correct view in this matter? Accepting the standpoint of the New Testament witnesses we will not take offense at the fact that God himself has prosecuted our cause. For, our thinking will be within faith in the mystery of revelation as such and not an idea or an experience of mystery in general.[118] We will recognize that Christ's uniqueness in this regard cannot be compared or interchanged with any idea or experience of uniqueness or singularity. From the first his particular history has a universal goal. It did not take place for itself; Christ was not elected for himself.[119] It took place for all persons. In this sense it comprehends the whole world of mankind. It comes with revolutionary force into the lives of each and every human being. In this way it reshapes the lives of men and women. This was an *event* which took place *extra nos pro nobis*.[120] Because Christ was the true Son of God, his human faithfulness was effective for us and is itself the possibility and limitation of the new life which creatures in themselves can now live as they see and accept this. This new history of human faithfulness to God is possible because God has taken our cause in his hand.

As we shall see, this *alone* is the possibility and limit of our *eucharistia*. Creatures as such, in themselves, did not become faithful instead of unfaithful to God. This was a possibility actualized by one who was very God as he was very man and in that unique way accomplished what had not been accomplished before in human history. Creatures today are called to live this new Christian life on the ground of this particular new beginning. Thus we are called not because we have now been given supernatural power or because we now have actualized an innate capacity for fellowship with God, but on the basis of grace alone, i.e., on the basis of our eternal election in Christ to be a covenant partner in and through him and therefore not in ourselves or in and through any created element. This new life to which we have been called corresponds to our election in and with Christ because it follows the divine transformation of our heart and person which took place in the history of Christ. Consequently, "The Christian life is founded, not when man takes the place of Christ as his own liberator, but when Jesus Christ takes the place of man to liberate him there."[121] Human beings, even Christians, must follow and cannot precede the Lord.

What actually occurred in the history of Christ is that God liberates us for faithfulness to him on our own part. This restriction is important because on a general or abstract definition of liberation, people may see themselves freed *from* all kinds of things. Yet this very view does not bind people unequivocally to God's revelation (grace). To that extent they are not actually free. Barth's insistence that there could be no abstract or general definition of the being of God then leads to the practical insight that there can be no abstract or general definition of liberation either. And this has another practical consequence. One could not "locate christology within ethics and not prior to it,"[122] if the truth of liberation means obedience to Christ, the Lord. But for liberation theologians who believe absolute norms are unethical and who exclude Christ as the only possible source of true liberation, this thinking makes no sense.[123]

For Barth, real knowledge of God, of Christ, and of the church cannot be described as a state; it is rather an *event*. Each is part of the human event of obedience enclosed in the mystery of the Trinity. Being a Christian then means *acting* in accordance with the knowledge of the truth attained in faith. To envisage our relation with God and Christ as it is seen and lived in the church as a state would imply identity between us and God rather than relationship. Event and action imply the need for *recollection* and *expectation* on the part of the community. The church therefore must actually pray for God to act according to his promise to be with it always.[124] This idea of history really existing in relationship with God, through the Holy Spirit, and in dependence on the Spirit is lost whenever identity is assumed or implied. This identity is the weakness of any pantheistic or panentheistic attempt to describe the creator—creature relation either in the doctrine of God or in the sacraments. This weakness seems particularly attendant on theologies which begin from "experience" as we have seen throughout our analysis thus far. It is now important to consider exactly how Barth could describe our inclusion in the Christ event without compromising divine or human freedom.

Notes

1. C.D. 4, 4, pp. 10–11.

2. Ibid., p. 11. It is instructive to note that Jürgen Moltmann in *The Way of Jesus Christ: Christology In Messianic Dimensions*, trans. Margaret Kohl (San Francisco: Harper San Francisco, A Division of HarperCollins Publishers, 1990, hereafter abbreviated: *The Way of Jesus Christ*), p. 68 explicitly rejects the idea that Jesus can be understood in light of a general metaphysics (classical Christology) or anthropology (Kant, Schleiermacher, and Rahner) and yet his own "ecological" theology represents just such an attempt to grasp Jesus in light of a synthesis of a general "relational" metaphysics and an anthropology, because Jesus becomes the particular instance of his "eschatology." For Moltmann therefore "The notion that there is an antithesis between an adoptionist and a pre-existence christology is a nineteenth century invention," p. 74. In fact, however, the opposition between adoptionism and a Christology which acknowledged Jesus' eternal pre-existence as the Son was stressed very early in church history by Irenaeus (cf. Adolf von Harnack, *History of Dogma*, vol. 1, trans. Neil Buchanan (New York: Dover, 1961), pp. 191ff. and Henry Chadwick, *The Early Church*, (New York: Penguin, 1967), pp. 86–7, and p. 114. Moltmann, however, cannot accept the traditional distinction between the immanent and the economic Trinity and so allows his understanding of Jesus' Sonship to be dictated by history as such rather than by the eternity of the Son revealed in and through history. Cf. also Paul D. Molnar "Moltmann's Post-Modern Messianic Christology: A Review Discussion," *The Thomist* 56 (1992): 669–693 and below.

3. Ibid.

4. Ibid., p. 12. See also C.D. 1, 2, pp. 50ff.

5. Ibid., p. 13.

6. C.D. 4, 4, *The Christian Life*, p. 252.

7. Here Barth maintains the distinction between Christ and others as he does in his Christology. See, e.g., C.D. 1, 1, pp. 141ff., C.D. 1, 2, pp. 136ff., and 155–58, C.D. 2, 1, pp. 272ff., and C.D. 2, 2, pp. 6ff., 10ff., 44, 53 and 509ff.

8. C.D. 2, 1, p. 152.

9. C.D. 4, 4, p. 13.

10. Ibid., p. 14.

11. See, e.g., C.D. 1, 1, pp. 402ff., C.D. 1, 2, p. 20, and C.D. 3, 2, pp. 54 and 444–47 and below, chapter six.

12. T.I. 4:237. Cf. also pp. 238f. and *The Trinity*, pp. 31-3.

13. Moltmann depicts this Christology very accurately in *The Way of Jesus Christ*, pp. 61-2 despite Pannenberg's criticism of him for comparing Rahner's "anthropological christology" to Schleiermacher's, *Systematic Theology Volume 2*, p. 294. Moltmann contends that traditional theology has emphasized duality, i.e., creation *and* redemption, creation *and* covenant, necessity *and* freedom, nature *and* grace. Accordingly, in his view, grace presupposes and perfects nature but does not destroy it. Moltmann says this is captured by Rahner's phraseology "that anthropology is 'deficient christology' and christology is 'realized anthropology,'" *Creation*, p. 7. He believes that the second part of the proposition fails to distinguish "grace and glory, history and new creation, being a Christian and being perfected" and has led to "triumphalism" i.e., "the glory which perfects nature is supposed already to be inherent in the grace," Ibid. Since, for Moltmann, both nature and grace will become complete in the kingdom of glory (*Creation*, p.8) he can argue that Rahner's Christology leads him into idealism (*The Way of Jesus Christ*, p. 63) *and* that God's grace is not a self-sufficient action of God *ad extra*. Rather God's action in Christ reveals God's own eventual need of redemption (cf. *Trinity*, pp. 39 and 53 and also *Creation*, pp. 82ff.). Interestingly, while such different theologians as Moltmann (*The Way of Jesus Christ*, p. 62) and Joseph Ratzinger (*Principles of Catholic Theology: Building Stones For A Fundamental Theology*, trans. Sister Mary Frances McCarthy, S.N.D. (San Francisco: Ignatius Press, 1987), p. 167 note that, for Rahner, acceptance of revelation amounts to human acceptance, Moltmann never actually escapes an idealist solution to this problem because his notion of suffering love (which involves the mutual conditioning associated with all human love) makes God's grace dependent on nature. And Ratzinger himself falls into an idealist solution to this problem at times because for him tradition becomes the mediator instead of Christ himself (Cf. Paul D. Molnar "Can Theology Be Both Contemporary And True? A Review Discussion of *Principles of Catholic Theology*" *The Thomist* 52 (1988): 513–537.

14. T.I. 16:55.

15. Ibid.

16. T.I. 14:290.

17. For more on this problem see Paul D. Molnar, *The Thomist* (1987): 588ff. and *TS* (1985): 254ff. and "Toward a Contemporary Doctrine of the Immanent Trinity . . ." *SJT*.

18. Cf. C.D. 2, 1, pp. 327–29ff. and above, chapter one.

19. See, e.g., Rahner, *Foundations*, p. 67. Being in general is the limit of all knowledge for Rahner. Hence: "Our proposition about the comprehensibility of being in itself did indeed arise from the fact that in the first question about being every possible object of cognition is already anticipated under the aspect of being in general. There can, therefore, be no existent thing that does not automatically and objectively fit into the context of being in general. For this very reason every thing is comprehensible," *Hearers of the Word*, trans. Michael Richards (New York: Herder & Herder, 1969, hereafter abbreviated: *HW)*, p. 96. The same ideas are expressed in *Foundations*, pp. 24ff.

20. See above and Paul D. Molnar, *SJT* (1989) and *TS* (1990). Even when he does speak of a distinction, eschatologically understood, his ideas that God depends upon history and that the immanent Trinity will not fully exist until salvation is complete belie this.

21. Jürgen Moltmann, *The Way of Jesus Christ*, p. 139. Cf. also pp. 136ff.

22. Ibid., p. 40. Wolfhart Pannenberg maintains the same view in *Jesus—God and Man*, pp. 320–21 and Eberhard Jüngel, while less critical of Barth's overall method than Moltmann and Pannenberg, holds the same view on this point in *God as the Mystery of the World: On the Foundation of the Theology of the Crucified One in the Dispute between Theism and Atheism*, trans. Darrell L. Guder, (Grand Rapids: Eerdmans, 1983, hereafter abbreviated: *God as the Mystery of the World*), p. 363, n. 39. For an accurate presentation of and assessment of Jüngel's views see John Thompson, *Modern Trinitarian Perspectives*, (New York: Oxford University Press, 1994).

23. Moltmann, *Trinity*, pp. 4–5, emphasis mine.

24. Moltmann, *The Way of Jesus Christ*, p. 140.

25. Ibid., p. 107.

26. Ibid., pp. 111–12, emphasis mine.

27. C.D. 4, 2, p. 658.

28. Markus Barth, *Rediscovering the Lord's Supper*, pp. 37–8.

29. C.D. 4, 2, pp. 667–68. Gordon Kaufman explicitly argues for secularization because his opposition to the Inquisition, the Crusades, and other forms of "imperialism" is not grounded in Christ alone but in his own moralistic framework. Cf. Kaufman, *T.I.*, chapters four and seven and *TNA*, pp. 61–2. In line with this thinking Kaufman not only argues that Christianity is one "world-view" among others, but that since the concept of God and human finitude are related, "If we can work out the dialectic of this relationship in contemporary (secular) terms, we will be able better to understand both the import of our relativity and the significance that talk about 'God' can have in contemporary life," *T.I.*, pp. 92–3. Among other things, we are taught that the idea that Christ is the One Mediator is evidence of Christian imperialism and idolatry (*TNA*, p. 50) and that salvation cannot have been accomplished in and through one

particular person (Jesus of Nazareth), *TNA*, p. 56.

30. C.D. 1, 1, p. 323.

31. Geoffrey Wainwright, *Doxology: The Praise of God in Worship, Doctrine, and Life, A Systematic Theology* (New York: Oxford University Press, 1980, hereafter abbreviated: *Doxology*), p. 407.

32. Ibid.

33. This does not imply that this human act of hearing and obeying is itself the cause of this divine possibility—perhaps in simultaneity with the divine act. This is what Barth would say *ex opere operato* assumes. For Barth, the human action *follows* the divine action and makes sense as a human change only in light of the divine change effected in Christ. For an interesting treatment of *theopoiesis* in Athanasius as it relates to this point see, e.g., Thomas F. Torrance, *The Trinitarian Faith*, (Edinburgh: T. & T. Clark, 1988), pp. 188-9. Torrance argues that our "deification" does not mean that there is "any change in divine or human being." What makes us "divine" is the fact that the Word acts in us. Our lost humanity is not only recreated but is lifted up in Christ "to enjoy a new fullness of human life in a blessed communion with divine life," p. 189. Also the concept *theopoiesis* "is closely related to the reception of the Holy Spirit." Thus, the actual atonement, i.e., Christ's self-sanctification was aimed at us. "When he received the Spirit, it was we who by him were made recipients of him," p. 190. Hence "This twofold movement of the giving and receiving of the Spirit actualised within the life of the incarnate Son of God *for our sakes* is atonement operating within the ontological depths of human being . . . Pentecost must be regarded, not as something added on to atonement, but as the actualisation within the life of the Church of the atoning life, death and resurrection of the Saviour," p. 190.

34. Cf. C.D. 1, 2, pp. 38ff. and p. 183.

35. Ibid., pp. 6ff., 291ff., 350, 374 and 542f. Cf. also C.D. 1, 1, pp. 420ff., 470f. and C.D. 2, 1, p. 41.

36. See, e.g., C.D. 2, 1, pp. 351ff. Any one of the divine perfections which Barth treats in this section in light of this insight indicates how theology may allow its general definition of reality to be determined by the particular revelation of God in Christ known in faith. For scriptural references concerning this divine change, see Gal. 3:27 and Rom. 13:14.

37. C.D. 4, 4, pp. 15-16.

38. Wainwright, *Doxology*, pp. 68-70.

39. Ibid., pp. 70ff.

40. T.I. 14:177.

41. Ibid., p. 178.

42. Ibid., pp. 180-81.

43. Ibid., pp. 169ff. Here Rahner stated his indebtedness to Teilhard's *Hymn of the Universe*. Rahner fashioned the same argument in T.I. 19:141-9 in "On the Theology of Worship." He modifies his earlier position by noting that the old sacramental view of God's grace entering history from outside is not to be completely rejected. But, by the time he finished his explanation of how the divine liturgy ought not to be construed as a "liturgy *in* the world, but as the divine liturgy *of* the world" (p. 149) it is clear that he meant that "worship is the explicit celebration of the divine depth of their [Christians'] ordinary life," p. 149

44. Ibid., pp. 169-70. See also Karl Rahner and Karl-Heinz Weger, *Our Christian Faith Answers for the Future*, trans. Francis McDonagh (New York: Crossroad, 1981, hereafter abbreviated: *Our Christian Faith*), p. 96: "God is not only the basis of a history of human freedom and does not merely support it in its own power . . . His method is to bring about (from the deepest centre of this world and of the history which he himself is) in this history an event which both itself expresses this divine world and history and makes it irreversible and also is its revelation."

45. Ibid., p. 167.

46. Markus Barth, e.g., makes this point well: "This relationship between the Lord's Supper and everyday life shows that Christ's table and meal have a social character that is related to the personal and political lives of all people. No sphere of life remains unaffected by it. The Supper is a missionary and a social happening. Either all Christian ethics is eucharistic . . . or Christians have nothing distinctive to 'do in remembrance' of Christ," *Rediscovering the Lord's Supper*, p. 76.

47. Paul Tillich, *The Shaking of the Foundations*, (New York: Charles Scribner's Sons, 1948), p. 57.

48. John Haught, *What is God? How to Think About the Divine* (New York: Paulist Press, 1986), p. 15 and John A. T. Robinson, *Honest To God* (Philadelphia: The Westminster Press, 1963), pp. 22 and 55ff. According to Robinson "The question of God is the question *whether this depth of being is a reality or an illusion*, not whether *a* Being exists beyond the bright blue sky, or anywhere else. Belief in God is a matter of 'what you take seriously without any reservation', of what for you is *ultimate* reality," p. 55.

49. Rahner, *Foundations*, pp. 59-60. T.I. 4:62. See also T.I. 11:153 and 156. Rahner wrote: "God is present as the asymptotic goal, hidden in itself, of the experience of the limitless dynamic force inherent in the spirit endowed with knowledge and freedom," p. 153. See also T.I. 13:123. Rahner indeed believed that the word God can be and is misunderstood. But according to his transcendental method it really made little difference what we name him at this stage since the term God refers to an experience on the basis of which that which we all experience (the term) is what "we call God", T.I. 11: 159.

50. Ibid., T.I. 4: 53.

51. Moltmann, *The Way of Jesus Christ*, chapter six.

52. Ibid., pp. 278–9.

53. Ibid., p. 279.

54. Ibid., p. 280.

55. Ibid., p. 282.

56. Ibid., p. 286.

57. Ibid., p. 290.

58. Ibid., pp. 118, 132, 251.

59. See Moltmann, *Creation*, pp. 204–14.

60. Moltmann, *The Way of Jesus Christ*, p. 291.

61. Barth rejected Teilhard's Gnostic Pantheism several times. Cf. *Letters*, pp. 116f. and 119f. and Eberhard Busch, *Karl Barth*, trans. John Bowden, (Philadelphia: Fortress Press, 1976), "Teilhard de Chardin is an almost classic case of Gnosticism," wrote Barth, p. 487.

62. Moltmann, *The Way of Jesus Christ*, pp. 296–7.

63. Moltmann, *Creation*, p. 211. Moltmann cites Teilhard de Chardin's view as an adequate account of this.

64. C.D. 4, 4, pp. 17–18.

65. C.D. 1, 2, p. 156.

66. T.I. 14:168.

67. Rahner, *Our Christian Faith*, p. 13.

68. C.D. 1, 2, p. 158.

69. C.D. 4, 1, p. 89.

70. Wainwright, *Doxology*, p. 60.

71. Ibid., p. 61. Ted Peters, *God as Trinity: Relationality and Temporality in Divine Life*, (Louisville: Westminster/John Knox, 1993), notes Wainwright's "subordinationist trinitarianism" (p. 45) and his attempt to support Nicea at the same time. Peters argues for an anti-subordinationist trinitarianism because the divinity of the Father and Son is mutually dependent. Yet Peters' thinking allows history to define God insofar as it emphasizes mutual dependence over God's free relatedness. Cf. also Molnar, *"Toward a Contemporary Doctrine . . ." SJT*.

72. Wainwright, *Doxology*, pp. 68–9.

73. Ibid., p. 59.

74. Ibid., pp. 79–80.

75. Ibid., p. 81.

76. Ibid., pp. 82–3.

77. Ibid., pp. 84ff.

78. T.I. 19:144–45.

79. Ibid., p. 147.

80. Ibid., pp. 148–9.

81. See C.D. 4, 4, pp. 17–18.

82. Cf. C.D. 1, 1, pp. 475–77.

83. See C.D. 1, 2, pp. 128–29, 172ff., p. 258 and C.D. 4, 3, pp. 88–91.

84. C.D. 1, 2, p. 125.

85. For a definition of this problem see C.D. 1, 2, pp. 122–131. The problem, of course, which cannot be resolved except in Christ is how it is that God and creatures can exist in union without dissolution of deity or humanity.

86. C.D. 4, 4, pp. 18–19.

87. Rahner's symbolic explication of God and Christ lead him to depict the church and sacraments as extensions of Christ's deity in time and space.

88. See C.D. 1, 2, pp. 136–38.

89. C.D. 4, 4, p. 19.

90. Ibid.

91. See C.D. 1, 1, p. 403 re: Christ and C.D. 4, 1, pp. 653ff. re: church.

92. C.D. 4, 4, p. 19.

93. Ibid.

94. C.D. 3, 2, pp. 8–11. Cf. also C.D. 4, 3, pp. 73ff. and 254ff.

95. Rahner, e.g., saw no problem in arguing that "We should arrive at a theology which from the outset takes as its starting-point man's experience of himself . . . a theology which from the outset has its place within an evolutive and historical '*Weltanschauung*,' however true it may be that the theology must provide a standard criticism for the '*Weltanschauung*' in that it imparts a radical dimension to it," T.I. 12:213. See also "Reflections on Dialogue within a Pluralistic Society" T.I. 6:31–42 where Rahner basically assumed that Christianity is in fact a universal world-view (p. 32) which must dialogue with other world-views in a pluralistic society. We may note that, while Rahner believed he had overcome Kant, and that theology's standard criticism of world-views is grounded ultimately in the Christian God, the logic of his own method precludes any reality to God beyond the ideas derived from experience. Hence, even though Rahner would insist upon the uniqueness of Christianity, insofar as he also maintains that Christianity is one world-view among others, Rahner essentially left himself in the same position as Gordon Kaufman. Kaufman has no intention of overcoming Kant's critique; he explicitly argues that God-talk

cannot begin in faith in a knowable and known divine revelation (*An Essay on Theological Method*, pp. 3 and 15, *TNA*, p. 18), and believes that all such talk "belongs to a specific world-view" and must be evaluated in relation to other world-views or frameworks created by people to organize their experiences, *TNA*, p. 23. Indeed for him "Christian faith is but one perspective, one world-view, among many vying for our attention and loyalty today," *T.I.*, p. 101. Its adequacy will be judged not by any unique revelation from God but by the way the world-view assists humans to create a better world.

96. C.D. 3, 2, p. 21. Cf. also Barth's introductory essay (pp. x–xxxii) in Ludwig Feuerbach, *The Essence of Christianity*, trans. George Eliot (New York: HarperTorchbooks, 1957) for an interesting discussion of this.

97. Wainwright, *Doxology*, p. 358.

98. C.D. 3, 2, pp. 22ff.

99. C.D. 4, 4, p. 20.

100. C.D. 1, 1, p. 402f., C.D. 1, 2, p. 20.

101. C.D. 4, 4, p. 20.

102. Cf. C.D. 1, 1, p. 345.

103. C.D. 4, 4, p. 20. The actual question of the church's catholicity, for example, is not seen if it is sought *directly* in its historical antiquity or modernity. See, e.g., C.D. 4, 1, pp. 703–04.

104. See Barth, *Protestant Theology*, pp. 106–107. As seen above Gordon Kaufman is an almost classical case of this Enlightenment thinking today.

105. See, e.g., C.D. 1, 2, pp. 11–12, pp. 493–94. See also, C.D. 1, 1, p. 106.

106. C.D. 1, 2, pp. 11–12.

107. Ibid., p. 13.

108. Cf. ibid., pp. 290–91. With this last comment Barth was rejecting the thinking of R. Seeberg and his school. For more on Barth's explicit critique of Ritschl see *Protestant Theology*, pp. 107 and 654–61. See also C.D. 1, 2, pp. 20, 123, 127, 290, 350.

109. Ibid., pp. 350–51.

110. T.I. 5:176.

111. Ibid., p. 175.

112. T.I. 1:165.

113. Ibid., p. 167.

114. Cf. ibid., p. 165.

115. Rahner, *Our Christian Faith*, p. 103.

116. Ibid., p. 113.

117. T.I. 6:238–39.

118. C.D. 4, 4, p. 20. See how Barth related this to his doctrine of the Word of God, C.D. 1, 1, pp. 62 and 65. In C.D. 2, 2, Barth argued that, because of sin, we actually take offense at God's revelation of himself in the form of a servant. See esp. C.D. 2, 2, pp. 10ff. and 166–93.

119. C.D. 2, 2, pp. 10ff., 25ff., 259ff. and 329.

120. Barth wrote "*qui propter nos homines et salutem nostram descendit de coelis.* This *pro nobis* or *propter nos* is to be taken literally and strictly," C.D. 4, 4, p. 21. This power comes only through the Word and Spirit.

121. C.D. 4, 4, p. 21. See also C.D. 1, 1, pp. 107–13 and C.D. 2, 2, p. 343.

122. Tom Driver, quoted in *No Other Name?*, p. 164.

123. Cf. Knitter, *No Other Name?*, pp. 163ff.

124. Cf. C.D. 1, 1, pp. 103f., C.D. 1, 2, pp. 116ff., 441ff., and 542ff.; and C.D. 2, 1, pp. 13 and pp. 37ff. and C.D. 2, 2, pp. 180ff.

IV

Resurrection, The Trinity, Barth and More Recent Theology

Resurrection—God's Act as Self-Grounded

How exactly is it that the Christ event can be efficacious for the historical and temporal life of every human being? It could not be divinely effective if it were conditioned in any way, either positively or negatively, by our affirmation or negation. Hence if the basis of God's claim on us were simply his power over us his claim "would still be without foundation. Even in the depths of hell it could still be flouted and despised." For this reason Barth rejected Schleiermacher's attempt to bring the Christian religion "under the common denominator of the concept of the 'feeling of absolute dependence'." This thinking is "an outrage to the essence of man . . . for it opens the door to the establishment of every possible kind of caprice and tyranny and therefore to the profoundest disobedience to God."[1] Further, if the basis of God's claim on us were merely the fact that God is the eternal good, then we could ignore the fact that while we are actually directed to cleave to God as our good we, from the very start, want "to be equal to God." Thus, any claim that the good may be found both in us (as Plato did) and in the infinite good would actually separate us further from God.

Finally, we might say that "God is simply the all-sufficient being 'whom I have selected as my supreme good'." Yet if this is the basis of God's claim on us then, while it is true that God gives himself as our complete satisfaction when he claims us, his claim would exist

> only in the setting and on the basis of the claim which man has first made on the God whom he has chosen. Every divine claim is ultimately only a confirmation, a condition, of the fulfilment of this human claim. It has the character only of an invitation. It is certainly not a claim which is grounded in itself. We hold to God because and to the extent that finally we want to uphold ourselves. The same man who to-day selects God as his supreme good may to-morrow wish to select a very different good.[2]

While the command of God does indeed promise and effect a reward, the divine command itself is not grounded in the reward or our desire for it, but is "grounded in itself."

Let there be no mistake: this imperative and therefore the justice and the real basis of the divine claim do not begin merely with our believing, nor are they conditioned or limited by it. There is obviously a circle—Luther often used to speak of it. God and faith, and faith and God, are two things which belong together . . . To this circle there belongs the fact that the claim of God is made on this or that man in particular and accepted by him . . . [yet] The basis of the faith which shows itself strong in this circle lies as such outside this circle. And God Himself is already God, and God for us, before this becomes a particular event for any man . . . The light and power of this specific, direct and personal encounter and movement fall into this circle from above. They are light and power in this circle because they are always light and power in themselves. That is why the light is so clear, and the power so irresistible. But they are not bound to what happens here or limited to it.[3]

It is because God is mighty, gracious, and good toward us in Jesus Christ that even when we reject it, ignore it, or do not even recognize it, we *may* believe it; its basis lies in the fact that God really is our creator, reconciler, and redeemer.

Implications for Phenomenology of Personal Presence: Symbolic Views

The significance of this might slip by with our unnoticed approval. Yet it is a view which literally cannot be sustained within a phenomenology of personal presence which often takes the form of a symbolic ontology. Here Barth's doctrine of God and Christology stress a notion of freedom consistent with his method. In his doctrine of election Barth argued that the divine claim upon us can neither be sought nor found in an idea or experience but only in God's election of all people in Christ. As we have just seen, from any other vantage, the divine claim would be dependent on our prior claim such as our human striving for the good considered apart from any recognition of revelation. Yet for Barth the divine command neither begins nor is conditioned or limited by any human affirmation or negation.[4] What is at stake here is an actual rather than an illusory perception of God's grace as free from us and for us. For Barth, God's grace is always his free action in his Word and Spirit and is never identical with any operation of human nature. By contrast, contemporary explanations of the sacraments that begin with experience tend to describe the grace of God disclosed in the sacrament as mutually conditioned. We have seen the christological implications of this above; now two examples will illustrate the sacramental implications.

First, as seen above, Rahner described the sacrament "as a case of an *intrinsic* and *mutual causal* relationship. What is manifesting itself posits its own identity and existence by manifesting itself in this manifestation which is distinct from itself . . . The sign is therefore a cause of what it signifies by being the way in which what is signified effects itself." The determining factor in Rahner's thinking is clearly "symbolic reality." Accordingly the church is an *opus operatum*:

> The Church in her visible historical form is herself an intrinsic symbol of the eschatologically triumphant grace of God; in that spatio-temporal visible form, this grace is made present. And because the sacraments are the actual fulfilment, the actualization of the Church's very nature, in regard to individual men . . . these sacramental signs are efficacious. Their efficacy is that of the intrinsic symbol. Christ acts through the Church . . . This visible form is itself an effect of the coming of grace; it is there because God is gracious to men; and in this self-embodiment of grace; grace itself occurs. The sacramental sign is cause of grace in as much as [*sic*] grace is conferred by being signified.[5]

Thus, the "relation between the Church as the historical visible manifestation of grace and grace itself, one of *reciprocal conditioning*, extends into the relation between sacramental sign and grace conferred."[6] It follows that the sacrament is not complete or full until the person responds or has the proper disposition.[7] Commenting on the relation between the *opus operatum* and *opus operantis* in connection with baptism Rahner wrote:

> the measure of grace from an *opus operatum* at least partly depends on the actual personal cooperation of the recipient. [Moreover] grace . . . is essentially the intrinsic raising and perfecting of a person, intended directly or indirectly to make possible his supernatural spiritual and personal activity . . . the measure of grace in the sacrament is regulated solely by the disposition of its recipient.[8]

We have already seen Barth's rejection of the popular Roman Catholic view of grace. The well known fact that Barth also rejected the Roman Catholic notion of cooperation with grace follows from this. But perhaps at this point, the seriousness of his objection can be seen. As there can be no independent study of Christ's humanity or ours, so there can be no independent study of "signs." Rahner assumed that Christ's humanity as such reveals his divinity and that persons have both an obediential potency and a "supernatural existential." It follows that the "effectiveness belonging to the sacramental sign . . . is not to be conceived of as something added on to its 'sign' function from without, but rather

is to be envisaged as an effectiveness inherent in the sign precisely *as* such."
This is why Rahner could describe the interaction between an individual's act and
God's grace by saying "it [the individual's act] is a cause to the extent that the
true cause, the interior decision of freedom, can posit itself in this its
promulgation."[9] It is our supernatural existential which enables us actually to
make a place for our reception of grace.

> We may therefore conclude that the sacrament itself confers grace for an
> increase of disposition and cooperation. In proportion as a man personally
> and concretely enters into its possibility, and is able to do so by the other
> psychological and moral circumstances, he makes a place and a capacity
> for the reception of grace (*consecutio gratiae*).[10]

For Rahner,

> This *free individual* brings himself to his fulness as an event of grace in
> this sense *in that* he expresses himself, and this expression is, in the sense
> explained the cause of the act imbued with grace and of the grace itself.[11]

This very analysis led Rahner to maintain that between the *opus operatum* and the
opus operantis (disposition) there is a mutual causal relationship in the full
completion of the sacrament.[12]

By contrast, when Markus Barth analyzes ways of being in communion in
light of 1 Cor. 10 he asserts that "The communion of the idol-worshipers with the
demons was *created* by participation in temple banquets." Hence, Paul is
convinced of the "causative, effective, creative—in short, sacramental—power of
pagan cultic actions." But he links communion with God's altar with divine
election arguing that the Israel of 1 Cor. 10:1-13 "is God's people, not because
they ate and drank bread and water miraculously provided by God . . . but by
God's love, election, and revelation, manifested in the calling of the patriarchs
and of Moses and by the liberation from Egypt." Thus the Lord's Supper is a
"strictly *interpersonal*" union which often includes "a physical expression of
unity." Jesus' death concerns those at the table so basically that "his death is
their death; that his suffering makes them willing and capable of suffering with
him; that his resurrection promises theirs; that their life is in him as he is in
them—he *is* their life. In the Parousia they will be with Christ." But since this
is uniquely grounded in Christ, "*koinonia* does not mean . . . a joining, a
common essence or function of diverse *things*—be they physical or heavenly
elements, forces, ideas, or symbols."[13] Thus, as we shall see, Markus Barth
opposes the doctrine of transubstantiation because Paul is not speaking of a

transformation of the bread and wine but of our typological participation in Jesus' death and resurrection.

By comparison, and in accordance with his theology of the symbol,[14] Rahner argued that the eucharistic elements are distinct from Christ's ontological presence only as an appearance is distinct from its original essence. The elements are, for Rahner, a permanent symbol as they are related to the words of consecration which in turn permanently refer back to Christ. Rahner insisted that although Christ is not *only* present in the *use* of the bread and wine, but *in* the bread and wine before use, Christ nonetheless "becomes present through the words of the anamnesis of the Lord's Supper . . . the coming to be of the presence is in the nature of an actual happening . . . the sacrament only becomes the body and blood of Christ when the word is spoken." The idea of "a 'universal presence' of a 'love not bounded by space'" Rahner rejected as Calvinist.[15] From this it follows that

> . . . Christ declares that what he offers (the Apostles) under the *appearance* of bread *is* his body. This means that if the words of consecration are to be taken in their strict and literal sense, and *if they bring about the event of the presence of the body of Christ*, then what Christ offers his Apostles is not bread, but his body. This statement, as it stands, must be accepted by all who refuse to give a vague, figurative meaning to the words of Christ.[16]

We shall analyze whether, in this reasoning, Christ's body takes the place of the bread or is identical with it below. Here we are contrasting Markus Barth's view of freedom as grounded in election and related to the sacrament (which is closely aligned with his father's opinion) with Karl Rahner's view which is grounded in his theology of the symbol. In the former we have a freedom for us which is not conditioned by us; in the latter we have one which is so conditioned.

Second, following Rahner's theology of the symbol and presenting a personalist view of the sacrament John H. McKenna writes:

> For a fully personal presence a response on the part of the other person is necessary. Presence in its deepest sense is a mutual *inter*personal presence. Thus it is not enough for the one person to offer himself to be known and loved. It is also necessary that the other person, to some extent at least, try to reciprocate . . . on this level presence is always mutual. It involves a mutual knowledge not just about, but of one another as persons . . . It . . . is no less real than the purely local presence . . . In fact, it is . . . this interpersonal encounter, which is most real. For only in the

context of mutual, reciprocal giving of persons to each other is there real presence in its fullest sense.[17]

McKenna carries this thinking to its logical conclusion:

> Christ's *sacramental* offer of himself finds its complete realization only in the *sacramental* acceptance of this offer by the faithful . . . Once one admits that a full, personal encounter must by its very nature be mutual, the believing response of the Church becomes a necessary element in the realization of the sacramental encounter . . . Thus, both the human and divine elements belong to, and are necessary for, the full symbolic reality. That it is God who takes the initiative, that he is absolutely free and sovereign in realizing the Eucharist, is undeniable . . . It is, nevertheless, also undeniable that the Church plays a role, however subordinate, in the realization of the sacrament. Without the Church's faith there is also no sacrament and no sacramental encounter.[18]

Why does McKenna present the divine freedom in this particular way? It is because he accepted Rahner's belief that "both realities are so interrelated that one can safely say: if one was not there, the other could not exist either or, at least, it could not be what it is."[19] This kind of mutual conditioning is exactly what Barth was here seeking to avoid.

Whereas Moltmann, e.g., rejects a restrictive idea of local presence[20] he nonetheless does believe that "Christ makes himself present in bread and wine" without compromising the once for all nature of his sacrifice on the cross. Even more importantly, however, Moltmann believes that "The breaking of the bread and the pouring out of the wine acquire a unique significance through the self-giving of the Messiah. They make the kingdom of God present in the form of Christ's body broken 'for us' and Christ's blood shed 'for us'. They make the kingdom of God present in Christ's person and his self-giving." While Moltmann speaks of God's sovereignty and of Jesus being the kingdom in his person, it is not at all clear that he makes a sharp and consistent distinction between a sovereign act of God in the history of Jesus and consequent acts of creatures who live their justification by faith in this particular human way. In his thought we have both the idea that "Like baptism, the Lord's supper emerges of its own accord from the messianic history of Christ," *and* the idea that the "Lord's supper confers fellowship with the crucified Jesus."[21] The former notion avoids the question of causality in relation to God's sovereign freedom which is here being discussed. The latter notion implies that since Jesus is present in the bread and wine (by the power of the Spirit), it is not he alone who unites us to the Father on our eschatological movement to the Parousia, but he can also say that "Because the fellowship of the table unites believers with the triune God through Christ, it also causes men to unite with one another in messianic fellowship."[22] What is the cause here? Is it the power of God or the human action of eating and drinking? Here it appears that, while Moltmann does not expressly affirm the symbolic views held by Rahner and McKenna, he certainly holds a view of mutual conditioning which follows from not making a clear and sharp distinction between divine and human activity at this point.[23]

While all of this reasoning might be perfectly sensible within a theology of the symbol, based upon an ontology of the symbol, it can only obscure God's grace as Barth envisioned it. The grace of God revealed in Christ is and remains *free* both positively and negatively in relation to the Lord's Supper. As there is no identity in his doctrine of analogy, there can be no reciprocal conditioning between the church and God's free action in his Word and Spirit. This pivotal point is exactly what a phenomenology of personal presence expressed symbolically can never admit. It constantly runs the risk of reducing the church to a socio-anthropological entity or of elevating the church to the status of a divine reality. Either way the distinction between the actual mystery (Christ himself) and our participation in that mystery by faith is obscured.[24]

Barth's View of God's Action

Attempting to avoid this kind of reasoning Barth argued that the Christ event has the power to affect our lives independent of our human actions and dispositions. The coming Lord therefore "does not come with a purpose whose execution depends, if not totally, then at least partially on the action, or at any rate the cooperation of Christians."[25] The kingdom of God is an act of God who creates righteousness and peace when he comes but whose coming is "unexpected and inconceivable" since it "comes down directly from above" and creates freedom. The Lord does not link up with the achievements of those to whom he comes as savior; "He does not ask for their opinion or advice. He does not have to explain himself to them or justify himself before them . . . He does not concur or collaborate with them. He simply goes his own way, the way of his own honor and our salvation."[26] Since we can only pray for the coming of this kingdom which, as an act of God is God's work alone "The kingdom would still be what it is even if there were never any such following and response anywhere."[27] This power is not some vague combination of humanity and divinity either in the form of a disposition or in the form of knowledge. It is nothing other than the very power of the resurrection. Christ's resurrection demonstrated that his temporal history was not transcended or outmoded by another history. From the resurrection as such we know with certainty that this particular history was not exclusively a past, transient history, and we know that it was also a history which is present to all earlier times because it happened once-for-all. In this specific way the Christ event is cosmically effective and significant history.[28]

Moltmann's View

While Moltmann also stresses the connection between the Eucharist and the resurrection,[29] he nevertheless traces the origin of the Lord's Supper to "the messianic history of Jesus and his messianic feasts with his disciples and with tax-collectors and sinners."[30] This allows Moltmann to locate both the origin and meaning of the Lord's Supper in the movement of history toward its "messianic" future in a general way. Hence, the causality here at work no longer must be traced exclusively and always to the specific history of Jesus Christ as the risen Lord acting in the present. It can be found wherever there are experiences of suffering and liberation. Thus, "His future is not a future happening; it is a power that liberates, determines the future and opens up new possibilities."[31] And, as seen above, following Unamuno's adage that "A God who cannot suffer cannot love either . . . only that which suffers is divine,"[32] Moltmann effectively eliminates the possibility of God *acting* freely in creation by arguing that it is not through supernatural interventions that God guides creation because, seen in terms of world history, the transforming power of suffering is the *basis* for the liberating and consummating acts of God. By contrast Barth insisted:

> Let us be clear that . . . we are again speaking of the Second Coming of *Jesus Christ*. Christian Eschatology is different from all other expectations for the future, whether they be worldly or religious or religious-worldly, in that it is not primarily expectation of something, even if this something were called resurrection of the flesh and eternal life, but expectation of the *Lord*. *He* awakens the dead; *He* gives eternal life; *He* is the Redeemer . . . Hope of our resurrection and of eternal life is therefore nothing at all, if it is not primarily hope of Him, and not of Him as the fulfiller of our wishes, but of Him Who carries out in us His *own divine* will. Therefore it cannot but be that in regard to its object hope is completely united with faith.[33]

It is not surprising then that Moltmann asks whether baptism and confirmation "ought to go on counting as the presuppositions for 'admittance' to the Lord's supper."[34] Since he deduces the actual meaning of the Trinity and of creation from panentheistic principles which clearly are not subordinate to the power of God actually disclosed in the resurrection, he is able to make the power of the resurrection a power inherent in the cosmos itself. Moltmann's starting point (experience) for analyzing the resurrection causes him to reach the conspicuously docetic conclusion that "Resurrection means not a *factum* but a *fieri*—not what was once done, but what is in the making: the transition from death to life."[35]

Ironically Barth's view is emphatically historical at just that point, insisting that the resurrection was a free act of God's grace (justification) which "did not follow from his death."[36] If, however, the resurrection does not refer to a fact, i.e., the fact of Jesus' Easter history, as Moltmann holds, then it can be detached from that unique history and allowed to function as a principle of becoming which Christians use to explain the transition from death to life. Moltmann argues that the resurrection is the foundation that "discloses the future and opens history" and that when we talk about Christ's resurrection we must talk about "*a process of resurrection.* This process has its foundation in Christ, its dynamic in the Spirit, and its future in the bodily new creation of all things."[37] But what dictates the meaning here? Is it a process of openness to new life which we experience and then find confirmed by Jesus' resurrection? Or is it the risen Lord himself? Moltmann contends that if we see the resurrection as a process we can integrate the ideas of Barth, Bultmann, and Pannenberg to correct their one-sidedness. In this *integrated whole* Moltmann discovers that Christ's resurrection is not an exception in the nexus of causality; it is the beginning of the gathering of mortality into the "immortal interplay of the eternal presence of God."[38] Looking at the resurrection of Christ "from the perspective of nature" Moltmann concludes that it does not interrupt "natural laws of mortal life," for if this were the case it would be a "meaningless miracle." Instead, the whole quality of mortal life has changed and with it the laws of its mortality. Accordingly, Moltmann concludes that the new creation which begins with the resurrection "issues from the cosmic annihilation of death."[39] Hence Christ's own death is *itself* already his new life.[40] And since there is a power of the resurrection even in the flesh, he identifies this as "the power of surrender" and ignoring the problem of sin argues that "Love is . . . the immanent power of resurrection in the flesh."[41] In other words Moltmann has clearly detached the power of the resurrection from the specific history of Jesus Christ and made it a principle inherent in nature itself. Since this leads him to the pantheistic idea that "loving and dying are simply the immanent sides of the resurrection and eternal life"[42] it is clear that he himself is unable to overcome completely the pantheism he criticizes in Troeltsch.[43]

We cannot discuss Moltmann's view of the resurrection in any detail here except to say that for him resurrection language interprets the "experience of

Christ's appearances," and the empty tomb does not signify the fact that Jesus actually rose from the dead but instead signifies the disciples' "experiences with Jesus." Thus Christ's resurrection "is still dependent on its eschatological verification through the new creation of the world,"[44] and resurrection language refers to the disciples' visionary or christophany experiences. Yet, in this view, the risen Lord cannot *act* in relation to the disciples during a specific Easter history, since the real power comes from the christophany experiences and is indistinguishable from those experiences. Believing in Christ's resurrection therefore does not mean affirming a fact. It means being possessed by the life-giving Spirit. The expressions "Christ appeared" and "was seen" do not then refer to facts within history existing independent of our faith (facts which actually govern our faith). Rather these expressions represent "the theological interpretation of these phenomena"; these "christophany conceptions" speak of a glory of the Lord which will appear only at the end of the world.[45]

In order to avoid this kind of predicament Barth specifically applied here the above mentioned notions of recollection and expectation as the manner of comprehending the grace of God revealed in history. For Barth, however, this human act of knowing is not self-sufficient and would be misconstrued if the resurrection were detached from the historical mediation of Jesus as the incarnate Word and were used as a principle to perceive Jesus' person and work before and after Easter. Hence, it is just because Moltmann has made the resurrection such a principle that he accuses Barth of de-historicizing the event of the resurrection. In fact Barth actually insisted that the "new creation" is a completed event in Jesus' history in which we *may* share by the *grace* of God through faith; hence it is to be distinguished *from* the experience of the disciples and our experiences as their *historical* foundation.[46] This may be known as we recall the Easter history and expect God to continue to act for us in the present and in the future. And Barth emphatically insisted on the historicity of the event of the resurrection, even though the Easter history cannot be explained in the usual historical sense.[47]

Pannenberg's View

Wolfhart Pannenberg consistently does the same thing, and it compromises Barth's concepts of revelation and of history. While Pannenberg claims to be presenting Barth's concept of revelation and of God's hiddenness,[48] his Christology from below does not actually begin and end with faith in Jesus as God and man. Rather, as seen above, he begins with history and faith in it by moving from a general anthropology to an understanding of revelation, and then he uses Jesus' resurrection as a principle by which to guarantee his uniqueness and our salvation.[49] But there is no clear attempt to let Jesus himself, as God and man, dictate the content and meaning of history and of the resurrection itself. In these ways Pannenberg's thinking clashes with Barth's notion of recollection and expectation. Barth himself criticized Pannenberg for this, as we have seen above.

Küng's View

Hans Küng also takes up Barth's notions of recollection and expectation in his Christology when he speaks of our dangerous memory of Jesus.[50] But it is clear from his presentation that, for him, it is not the specific history of Jesus, God and man, which sovereignly effects our true justification, but it is our memory which has the capacity to situate and fulfill the process of revelation itself. Thus, for Küng, the special feature of Christianity is that "it considers this Jesus as ultimately decisive, definitive, *archetypal* for man." In Küng's analysis, this ebionite foundation allows him to hold that Christianity can be relevant "only by activating—as always, in theory and practice—the *memory of Jesus as ultimately archetypal* . . . "[51] Here ebionitism issues in the docetic idea that *we* can make Christianity relevant by activating our memory of Jesus as our archetypal ideal. While Küng argues that Christ cannot be reduced to a principle since he is a historical person; he nevertheless has done just that by reducing him to a historical figure who is "ultimately decisive." Still, the fact that Barth's notions can be misunderstood is no reason why their real worth cannot be seen.

Barth himself argued that, in light of the resurrection, we know that this particular history, i.e., the history of Jesus Christ, was the object of the Old Testament expectation. From the same event we know that the identical historical person was the object of recollection of the New Testament. It is only as we today recollect this particular historical object of the Old and New Testament witness that we may hope in the same power which made that historical event a revelation to Christians. And that power is the power of the resurrection, namely, the power of the Holy Spirit of the triune God.[52] Thus, using these notions, Barth argued that the only way we can say anything about the direct *miraculous* action of God in his revelation is in recollection and expectation. That, for Barth, is how we actually know God in the present without being assimilated to the Holy Spirit.

> The man who so hears their word [of the prophets and apostles] that he grasps and accepts its promise, believes. And this grasping and accepting of the promise: Immanuel with us sinners, in the word of the prophets and apostles, this is the faith of the Church. In this faith it recollects the past revelation of God and . . . expects the future revelation that has yet to come. It recollects the incarnation of the eternal Word and the

reconciliation accomplished in Him, and it expects the future of Jesus
Christ and its own redemption from the power of evil . . . [it] is to be
understood only as an event. In this event the Bible is God's Word . . .
The fact that God's own address becomes an event in the human word of
the Bible is, however, God's affair and not ours. This is what we mean
when we call the Bible God's Word . . . It is not in our own power to
make this recollection, not even in the form of our grasping at the Bible.
Only . . . as the Bible grasps at us, when we are thus reminded, is this
recollection achieved . . . all this is grace and not our work. The Bible is
God's Word to the extent that God causes it to be His Word, to the extent
that He speaks through it.[53]

All of this clearly means that we cannot control our present since we are in God's
hands; we recognize the Bible as God's Word in faith, not however "as a
description of our experience of the Bible [but] of God's action in the Bible."[54]

Rahner's View

It does not mean, as Rahner believed, that we can deduce the reality of God
and the meaning of revelation from an experience of not being in control.[55]
Rahner's thinking led him to conclude that the resurrection "is an inevitable part
of the interpretation of my existence imposed on my freedom . . . The message
of Jesus' resurrection says in addition that his definitive identity, the identity of
his bodily history, has victoriously and irreversibly reached perfection in God."[56]
But what is it that determines our knowledge and hope here? Is it the fact that
Jesus rose from the dead and in the power of his Spirit opens us to a knowledge
of our reconciliation in him? Or is it that our transcendental hope is already
"graced" and therefore the foundation for our hope is our hope itself and the
resurrection merely represents the historical event in which we perceive this as
irreversible? That this latter concept was determinative for Rahner is obvious
when he wrote: "If one has a radical hope of attaining a definitive identity and
does not believe that one can steal away with one's obligations into the emptiness
of non-existence, one has already grasped and accepted the resurrection in its real
content."[57] It is evident that, as one can grasp the existence of God by analyzing
the experience of not being at one's disposal, one can also grasp the "real
content" of the resurrection without adverting to the resurrection narratives *first*
and through these to the Easter history where the risen Lord meets us as the
condition of faith and hope. Hence

Although we ourselves may always remain dependent on the testimony of
the first disciples in order to be able to connect our experience of the spirit
. . . with Jesus, we may nevertheless say with confidence that wherever
and whenever we experience the unshakeableness of our own hope of a
final victory of our existence, there takes place, perhaps anonymously, that
is, without reference to the name of Jesus, an experience that he has risen.
For this power of the spirit that we experience in this way as life's
victorious defiance of all forms of death is the power of the Spirit which
raised Jesus from the dead and thereby displays its victorious power to the
world in history.[58]

Rahner did not clearly distinguish the resurrection event in Jesus' life from the
disciples' experience either.[59]   And those who follow him tend to think in a
similar fashion.

Dermot Lane's attempt to deal with the resurrection is instructive in this
regard.   He wants to avoid "subjectivism" and "objectivism."   Addressing
Barth's rejection of Bultmann for reducing the Easter event to the "Easter faith"
of the disciples, Lane formulates the view, based on an interpersonal model of a
"person-to-person transforming experience" that "The issue here cannot be
reduced to either 'faith creates resurrection' or 'resurrection creates faith'.
Rather, these are *intrinsically* related dimensions of the *same transforming
experience*."[60]   And Lane really believes that this obvious confusion of "cause"
(resurrection) and "effect" (the apostles' experiences of the risen Lord)
adequately presents the resurrection as the actual foundation of the church and
sacraments.   This finally leads to his belief that what happened in Christ's death
and resurrection was already anticipated in our experiences of the world.   Thus,
the resurrection is now seen as reasonable:

> Is it not reasonable to ask whether there is any point within the history of
> mankind in which these deeply-rooted aspirations and hopes of mankind
> have been fulfilled and realised? . . . Within such an horizon the
> resurrection appears not as some exception or isolated incident but rather
> as the *realisation and crystallisation of man's deepest aspirations* . . . nor
> is it a violation of the laws of nature . . . the resurrection is, in the case of
> Jesus, the full realisation and actual fulfilment of those *seeds of
> indestructibility* which exist within the heart of every individual.[61]

It is obvious from this reasoning that the seeds of indestructibility within the heart
of every person are the basis of and foundation for both the reality of and
meaning of Jesus' own resurrection. The horizon, constructed on this foundation,

leads to a denial of the miraculous element in the resurrection of Jesus; it blurs the distinction between his activity and our experiences and aspirations; and finally it makes Jesus' resurrection a particular instance of the general experience of hope found within everyone.

Nor does it mean, as Pannenberg believes, that one "only needs to look at what happened then and ask how it stands the test of present-day reality."[62] Pannenberg correctly asserts that there is no direct experience of revelation. Yet he fails to note that our view of present-day reality, even when seen historically, may be an attempt to deduce the meaning of revelation from a direct experience of what we perceive history to be, rather than from a genuine knowledge of revelation. Thus, for him, the assurance of faith does not always and everywhere come from Jesus, the incarnate Word. Rather, "The recognition [of Jesus as God's unique historical revelation] cannot for them [believers] be a matter of a decision of faith, for that recognition is the ground of their trust in God and in Jesus Christ."[63]   For Barth this knowledge itself is an event enclosed in the freedom of God; thus prayer is necessary and faith always specifically means faith in Christ himself as the One Mediator.[64]   And the truth of this faith is dictated by the present sovereign action of the Holy Spirit and not by our recognition of it.

Implications of Barth's View of the Power of the Resurrection as God's Act

Barth's understanding here is dictated by three patristic principles which he developed in connection with the doctrine of the Trinity.[65]   These principles, *opera trinitatis ad extra sunt indivisa*, *perichoresis*, and *appropriation* reflected Barth's attempt to take seriously the indissoluble union and indestructible distinction of the Father, Son, and Spirit. He argued that because the power of the resurrection is the power of the one God who exists in indissoluble unity even as he is distinct as Father, Son, and Spirit *ad intra* and *ad extra*, we do not have to do now with a second history of Christ or with a different content. This same insight is what Rahner, Moltmann, and others seek to uphold in identifying the immanent and economic Trinity. But, as we have seen above and shall see with a different emphasis in the next chapter, each in his own way also detaches the power of the resurrection from God's Word and Spirit and locates it in history as well. That is the issue here.

Barth rejected such an identity precisely because he believed Christ's humanity and divinity should be distinguished but not separated. Therefore God's revealing activity was not wholly a property of the man Jesus as we saw above in connection with Christology. Any view that Jesus' humanity as such revealed his divinity then has allowed "man to set himself on the same platform as God, to grasp him there and thus to become His master." Any assumption of such an identity here in Barth's eyes means we have failed to grasp God's holiness, i.e., his right to make himself known as he so chooses, while at the same time "He still inhabits and asserts the sphere which is proper to Him and to Him alone."[66] Thus, "the Godhead is not so immanent in Christ's humanity that it does not also remain transcendent to it, that its immanence ceases to be an event in the Old Testament sense, always a new thing, something that God actually brings into being in specific circumstances."[67] As seen above in the last chapter this pivotal point is consistently denied in a Christology from below which stresses Christ's humanity. In addition, it led Moltmann, Küng, Pannenberg, and Rahner to make the power of the resurrection a power inherent in history and experience, as we have just seen. This problem of course relates to the connection between the immanent and economic Trinity which will be discussed more below.

Moreover Barth argued that the resurrection was not the continuation of Christ's first history on some other worldly level. Christ's history *needs* no such completion or continuation because what he did in his particular history was done in perfect obedience. For that reason "His resurrection was rather the beginning of the manifestation of what He was and did perfectly there and then: perfectly both in itself and in its scope for each and every man."[68] In this insight Barth was careful to avoid any adoptionist perspective which he believed typified so-called two stage Christologies.

> It was neither a 'historical Jesus' nor a 'Christ of faith' which they [the apostles] knew and proclaimed, neither the abstract image of one in whom they did not yet believe nor the equally abstract image of one in whom they afterward believed . . . A twofold Jesus Christ, one who existed *before* and another who existed *after* Easter, can be deduced from the New Testament texts only after he has been arbitrarily read into them.[69]

Since Christ's particular history is the limit here, the church's action in the Lord's Supper cannot claim to be a continuation of Christ's unique history. Instead, the church's action points beyond itself to this completed history in an historical and limited way. In that fashion revelation is perceived without compromising its divinity or the true humanity of the creature's free act corresponding to the knowledge of faith. In this manner the church lives as Christ's earthly-historical *form* of existence.[70]

This is to be sharply contrasted with Jürgen Moltmann's view of the matter. He thinks that *both* nature and grace will be completed in the kingdom of glory. Since Christ's resurrection is the beginning of the new creation of the world we must speak of nature and grace in a "forward perspective in the light of the coming glory, which will complete *both nature and grace*."[71] He also believes that Christ's Lordship is provisional; it will be complete only in the kingdom of glory when the Son transfers the, as yet, incomplete kingdom to the Father.

> With this transfer the lordship of the Son ends . . . it means the consummation of his sonship . . . all Jesus' titles of sovereignty—Christ, kyrios, prophet, priest, king . . . are *provisional* titles, which express Jesus' significance for salvation in time. But the name of Son remains to all eternity.[72]

And he believes all of this can be grounded in Paul's theology as a "two-stage" Christology.[73] In Barth's view this very reasoning neglects the fact that the resurrection was the beginning of the manifestation of what Jesus was and did perfectly there and then. For Moltmann Jesus' history itself will not be perfected until the kingdom of glory arrives. For Barth that kingdom, which has already arrived in the completed event of Christ's death and resurrection, will be complete for the rest of history at the second coming. Whereas Moltmann believes that Christ's resurrection inaugurates a cosmic and anthropological process of becoming which can be discerned in the experience of suffering,[74] Barth refused to detach the power of the resurrection from the historical Jesus who is at the right hand of the Father while ruling on earth through the Spirit.

In his resurrection then this perfected history came to light. This is Jesus' uniqueness. There really is and will be no other like him. There will be no other Christ(s) but only Christians, i.e., those who believe and live in his perfected history. Invisibly the church's existence is hidden with Christ as it exists by grace and not nature. Therefore the visible church exists in correspondence to Christ rather than in *parity* or *identity* with him. Even in its invisible essence "it [the church] is not Christ, nor a second Christ, nor a kind of extension of the one Christ." The church is "His body, His earthly-historical form of existence. It is indeed in the flesh, but it is not, as He is, the Word of God in the flesh . . ."[75] For Barth "The children of God . . . are not Jesus Christ Himself, but the earthly members of the earthly body of this their heavenly Head and Lord."[76] It is just because Barth rejected analogies of parity in his doctrine of God that he made this distinction here and insisted that the command to love God and to love one's neighbor cannot be confused.

> It became visible, first to His own, then, in the mirror of their witness, to many. There was here disclosed the accomplished fulfilment of the covenant between God and man in the obedience rendered to the Father by the Son, the reality of His dominion over the quick and the dead as the Representative of all men and therefore as the Liberator of all men. In the

resurrection of the man Jesus from the dead, God publicly confessed the power at work in His history . . . Beyond the fact that it took place, and did so for all, the history of Jesus Christ had become the living Word to all . . . The future into which Jesus Christ went forward from His resurrection was His action as the Revealer, Proclaimer, Prophet and Apostle of the salvation history of all men accomplished in His death, who is alive as such in every age and place, and who is powerful because, as the One whom God has raised from the dead, He has been confirmed in this power by God.[77]

It is simply because all of this actually happened that all persons are in a position to receive this salvation. What is revealed in this happening "is not merely ordained for all," but "does in fact reach all and may be received by all." There are no closed doors to the Word of salvation "who makes himself present to all men in all ages, to His 'Peace be with you'(Jn. 20:19)."[78] With this insight Barth carefully argued for the union and distinction between the command to love God and neighbor; love of neighbor was the form in which Christians actually loved God.[79] But he decisively opposed the idea of two absolute commands or two identical commands. By comparison Rahner spoke of the "radical identity of the two loves," and even argued that they are "one and the same thing."[80]

For Barth the simple fact that Christ himself and no other is the true light which has actually come into the world means that he himself is the *Pledge* and *Promise* to all, whatever their attitude toward him may be. This is a fact which has universal significance whether people know it or not.[81] While this insight seems identical to Rahner's view on this subject, it is actually quite different. For, as seen above, Rahner believed he could verify the truth of this insight by analyzing religious experience in itself, both Christian and non-Christian.[82] Barth believed this kind of analysis must end in an apotheosis in which Christ has become a principle rather than the One Mediator; he strictly adhered to the fact that we cannot interpret the universal significance of Christ in the church or the world without *first* knowing the particular significance of the resurrection. For Barth it is by the power of the resurrection that what happened in the history of Christ long ago can once again become a historical event for us here and now. We can be renewed and participate in the covenant experiencing communion with the "totally other," in Christ, by the power of the resurrection.

This positive insight is compromised by Pannenberg's assertion mentioned in chapter two that Jesus' resurrection caused him to be at one with God in eternity. In this thinking Pannenberg introduces the fruits of his christological method which refuses to think about Jesus from the start as divine and human.[83] Barth was actually saying that, while the resurrection revealed the eternal truth of who

Jesus was before Easter and in eternity as the pre-existent Word, the truth of this eternal existence cannot be identified with the historical event of the resurrection as Pannenberg does. This would confuse the development of thinking on the part of the disciples with a corresponding development in the being of God himself and would end in adoptionism. And this is just Pannenberg's predicament as he begins his Christology without acknowledging Jesus' divinity.

It is interesting to note that while Moltmann criticizes Pannenberg's view that Jesus' resurrection had a "retroactive power" on his history as a "violent assumption,"[84] his own view of the matter is materially no different. Hence Moltmann holds that "Jesus *is* the Lord because God *has raised* him from the dead."[85] The only genuine difference seems to be Moltmann's more "holistic" view which sees present experience as harmonious with what was already happening in Jesus' history (i.e., he was becoming the messiah). Moltmann does not want to impose a retroactive power *onto* a history that was not already being experienced as having a power. Yet in his trinitarian doctrine he actually believes that "the surrender of the Son for us on the cross has a retroactive effect on the Father and causes infinite pain."[86] Clearly, the events within the economy, according to this thinking determine who God is in eternity. Hence God can, according to the mystical doctrine of the Shekina, make "himself in need of redemption"; and "the unity of the triune God" can be described as "the goal of the uniting of man and creation with the Father and the Son in the Spirit"; Moltmann even concludes that "After the Son's exaltation the relationship between the Father and the Son is no longer absolutely the same as before . . . God experiences . . . pain . . . this is a new experience for God . . . God experiences the cross, but this also means that he has absorbed this death into eternal life . . ."[87] While Eberhard Jüngel is more positively disposed toward Barth's method, he does, however, take a similar view of the resurrection: "What is true in God's eternity is decided with retroactive validity only from the perspective of what occurs temporally with the importance of the ultimate . . . thus the truth of the incarnation—is also decided only retroactively from the perspective of Jesus' resurrection . . ."[88] By contrast, Barth argued that

> He is the One for whom it was impossible that the resurrection from the dead should not take place . . . He did not have to become this. He is from the very beginning the possessor of 'the power of an endless life,' (Heb. 7:16) . . . Jesus Christ is not merely the bearer and executive of a power of God which is given Him but which is not originally and properly his. On the contrary, Jesus Christ has the power of God because and as He Himself is it.[89]

Pledge and Promise

In describing Christ as pledge and promise, Barth emphasized that what Christ was and did, he was and did for everyone. This is his pledge. "In Me you are God's child. In Me you are justified before him, sanctified for him, called to His service."[90] For Barth the common testimony of the Old and New Testaments points nowhere but simply says *"I am the way, the truth and the life."*[91] This is a promise to everyone since what Christ was and did for all we already have and are in him. This new life "shall and will, in the same divine power as that in which I was raised from the dead, be manifested and brought to light as the reality of your poor life, as your eternal life."[92]

When the Lord's Supper attests this unique history as its saving history here and now it attests our being in Christ. In this way it does not claim to be more than a human action responding subjectively to its objective inclusion in Christ's history. In this fashion the church's action is limited by the mystery of revelation itself. It is limited then by Christ who lives in the power of his Spirit as a pledge and promise for all men and women. The concepts of pledge and promise enabled Barth to apply his view of analogy as an *analogia relationis* insisting that God gives us meaning according to his pledge and promise. Thus, we do not *possess* this but exist in relation to the divine act. In that specific way our human existence changes from faithlessness to faithfulness. All of this is real and actual only because Jesus was and is the one Word of God *in se* and *ad extra*. In this particular *esse* he is present for, with, and in every creature.[93]

From the resurrection and ascension we know that Christ is at the right hand of the Father. But this does not mean that he has returned to a state of divine rest.[94] Barth took a similar position in his doctrine of creation insisting that the sabbath rest meant that God was to be distinguished from a world principle or a self-evolving infinite sequence.[95] We shall see below how Moltmann interprets the sabbath from within his eschatological perspective. While he is quite clear that our existence here below is not identical with the kingdom of glory, it is not at all clear that he is able consistently to distinguish God from a self-evolving sequence. We shall also see exactly how Barth interpreted Christ's session at the right hand of the Father later.[96] Here Barth meant that "in His human history in His person He is manifested and visible and comes to all as the kingdom which is coming, which has already come, which is secretly present."[97] Again, Moltmann's own eschatology enables him to distinguish the church from God's glory, but it also causes him virtually to ignore the fact that the kingdom actually has already come in the history of Jesus Christ. Hence "The Spirit and the Word therefore point beyond themselves to the consummation."[98] If, as Moltmann insists in other contexts, the kingdom is identical with Jesus, then the Word and

Spirit do not point beyond themselves but rather to the consummation which they themselves have effected, are effecting, and will yet effect.

One brief example may clarify how Barth's concept of analogy shaped this insight. In his doctrine of the Word of God Barth argued that no sign, including scripture, has the attribute of being the Word of God because God is not an attribute of anything else.[99] Thus, God is free in relation to signs, including scripture. God is not bound to scripture or to the Lord's Supper. It is the other way around. God is Lord over and in scripture and the Lord's Supper. Our certainty consists therefore in the promise which the Bible and the Lord's Supper attest, i.e., the uniqueness of Christ *extra nos pro nobis*. Signs differ from the being of Christ. For a sign actually to point to the divine promise, its being requires the promise and faith. This means that, while the being of Christ does not require the promise and faith, signs must continually become signs of the eternal presence of Christ in the power of the Holy Spirit. As the One Mediator, he is the promise and the content of faith. In the oneness of his humanity and divinity, he is the fulfillment of the covenant and the object of scriptural faith. The *event* of faith must occur again and again in the freedom of God. On any other view we would have a false concept of analogy determining the relation between creator and creature.[100]

Jesus Christ, the eternal God, is once and for all part of human history. He himself *alone* is the factual possibility and limitation of divine transcendence and immanence.[101] This cannot be over-emphasized. Because of this particular history it is now the essential nature of the person in every age to be the *addressee* and *recipient* of this particular divine pledge and promise.[102] This was not just offered but actually given to humanity in the history of this man. It is precisely in knowing this fact that we know that there are and will be no other divine pledges and promises. But the positive content of this insight is lost the moment Christ and creatures and nature and grace are not sharply distinguished and united in faith.

Implications for Revelation

For example Rahner interpreted this to mean that, since the incarnation, creatures have been inherently changed ontologically so that the very structure of their consciousness is orientated toward God. Thus through his notion of quasi-formal causality Rahner proposed that transcendental revelation refers to "a transcendental divinization of the fundamental subjective attitude, the ultimate horizon of man's knowledge and freedom, in the perspective of which he accomplishes his life."[103] This is our grace-given supernatural existential which itself is the beginning of the *visio beatifica* in this life. As God's self-communication to the creature then, this revelation cannot be confined to words. It must also be the giving of grace, i.e., "an inner, objectless though conscious dynamism directed to the beatific vision."[104]   The beatific vision is the direct apprehension of God, given by God, which is in reality no different from the object of our initial dynamism of spirit which discerns being in general.   Hence,

> In his intellectual and transcendental dynamism, Maréchal considers man (as spirit, i.e. in his 'nature') in the inmost heart of his being as *'desiderium naturale visionis beatificae'*—to use the words of St Thomas. This desire is conditional and so there is no necessity for the actual call to the vision by grace.   But it is a real longing for the absolute being and one which is present in every spiritual act as its *raison d'être* . . . it is the *a priori* condition of all knowledge where a finite object is grasped.[105]

From this insight he proceeded to describe grace as noted above (as an element in human being) and concluded that

> The experience of God to which we have appealed . . . is not necessarily so a-Christian as appears at first sight.   On the contrary . . . it is precisely Christianity which makes real this experience of God in its most radical and purest form, and in Jesus Christ achieves a convincing manifestation of it in history . . . this experience of God . . . really constitutes the very heart and centre of Christianity itself and also the ever living source of that *conscious manifestation* which we call 'revelation' . . . through this experience of God Christianity itself simply achieves a more radical and clearer understanding of its own authentic nature.   For in fact in its true essence it is not one particular religion among others, but rather the sheer objectivation in history of that *experience* of God which exists *everywhere* in virtue of God's universal will to save all men by bestowing himself upon them as grace.[106]

But the problem in relation to Barth's analysis is that once this supposition is made, creatures may then rely on their experiences, whether religious or not, to lead them to the truth which Christians believe.   Yet the actual positive content of the incarnation can be perceived only in Christ and by faith in him.   Hence, while Rahner could speak about a true revelation apart from Christ, using his notion of transcendental revelation, Barth systematically excluded any such idea.

For Barth revelation is Christ and Christ is revelation.   In his humanity our humanity is addressed and promised salvation.   Both Barth and Rahner agree that we are not only offered salvation but given it in virtue of the incarnation.   But

Barth insisted that it is given in Jesus *alone* while Rahner was willing to seek and to find the gift apart from Jesus and then in him. Rahner presupposed "a general supernatural divine will to salvation which is really efficacious in the world. This makes possible a belief in supernatural revelation everywhere, i.e., in the whole length and breadth of human history."[107] Here general revelation is equated with the object of the experience described above and Christ and the Spirit become particular instances of this general ontology. Thus revelation and salvation are equated with the experiences of all creatures without any specific advertence to Christ and the Spirit, and the particularity of the pledge and promise of salvation is resolved into transcendental revelation as that conscious dynamism toward absolute being present within all religious people. Faith, grace, and revelation have all been equated with being in general as objectivated on the basis of this experience. It is not at all surprising then that Rahner began his chapter on Jesus Christ in *Foundations* by first ascribing what is specifically Christian to everyone as an existential of their being in freedom. Hence his first task was to present the anonymous Christian and all people who accept their orientation toward "absolute being," not Jesus Christ as the unique God-man; they develop an a priori doctrine of the God-Man which allows them to make sense of the historical Jesus. To this extent an "ascending Christology" sees the incarnation of the eternal Logos as "the end and not the starting point of all Christological reflection,"[108] even though ascendent and descendent Christologies are mutually related.

While Wainwright finds Barth's insistence on Christ's uniqueness at this point "perverse," insofar as it does not tend "towards the universality of ultimate salvation,"[109] and Moltmann finds it "too narrow" arguing that this narrowness must be overcome in his "trinitarian understanding"[110] of the sacrament, the real problem that emerges at this point is whether or not theologians are willing to admit that Jesus is utterly unique as the one and only Word of God. If he is, then neither a trinitarian understanding which sees God needing the world (Moltmann) nor an understanding which resolves Christ's uniqueness into a pattern for universal human values (Wainwright) nor a view that resolves revelation into the universal conscious drive toward the absolute (Rahner) can solve the problem here. We are left with a decision with respect to Jesus himself at this point.

By comparison Barth argued that it is in this specific way (in relation to Christ as the pledge and promise of salvation) that the divine change which took place in the history of Christ becomes the concrete and dynamic relation between creator and creature. In this *event* the creature becomes and is a faithful covenant partner. As such, creatures are called into the body of Christ.[111] As we shall see, it is only in *this* concrete calling and action that *eucharistia* can be grasped as a real response of the earthly body of Christ to the transcendent pledge and promise which is the basis and goal that determines its meaning as a human action.

This explains how it is in Barth's view that we creatures who, in ourselves are unable to be faithful to God, nonetheless become faithful by the divine judgment. It is in the historical *event* of Jesus Christ that we see "the event of the foundation of the Christian life."[112] This explanation views the Christ event from the perspective of the antecedent existence of the triune God who loves in freedom; this is the prior divine action in which human beings as such are included.[113]

Still to be answered is the question of how this event, which occurred at a specific time in the history of Jesus, is to become an event of renewal in the lives of others existing at other definite times and places. It is, of course, this renewal of communion between God and creatures which is the basis and goal of the Lord's Supper.

In answering this question, Barth insisted that the power "which makes men free, able, willing and ready to give this event a place" is nothing other than the power of the history of Christ demonstrated in his resurrection. For Barth this power permits, enables, and orders people. It commands and liberates them through the history of Jesus Christ to become "responsible subjects of their own human history, which renewed by the presence of the living Jesus Christ, has become a history of salvation rather than perdition."[114]

It is important to note that Barth had in no way changed his position on analogy as he developed it originally in his doctrine of God, though Hans Urs von Balthasar thinks that Barth eventually adopted the Roman Catholic doctrine of *analogia entis* in his doctrine of Creation.[115] Yet, Grover Foley correctly notes that this is a misunderstanding of Barth's own intention and of the meaning he attached to analogy. Even in his ethics Barth argued that only the special presence of Christ known in faith can lead to knowledge of salvation and therefore to a history of salvation rather than of perdition. Since being in general makes no sense interpreted *in se* or apart from this particular knowledge of faith, Barth argued that *any attempt* to describe this renewal as a general happening—discernable and actual apart from Christ, meant abstraction from faith, grace, and revelation. This calls the objectivity of God into question and renders true knowledge and action impossible. Barth consistently maintained that this thinking is what an abstract definition of the *analogia entis* supposes.

Action of the Triune God/Event

Everything depends upon the fact that this event is the same from below (i.e., in the sphere of immanence in which we live historically as it was from above i.e., the sphere of transcendence proper to God *in se*). Because this action *ad extra* is the action of the triune God,[116] it cannot be interpreted as a power native to the creature as such. Nor can it be claimed as a property of the sphere of immanence at all, whether inanimate, as in the numinous of Rudolf Otto,[117] or animate, as in the collective unconscious of Jung.[118]

For Barth, especially as it relates to the Eucharist, the power of the resurrection is the power of the one who loves in freedom. Thus, it cannot be ascribed either to the human acts of eating and drinking or to the elements of bread and wine. Both claims assume what is factually excluded in light of the history of Jesus Christ, very God and very man. They suppose that in the history of Christ, God handed over his divine power to humanity in general so that creatures as such now possessed the same power which is proper to God alone.[119] Abstracting from faith, this view fails to note the absolute priority of the sphere of primary objectivity (God *in se*) in relation to the sphere of secondary objectivity (God acting *ad extra* in and through creation).[120]

It is true that the stress is on the fact that creatures themselves do indeed become faithful to God and may truly act accordingly. The liturgy certainly is the place where human and divine action ought to be most clearly stated because it is here that the community specifically, decisively, and directly attests God and the covenant established by God. Here the church confesses what it lives each day.[121] But this particular possibility is the *goal* of the self-revelation of Christ in his resurrection from the dead. Consequently this specific possibility did *not* come from *within* history.[122] It is a divine working which came from and is effective as an action of the immanent Trinity.

The emphasis here cannot be on the fulfillment of our religious, psychic, moral, intellectual, and physical possibilities. Rather the accent is on the divine change which God has brought about for humanity in Christ. Christ always is and remains *distinct* from creatures as such, even though he is in closest union with them. The two never are mixed and cannot be reversed. Only as our human lives and our human works are enclosed in this prior divine act can we avoid ascribing this possibility to creatures in themselves apart from the triune God. This particular possibility is itself our limitation because this possibility can be no more than a fully human response to a fully divine act.[123] It is humanly possible only as it is enclosed in the mystery of the Trinity.

This suggests that the human act *cannot precede* the divine act either noetically or ontically; and this is the pivotal insight which determined Barth's rejection of natural theology. Never rejecting its actuality he rejected the idea that it could be used as a point of departure for understanding Christian revelation. The starting point for natural theology is itself the denial of grace insofar as it assumes there may be epistemological or ontological points at which creatures do not need faith, grace, and revelation as the sole criterion of truth. Thomas F. Torrance sees this point and treats it with great care so as not to deny the fact that people have some knowledge of God apart from revelation, but he insists that the substance of their knowledge of God must take place from Christ and in the Spirit. Hence

> Justification by the grace of Christ alone calls in question not only all natural goodness but all *natural knowledge.* Natural knowledge is as much the work of the flesh as natural goodness . . . Justification puts us in the right and truth of God and therefore tells us that we are in untruth . . . [it] . . . does not mean that there is no natural goodness in man, but that man with his natural goodness is called in question. Jesus Christ died for the whole man (with his good and his evil) not for part of him, the evil part . . . He died for all men, the good and the bad . . . *Justification . . . does not mean that there is no natural knowledge—what natural man is there who does not know something of God* even if he holds it down in unrighteousness or turns the truth into a lie? But . . . the whole of that natural knowledge is called in question by Christ who when he comes to us says: 'If any man will come after me, let him deny himself, take up his cross and follow me.' The whole man with his natural knowledge . . . is summoned to look away from all that he is and knows or thinks he knows to Christ who is the Way the Truth and the Life; no one goes to the Father but by him. The theology of Barth can be described, then, as the application of justification to the whole realm of man's life, to the realm of his knowing as well as the realm of his doing.[124]

Holy Spirit

The fact that this human action is a free decision to be faithful to the divine change revealed in the history of Christ can only be understood as the work of the Holy Spirit.[125] Moltmann surely says the same thing, but he deduces the Spirit's work not only from the immanent Trinity acting *ad extra,* but from the spirit of the cosmos which he eventually equates with the Holy Spirit.[126] Only the Holy Spirit enables creatures to be open, seeing, and comprehending in this matter.

> In the work of the Holy Spirit it comes about that the man who with the same organs could once say No thereto, again with the same organs, in so far as [*sic*] they can be used for this purpose, may and can and must say Yes. In the work of the Holy Spirit that which was truth for all, and hence for him too, even without his acceptance, becomes truth which is affirmed by him. The pledge which was previously given to him and to all becomes the pledge which is received by him. The promise which was good for him and for all becomes the promise which is grasped by him.[127]

A clear understanding of what Barth meant is crucial at this point. It is precisely because creatures actually may become the ones who say Yes to God, in the power of his Holy Spirit, that they cannot "fade away in favour of some other being, divine or semi-divine, which is organised and equipped differently."[128] In the work of the Holy Spirit, communion, fellowship, and communication between God and creatures, neither entity ceases to be what it is. Creator and creature do not become confused in this encounter between divinity and humanity. Transcendence and immanence are not merged into each other according to some generally discernable pattern which might perhaps be illustrated according to the presuppositions of Rahner, Wainwright, or Moltmann as presented above. It is expressly as persons who are faithful to God that human beings occupy the place appropriate to them. They cannot do this by trying to take God's place. Creatures literally cannot become more than human.

Contemporary theologians are quite aware of the need for an accurate doctrine of the Holy Spirit. Barth himself believed that such a doctrine would have helped a theologian like Schleiermacher to distinguish nature and grace where he failed to do so.[129] Since this is such an important issue, it is worth comparing and contrasting Barth's premise and conclusion with Rahner's. This is no idle comparison as we already saw above. I think it exemplifies exactly the predicament Rahner and the many Catholic and Protestant theologians who follow him face by applying his transcendental method, which starts from experience, to the various Christian doctrines. Here we are particularly concerned with his doctrine of grace. Rahner began his description of the creator—creature relationship by ascribing to creatures an obediential potency and a supernatural existential.[130] Much has been said and written to justify both of these notions. By obediential potency Rahner meant creatures are by nature ordained "to hear a possible *speech* of God, should it take place . . ."[131] What he meant by the supernatural existential is just as clear. As seen above, it is the fact that human nature as it exists in the concreteness of history is embedded in the supernatural or what he calls grace. This is why, for instance, a recognized Rahner commentator can title a book of essays on Rahner's theology, *A World of Grace*.[132] But whenever Rahner or his students are confronted with the obvious problems involved (analyzed above) in asserting such an existential, their explanations of what they really mean by this term become so vague, confused, and confusing that it could be said that it is literally impossible to know whether they really intend to speak of grace as a supernatural reality that transcends all spiritual and natural creation, or as a deeper level of the spirit (which is assumed to be supernatural) as it exists within history.[133]

Ultimately this problem stems from Rahner's assumption that "In any act of cognition it is not only the object known but also the knowing subject that is involved."[134] This statement could be interpreted to mean exactly what Barth stated above. But it cannot mean this for Rahner since, as we have already seen, he could only conceive of nature and grace as embedded in a historical process that reaches its climax in Christ. Thus, for Rahner, creatures cannot inquire about the "totally unknown . . . The being of that which is and the knowledge thereof are thus interdependent, because originally they are one and the same in their cause . . . Being and knowledge form an original unity . . ."[135] This thinking then leads to the idea that metaphysics studies "things which we 'always know and always have known.'"[136] So while Rahner might hesitate to claim that we have innate knowledge of God by nature, these very presuppositions forced him to maintain that we do have such knowledge while at the same time denying it. Even more importantly, however, this series of epistemological assertions led Rahner to conclude that God "makes his own further Word dependent upon the way in which man does in fact freely answer."[137] Thus, for Rahner, creatures have the capacity to place themselves at the disposal of grace and to cooperate with grace in a mutually conditioning fashion in the manner described above.

Concerning revelation Rahner wrote: "The revealed Word and natural knowledge of God mutually condition each other."[138] We neither have the time nor the space to extend a discussion of natural theology here. But we have already seen Barth's reason for rejecting natural theology as a prolegomenon to theology. Natural theology begins by assuming a knowledge of God's being which is not dictated by the grace of God revealed in Christ. Thus it can hold, as Rahner did, that there is an original unity between God and creatures, which is knowable through natural theology. But, it is this assumed knowledge of God which led to Rahner's description of nature and grace as mutually conditioning and mutually conditioned as well.[139] This, for Barth, is the clearest indication of a confusion of nature and grace and of theology and anthropology.

And here is where the comparison is revealing. Barth was attempting to show how creatures who are unable *in themselves* to relate with God (because of God's transcendence and Adam's sin) are enabled by God to do so without changing their actual humanity. Thus, Barth argued that knowledge of the Holy Spirit means realizing that the creature who lives by grace really does not fade away in favor of some semi-divine or semi-human being organized and equipped differently. By contrast, Rahner argued that God's relation to creatures through "created grace," a concept Barth obviously would reject, "can only be conceived of as founded upon an absolute entitative modification of man himself."[140] In other words, "Grace, being supernaturally divinizing, must rather be thought of as a change in the structure of human consciousness."[141] This, once again, leads to the heartbeat of Rahner's method as he adopted Maréhal's analysis cited above. Just because Rahner thought of God's grace by thinking of a structural change in human consciousness he failed to perceive God's actual transcendence and immanence as Barth described it.

It has been pointed out by others how Rahner's method actually fails to grasp Thomas' notion of being;[142] and I have discussed how this thinking relates to his reinterpretation of scripture and the tradition.[143] Perhaps at this point the seriousness of Barth's objection to the method of natural theology can be seen. While he tried to take seriously our humanness in relation to the Holy Spirit and grace from the very start of his reflections, Rahner was forced to assume by his very method which begins from our transcendental experience, that we are indeed more than human, since we are embedded in a world of grace. This very point led to Rahner's insistence that we have proper rather than appropriated relations with each of the trinitarian persons.[144] Moltmann takes a similar view.[145] But the problem is that Barth followed Thomas here and argued that a denial of appropriation meant a dissolution of the distinction between nature and grace.

The purpose of this discussion of the relationship between nature and grace is to illustrate the profound difference between Barth's *analogia fidei* and Rahner's *analogia entis* and to show that this difference indeed has a bearing on one's interpretation of the sacraments. At this point it is worthwhile to recall that according to his analogy of faith Barth argued, against all philosophical attempts to apprehend the God of Christian revelation, that the *terminus a quo* and the *terminus ad quem* of human knowledge is the immanent Trinity known in and through Jesus Christ and the Holy Spirit. For Barth this suggested that three insights, which stand in stark contrast to Rahner's views, had to be in evidence.

First, our knowledge of God is not based on any obediential potency or on our viewing and conceiving as such. Any such view would be Pelagian in origin and outcome since it could not trace its real knowledge of God both from and to the Holy Spirit as distinct from our human spirit elevated to the level of an absolute. This insight contradicts Rahner's *Vorgriff* and his entire attempt to explain our readiness for God in term's of an obediential potency and then as part of the structure of human consciousness, i.e., as a supernatural existential.[146] Second, we have no innate capacity for relating with God. This differs from Rahner's idea that being in itself is *luminous* with respect to the trinitarian God and that there is an original unity between God the creator and his creatures. When we do relate with God it is due to the miraculous action of his free grace. Third, true knowledge or true Christian behavior (obedient thinking and acting) do *not* come about *through* our work. We cannot cooperate with the divine act in this sense because human being *never* receives ability to relate with God as part of its *structure*. This contradicts Rahner's idea that creatures can activate or complete God's action using key words or sacraments. For Barth, we can only think obediently and act in accordance with God's prior action in Christ and his Spirit as we hear the Word of God and believe it by the power of his Holy Spirit. This insight is decisive in relation to the church's action in celebrating the Eucharist. Only if the incarnation is seen as a general theory, which creatures discover for themselves, can the Eucharist be seen as a particular instance of our general metaphysical participation in the divine being. For Barth this is just what revelation demonstrates to be impossible. This is the very limit within which the *analogia fidei* works.[147] It allows itself to be informed by grace here rather than by what can be demonstrated from nature. Insofar as we have seen that Moltmann accepts Rahner's basic position, with the reservation that theology must be placed more decisively within his eschatological context, we have seen that he too moves beyond this particular limit.

The work of the Holy Spirit does not mean that the human spirit, mind, knowledge, and will are paralyzed or dismissed. Barth observed

It has often been depicted thus. Attempts have been made to achieve it by strangely resigned twistings of human thought, feeling and effort. It has been overlooked that the attempt to sacrifice the human intellect and will is also an enterprise of the human spirit, that this attempt is impracticable, that the work of the Holy Spirit cannot be forced thereby . . . that the very intention of the Holy Spirit is to bear witness to our spirit, not to a non-human non-spirit but to the human spirit, that we are the children of God (Rom. 8:16), and to help us to our feet thereby.[148]

Creatures as such are opened to the history of Jesus Christ as their salvation history. In that way they begin to cry Abba, Father (Ga. 4:6; Rom. 8:15) "This completely new thing does not mean, however, that he takes leave of his wits and starts raving."[149] Rather, it is only in this way that creatures actually come to rationality and to their senses. This is the sense of the *credo ut intelligam* which Barth never ceased stressing since his treatment of Anselm. For Barth, *Credo* is not the last step that we creatures take when we cannot reason further. It is the *first* step which actually leads to clear reasoning. And clear reasoning here means precisely avoiding individuals or communities who seek the Spirit of Jesus in experiences, contrary to this kind of rationality. Thus, it is only in this particular way that creatures actually may know the eternal decision of God to be their Friend and Helper.[150] Only in this way can we know of our election to be God's covenant partner.[151] Here, in connection with the sacrament, Barth has simply applied his notion that faith does not just mean trust, though it certainly means that, but it also means *knowledge of the truth*.[152]

God's will for us in Christ is that everyone should be brought subjectively to the truth that they are saved in him.[153] Barth avoided any idea of self-justification by stating quite simply that the truth of salvation is a historical reality in him. As we are in him we live this. As we rely on ourselves we contradict our election in him. Since, however, God's will is not something general but a specific historical event in Christ, creatures cannot know it except in him.[154] This does not mean that the risen Lord does not work outside the visible church.

> Nothing that we can do in fulfilment of the will of God is higher and deeper than to love Jesus and therefore to keep His commandments . . . And whatever is done in line with and in the sense of this action even *where Jesus is no longer or is not yet known*; whatever bears in itself something in the nature of this action and is therefore an actual witness to the fact that Jesus lives and reigns and conquers, is definitely a fulfilment of the will of God. *In all ages the will of God has been fulfilled outside the Church as well.* Indeed, to the shame of the Church it has often been better fulfilled outside the Church than in it. *This is not in virtue of a natural goodness of man.* It is because Jesus, as the One who has risen from the dead and sits at the right hand of God, is in fact the Lord of the whole world, who has His servants even where His name is not yet or no longer known and praised.[155]

It does mean, however, that we have no knowledge of its truth apart from what the church knows and preaches, i.e., apart from the death and resurrection of Jesus Christ. This belief differs significantly from Rahner's notion of the anonymous Christian as we have already seen above. For Rahner creatures have already said yes to Christ in saying yes to themselves. And since God is implicitly known in each act of self-transcendence Rahner, at times, simply equates ethical goodness with living the Christian life. Geoffrey Wainwright takes a similar position when he argues that Christians pray for the establishment of kingdom *values* and that "Worshippers may glimpse the character and purposes of God and learn and experience the value-pattern of his kingdom in the Christian assembly."[156] This statement and the ideas that Christ is unique in a pattern setting way, as described above, and that where similar values are found outside of Christianity there we may seek and know Christ, make Wainwright's position similar to Rahner's.

Moltmann's idea that the risen Lord may work outside the visible church blurs the distinction between the church and those outside it who do God's will, by equating different experiences with experiences of the Spirit:

> Wherever this [experience] takes place through the workings of the Spirit, there is the church. The true church is the song of thanksgiving of those

who have been liberated . . . The church participates in the uniting of men with one another . . . Wherever unions like this take place . . . there is the church. The true church is the fellowship of love . . . in suffering and under the cross the church also participates in the history of the divine joy . . . Wherever the joy of God can be heard, there is the church.[157]

This is why, for Moltmann, Christians can seek the lordship of Christ "in themselves," and speak of Christ's own lordship as having been "ascribed to him" by the community based on its own experiences of liberation.[158] Clearly, for Moltmann, it is experience, such as the experience of liberation which, as a "fundamental experience" becomes the norm and source of true theology. Hence his whole Christology is founded on the idea that the church's Christopraxis is the source for understanding and his doctrine of God is founded on the idea that experiences of suffering yield both a knowledge of and union with the Trinity.[159]

In opposition to this thinking Barth was simply stating the fact that the objective truth of salvation is operative in the church and in general in and through the action of the risen Lord. It can in no way be detached from this sovereign action and described without specific reference to him and obedience to him. Thus, it is in the knowledge of faith that creatures can be free to be faithful to him. This, however, is not the work of creatures but the work of the Holy Spirit. And this work of the Spirit cannot be construed as a second work alongside Christ's work of reconciliation which was manifest in his resurrection. The work of the Holy Spirit is the *one* divine work in its movement toward all creatures. The condition of the possibility of living and acting as a Christian therefore is the prior and determinative divine action of God himself in Christ (resurrection and the Holy Spirit as the subjective apprehension of the mystery of revelation and salvation).[160] The Holy Spirit is holy precisely because he is of the essence of the Father and Son. As the theologians of the Enlightenment failed to heed this limitation in their thinking, they tended to identify the divinity of the Spirit with human feelings, experiences, and with belief itself.

Barth's point here is important. His belief was that any conception of human knowledge of God as an alteration in the structure in the realm of creation would reveal that we had conceived the work of the Spirit as a second work alongside Christ's work of reconciliation. It would compromise the truth that the Holy Spirit is of the same essence as the Father and Son.[161] When Barth argued that all human knowledge of God was indirect and mediated through created realities he intended to preserve just this notion. Since the triune God never abandons his transcendent power *to* creatures, this insight literally cannot be understood according to the phenomenology of symbolic reality. Within such a philosophy the medium is essentially related to the reality symbolized. To that extent, they are mutually necessary. Knowing God who is and remains free, however, precludes this view, because human mediation cannot supply, create, or guarantee what only God himself can create, supply, and guarantee; such as the unity of the church.[162] For Barth human belief is the work of the Holy Spirit, even though it is a fully human work as well.[163] Thus the spirituality of the Word of God means that it is spoken by God himself and actually heard by creatures in specific human experiences, attitudes, and thoughts. These experiences, however, cannot create or guarantee the presence of the Word of God; nor can they be necessary and unequivocal signs of its reality simply because "God is known only by God; God can be known only by God."[164]

Barth spelled this insight out quite clearly in describing God's hiddenness. He maintained that the truth and certainty of our knowledge of God is God himself by insisting that at no time can it be said or implied that we, in ourselves, are capable of fellowship with God, either noetically or ontically. There is therefore, no sign, no analogy, and no created reality at all which is true in itself. Here Barth's thinking is most opposed to Rahner's philosophy and theology of the symbol; it is also opposed to Moltmann's attempt to blend experience with our knowledge of God and God's experience with us and then to reinterpret the divine being from within a panentheist perspective. Because of his presuppositions, Rahner not only claimed for us an obediential potency for revelation, as well as a supernatural existential, but he even believed there are certain words which in themselves have the very power Barth here insisted can only come from the Holy Spirit.[165] For Barth the only guarantee that our speaking of God is true speaking, no matter what the concepts, is and remains the Holy Spirit.[166] But, because it is the Spirit of Christ and neither a second work alongside Christ's work nor some other spirit, we know it *indirectly*, in faith in the particular mystery of God as it is divinely disclosed in the history of Jesus and the history of the church. Human knowledge which does not admit this limitation either has not yet or no longer grasps the truth revealed by the trinitarian God in his action *ad extra*.

It is important then, that we realize that we are here dealing with a single act of the one who loves in freedom. In the resurrection of Christ he disclosed his history to all creatures. But, based on the analysis just offered, it is not something that can be seen and grasped generally and directly. For Barth, it can literally only be seen indirectly and in faith. In the Holy Spirit God opens specific persons for his history and in that way enables them to live their eternal election of grace as a testimony for others. Without the resurrection and outpouring of the Holy Spirit, living as a Christian would merely be an ideal and postulate. So also would Christian worship and celebration of the Lord's Supper. But it would not be a true human *event* (act) enclosed in the mystery of the Trinity.[167] Now we must look more closely at the relationship between the Lord's Supper and the doctrine of the Trinity by examining the relationship between the immanent and economic Trinity showing how a correct understanding of this relation may lead to a better grasp of the Lord's Supper as a work of the Holy Spirit.

Notes

1. C.D. 2, 2, pp. 552–55.

2. Ibid., pp. 555–6.

3. Ibid., p. 556.

4. Ibid., pp. 556ff.

5. Karl Rahner, *C.S.*, pp. 38–9, emphasis mine.

6. Ibid., pp. 39–40. Emphasis mine.

7. See, e.g., Karl Rahner, T.I. 2:109–133 "Personal and Sacramental Piety," at pp. 124–5.

8. Rahner and Häussling, *The Celebration of the Eucharist,* trans. W. J. O'Hara, (New York: Herder and Herder, 1968, hereafter abbreviated: *CE*), pp. 68–9. For similar ideas see T.I. 2:124–5. See also, pp. 129–30.

9. T.I. 14:177–78.

10. Karl Rahner, *CE*, pp. 76–77.

11. T.I. 14:178.

12. T.I. 2:129–30.

13. Markus Barth, *Rediscovering the Lord's Supper*, pp. 36–8.

14. T.I. 4:221ff.

15. T.I. 4:295.

16. T.I. 4:297, emphasis mine. Rahner of course holds that transubstantiation is a *logical* rather than an *ontic* explanation of the words of Christ recorded in scripture. A logical explanation clarifies some statement on its own terms without reference to something else. An ontic explanation clarifies some statement by appealing to some other matter which would explain the statement. Thus if I explain darkness which is before me by the fact that the light was turned out, this would be an ontic explanation, T.I. 4:300ff.

17. John H. McKenna, *Eucharist and Holy Spirit*, pp. 177–8f.

18. Ibid., pp. 191–3.

19. From T.I. 4:285, quoted in McKenna, p. 193.

20. Jürgen Moltmann, *The Church in the Power of the Spirit: A Contribution to Messianic Ecclesiology*, trans. Margaret Kohl (New York: Harper & Row, 1977, hereafter abbreviated: *The Church in the Power*), pp. 254–5.

21. Ibid., pp. 249–53.

22. Ibid., p. 257. See pp. 251ff. for similar problems.

23. I have explored the problem of mutual conditioning in Moltmann's understanding of God and creation in the *SJT* and *TS* articles cited above. Also, see chapter three above for how the notion of mutual conditioning operated at the heart of Moltmann's Christology.

24. For more on why the idea of mutual conditioning is so problematic in distinguishing nature and grace see C.D. 2, 1, pp. 69ff. and 569–71.

25. Barth, *The Christian Life*, p. 237.

26. Ibid., p. 235.

27. Ibid., p. 240.

28. C.D. 4, 4, pp. 23–24. This fact is the limitation of the community in relation to Christ (cf. C.D. 4, 2, pp. 614–660). Thus, it is also the limitation of the church's eucharistic celebration.

29. E.g., Moltmann, *The Church in the Power*, p. 256. He writes: "For the participants [in the Lord's Supper] this means that in this meal they *remember* the death of Christ, through which God reconciled the world once and for all; *acknowledge* the presence of the risen Lord in their midst; and *hope* with joy for the coming of his kingdom in glory." And he writes: "The Christian service was originally and still is the feast of Christ's resurrection," p. 273.

30. Ibid., p. 249.

31. Ibid., p. 254.

32. Moltmann, *Trinity*, p. 38.

33. Karl Barth, *Credo*, trans. Robert McAffee Brown (New York: Charles Scribner's Sons, 1962), pp. 166–67.

34. Moltmann, *The Church in the Power*, p. 259.

35. Moltmann, *The Way of Jesus Christ*, p. 241.

36. C.D. 4, 1, 302–304.

37. Moltmann, *The Way of Jesus Christ*, p. 241.

38. Ibid., pp. 242–3.

39. Ibid., pp. 250–52.

40. Ibid., p. 249.

41. Ibid., pp. 262–63.

42. Ibid., p. 260.

43. Ibid., p. 232.

44. Ibid., pp. 222-23. This problem of beginning with experience is very evident in Moltmann's analysis of the trinitarian missions. Cf. *The Church in the Power*, pp. 52ff. For Moltmann "In the eschatological anticipation of history, however, the unity of God contains within itself the whole union of creation with God and in God," p. 61. This very confusion of the immanent and economic Trinity leads Moltmann to argue that creation is inherent in the Father's love for the Son in eternity and that creation and incarnation are necessities grounded in the nature of selfless, suffering love (cf. Molnar, *TS* and *SJT*). Here there can be no distinction between God's eternal, self-sufficient love and his action *ad extra* in the distinct events of creation, reconciliation, and redemption.

45. Ibid., pp. 218-19.

46. C.D. 4, 1, 340-1.

47. C.D. 3, 2, 439-454.

48. Cf. Wolfhart Pannenberg, *Faith and Reality*, trans. John Maxwell (Phila.: The Westminster Press, 1977), pp. 60, 62, and 64ff. and also Molnar, *SJT,* pp. 387ff. and "Some Problems With Pannenberg's Solution . . ." *SJT* (1995).

49. Pannenberg, *Jesus—God and Man*, pp. 34ff.

50. Hans Küng, *On Being a Christian*, pp. 119ff. See above, chapter two.

51. Ibid., pp. 123-24. See also p. 174.

52. See C.D. 1, 2, pp. 63-64 for how this thinking affects Barth's understanding of scripture as the Word of God. See also C.D. 1, 2, p. 503.

53. C.D. 1, 1, pp. 108-9.

54. Ibid., p. 110.

55. Rahner, *Foundations*, p. 44, T.I. 4:52 and T.I. 11:151. See also P. D. Molnar, *The Thomist* (1987), pp. 579ff.

56. Rahner and Weger, *Our Christian Faith*, p. 111.

57. Ibid. p. 110.

58. Ibid., p. 113. Rahner believed "that the knowledge of man's resurrection given with his transcendentally necessary hope is a statement of philosophical anthropology even before any real revelation in the Word," T.I. 17:18, "Jesus' Resurrection." This same thinking is repeated in T.I. 7:168: "But it certainly will be maintained here that he who really does this [remains true to his own conscience] whether he realises it explicitly or not does in fact believe in the risen Lord even though for him he is nameless."

59. Thus he wrote: "There is such a thing as Easter faith. Those possessing it are beyond all reckoning. It is present first in the disciples of Jesus, and the witness *which they bear to their Easter experience* and their Easter faith is to acknowledge him who was crucified . . . It may be that we of today cannot draw any clear distinction within the Easter event as understood here between Easter itself (precisely the fact of the risen Christ) and the Easter experience of the disciples . . . In the case of Jesus' disciples their Easter faith and their Easter experience (their belief and the grounds for that belief) are already blended into each other indissolubly," T.I. 7:164 "Experiencing Easter."

60. Dermot Lane, *The Reality of Jesus*, p. 61. Emphasis mine.

61. Ibid., p. 64, emphasis mine. Rahner's position is very similar in T.I. 17:16–23, "Jesus' Resurrection."

62. Pannenberg, *Faith and Reality*, p. 64.

63. Ibid., p. 67.

64. Much of C.D. 3, 2, presumes and explains this meaning of the resurrection while C.D. 2, 1 pursues a concept of the *analogia fidei* which presupposes this understanding.

65. C.D. 1, 1, pp. 348–383.

66. Ibid., pp. 322–23.

67. Ibid., p. 323. Thus Barth rejected any "divinization" of Christ's human nature (cf. C.D. 4, 1, pp. 132ff. and C.D. 2, 1, p. 309) and argued that in becoming man Christ's divinity in no way ceased, C.D. 4, 2, pp. 40ff.

68. C.D. 4, 4, p. 24.

69. Karl Barth, *Evangelical Theology*, pp. 29–30. Edmund J. Fortmann, *The Triune God*, (Philadelphia: Westminster Press, 1972), p. 13 offers a similar interpretation of Acts 2: 32, 36. This is a text which is sometimes used to validate the idea that adoptionism was the earliest form of Christology. John Knox, *The Humanity and Divinity of Christ*, maintains "It is not too much to say that the disinterested critical reader of the New Testament is almost bound to conclude that, for however short a time—and however rightly or wrongly, adequately or inadequately—Jesus was at first regarded simply and naturally as a man," p. 75. Cf. also ibid. pp. 8–9.

70. For more on this and how it relates to Barth's concept of analogy, see C.D. 4, 3, pp. 597–600 and 727–29.

71. Moltmann, *Creation*, p. 8, emphasis mine.

72. Moltmann, *Trinity*, p. 92.

73. Ibid., pp. 86–88ff.

74. Ibid., pp. 4–5.

75. C.D. 4, 3, p. 729.

76. C.D. 1, 2, pp. 412–13.

77. C.D. 4, 4, pp. 24–5.

78. Ibid.

79. C.D. 1, 2, 402ff.

80. T.I. 6:233 and 236.

81. C.D. 4, 4, p. 25.

82. Cf. Rahner and Weger, *Our Christian Faith*, chapter one and T.I. 17:48. Moltmann skillfully analyzes this approach in *The Way of Jesus Christ*, pp. 61–2.

83. Pannenberg, *Jesus—God and Man*, pp. 34–35.

84. Moltmann, *The Way of Jesus Christ*, p. 76, cf. n. 9. See Pannenberg, *Systematic Theology II*, p. 303 where he responds to Moltmann's criticism.

85. Ibid., p. 40.

86. Moltmann, *Trinity*, p. 160.

87. Moltmann, *The Church in the Power*, pp. 61–3.

88. Jüngel, *God as Mystery*, p. 363, n. 39.

89. C.D. 2, 1, p. 606.

90. C.D. 4, 4, p. 25.

91. C.D. 1, 2, p. 105.

92. C.D. 4, 4, p. 25.

93. Ibid. This same point is made in C.D. 1, 2, p. 106. Barth noted that Christ is the true mediator between God and creatures because he himself acts divinely.

94. Ibid., p. 26.

95. C.D. 3, 1, p. 215.

96. Cf. C.D. 4, 1, p. 661.

97. C.D. 4, 4, p. 26.

98. Moltmann, *The Church in the Power*, p. 204.

99. C.D. 1, 2, p. 513.

100. Barth's view of the visible and invisible church (C.D. 4, 1, pp. 653–680), of veiling and unveiling as the manifestation of revelation (C.D. 1, 2, pp. 41ff.) and of the hiddenness of God (C.D. 2, 1, pp. 179–204) express this same insight.

101. Cf. C.D. 2, 1, pp. 150ff., 284–6 and 305ff.

102. This fact of grace, however, cannot be seen and described generally. See, e.g., C.D. 3, 2, pp. 148–51ff.

103. Karl Rahner and Joseph Ratzinger, *Revelation and Tradition*, trans. W. J. O'Hara (New York: Herder and Herder, 1966), p. 16.

104. Rahner, T.I. 4:61.

105. Rahner, "Nature and Grace," T.I. 4:169.

106. T.I. 11: 164. Some emphases mine.

107. Rahner, T.I. 17:40, "Jesus Christ in the Non-Christian Religions." While Joseph Ratzinger adopts Rahner's basic theological method, (*Principles of Catholic Theology*, pp. 163ff.) he does criticize Rahner on this point when he writes regarding Rahner's "spirituality" that he "is led into the freedom of universal philosophy and its rationalism . . . The weary Christian who groans under the burden of Christian history and ecclesial bonds is also freed by these theories. Self-acceptance—just being human—is all that is required," p. 167. This leads to "pseudo-liberation," p. 167. Ratzinger replies: "Just to accept one's humanity as it is (or, even, 'in its ultimate unconditionality')—that is not redemption; it is damnation," p. 167.

108. Rahner, *Foundations*, p. 177. See chapter six.

109. Wainwright, *Doxology*, p. 385

110. Moltmann, *The Church in the Power*, pp. 199–206.

111. See C.D. 4, 1, pp. 650–51 and pp. 661ff.

112. C.D. 4, 4, p. 26.

113. C.D. 1, 1, pp. 414–47. Moltmann thinks this view is determined by metaphysics in *The Way of Jesus Christ*, e.g, pp. 48ff.

114. C.D. 4, 4, pp. 26–27. For more on Barth's understanding of responsibility see C.D. 2, 1, pp. 641ff. For how this relates to the divine command see C.D. 2, 2, pp. 511ff. and 609ff. as well as Karl Barth, *Ethics*, ed. Dietrich Braun, trans. Geoffrey W. Bromiley (New York: The Seabury Press, 1981).

115. See von Balthasar, *The Theology of Karl Barth*, pp. 137–8, 226, 264–5 and Grover Foley, "The Catholic Critics of Karl Barth in Outline and Analysis," *SJT* (1961):139ff. Colin E. Gunton mentions this in *Becoming and Being*, pp. 174f.

116. Cf. C.D. 1, 1, p. 479 and C.D. 2, 1, pp. 257–321.

117. C.D. 2, 1, pp. 360f. Wainwright, e.g., *Doxology*, sees no problem here, as long as it has a specific Christian reference.

118. Paul Knitter, *No Other Name?*, argues that Jung has discovered our true selves and indeed the essence and truth of Christianity in discovering the fact that we need religious concepts to adequately express our deepest individual and

collective selves. Not only is this approach one which presupposes some type of self-justification, but it distorts what Christianity teaches in at least three ways: 1) it denies the traditional doctrine of original sin, 2) it claims an innate knowledge of the true God, and finally 3) it perceives Christ as only one symbol among others manifesting this same truth. See P. D. Molnar, *The Thomist*, (1991): 475ff.

119. Cf. C.D. 1, 2, p. 38.

120. See C.D. 2, 1, pp. 16–62.

121. Cf. C.D. 4, 2, pp. 676–710.

122. C.D. 1, 2, pp. 34, 58, 134 and pp. 360–61. Cf. also C.D. 1, 1, pp. 402ff.

123. Cf. C.D. 4, 4, p. 27 and esp. C.D. 2, 1, pp. 309–12.

124. T. F. Torrance, *Theology in Reconstruction*, (London: SCM Press, 1965), pp. 162–3, some emphases mine. In *The Trinitarian Faith* Torrance makes excellent use of Athanasius' important phrase "'It would be more godly and true to signify God from the Son and call him Father, than to name God from his works alone and call him Unoriginate'" (p. 49) to argue, among other things, that if we try to understand God from a point outside of God, we "are inevitably flung back upon ourselves. Even if we relate God negatively to what we are in ourselves, we are nevertheless quite unable to escape using ourselves as some sort of measure for what we think and say of him," p. 51. See also pp. 6ff. and *Karl Barth Biblical and Evangelical Theologian*, where Torrance notes that "in Karl Barth we have been given another Athanasius *contra mundum*, doing battle against modern Sabellians and Arians alike . . ." p. 22. While Torrance agrees with Barth's view of natural theology, he does hold a somewhat different view of the relation of theological science to natural science than does Barth; this leads to a modified view of natural theology as well, in *The Ground and Grammar of Theology*, (Charlottesville: University Press of Virginia, 1980), pp. 94ff.

125. C.D. 4, 4, p. 27. On the proper relationship between faith and works see C.D. 1, 2, pp. 366ff. and C.D. 2, 2, pp. 536ff. and 546–83.

126. See P. D. Molnar, *TS* (1990). Torrance argues against such a view of the Holy Spirit as noted above.

127. C.D. 4, 4, pp. 27–8. In C.D. 2, 1, pp. 70ff. Barth spells out his view of the divine and human relationship as it relates to this insight.

128. C.D. 4, 4, p. 28.

129. Cf. *Protestant Theology*, pp. 459–60.

130. Cf., e.g., *HW*, pp. 3ff., 10ff., 22, 25, 161ff., 175ff., T.I. 1:303, 315–16, T.I. 4:167ff., 186–7 and T.I. 9:28ff. Cf. also *Foundations*, pp. 47–52ff. and 126–33.

131. *HW*, 22. Cf. also p. 16. Rahner's philosophy of religion is an "ontology of the *potentia oboedientialis* for the free revelation of God," *HW*, p. 22.

132. Leo J. O'Donovan, editor, *A World of Grace: An Introduction To The Themes and Foundations of Karl Rahner's Theology*, (New York: Crossroad, 1981). In chapter three, "Within the Holy Mystery" Michael J. Buckley can say that "God is the context of all reality and experience," p. 31; that God is "the nameless, silent context for everything we name," p. 32; and that "God is the orientation of the mind when it is geared to ultimate reality," p. 35. In chapter one, "Theology in a New Key" William V. Dych notes that neither God, nor Christ, nor scripture can be a starting point for theology today since modern philosophy and science have raised questions about their reality, pp. 2–3. But he believes Rahner offers a starting point which touches everyone, i.e., our "shared human existence." Thus our unthematic transcendental experience of mystery is Rahner's starting point for talking about God. Since human experience is open and undetermined we can say "Human beings by their very nature are listeners for and possible hearers of the word of salvation and grace," p. 9. This is our obediential potency. In Rahner's transcendental theology of grace, the key concept is the "supernatural existential." This is "not a 'thing,' but a concept used to explain how it belongs to concrete human existence to be called to what transcends our existence, to life with God. Hence grace is an 'existential' . . . it belongs to the very essence of concrete human nature to be called to grace, to be able to find God . . . ," p. 13. In chapter five "The Invitation of Grace" John Galvin notes that an existential is "a dimension pertaining to the whole [person] . . . The adjective 'supernatural' is added in order to indicate that this existential, unlike others, is not given automatically with human nature, but is rather the result of a gratuitous gift of God. The divine offer of self-communication forms a constant dimension of human existence, always present, yet not part of human nature as such . . . directing us toward unsurpassable nearness to the triune God of grace and eternal life. The supernatural existential is the initial effect of the offer of grace, even prior to human response. It is present and operative universally . . . ," p. 72. How a self-communication of God can be "always present" and as an effect of grace be directing us toward the triune God who transcends nature is a problem inherent in this reasoning. Sometimes Rahner himself describes this supernatural existential as grace and sometimes he insists that it is not grace but an orientation of nature. That is the problem in detaching God's self-communication from God's action in Christ and the Spirit and ascribing it to humanity as an "offer" universally present. For an excellent analysis and critique of Rahner's "supernatural existential" see Stanley J. Grenz and Roger E. Olson, *20th Century Theology: God & the World in a Transitional Age*, (Carlisle: The Paternoster Press, 1992), pp. 246–7.

133. Cf. T.I. 1:305-317. This problem can be seen in the preceding note.

134. T.I. 11:87. Here Rahner sees this as a mutually conditioning relationship.

135. Rahner, *HW*, pp. 38-9.

136. Ibid., p. 31.

137. T.I. 1:111.

138. T.I. 1:98 and 107.

139. See, e.g., T.I. 6:73. Thus, "Grace exists by affecting a spiritual, personal substantiality, by being the divinising condition *of the latter* (nature), and hence presupposes and incorporates into itself the whole reality of this person as the condition of its own possibility and makes it part of the factors of its own concrete being." Speaking of God's relation to us Rahner even said that "grace, understood as the absolute self-communication of God himself, must always presuppose as a condition of its own possibility (in order to be itself) someone to whom it can address itself and someone to whom it is not owed," p. 75.

140. T.I. 1:324.

141. T.I. 5:103.

142. J.F.X. Knasas, "Esse as the Target of Judgment in Rahner and Aquinas," *The Thomist* (1987): pp. 222-245.

143. See Molnar, *TS* and *The Thomist*.

144. Rahner, *The Trinity*, p. 34. Cf. also T.I. 1:323 where Rahner wrote that the "conjunction of the Holy Spirit in particular with man is a proper and not merely an appropriated relationship." Cf. Molnar, *TS*, pp. 238ff. for how Rahner's notion of quasi-formal causality caused him to unite the triune God with the "nameless" discovered in his philosophy.

145. Moltmann, *Trinity*, p. 112 writes: "Contrary to the Augustinian tradition, it is not that the work of creation is only '*appropriated*' to the Father, though being actually the work of the whole Trinity. On the contrary, creation is actually a product of the Father's love and is ascribed to the whole Trinity." Of course the very way Moltmann conceives of creation is inherently emanationist because he believes the very nature of God's love leads him to create and that God cannot have been without the world because of this. See Molnar, *TS* (1990).

146. See Rahner *HW*, p. 10, T.I. 1:302, 312, 313-15; 2:240; 4:200; 6:78. It is not insignificant that Wainwright, who presents a modified Rahnerian position, is opposed to "extreme augustinianism and full pelagianism" in understanding our relation with God, but he says "there is room for a variety of accents in between," Wainwright, *Doxology*, p. 84.

147. C.D. 2, 1, pp. 138–39, and 385. Cf. also C.D. 1, 2, p. 234. Here Barth is most opposed to the thinking of Schleiermacher.

148. C.D. 4, 4, p. 28.

149. Ibid.

150. C.D. 2, 2, pp. 26ff. and p. 187. Also C.D. 1, 2, pp. 465ff.

151. C.D. 4, 4, p. 28.

152. C.D. 2, 1, pp. 3–31. Also Karl Barth, *Anselm: Fides quaerens intellectum. Anselm's Proof of the Existence of God in the Context of His Theological Scheme.* (Richmond: John Knox Press, 1960), p. 84, pp. 92ff., and 102ff.

153. C.D. 4, 4, p. 29.

154. Cf. C.D. 4, 3, pp. 726–28.

155. C.D. 2, 2, p. 569.

156. Wainwright, *Doxology*, pp. 355–6.

157. Moltmann, *The Church in the Power*, p. 65.

158. Ibid., pp. 104 and 280ff.; also *The Way of Jesus Christ*, pp. 40ff. and 70ff.

159. Cf. Moltmann, *The Way of Jesus Christ*, p. 41 and *Trinity*, p. 4. Moltmann intends to speak of God's experience with us as well as our experience with God, but since his idea of the Trinity is shaped by his panentheism rather than the Word incarnate, he blends the two together into an indistinguishable synthesis.

160. C.D. 1, 2, pp. 130–32 and C.D. 1, 1, pp. 415, 418ff., 422, and 439.

161. Cf. e.g. C.D. 1, 1, pp. 125–32, p. 321 and pp. 448–89.

162. Cf. e.g. C.D. 4, 1, p. 671.

163. C.D. 1, 1, p. 183, p. 461 and C.D. 4, 1, p. 697.

164. C.D. 2, 1, pp. 183 and 205ff.

165. Rahner, T.I. 8:219ff. Rahner believed we must seek unifying words to conjure up the truth of the original unity revealed in Christ. This original unity is already part of the structure of human being in accordance with assumptions concerning the original unity of knower and known. Rahner writes, "Such key-words do exist, with their power to adjure to epitomise and to unify," p. 220. While the Logos was probably one of these words, we must always search for new key words. "But woe betide that age which no longer possesses any word imbued with a quasi-magical force of this kind to epitomise all in one!" p. 220. Rahner's intention in this context was to apply this thinking to the Sacred Heart.

166. Cf. C.D. 1, 1, pp. 448–89 and C.D. 4, 1, pp. 151ff.

167. Cf. C.D. 1, 1, p. 462 where Barth writes: "This being of ours is thus enclosed in the act of God."

V

The Relationship Between the Doctrine of God and the Lord's Supper

In view of what has been established so far, we can now say that the correlation between Barth's doctrine of God and the Lord's Supper consists in the fact that it is the *same* Christ whom we know in both places.[1] This fact is what calls for the *distinction* in union between God and creatures and between divine and human action throughout the *Church Dogmatics*. Human knowledge and action are possible only as they represent and attest the being of God himself. Thus neither true knowledge nor true action is possible outside the sphere in which God seeks and effects communion with his creatures, namely, outside of faith. Before concluding this chapter with the implications that this insight has for church practice in the Lord's Supper, it is important to show how Barth's perception of the relationship between the immanent and economic Trinity shaped his view of analogy and how that view of analogy governed what he said about the sacrament.

Barth's insight that our being is enclosed in the act of God already bears the stamp of the *analogia fidei*. When he spoke of the veracity of human knowledge of God, Barth maintained that the *terminus a quo* and the *terminus ad quem* of genuine knowledge of God is God himself, i.e., the immanent Trinity. Thus, knowledge of the immanent Trinity occurs for us, who are not God, indirectly and in faith. "Knowledge of God is then an event enclosed in the bosom of the divine Trinity."[2] This means that it has no immanent *terminus a quo* or *terminus ad quem*. Here Barth maintained his insight that there is an absolute priority of the divine in relation to human action in which both the freedom of God and of the creature are maintained without any confusion. For this reason Barth made a sharp distinction between baptism of the Holy Spirit and baptism of water, which denotes the divine act of being cleansed by the Holy Spirit. The former corresponds noetically and ontically with an act of God. The latter corresponds with an act of creatures which is called for by God, initiated by God, and indeed sustained, and brought to completion by God.

As this thinking relates to the Lord's Supper it is clear that a deliberate and sharp distinction must be drawn between the working of the Holy Spirit and creatures as they are enabled to recognize Christ actively present and bringing them to knowledge of himself, and thus to knowledge of the truth. The purpose of this distinction is to see the *actual* communion between God and creatures established and maintained by God alone. This relationship between God and humanity in Christ is a communion which can never be construed as a dissolution of divine into human being or an elevation of human being into divine being or a combination of these into some *tertium quid*.

Prayer

It is significant that, for Barth, theology could only take place as a prayer.[3] Even the coming kingdom for which people pray is marked by "pure prayer" since it is done in free obedience to God the Father, because

> in it they turn to God, with whom alone it rests that his kingdom should come . . . The prayer for the coming of the kingdom, however, looks directly and exclusively beyond all that people can and should do for the betterment of the human situation to the change which it can be God's business alone to effect . . . [and because pure prayer] carries with it the unreserved certainty of being heard.[4]

If prayer were merely the arbitrary request for the strengthening of our human efforts for a better society then it would be filled with doubt and uncertainty; but if it is ventured in "obedience to God's command as a prayer for the new thing which is to be expected from God alone, it has an objectively and subjectively solid basis that is protected against all doubt." For Barth prayer is bounded by the history of Jesus Christ as the present and future kingdom and if this is not seen or ignored then we are merely "blowing bubbles." For this reason prayer is not "the expression of a hope manufactured by people and cherished by the human race as such . . . It is not the exponent of wishful thinking, whether metaphysically speculative or mythologizing."[5]

Relation of Immanent and Economic Trinity

The dogmatic reason for the distinction in union between God and creatures for which Barth argued is the fact that the immanent Trinity is the indispensable presupposition of the economic Trinity.[6] Thus, in encountering the economic Trinity (the historical humanity of Jesus Christ) we meet nothing other than God himself in his inner trinitarian life. But because the two are not directly identical, i.e., God *in se* was not merged *into* a reality distinct from him (the *oikonomia*), Barth maintained, in his Christology, that the humanity of Christ is what it is only in virtue of the prior and determinative act of the Logos. Christ's humanity really is the locus of revelation to and for humanity, but not of its own power. This truth is the basis of the distinction in the union of humanity and divinity in Christ.

Barth stressed the fact that there is a genuine distinction in union between the immanent and economic Trinity in his doctrine of God and in his Christology by stressing the union and distinction of the divinity and humanity of Christ. In his ecclesiology, this enabled Barth to maintain that creatures in the church are what they are only as they are at one with Christ without being assimilated into him. But this is not a human possibility. It is a divine possibility given to us in Christ by the Holy Spirit. Consequently the body of Christ (the church) cannot be interchanged with the head, very God and very man, who absolutely precedes and determines the truth of the community's existence. They are *not identical*, even though the one cannot be understood without the other. Finally, because of the distinction in union maintained by Barth in his doctrine of God, Christology and ecclesiology, he maintained a clear distinction between the working of the Holy Spirit and the human response to that divine happening in describing the sacrament. This, because the Holy Spirit is none other than the Spirit of the Logos and Father. The Spirit is one in essence with the immanent Trinity. He opens people up to be faithful to the same triune God which he is *ad intra* and *ad extra*. In meeting this Spirit, people encounter the immanent Trinity *indirectly*, i.e., in and through the human testimony to the truth of the resurrection which began with the apostles. The church is the *oikonomia* of salvation and as such is not identical with Christ or his Spirit. The immanent Trinity is not enclosed by the *oikonomia*—it is the other way around.

Rahner's Axiom of Identity

Here we must at least call attention to the fact that Rahner's axiom concerning the identity of the immanent and economic Trinity led him to a view of divine and human being and action which defines the immanent Trinity *by* the historical events in and through which God has acted and acts *ad extra*. It is difficult to know whether the axiom came from experience or the axiom led to Rahner's particular interpretation of experience. Of course there is a sense in which Rahner's axiom rightly opposes separating God *in se* from God acting for us *ad extra*. But his axiom is also shaped by his methodological and ontological presuppositions. That is the problem.

Moltmann accepts Rahner's axiom but contends that it remains open to misunderstanding "as long as we cling to the distinction at all."[7] Clearly, Moltmann still recognized that Rahner himself knew that some distinction between the immanent and economic Trinity was in order, at least theoretically. Yet Moltmann believes he has overcome this problem by transferring the identity between the immanent and economic Trinity to a process in which divine and human being are, together, proceeding toward their common redemption in which

God will eventually be all in all. By arguing that the economic Trinity not only reveals the immanent Trinity but has a retroactive effect upon it, Moltmann clearly introduces the necessities inherent in created being into the Godhead. Hence he argues that God needs the world and creatures;[8] that the incarnation means an "increase of his riches and his bliss;"[9] and that what "the incarnate God, did in time, God, the heavenly Father, does and *must do* in eternity."[10] As seen above, he argues that we must speak of nature and grace within a "forward perspective" in light of the "coming glory, which will complete *both nature and grace.*"[11] And finally, he argues that God's self-communication of his goodness to creation is not a matter of his free will but a matter of the essential emanation of his goodness which he cannot keep to himself.[12] Furthermore, while he rejects what he regards as Tillich's pantheist understanding of the *creatio ex nihilo*, he himself maintains Tillich's essential insight that creation is necessary to God. John Thompson offers an interesting evaluation and critique of Moltmann's view that God must suffer because he is love. Instead of saying, with Barth, that God suffers for us in Christ while remaining Lord over it, Moltmann "reverses this and sees suffering as being *in* God in a manner bordering on pantheism."[13]

Wolfhart Pannenberg thinks that Rahner's axiom of identity does not go far enough and argues that "The maker himself is changed by the production and shaping of another being. The change cannot be held remote from God's inner being,"[14] as he believes Rahner does when he contends that God is unchangeable in himself but can become subject to change in another. While Rahner's notion that God needs another outside himself to change clearly reflects the problems of his view that the immanent and economic Trinity can be understood "symbolically,"[15] Pannenberg's view that God is changed by the production of creation presents its own version of mutual conditioning. Hence, while Pannenberg faulted Barth for having a "pre-Trinitarian, theistic idea of God" which determined his trinitarian doctrine and led him to modalism,[16] his own Christology from below, which he thinks avoids subordinationism, actually is entirely determined by it. In fact his own aversion to what he assumes is Barth's modalism leads him to reject completely the *actual* existence of an immanent Trinity which can be distinguished from Jesus' history. Of course Pannenberg knows that without the immanent Trinity, statements about God's actions in history are meaningless. In fact he attempts to ground his own view of revelation in the immanent Trinity. But since his thinking cannot allow for an immanent Trinity *actually* to exist prior to and apart from history, without becoming dependent on history, it appears that the immanent Trinity merely describes Pannenberg's own idea of revelation grounded in his view of history.

He believed that Barth's doctrine of the Trinity, like Augustine's, was determined by natural theology, in spite of Barth's denial.[17] Yet his own correction of Barth is instructive. It is not based on Jesus of Nazareth as the Word incarnate but on his "idea of revelation" as the point of departure for Christology.[18] For that very reason, however, it falls directly into the docetism which Barth actually avoided by acknowledging, from the very outset, that Jesus' humanity in its union with the Word was the sole point of departure for Christology.[19] Pannenberg grounds Jesus' sonship in his "message of the nearness of the Father's lordship,"[20] and concludes, in typical adoptionist fashion, that "Jesus was and is the Son of God because he lived out his mission and message by sanctifying the name of the Father among humans . . . Jesus' active self-differentiation from God made him the Son . . ." Or as Roger Olson puts it: "Jesus is God, then, because of his mediatorship, not vice versa." It is puzzling, that in spite of Pannenberg's rather overt adoptionism (contradicting his own theoretical rejection of subordinationism and modalism), Olson says "It might be easy to label this account of Jesus' sonship 'adoptionistic' and dismiss the doctrine of the Trinity based on it as merely 'economic' were it not for Pannenberg's insistence that there is a reciprocal relationship between the Son and the Father by which the Father also receives his deity from Jesus the Son."

The problem with this reasoning stems from the fact that "Pannenberg recognises no personal 'Son of God' distinct from the man Jesus of Nazareth."[21] And if this is in any sense true, then the fact that he maintains that there is a reciprocal relationship in which the Father receives his deity from the Son solves nothing at all since what the Father receives is a meaning, truth, and reality conferred upon him by history itself. The fact that this history might be the history of Jesus of Nazareth becomes irrelevant the moment his humanity is separated from his divinity, as must be the case, according to Pannenberg's own method.[22] That is the ultimate predicament of a theology which refuses to acknowledge the *reality* of the immanent Trinity while at the *same time* not rejecting an independent natural theology as Barth himself actually did. Pannenberg's own *historical* natural theology leads him to adopt Rahner's axiom, to modify it, and to argue that in the history of Jesus we are led beyond the doctrine of appropriation.[23] The result is a concept of God whose "deity is radically dependent on the creation and its history."[24] We have discussed this notion of mutual dependence at length already and there is no need to repeat it here. We simply note that a denial of appropriation means confusion of nature and grace as well as of the immanent and economic Trinity. What results is the idea that God really cannot have ever existed without his actions *ad extra* and still have been God. And thus, Pannenberg can argue that Christ's resurrection determines the nature of the eternal Godhead. This very thinking makes God dependent on the world and on his works within the world. And we saw in the last chapter that a God who is so dependent is not really free at all.

We cannot go into all the details of Eberhard Jüngel's view of the relationship between the immanent and economic Trinity here except to note that he gives "unqualified agreement" to Rahner's thesis that *"The 'economic' Trinity is the 'immanent' Trinity and the 'immanent' Trinity is the 'economic' Trinity."*[25] And the problem here is that it leads Jüngel to think beyond Barth's view that the immanent Trinity is the indispensable premise of the economic Trinity, and instead to argue that "the economic doctrine of the Trinity deals with God's history with man, and the immanent doctrine of the Trinity is *its* summarizing concept."[26] The problem with this reasoning, however, is that, as it is logically followed, the immanent Trinity is given only so much independence as we are willing to give it based on our own experiences of faith in the crucified and risen Jesus. As John Thompson notes, this is against Jüngel's intention which is to maintain God's freedom for us in Christ.[27] But we have already seen the problems of interpretation which follow this kind of grounding of the mystery of the resurrection in experience in the last chapter. What happens is that our interpretations are detached from the historical event of Jesus' own life and used to redefine this from the general constructs adopted from some favorite source, such as transcendental experience, eschatology, love, the idea of revelation, or even trinitarian thinking shaped by panentheism.

While Thomas F. Torrance rejects any logical necessities which he thinks Rahner may have introduced into the immanent Trinity, he believes Rahner's axiom might be acceptable; he even believes it might lead to a "rapprochement between Roman Catholic theology and Evangelical theology, especially as represented by the teaching of Karl Barth."[28] While space and time prohibit an extensive treatment of the differences between Torrance's interpretation of this axiom and Rahner's, it is clear from his major work on the Trinity[29] that Torrance follows Athanasius and argues that we must not attempt to understand God by falling back upon our own reflections on ourselves and our world. Rather we must understand God from a center within his own personal being, i.e., from the immanent Trinity and therefore through the historical Jesus known to us through faith and by the Spirit. Thus, his own conception of this axiom clearly indicates that he thinks we cannot isolate the Son from history (as in dualism) just as we cannot define the Son by history (as in pantheism). He maintains Barth's notion that the relationship between the economic and immanent Trinity is irreversible and in that way he presents a powerful and accurate interpretation of how God can be God in his own unique way *ad intra* and *ad extra* without being defined by any logical necessities. When he thinks of the identity of the immanent and economic Trinity it seems clear that he means that one cannot separate divinity and humanity as they actually have been united in the history of Jesus Christ. When Rahner thought of the identity of the immanent and economic

Trinity he meant that in one's experience of grace one is enabled to unite conceptually the efficient cause known in natural theology with the Father of Jesus Christ known through revelation. His starting point was the experience of the self and of the nameless. His conclusion was that Christ is the highest symbolic representation of God in history and that both the immanent and economic Trinity act in accordance with his theology of the symbol. Yet, as we have seen, this left him in a position where he both compromised God's freedom and fell into pantheism and subordinationism.[30]

To return to Barth's own thought then, we may say that because it is the economy chosen by God as the place and manner of revealing himself, we creatures are bound to *this* economy in order to understand the immanent Trinity. The immanent Trinity is the indispensable presupposition of the existence of Christ and the church, i.e., the existence of Christians as those who choose to live in accordance with their eternal election in Christ to be faithful covenant partners. In this manner they constitute the earthly-historical form of his body. But because the immanent Trinity is not identical with the economy of salvation (i.e., the history in which creatures recognize their salvation in Christ) the latter cannot be known without the preceding and determinative action of the former.

From the antecedent and determinative action of the immanent Trinity we also know that God still remains free in relation to the *oikonomia*. He is still Lord of history, including the history of salvation. He is not unconditionally bound to the *oikonomia* in the same way we creatures are. That is why the Holy Spirit and the human spirit are not interchangeable even in baptism or the Eucharist. The one must be distinguished from the other in order to see the truth of both. Only by actually recognizing the act of the triune God in faith is it possible to perceive the human action in the Lord's Supper as a faithful attestation of God's *pledge* and *promise*. Because the immanent and economic Trinity is indissolubly *one*, yet distinct, our human action in the Lord's Supper is not merged into God's action in his Spirit. Nor does it precede the divine action as its subject. Its truth lies precisely in recognizing its distinction from and dependence upon the triune God himself.[31]

This distinction between the immanent and economic Trinity which Barth carried through into the rest of his theology shaped his view of analogy. We cannot choose analogies we think are appropriate. Instead, analogies are true only if they actually acknowledge that their *terminus a quo* and *terminus ad quem* is God, the immanent Trinity acting *ad extra*, and not created being as such, i.e., the *ad extra* sphere. In order to stress this point Barth consistently maintained in *C.D.* 2 that the relationship between creator and creatures as established by God alone was and is an irreversible relationship explainable only by God's grace. That is why all human knowledge of God is mediated and indirect. It can only point obediently to God's preceding act of graciousness; its locus can never be found directly *in* the mode of secondary objectivity (creation) since creation never becomes identical with the act of God (grace) which precedes it always.[32] This is what Barth meant when he said that our readiness for God is real only when it is enclosed and preceded by God's readiness for us. Any reversal here confuses divine and human reality. In order to avoid this, Barth asserted that the *analogia entis* is real only as it is enclosed by the *analogia fidei*. For Barth, then, true Christian knowledge of God must always bear the mark of an encounter with this God by never attempting to ground its knowledge in itself; thereby attempting to precede its Lord by setting up another word independently and alongside his one Word of revelation. Whenever this reversal (mutual conditioning) takes place, creator and creature have already been identified, and theology becomes impossible since we have no way of knowing who is God, the creator and who is the creature.[33] Five implications for understanding the human action in the Lord's Supper follow from this view of analogy.

Implications For Understanding the Lord's Supper

1. Christ alone is the author and finisher of faith.[34] This means that he, in the power of his Spirit, attests himself and imparts himself to persons of every age. This prophetic action is not in any sense given over to anyone or anything else.[35] Practically speaking this means that the church is neither the author, dispenser, nor the mediator of grace and revelation.[36] The church, in its eucharistic action and in all other forms of its work stands or falls with the self-attestation and self-impartation of Christ. The church can only participate in this secondarily, namely, as it follows and does not attempt to precede its only Lord. There really is only *One* Mediator between God and creatures today as there was yesterday and will be tomorrow.[37]

In no sense can it be implied either that the church's action or any element in creation (including bread and wine) is *identical* with the divine action of the Holy Spirit. As people actually become Christians in the fact that they request and receive baptism with water, so they confirm and express their communion with God by celebrating the Lord's Supper. This is a human action corresponding to God's action in his Spirit as described above. In this action people attest their real communion with God established and maintained by God. They do this by coming together with the community in public convocation. They do *not*, however, *become* Christians *through* baptism with water or *through* their human decisions.[38] This, in Barth's view, is either an *ex opere operato* or an *opus operatum* understanding to be rejected because wherever there is true knowledge of God or Christian action, it can only be traced back to God and neither to the work working nor to the disposition which may or may not be in evidence. Thus, speaking of the union of Christ and Christians, Barth wrote, "union does not mean the dissolution or disappearance of the one in the other, nor does it mean identification . . . The union of the Christian with Christ which makes a man a Christian is their conjunction in which each has his own independence, uniqueness and activity."[39]

Since Jesus Christ is the one in whom reconciliation, justification, and sanctification were accomplished "He has no assistant nor fellow-worker to accompany Him, let alone any *corredemptor* or *corredemptrix* . . . Without them [others], He intervenes for them;" Christ actually makes common cause with Christians as he "attests to the world the reconciliation to God effected in Him . . . He refreshes them by offering and giving Himself to them and making them His own." This is the "ratio" of the Lord's Supper. It can be understood in analogy "to the mystery and miracle of Christmas . . . We are concerned with the fact that He as the one Word of God takes up His abode in the called, that His life becomes their life as He gives Himself to them. This is the mystery and miracle of His union with them."[40] Correspondingly, it is not *through* the human actions of eating and drinking or any ritual action, that creatures are brought into communion with God in Christ. It is not through *any human* consecratory word that the bread and wine become holy food and drink. Since events in themselves are *not* revelatory (as in a symbolic ontology) we may miss God who reveals himself in Christ when looking at events such as birth and death or in this case when viewing water baptism or the Lord's Supper.[41]

It is here that Barth applied his insight developed in the doctrine of God that no analogy is true in itself. He maintained the same position in his ecclesiology by insisting that the church has no holiness in itself; and the logical application of this insight in this context is that there is no holy action or holy element *in se*. Hence in considering the union of Christians with Christ that takes place at the Lord's Supper Barth believed it was unwise to interpret eucharistic New Testament references such as Jn. 6:53 to refer to "an extension of the incarnation in relation to the Christian's *unio cum Christo* and then in relation to the Lord's Supper. We are concerned rather with the extended action in His prophetic work of the one Son of God who became flesh once and for all and does not therefore need any further incarnation."[42] This understanding could shed some light on the problem of eucharistic epiclesis and on how to understand correctly eucharistic real presence without making God's active presence to us a static presence absorbed by and identified with our own historical responses.[43]

In no way can the ecclesial action of the Lord's Supper be conceived as a basis or guarantee of the covenant of grace. The truth of the Lord's Supper is seen only as the church recognizes that its basis and guarantee are and remain in God himself in his action *ad extra*. Christ does not delegate his divine work even to the community. What the church is in reality is invisible; its true being is grounded in grace—in its relationship with Christ. Between the church and Christ

> there is indeed correspondence but no parity, let alone identity. Even in its invisible essence it is not Christ, nor a second Christ, nor a kind of extension of the one Christ . . . it is His body, His earthly-historical form of existence . . . Thus to speak of a continuation or extension of the incarnation in the Church is not only out of place but even blasphemous.[44]

The community is his, only as it lives as his body, that is, only as it recognizes his active presence and *not* its own *idea* or *experience* of divine presence. Christ is the transcendent head of his body on earth.[45] The work of the Holy Spirit is Christ himself as the guarantor of God's faithfulness and of his own faithfulness to God.[46]

2. This self-impartation of Christ, i.e., this action of the Holy Spirit is the form of grace which actually reconciles the world to himself.[47] This is the form of grace which is addressed to particular persons at specific times and places. Markus Barth applies this point well when discussing 1 Cor. chapters 8–14,

> Obviously, love is not a virtue that can be applied equally to this or that subject. Rather, the content and substance of love consists in human beings, those who may be hard to bear because of their specific character, conduct, and public repute. This means that to love is to accept just such an unlovable person. Humanity as such, all people of the world or faraway groups that suffer hunger and injustice cannot really be loved. A neighbor or a family member, even an enemy, who has to be loved according to God's will, is always a person known well and loaded with specific, perhaps repulsive, idiosyncrasies.[48]

Those who constitute the earthly-historical form of this self-impartation respond with baptism of water and the Lord's Supper. Consequently the corresponding human decision is not identical with grace and cannot precede and condition it. The human decision and action can only follow grace.

Therefore as water baptism is not to be equated with grace, so also the human activity of eating and drinking in thanksgiving for the oneness and fellowship we actually have in Christ, cannot be equated with grace. On the contrary, baptism with the Spirit is the active "actualising" of the grace of God in creatures. Water baptism follows this but is neither identical with it nor is grace dependent on the human action. The action of the Spirit in cleansing the "old man" is the decisive and determinative point in relation to baptism. It is not just a metaphoric image or symbol of something else; this action of God on and in creatures is "divinely effective."[49] Similarly, in the Lord's Supper the community's action, insofar as it is the earthly-historical form of Christ's self-impartation, is determined by what took place in the baptism of each individual and what continually takes place anew each day in the power of the Spirit.

The presence and activity of God proclaimed by the church in the Lord's Supper are not something new and different from the power of the Spirit in which people first become Christians. If it is seen or described as something essentially different, then the essential unity of the triune God as such is denied. Herein lies the basic union of both baptism and of the Lord's Supper. The action of the Spirit of Christ in imparting Christ himself to creatures is the form of grace which those baptized with that Spirit confess and live in their action of *koinonia* and *eucharistia*. This fellowship and thanksgiving cannot attest anyone or anything other than the triune God in his act of revealing himself *ad extra* to us. As it does attest anyone or anything else, it ceases to be the body of Christ and so also an obedient and true ecclesial act of worship.[50] We have already seen the implications of this above in relation to Moltmann, Rahner, and Wainwright. To the extent that Christ's uniqueness is redefined by each of these theologians in his own distinctive way to refer to more universally acceptable notions of grace and salvation, this insight compromises the notion of worship built on this foundation. Indeed this redefinition of Christ's uniqueness really ignores the necessary distinction between the immanent and economic Trinity discussed above.

What happens in the Lord's Supper is not just a reference through image and symbol to something generally discernible by us. Markus Barth himself argues that the New Testament references to meals "do not hint at a specific presence that would be different from Jesus' pre- and post-Easter presence in Galilee and Jerusalem, or from Jesus' advent in the Parousia." Indeed he contends that the many disputes about Christ's real presence in the Eucharist have "little or no foundation in the New Testament itself." Hence even with regard to the idea that Christ's presence is symbolic, he concludes "it would be difficult to demonstrate that biblical thought and diction are built upon this or another conception of symbol." Indeed he believes that Paul does not hold that Christ is present "in the person of the priest or in the substance of bread and wine."[51] Moreover, there is no "secret identity" between Christ and Christians being advocated by Paul.

Therefore the referent here is the actual living fellowship willed and effected by God in Christ and rendered actual here and now in the power of his Spirit.[52] The church is not directed to an image or a symbol when it is called to the Lord's Supper. It is directed by the Spirit of Christ to recognize and attest the communion established and maintained by the triune God himself. Its attention is directed to the covenant fulfilled in the history of Christ; thus, it is pointed to the divine command and promise. The command received by the Christian in baptism is *not* a partially adequate grace which may be diminished by our disobedience. It is wholly adequate and remains in itself an effective command which we must obey.[53] As seen above, this is exactly what cannot be held according to a phenomenological view of presence; or according to a view of the God-world relation which introduces the idea of mutual conditioning into the discussion of the sacraments, or nature and grace, and reason and revelation. Against any notion of mutual conditioning Karl Barth argued that it is precisely in this very human act of obedience that the creature actually lives his or her communion with God and his or her fellow creatures. To the extent that Moltmann, e.g., can no longer describe the act of Christians as obedience, his own theology tends to blur just this distinction, as noted above. To the extent that the church is seen as the guarantor of the Spirit's power, obedience to the church rather than to Christ tends to become the preferred view.

3. This particular action of the Holy Spirit of Christ demands *gratitude*.[54] It is God's action on and in us which we did not produce for ourselves. This does not mean that the creature is just a "cog" set in motion but that creatures, in the freedom appropriate to them, decide to determine their existence in accordance with the Word heard and believed.[55]

> What the free God in His omnipotence wills and fashions in Jesus Christ in the work of the Holy Ghost is the free man who determines himself under this pre-determination by God, the obedience of his heart and conscience and will and independent action. Here man is taken seriously, and finds that he is taken seriously, as the creature which is different from God, which is for all its dependence autonomous before him . . . he is empowered for his own act, and invited, commanded and encouraged to perform it.[56]

In this way creatures are set directly before the command of God by God himself.[57] They are claimed in their human self-determination for service of the Word heard and believed. There is no escape from this command and no excuse which can weaken this confrontation of creatures by God. God has liberated weak and impotent creatures for obedience to himself.[58] The only possibility for the person confronted by grace is a corresponding human decision to be faithful in his or her human being, action, and conduct to God's faithfulness. This obedience, however, is not a mechanical consequence of a person's being confronted by God. Even the slightest idea of this and it would not be God who confronted the person. In fact any deviation from Christ himself at this critical point will lead to the same problems that arise in connection with predestination when it is detached from Christ himself.[59] This is exactly the problem, as we saw above, with the various attempts to reconcile Christ's uniqueness in relation to non-Christian views of salvation.

4. As in baptism, creatures are not left to themselves, but called into the *communio sanctorum* by the Spirit of the risen Christ. As they confess God, so in the unity of faith, love, and hope they confess the particular community into which they are called historically.[60] For Barth, the true basis and guarantee of the church's unity is "The Lord who attests Himself in the prophetic and apostolic word, who is active by His Spirit, who as the Spirit has promised to be in the midst of every community gathered by Him and in His name."[61] Thus, it is *not because* the community gathers in his name that Christ is present. Rather it is because he has promised to be present and in the power of his Spirit is actually present that two or three may confidently gather in his name.[62]

Just as the immanent and economic Trinity and the humanity and divinity of Christ are neither identical nor separate on the basis of God's free grace, so revelation is not identical with the scriptural testimony. We can only have revelation *indirectly*, in faith, in the historical words of the Old and New Testaments. Just because they are distinct in their unity they are not dissolved in their created character in relation to the creator. For Barth, then, the nature of the church's unity consists in the fact that in its plurality the church responds to the *one* God revealed and active for us in Christ and the Spirit.[63] In this way the church also participates in Christ's own ministry.[64] The norm for the church's unity, then, is not a general definition of being, but the one being of the triune God active in his Word and Spirit. While Moltmann, Pannenberg, and Rahner each attribute their distinctive explanations of the church's unity to God's Word and Spirit, we have seen that, in various ways, it is not this particular Word and Spirit which actively determines their respective explanations of the church's actual unity. To that extent it is clear that a general notion of being dictated by experience within history has become determinative.

This point must be stressed since, for example, Hans Urs von Balthasar assumed that Barth's norm was being in general.[65] Von Balthasar believed that for Barth salvation is the "fulfillment of being" and missed Barth's main point; he assumed that Barth had defined the analogy between God and creatures on the basis of parity between the two. As seen above, however, Barth rejected this understanding in his doctrine of God, Christology, and in connection with the sacrament and he did not adopt this understanding here. Rather, in what preceded and followed the excerpt from the *Church Dogmatics* cited by von Balthasar, Barth insisted that only being as the being of God is what faith can speak about in this way.[66] Thus in virtue of God's free inclusion of human being in his triune self-knowledge, which is revealed in the incarnation, human being has a place in relation to God. But the two do not arise from a common ontological sphere.

Divine being absolutely precedes and determines the possibility and limit of human being. Humans in general cannot know this without the specific divine action of reconciliation in Christ. This is precisely what von Balthasar could not say and in fact did not say in this context: "the salvific happening that takes place between God and the world is being, being in its fullest sense."[67] But "Being in the fullest sense" need have nothing to do with the being of the triune God and to that extent directs our attention away from God instead of toward him. As this idea of being does this, it is not only useless to theology, but contradictory to it. Thus, the decisive feature here, as elsewhere in Barth's thought, is determined by his view of the *analogia fidei*.[68] It is just this point that is compromised by Eberhard Jüngel's modification of Barth's method with the idea that we can better understand God's love when "we first ask generally what love is."[69] Among other things this method eventually leads Jüngel to conclude that "In the event of love, God and man share the same mystery."[70] It is noteworthy that Jüngel's own attempt to reconstruct Barth's doctrine of analogy, at least in part, is indebted to the thinking of Hans Urs von Balthasar.[71]

People, therefore, enter the community and participate in its worship of the triune God in their own ways and with their own commission. Consequently as being a Christian is not a private affair, so the Lord's Supper is *not* a private affair. For Barth, individuals are called and separated into the body of Christ on earth by the Holy Spirit. As individuals they are awakened to faith in him.

> Where and when He calls these men—and not others, addressing and setting aside this man or that woman as His own, it does not mean, as the matter has often been put, and is still put, in a very doubtful way, that there arises between Him and them a private relationship. The fact that these individuals can as such partake of His grace and live with Him and for Him has no autonomous or ultimate significance. It has significance only as in so doing they become members of His body, or, rather, are revealed to be such to themselves and others.[72]

Participation in the Lord's Supper then consists in the same obedient service that is required of all persons. This relationship with fellow creatures in which all are involved in doing God's will is not identical either with water baptism or with the human action of eating and drinking which takes place in the Lord's Supper. This relationship is the work of the Holy Spirit. This is a most important point. Baptism with water and the human celebration of the Eucharist are human actions called for by this Spirit. They therefore follow from this call and are real as enclosed within it. They are, however, in *no way identical* with it. They neither lose their human character nor does the Spirit lose its divine character. One does not become semi-human or semi-divine. We saw the implications of this above in relation to Rahner's notion of the supernatural existential. We shall discuss the further implications of this in relation to transubstantiation below in Part Two.

Being a Christian, i.e., one who is called to attest his or her oneness with the triune God and with one's fellow creatures in his or her behavior and public worship[73] certainly does not mean

> donning a uniform and clapping on a helmet and as a member of the community, as one specimen among many others, being subjected to the same regimented spiritual and ethical drill . . . . The Holy Spirit, being the Spirit of the one, but eternally rich God, is no compactly uniform mass.[74]

Consequently each person who is called by the Spirit has his or her own special task within the community. In that way the one God is attested without dissolving the multitude of the gifts of the Spirit. Thus,

> The criterion of the authenticity of the discharge of all institutional office in the Church is always and everywhere the question whether the one who serves in this or that office is a recipient and bearer of the *charisma* indispensable to his work, and first and finally whether he is a recipient and bearer of the love which is above all spiritual gifts. At no time then . . . can one dispense with the petition: *Veni Creator Spiritus.*[75]

5. Baptism with the Holy Spirit is a new *beginning*. "It is not perfect. It is not self-sufficient, definitive, or complete."[76] Being a Christian means further work, further renewal, and further growth in Christ. Yet, how does one know whether one is growing in Christ or growing in accordance with some idea or experience which is at variance with his Word and Spirit? The answer is simple. Whenever that growth or renewal is seen as taking place *automatically* in accordance with the development of the person, it cannot be growth in Christ. Whenever that growth or renewal has for its norm an idea or an experience, it cannot be growth in Christ; because no idea or experience has the power which the triune God who loves in freedom has. Hence God alone remains the sole criterion by which ideas and experiences are to be evaluated. This can never be reversed as in the Protestant theology of the nineteenth century.[77]

The prompting of the Holy Spirit is always something radically new which calls for ever more radical conversion;[78] it is not and must never become indistinguishable from the human spirit. There may be curable and perhaps incurable setbacks for the Christian, but one must constantly seek renewal according to the impulses of the Holy Spirit and not the impulses of one's heart or mind. Renewal includes the person's mind, heart, and spirit, but it does not derive from these, as in Pietism. In this sense renewal and growth in the Spirit of God mean a constant search for the divine invitation and command; living in prayer in accordance with the promise that God will make himself known and present again and again in his power according to his will.

In the church, we are thrown back entirely on the divine promise exactly where we are tempted to see directly;[79] in the Lord's Supper, we are in the corresponding position. Indeed "As we can only believe the Christian community as such in its identity with the holy community of Jesus Christ, so we can only believe ourselves and others as its holy members."[80] Whatever the advances that are made in the life of the Spirit, it must be remembered that it is not yet the perfect life which is the final goal of the Christian. While we have seen that Moltmann emphasizes this eschatological side of theology and also the fact that the church is not yet the church triumphant, he also consistently identifies the Holy Spirit with the cosmic spirit and even with the spirit of liberation and union found in the world at large. In these ways he clearly compromises the special nature of the Spirit which is being spoken of here.

For Barth, the final goal of the Christian is to live as a witness with the first fruits of the pledge of the "perfection in which he will one day be manifested when Jesus Christ shall come, when He shall manifest himself as the Pantocrator of all life, and hence of his mortal life, when He shall awaken him from his life in partial knowledge of God to life in the knowledge which is no longer in the riddle of a reflection, but 'face to face.'"[81] For this reason Barth called the church "the provisional representation of the new humanity in the midst of the old."[82] Humanity's absolute future is this very God who is the same yesterday, today, and tomorrow.[83] The key point in connection with the Lord's Supper is that as one is led by the Holy Spirit to this particular future as a member of the pilgrim community, "the Holy Spirit feeds him with the body of Jesus Christ which was given for him, and strengthens him with the blood of Jesus Christ which was shed for him."[84] There is a constant being apprehended by Christ and a continual prayerful seeking to apprehend the kingdom which is to come; the power of the life to come is already the power of one's present life in the world.

By comparison, Jürgen Moltmann can only speak of Christ as Pantocrator *after* the resurrection and *until* he has handed over the kingdom to his Father.[85] Even in Christ's incarnation there is no room for the divine action of the Word; in Moltmann's thought, Jesus becomes the Son of the Father as he lives out his messianic history. He is not this Son from eternity, in time, and after the end of time.[86] The future conceived by Moltmann is very different from that portrayed by Barth. Barth takes account of the fact that the future for which we hope entails an *act* of the triune God (Christ's second coming) which cannot be separated from his being as Lord. For Moltmann, our future hope is not solely defined by this particular act. Indeed, their views of God's sabbath rest show how Barth's conception of God's act and being enabled him to distinguish God from creation in a way that Moltmann cannot.

Barth portrayed God's sabbath rest as an *act* of God by which he ended his work of creation, distinguished his free act of love from an evolving world principle which is neither free nor loving, and was immanent within his creation, as Lord of the covenant.[87] In Moltmann's conception of the *zimzum* and of the sabbath rest, his image of the future redemption incorporates the very pantheism which he actually attempts to avoid. He adopts the doctrine of the *zimzum* from Isaac Luria to explain the *creatio ex nihilo* and our future redemption.[88]

Intrinsic to the doctrine of the *zimzum*, God must create a primal space (which Moltmann later calls Nothingness) in order to act *ad extra*. From this Nothingness it is then adduced that God himself needs to be redeemed and that he then becomes part of the process of redemption as he releases a certain sector of his being. The very fact that Moltmann describes the act of creation as an issuing forth rather than as an act by which God posits a reality distinct from himself sheds light on his view that the sabbath rest rather than God himself is the final goal of creation. But the obvious problem in this reasoning is that if there is a primal space into which God issues when he creates, then the sense of the *creatio ex nihilo* has already been negated. For the point of the doctrine is, according to Moltmann's own analysis, to insist that God is free; a point which emanationist theories like the *zimzum* cannot acknowledge.

The sabbath blessing then "does not spring from God's activity; it springs from his rest. It does not come from God's acts; it comes from his present Being."[89] Since, for Barth, God's action *is* his present being, there can be no such separation of God's act and being. Any such separation would indicate a fusion of divine and human being and a denial of the divine freedom. Yet this explains why Moltmann describes the "eschatological moment" as the ending of God's self-restriction which took place in creation. Heaven and earth therefore find their final form in God's "unrestricted omnipresence itself." While Moltmann distinguishes God's "absolute eternity" from "relative eternity" which he describes as aeonic time, the fact is that such a distinction allows him to say that "Eternity is one of life's dimensions: it is life in depth. It means the intensity of the lived life, not its endless extension."[90] Yet if eternity is one of life's dimensions, how can God really be distinguished from creatures at that point? Are they not relatively what God is absolutely? Why would we need to believe in and hope for an eternal life which will result from an *act* of God whose Holy Spirit governs our life now and which will be a new beginning?

Divine/Human Freedom

In presenting the Lord's Supper as a work of the Holy Spirit of Christ, we have seen that the freedom of God and human freedom remain. By perceiving the absolute priority of divine in relation to human action, including the human action which takes place in the Lord's Supper, it is possible to see a real relation and distinction between human and divine action. Now this must be made more precise from the perspective of the human action itself. In light of the absolute priority of the triune God in relation to creatures, including those transformed (from faithlessness to faithfulness) in Christ, it remains for us to consider the basis, goal, and meaning of the church's action in the Lord's Supper. In other words, given the perception of the divine and human freedom which can be seen according to Barth's *analogia fidei*, we must see just how the historical event of the Lord's Supper actually participates in the movement of the immanent Trinity *ad extra*.

The person who is baptized by the Holy Spirit is one who is called into the church by God himself, i.e., one of those who confess their election in and by Jesus Christ for fellowship with God and with their fellow creatures. These individuals constitute the community which is called to be Christ's body on earth until he returns. As such it is his "special presence" on earth. This is the place and manner in which God wills to be known as the one who loves in freedom between the time of the resurrection and the second coming.[91] This is what the church lives in its ethical decisions and confesses in the Lord's Supper. It lives its baptism by the Holy Spirit. It confesses its renewal by the Holy Spirit. This divine action is the basis, goal, and the possibility of meaning for water baptism which needs no repetition. What needs repetition is the human confession of this divine action. This confession leads to the question of right liturgical action and right ethical action.[92] In this way God upholds us in our self-determination as people who are now obedient to the triune God. This is what the church lives as it attempts to conduct itself in accordance with the will of its only Lord. This is what the church confesses in its liturgy.[93] As with the church's oneness, holiness, catholicity, and apostolicity, those gathered in the name of Christ are what they are as his body *only* because he is who he is. This decisive fact can *never* be reversed either theoretically or practically without abstracting from faith and leaving the sphere of the *analogia fidei*. We shall see that this has particular significance in connection with the meaning of the Lord's Supper.

Notes

1. Cf. C.D. 1, 1, p. 332. God reveals himself as the Spirit of the Father and the Son and not just as any spirit. Thus, the deity of the Holy Spirit could be contested theoretically or practically only if the deity of Christ is contested. Cf.

C.D. 1, 1, p. 460 and C.D. 4, 1, p. 147.

2. C.D. 2, 1, p. 205. Cf. also C.D. 2, 1, 181, and C.D. 1, 1, 462.

3. Cf. Barth, *Anselm: Fides Quaerens Intellectum*, pp. 35ff. The necessity of prayer shows that God and no one else is the source of true theological knowledge. See also C.D. 4, 2, pp. 704ff., C.D. 3, 3, pp. 265-88, C. D. 3, 4, pp. 87–115, C.D. 2, 2, pp. 763 and 780f. and Barth, *Prayer*, ed. Don Saliers, trans. Sara Terrien, (Philadelphia: The Westminster Press, 1985).

4. Barth, *The Christian Life*, p. 245.

5. Ibid., pp. 246–47.

6. C.D. 1, 1, pp. 172 and p. 479–81.

7. Moltmann, *Trinity*, p. 160.

8. Ibid., p. 58.

9. Ibid., p. 121.

10. Ibid., pp. 31–33. Emphasis mine.

11. Moltmann, *Creation*, p. 8, emphasis mine. This has disastrous consequences for Moltmann's eschatology because, while Barth maintained a clear distinction between time and eternity (C.D. 2, 1, 608ff.), Moltmann argues that creation will be "relative eternity" rather than "absolute eternity" and concludes that "Eternity is one of life's dimensions: it is life in depth. It means the intensity of the lived life, not its endless extension," in *The Way of Jesus Christ*, pp. 330–31.

12. Ibid., 82ff.

13. John Thompson, *Modern Trinitarian Perspectives*, p. 63.

14. Pannenberg, *Jesus—God and Man*, p. 320.

15. See Molnar *TS* (1985), pp. 242ff. and "Toward a Contemporary Doctrine of the Immanent Trinity . . ." in *SJT*.

16. Roger E. Olson, "Wolfhart Pannenberg's Doctrine of the Trinity," *SJT*, 43, (1990): 175-206, pp. 184ff. This is spelled out by Pannenberg in *Systematic Theology I*, pp. 45, 75, 299, 303ff.

17. Pannenberg, *Systematic Theology I*, p. 304. For a discussion of how this thinking relates to "anticipation" cf. Paul D. Molnar "Some Problems with Pannenberg's Solution to Barth's 'Faith Subjectivism'" *SJT* (1995).

18. This idea includes five features which Pannenberg finds in scripture (*Systematic Theology I*, p. 206) and is meant to imply that when God revealed his name (Ex. 3) it was a "provisional disclosure" because the name "will take on its content only from God's future action in history," p. 207. This he opposes to the idea that God's revelation is a disclosure of "God's own self that can never be

surpassed" and leads him to make God *dependent* on history which, in certain ways, helps to constitute revelation, cf. p. 329.

19. See Molnar, *SJT* (1989), p. 389.

20. Olson, *SJT* (1990), p. 186. Cf. also Molnar "Some Problems with Pannenberg's Solution . . ." in *SJT*.

21. Ibid., pp. 187–88. Cf. also Pannenberg, *Systematic Theology I*, pp. 321ff. In fact, however, Pannenberg explicitly maintains that "The eternal Son is first . . . an aspect of the human person . . . Hence his self-distinction from the Father is constitutive for the eternal Son in his relation to the Father," p. 310.

22. Pannenberg, *Jesus—God and Man*, pp. 34ff.

23. Olson, *SJT* (1990), p. 197. See also Pannenberg, *Systematic Theology I*, p. 329, n. 5.

24. Ibid., p. 199.

25. Jüngel, *God As The Mystery Of The World*, pp. 369–70. I have discussed the implications of this in relation to Jüngel's theology in *SJT* (1989): 390–99.

26. Ibid., p. 346. Cf. Molnar "Toward a Contemporary Doctrine of the Immanent Trinity . . ." forthcoming in *SJT* for how this relates to recent views which see the immanent Trinity in this way.

27. Cf. John Thompson, *Modern Trinitarian Perspectives*, pp. 32f. and 58–61.

28. Thomas F. Torrance, "Toward an Ecumenical Consensus on the Trinity," in *Theologische Zeitschrift* (Basel) 31, (1975): 337–350, pp. 337 and 339. This article is published in later form in Thomas F. Torrance, *Trinitarian Perspectives: Toward Doctrinal Agreement*, (Edinburgh: T & T Clark, 1994), chapter four.

29. See Thomas F. Torrance, *The Trinitarian Faith*.

30. Torrance is clearly aware of this problem since he indicates that the Colloquium held in Switzerland in 1975 which analyzed Rahner's views found that Rahner expressed the economic Trinity as it is in God "in such a way that it precinds [*sic*] from God's free self-communication," *Trinitarian Perspectives*, p. 79. He thinks this problem results only from a logical movement of thought which arose from Rahner's attempt to reconcile official Church declarations with a desire to free himself from scholastic dogmatic formulations. I believe the problem is deeper than that, and is linked, as I have indicated, to Rahner's transcendental method which begins from our self-transcending experiences and then attempts to make the doctrines credible. It may well be the case that what Rahner intended "in his own way is basically in agreement with St Athanasius on the one hand and Karl Barth on the other," but the fundamental differences of method between Barth and Rahner show little concrete evidence of such a

convergence. As we have seen, Rahner's symbolic view of Christology is quite different from Barth's in starting point and conclusion. Torrance notes additional difficulties such as 1) Rahner's apparent ambiguities in speaking of the Father as God rather than of God manifested as Father, p. 82 and 2) that Rahner is misled "by a rational analysis of merely inter-human connections" when he speaks of "the inter-personal relations in God," p. 91. But when Torrance says that the doctrine of the Trinity should be "grounded in a living experience of the Father, the Son and the Holy Spirit within the life and worship of the Church," p. 100, does he not counter his basic insight that the ground of our understanding is not a center in experience but in God?, p. 85.

31. Among contemporary theologians, John Thompson, *The Holy Spirit in the Theology of Karl Barth*, (Allison Park: Pickwick Publications, 1991), is very clear about this. In *Modern Trinitarian Perspectives* Thompson argues convincingly for the union and distinction of the immanent and economic Trinity.

32. C.D. 2, 1, p. 31. Here Torrance is certainly more in accord with Barth's actual theology, than Moltmann, Pannenberg, and Jüngel.

33. For more on this point see C.D. 2, 1, pp. 20–44. Grover Foley, *SJT*, pp. 138ff. is very clear on this point.

34. C.D. 4, 4, pp. 31–32. See also C.D. 1, 1, pp. 461–62ff.; C.D. 3, 2, pp. 68–71, 152, 212ff., 445; C.D. 3, 3, pp. 135ff. and C.D. 4, 1, pp. 146ff.

35. C.D. 4, 3, pp. 347ff.

36. C.D. 4, 4, p. 32. Cf. also C.D. 4, 1, pp. 672–73 and C.D. 4, 3, pp. 605–608, p. 792. This is the point in Rahner's theology that Barth would here reject.

37. C.D. 4, 1, pp. 122ff., and 4, 3, pp. 275ff.

38. C.D. 4, 4, pp. 32–3.

39. C.D. 4, 3, p. 540.

40. Ibid., pp. 541–43.

41. Cf. C.D. 4, 3, p. 737.

42. Ibid., p. 543.

43. Cf. John H. McKenna, *Eucharist and Holy Spirit*, chapter seven. This is certainly his aim in coming to grips with the "Scholastic" approach which, among other things, did not do adequate justice to the "interpersonal, sacramental context of an encounter between Christ and the faithful," p. 176. We shall consider Barth's view of God's active presence more deeply in Part Two.

44. See esp. C.D. 4, 3, p. 729.

45. C.D. 1, 2, pp. 412–13.

46. C.D. 4, 4, p. 33. See "Real Presence" below, Part Two. In this regard, Joseph Ratzinger criticizes the pre-Vatican II divorce of sacramental power ("the power of transubstantiation") and "juridical power over the Mystical Body" as leading to "individualization of the priestly ministry" as against *communio.*" He appeals to the gospel as the principle of the church's life. Hence "the point of departure is the mission of the apostles, but this mission is the handing on of the gospel," *Principles of Catholic Theology*, p. 243. Yet, this reasoning does not lead Ratzinger back to the exclusive action of the Spirit as the guarantor of Christ's presence. Rather "the sacrament of holy orders is the expression and, at the same time, the *guarantee* that the bishops are faithful to what has been handed on . . ." p. 244, emphasis mine. One is not alone as a priest but "enters into the *presbyterium* of a bishop." This communitarian factor excludes individualism and Ratzinger argues that it cannot obscure the need for the Spirit since "The community can do nothing of itself," p. 244. But his final conclusion expresses the very idea which Barth was here contesting: "On the other hand, however, the community of the whole Church . . . is, for the individual, the place of the Spirit and the *guarantee* of union with the Spirit," p. 244, emphasis mine.

47. C.D. 4, 4, p. 33; C.D. 4, 1, pp. 44ff.

48. Markus Barth, *Rediscovering the Lord's Supper*, pp. 64–65.

49. C.D. 4, 4, pp. 32–4.

50. C.D. 1, 2, pp. 347–61; C.D. 2, 1, p. 161; C.D. 3, 3, pp. 270, 283ff.; C.D. 4, 1, p. 41.

51. Markus Barth, *Rediscovering the Lord's Supper*, pp. 52–3.

52. C.D. 1, 2, p. 359; C.D. 1, 1, pp. 466–67, C.D. 4, 3, p. 543.

53. C.D. 4, 4, p. 35.

54. Ibid., pp. 35ff. Also see C.D. 4, 1, pp. 41ff. and C.D. 3, 2, pp. 168–70ff.

55. C.D. 1, 1, pp. 88–162; C.D. 2, 2, pp. 546ff. and also C.D. 4, 3, pp. 548ff.

56. C.D. 4, 4, p. 35.

57. See C.D. 2, 2, pp. 557–65, 585ff. and p. 603.

58. C.D. 4, 4, p. 36.

59. On this point see all of C.D. 2, 2.

60. C.D. 4, 4, p. 37. See C.D. 1, 2, pp. 371–454 re: love of God and of neighbor.

61. C.D. 4, 1, pp. 674–75.

62. Cf. C.D. 4, 3, pp. 791ff. Barth worked out the implications of this same point in his doctrine of the Word of God (C.D. 1, 2, pp. 492ff.) and in his ethics

(C.D. 2, 2, pp. 546ff.)

63. C.D. 4, 1, pp. 668-69.

64. C.D. 3, 3, 278-80.

65. Hans Urs von Balthasar, *The Theology of Karl Barth*, p. 272.

66. Cf., e.g., C.D. 2, 1, p. 564.

67. Von Balthasar, *The Theology of Karl Barth*, p. 272. For a fine analysis of this point see Grover Foley, *SJT* 14 (1961): 136-55.

68. For more on this point see Barth's analysis of the church as the body of Christ, *Credo unam ecclesiam*, in C.D. 4, 1, pp. 668-85.

69. Jüngel, *God as the Mystery of the World*, p. 317.

70. Ibid., p. 392.

71. Ibid., p. 282.

72. C.D. 4, 1, pp. 687-88. For more on Barth's view on the relation between the individual and the community see C.D. 2, 2, pp. 410ff.; C.D. 1, 2, pp. 479ff.; C.D. 4, 2, pp. 627, 705 and 727ff.

73. See esp. C.D. 4, 1, pp. 638ff. and 695-710.

74. C.D. 4, 4, pp. 37-38.

75. Ibid., p. 38. This prayer for the creator Spirit is compromised by Moltmann's conception of the Spirit. He argues that the Spirit can no longer be seen as creator in the traditional sense but must be seen as engendering and bringing forth Jesus Christ: "If the messiah is called the Son of God, then to be consistent we have to talk about the Spirit as his divine 'mother,'" *The Way of Jesus Christ*, p. 86. This reasoning is in accord with Moltmann's panentheist reinterpretation of the Trinity and of creation, but it leads to the emanationism he himself holds that Christians cannot accept. Cf. Molnar, *TS*, 1990.

76. Ibid.

77. See Barth, *Protestant Theology*, and C.D. 2, 1, pp. 270, 288ff., and 293.

78. C.D. 4, 4, p. 39.

79. Cf. C.D. 4, 1, pp. 650-725. This is especially clear in connection with the doctrine of Providence in C.D. 3, 3, pp. 33-57. See also C.D. 4, 2, p. 648.

80. C.D. 4, 1, p. 698.

81. C.D. 4, 4, p. 40.

82. C.D. 4, 2, p. 642. Cf. Also C.D. 2, 1, pp. 160ff.

83. See C.D. 2, 1, pp. 608-43. See also C.D. 4, 3, pp. 902-42. See C.D. 3, 2, pp. 210-21 for Barth's application of the same idea. Unless this goal is seen as the triune God himself, we might mistakenly suppose that it is our own spirit

which is the goal here. We might confuse the Spirit of God with Hegel's absolute idea and thus slip once more into the error of self-sanctification.

84. C.D. 4, 4, p. 40.

85. Hence "Even the raised Christ himself is 'not yet' the pantocrator. But he is already on the way to redeem the world . . . Anyone who confesses Jesus as 'Christ of God' is recognizing the Christ-in-his-becoming, the Christ on the way . . . The risen Lord is on the way to his rule . . ." Moltmann, *The Way of Jesus Christ*, pp. 32–33. Cf. also pp. 191, 194, and 280ff. Since Moltmann believes that Christ is becoming the messiah, he also detaches the process of "new creation" from the historical action of God's Word and Spirit and argues that Christ's parousia is not merely historical in the sense of an end of the world but that "It must also be conceived of and awaited as the final coming forth of the Pantocrator hidden in the cosmos . . . the cosmic Wisdom-Christ will come forth from the heart of creation," pp. 280–1. For Barth's view see chapter four above.

86. Moltmann, *The Way of Jesus Christ*, chapter three.

87. C.D. 3, 1, pp. 214–228.

88. Thus, "The existence of the universe was made possible through a shrinkage process in God." Creation refers to a sector of God's being, i.e., "a kind of primal, mystical space" into which "he can issue from himself in his creation and his revelation." God first withdraws from himself into this space in this first act which was not an *actio* but a *passio Dei*. This act is not a revelation of God but a veiling; it is "a limitation on God's part, not a de-limitation." In Act Two "God issues from himself as creator into that primal space which he had previously released in Act I." God "creates by withdrawing himself, and because he withdraws himself. Creation in chaos and out of nothing . . . is also a self-humiliation on God's part." This idea of creation allows us "to think of *the world in God* without falling victims to pantheism," Moltmann, *Trinity*, 109–110. Cf. also Moltmann, *The Way of Jesus Christ*, p. 329 and esp. *Creation*, pp. 86ff.

89. Moltmann, *Creation*, p. 282.

90. Moltmann, *The Way of Jesus Christ*, pp. 329–31. Moltmann wants to correct the one-sided view that creation is only a work to be distinguished from God: "Creation is also the differentiated presence of God the Spirit, the presence of the One *in* the many," *Creation*, p. 14.

91. C.D. 4, 2, pp. 641ff.

92. Ibid., p. 706.

93. C.D. 4, 3, pp. 830–901, esp. 866ff.

Part Two

The Lord's Supper as the Work of Creatures

VI

The Basis of the Lord's Supper as the Work of Creatures

Beginning with this chapter we shall consider the Lord's Supper by focusing on the activity of the people who celebrate it. We have established that the foundation for what can be said here is the activity of the Holy Spirit in mediating Christ's reconciling truth to us and including us in the covenant of grace. We shall now examine the basis, goal, meaning, and significance of the Lord's Supper in order to understand how the work of the Holy Spirit includes *us* in a genuine relationship with God without compromising divine or human freedom.

Following Barth's doctrine of analogy, there can be no other basis for the Lord's Supper than the simple fact of Jesus Christ; he is the possibility of knowledge and action that is within faith. The knowledge of the truth which takes place in faith

> does not start from the believing man but from Jesus Christ as the object and foundation of faith . . . as the one and only man ready for God, Jesus Christ has not only lived, died and risen for us once in time, so that the abounding grace of God might be an event and at the same time revelation among us, but that as this same One He stands before His Father now in eternity for us, and lives for us in God himself as the Son of God He was and is and will be . . . Jesus Christ Himself sees to it that in Him and by Him we are not outside but inside. He Himself sees to it that His readiness is valid for us who are not identical with him, and who in ourselves are not ready for God . . . It is not another work that begins at this point, a work that will have to be ours. We do not here fall into the hands of another God . . . As His work, the work of God's Son, this representing of Jesus Christ is an eternal representing and therefore one which is contemporary to all time.[1]

Any other statement at all in this context, then, means abstracting from faith and calling God's primary objectivity into question by a reality distinct from him and dependent upon him. Such a reversal of creator and creatures frustrates true knowledge by reducing theology to anthropology.

We have already seen that the sole basis and criterion for the church's celebration of its communion (fellowship) with God, established and maintained by God alone, cannot be an idea or experience, even of Christ. Such a starting point leads to docetic and ebionite Christology, respectively,[2] and adversely affects ecclesiology and sacramental theology.

Insofar as the *idea* or *experience* of Christ becomes normative in this way for understanding revelation, church, and sacrament, revelation can no longer be viewed as grounded solely in God and not in creatures or in a relationship between God and creatures. We have seen what this means to Rahner, i.e., grace implants in us the free tendency toward our own salvation and revelation means a modification of our transcendental awareness and is therefore a "permanent element in our consciousness."[3] Yet, as long as revelation is not grounded solely in God, the Lord's Supper cannot be seen as grounded solely in God; then it is based, at least partially, in creatures or in some idea or experience of "sacramental reality" conceived apart from the mystery of revelation, i.e., grace itself (Jesus Christ). We have seen some of the implications of this insight in connection with the theology of Moltmann and Wainwright above.

Moltmann begins his theology with the experience of suffering, traces his Christology to "Christopraxis" instead of to Christ, argues that Christ grows into his messiahship, that Jesus is dependent on faith in order to heal, and that "The breaking of the bread and the drinking of the wine make the kingdom of God present in the form of Christ's body given 'for us' and the blood shed 'for us'."[4] Moltmann even thinks that "The unity of the triune God is the goal of the uniting of man and creation with the Father and the Son in the Spirit."[5] Wainwright's Christology is distinctly ebionite because he believes that Christ's uniqueness can be seen as a quality ascribed to him so that he becomes the focal point of human self-sacrificing love. Wainwright's thinking ends with the docetic idea that Jesus' uniqueness can be equated with the fact that he is not the only way to the Father because he *is* the Son (beside whom there is no other), but he is the pattern for the self-giving love which we already know and experience within the world.

We have already seen that sacramentalism and moralism cannot abide a clear distinction between the immanent and economic Trinity. Here, the importance of a clear doctrine of God can be discerned. If identity (as discussed in the last chapter) can be maintained at *one* point in our thinking, then there is no logical reason why it should not be maintained in each of our reflections. Of course the danger then would be a pantheistic or panentheistic description of the sacrament which would make God's action indistinguishable from the church's action. This danger continually threatens a theology which is based on the identity of the immanent and economic Trinity. We have already seen how this leads Rahner to speak of the church's worship in relation to a "divine world" and of the world as "permeated" by grace (chapter three). We have seen how this thinking leads Moltmann to blend human and divine experience into his notion of suffering love.

Apart from us and our ideas and experiences then, Jesus Christ himself *is* the mystery of revelation and the distinction between Christ and us must always be maintained.[6] Only he is very God and very man and as such the fulfillment of God's covenant of fellowship with men and women. Creatures as such, apart from Christ, have no claim to fellowship with God. Because he has been revealed as this transcendent other, in the power of the resurrection and the outpouring of the Holy Spirit, the church can count on his promise and obey his command. This truth precludes Rahner's anonymous Christianity and Wainwright's attempt to reconcile Christ's uniqueness with other religious viewpoints which cannot accept Jesus as the *only* one in whom God's covenant has been fulfilled. Here it is important to see that the docetism toward which both theologians are led stems from beginning theology with our self-experience rather than with Jesus himself as the mystery of revelation.

Possibility and Limitation of the Lord's Supper

Several clarifications are needed before specifying the nature of the *command* and *promise* which set the possibility and limitation of the Lord's Supper as a human act. First, it is the object of faith alone which determines the possibility and limitation of human obedience.[7] This means that the possibility and limitation of human obedience is and remains distinct from humanity as such. Thus, the human action of the Lord's Supper can be no more and no less than human obedience (witness) to the Word heard and believed in the power of the Spirit of Christ; it must follow the object of faith. Consequently if the human action of the community were capricious or vague it would not have for its norm the object of faith, i.e., God himself.[8] The community can never seek its basis in its action or in creation as such. Consistently and discernibly it must be a human response of faithfulness to the faithfulness of God demonstrated in Christ's history.

Because of Christ, God's address and the human response must be seen together. They are indissolubly united, even though distinct.[9] As we have seen, this is why Barth maintained that no analogy is true in itself. We neither invent theological analogies freely nor do we invent our liturgical action freely. Both take place in obedience to the Word heard and believed. Barth worked this insight out specifically in his doctrine of reconciliation.[10] The reason for all this is the fact that both the unity and distinction are grounded in God's act of grace, namely, in Christ himself. This christological fact is the possibility and limitation of the Lord's Supper. Its possibility is that it may truly point to God himself insofar as he is the object of its thought and action. Its limitation is that the Church's worship can never be more than a prayer ventured in recollection of God's past faithfulness and in expectation that he will be faithful again.

Furthermore, God absolutely precedes and the church unequivocally follows. *Exclusively* in this way the Lord's Supper actually can attest the One who is loving as well as free. This means that even in the Eucharist, we do not see God *directly*. Faith, which does not cease, knows that God actually cannot be encountered any other way because he has not willed to be known *directly*, but *indirectly*, i.e., in and through the sphere of creation. In this way the Eucharist is a real human participation in Christ's action. There is a real similarity (analogy) here, but not an identity. [11]

Like its knowledge, the church's action is enclosed in the mystery of the Trinity. This means that the positive (the fact that God is loving) and negative (the fact that God remains free) aspects of the divine freedom must be clear at all times. Herein, as we shall see below in consideration of the meaning of the Lord's Supper, lies the connection between Barth's concept of analogy developed in his doctrine of God and his view of the Lord's Supper. In his Christology Barth attempted to maintain the positive and negative aspects of the divine freedom by using the patristic notions *enhypostasis* and *anhypostasis*. [12]

Role of the Created Elements

Since there is no theology of water or phenomenology of water in scripture, none is called for in connection with water baptism. In this regard, we are not called by the Holy Spirit to focus on the elements as such. This, as we shall see, is for Barth a key error in grasping Christ's real presence. In connection with this position Barth opposed G. van der Leeuw when he wrote

> Certainly there is no theology of water as such in the New Testament. There is no hint of any special power or even symbolical force attaching to its elemental nature and effects. To try to see connexions between baptism and creation in virtue of the baptismal water, even if only by way of recollection that Jesus Christ is Lord of nature too and consequently of water, is an unpromising and far too arbitrary enterprise from the standpoint of the New Testament. We need not return to this even in the form of controversy with van der Leeuw and similar ingenious contemporaries. The water of baptism is important only because man usually washes or is washed with water. [13]

Similarly, there is no theology of meal or phenomenology of bread and wine called for in connection with the Eucharist. Neither of these positions takes seriously the fact that water, bread, and wine are significant *only* insofar as they are used by people in faith. This means that these phenomena, as well as the human fellowship of eating and drinking have no *independent* significance whatsoever. Their significance lies in the extent to which they actually attest the mystery of revelation and our human inclusion in the covenant secondarily, i.e., in faithfully following Christ. It was in his history that the divine act became a human possibility.[14]

What exactly is Barth's point here? We have seen that any attempt to explain our relationship with God on the basis of a general apprehension of reality through phenomenology necessarily abstracts from faith.[15] It assumes that what is known *indirectly* in faith (the being and activity of the triune God himself) can be perceived *directly* in the phenomena themselves or by an analysis of the phenomena in themselves. We compared this with Rahner's theology of the symbol above in order to show that such an assumption assumes that God is inherent somehow in created reality as such. Inasmuch as created reality is thus given independent significance in relation to God, God's freedom is compromised.

Rahner's notions of an obediential potency and a supernatural existential presume not only that people have the capacity for revelation and faith, but that grace is part of the structure of their quest for absolute being. To that extent we already know God whenever we reflect on our transcendental experiences and these experiences become the source of our knowledge of God, revelation, and grace.[16] This kind of independent investigation of God's being and action shows that this idea may be necessary to an ontology or theology of the symbol, but it ignores the one who loves in freedom and shows how faith and reason can reach different conclusions.

Reason, left to itself, compromises the truth of the *analogia fidei* at the outset with this kind of thinking. As we saw in chapter one, analogies of parity, disparity, or synthesis compromise the fact that *only* God can reveal God. They start with something in the created realm rather than the Word of God revealed in the *history* of Christ; they start with the phenomenal realm rather than with faith in the Word and Spirit acting within the phenomenal realm (and not in identity with it).

Starting from phenomena in an attempt to understand the basis of the Lord's Supper means a corresponding focus on the church as an *opus operatum*, the individual's *opus operantis*, and the elements which in some sense are supposed to have an inherent revelatory significance. Here reason and revelation are opposed, according to Barth's analysis. While Rahner's theology of the symbol saw the church and grace related in a non-magical but mutually causal way,[17] Barth insisted that created signs and grace are not in any sense dependent on each other and that signs in no sense cause grace. This thinking, in Barth's view, compromises the freedom of grace by making God's action in Christ and the Spirit in some sense identical with and dependent upon the church or the sacraments. Hence, while Rahner insisted that the relation between the historical church and grace is one of "reciprocal conditioning" and that "the manifestation [of grace] necessarily renders present what is manifested,"[18] Barth argued that God is freely bound to the church and its sacraments. Thus, the manifestation of grace is entirely dependent upon God's free actualization of his sovereign power to be present; only this divine power is determinative here. God infallibly promises to be present in his Word and Spirit, but the mere fact of the sacrament does not guarantee this; the guarantee is his personal presence which can be seen and understood only in faith as the presence of one who may make himself present and known and does so, but who also may not disclose himself. This does not imply arbitrariness, but God's freedom to be neither identical with nor dependent upon any created phenomenon for his being, action, or meaning.

Analogia Fidei—Christology

Faith knows that God seeks and creates fellowship with people as one who is by nature inaccessible to them. As he is transcendent, only he can reveal himself. This fact is *not* dissolved in Christ, but given a specific form. To think of God as inherent in the reality created by him and completely dependent upon him compromises this divine being in freedom. If the truth and certainty of this particular divine action is compromised, so also is the truth and certainty of human existence as such. For on this view creatures ultimately may be absorbed into the deity, variously conceived, and would lose their actual human dignity given them by God himself. The church, as the body of Christ, then would be indistinguishable from its transcendent head. We have already seen the implications of this in chapter two, especially as it relates to Christology, i.e., it ascribes God's free action directly to the phenomena; it describes Christ's relation with the phenomena in terms of mutual conditioning; it separates Christ's humanity from the Word; and it makes Christ the highest instance within a particular ontology or theology. Now we must relate this to Christology from the side of Christ's humanity. For Barth there is a *communicatio idiomatum* in Christ. If, however, this is conceived phenomenologically, then both God's freedom and the solid foundation we have for actually distinguishing God's action in creation from creation itself are lost.

Once God's freedom is compromised, a false notion of the *communicatio idiomatum* becomes possible.[19] Both the Lutheran and Roman Catholic concepts of grace which Barth rejected (chapter two above), are traceable to their conception of a *reciprocal* relationship between creator and creature evident in their respective grasp of the *communicatio idiomatum* as mutually conditioning. Barth insisted that such a view no longer sees the relationship between creator and creature as a one-sided *egeneto* grounded exclusively in the *Word* assuming a human nature. Instead of describing the reality of the incarnation as definitively and exclusively a divine action of the Logos *in* all *its* stages, in which the divine being and action absolutely precede and determine the positive and negative validity of human being and action, this conception supposes that there was a mutual interchange of divinity and humanity in the person of Christ.

This is why Rahner believed he could investigate the actual meaning of Christ's humanity in abstraction from the Word.[20] What he discovered was that humanity, in its ability to transcend itself, already is the mystery of God's eternal love expressed in the incarnation, since all theology is eternally anthropology.[21] Hence for Rahner we do not have to make a specific decision with respect to Jesus in order to speak of revelation; all we have to do is accept our own existence as meaningful and since "the grace of God and Christ are in everything, as the secret essence of all eligible reality,"[22] we have already accepted Christ in his uniqueness as the Word incarnate. Here Rahner has proven by his own analysis how dangerous it really is to abstract from the Word of God in himself when considering the meaning of the incarnation. His own view of the incarnation is not defined by God's act. God's act is defined by human self-transcendence in such a way that the mystery of God is indistinguishable from the human mystery. The very notion of the *communicatio* which allows for the idea that all theology is eternally an anthropology demonstrates exactly the confusion of nature and grace Barth could avoid by insisting on the irreversibility of divine and human being in Christ.

Moltmann objects to Rahner's Christology and anthropology[23] because they lead to "Jesuology," i.e., to anthropologizing Jesus and to the worship of our own humanity projected onto the man Jesus. He links Rahner with Schleiermacher and argues that Schleiermacher basically reduced Jesus' uniqueness to his God consciousness while Rahner reduced it to his being the truly self-transcendent human being; Rahner's self-transcendent Christ does not relate to the external conditions which give rise to these experiences and is thus "idealistic." In his view, Rahner's Christology is individualistic because salvation is "localized in the human heart" via "self-transcendence."

> Modern christology is soteriologically related to this existential experience of the individual self, but not to the external conditions of society which evoke these inner experiences and crises. In this respect, it has to be termed idealistic. This relegation of salvation to the inward realm of 'the heart' (and its presupposition in modern Jesuology) finds its sociological equivalent in the privatization of religion . . .[24]

Moltmann's analysis and critique of Schleiermacher, Kant, and Rahner is well founded, profound, and at times quite interesting.

Yet Moltmann's own solution is to see Jesus as "'the messianic human being' on the way to [his] redeeming future."[25] His analysis of Rahner discloses a basic weakness in Moltmann's method; the external conditions which set the question and provide its solution for Moltmann are the conditions of society and not revelation. Consequently, instead of asking who Christ is in himself and what his particular action in history might mean for us who need his assistance, Moltmann asks: "Who really is Christ for the poor of the Third World?," "Who really is Christ for us today, threatened as we are by the nuclear inferno?," "Who really is Christ for dying nature and ourselves today?" And his answers show that while he says that neither metaphysical theology nor anthropology dictate his explanation,[26] his very position is indeed dictated by a synthesis of metaphysical theology *and* anthropology. In his theology we meet a Christ who cannot *be* the eternal Son of God who becomes man for us and for our salvation; instead we meet a man on a messianic mission which, after the resurrection, discloses his divinity as a divinity which needs others to be what it is. Moltmann cannot accept the traditional christologies partly because he thinks that "The notion that there is an antithesis between an adoptionist and a pre-existence christology is a nineteenth-century invention."[27] This leads to Moltmann's own rather overt adoptionism:

> The continuing presence of the Spirit in Jesus is the true beginning of the kingdom of God . . . This presence of the Spirit is the authority behind his proclamation . . . The divine Spirit who indwells Jesus, initiates and makes possible the relationship of the Father to the Son, and of the Son to the Father. In the Spirit, God experiences Jesus as the messianic child, and Jesus experiences God as 'Abba'. . . Filled with the Spirit, Jesus becomes the messianic Son of God.[28]

For him Christ needs the poor and indeed can only be revealed to the poor of society. Christ needs the cosmos and indeed the cosmos completes his actual being as the Christ. Hence in our present ecological crisis Moltmann holds Sittler's view that "With every new conquest of nature a piece of God dies" and "Unless *the* whole cosmos is reconciled, Christ cannot be the Christ of God and cannot be the foundation of all things."[29] While Moltmann wishes to extend Christ's reconciling act from individual experience to the cosmos so that we would have respect for nature, the problem in his analysis is that Christ cannot be the Christ of God simply because he *is* the Christ, i.e., God and man and as such the reconciler. Rather, even reconciliation cannot be complete until Christ turns over the kingdom to his Father and God is "all in all." Thus the eternal kingdom does not actually begin until Christ's parousia.[30] Instead of Christ's resurrection disclosing the completed event of salvation which had taken place in his history on our behalf, it points beyond itself to the coming kingdom of glory.

The ironical fact then is that by compromising Christ's divinity, for the purpose of emphasizing the significance of his humanity, it is humanity in the long run which is compromised. If his humanity is interchangeable with his divinity, then we have no way of knowing when we are speaking of one or the other. Then it remains an open question as to whether God really was a man like us in all things but sin. Our human justification and sanctification are jeopardized. Moreover, such an assumption conceives the nature of the *unio* in Christ as a state rather than as an *event*. It does not matter whether this state is conceived as a process or in some static way. Barth rejected any attempt to ascribe independent validity to humanity, including the humanity of Christ, by rejecting this conception; he also believed that the modern argument, also used by some today to support this undertaking, i.e., that personality really belongs to true human being, is primitive and leans toward docetism.

Barth's critique of this modern argument is significant. He believed that the modern position was primitive because it turned on a misunderstanding of the Latin term *impersonalitas* which was used occasionally for *anhypostasis*. According to the early doctrine, Christ's human nature did not lack what we call personality and they called *individualitas*; personality belonged to true human nature. *Personalitas* was their word for what we call being or existence. By the term *impersonalitas* they denoted the negative perception that Christ's flesh had no existence *in* itself. This negative was asserted in the positive interest of noting that Christ's flesh actually had its existence in and through the Word who is God acting as revealer and reconciler. Barth's description of the *unio hypostatica* as a *completed* event and a completed *event* seeks to make the same point;[31] his position on the sacrament then is traceable to his Christology and ultimately to his *analogia fidei* as developed in his doctrine of God.

Interestingly Moltmann assumes that in the traditional Christologies, *anhypostasis* meant that Christ's human nature was "non-personal, because the centre that constitutes its personhood is the eternal Son himself."[32] He thus replicates this modern misunderstanding without ever mentioning Barth's view and sees this as one of the impasses of the traditional Christologies which inhibits Jesus from being genuinely historical in the modern sense.

At this point, and with specific regard to sacrament, a choice of priorities is necessary since what we say about Christology has real meaning for sacramental theology. Is the norm for true sacramental action the reality created by God and distinct from him or God himself in his action *ad extra*? If it is the former, then all kinds of models for understanding Christ's presence will be thought possible. Yet each one will be betrayed by the fact that it will perceive itself as in some sense *mutually necessary* to God's action *ad extra*. If it is the latter then it will be necessary to correlate and distinguish human and divine action clearly and decisively. This of course is the major problem with Rahner's symbolic explanation of God, Christ, church, and sacrament.[33] As Rahner asserts, a symbolic identity and distinction can only make sense as one which is *mutually conditioned*. This affects all of his theology and is particularly evident in his presentation of the sacrament, as we have seen. We have also seen that this problem of mutual conditioning is intrinsic to Moltmann's theology.

For Barth it is only in light of a clear knowledge of the being and activity of God himself that the Lord's Supper can be understood correctly. As no analogy is true in itself, so no human action (including the church's action in worship) is true in itself. Both may also not serve revelation.[34] To this extent the Lord's Supper has no perduring truth in itself. Its truth always must come to it anew in the freedom of God. The church's action can and must be ventured only in the light of the divine promise which is loving but *free*. It is a promise of one who remains transcendent, even in Christ. Therefore people cannot *control* their being in Christ noetically (with a concept of analogy) or ontically (with a self-validating experience or ritual).

No phenomenology of community, of faith, or of humanity can reveal what only God himself can reveal in his Word and Spirit. Bread and wine and the human eating and drinking are significant *only* because the community does so in faith, i.e., in the knowledge that God has been faithful to humanity in Christ and in the hope that he will do so in the future, according to his promise.

As apostolic authority cannot mean a transferral of power or competence which only God in his freedom can give, so there is no such transferral in the church's baptismal or eucharistic action.[35] This means that the Eucharist must not be associated with office. It is the celebration of the community of God, i.e., the visible human expression of Christ's invisible presence in the power of his Spirit. God's special presence cannot be seen directly but is visible only to faith.[36] That is why the church's only command is to follow the object of faith, i.e., *vere Deus vere homo*. Knowledge of God is now lived as an *event* of Christian worship. While Moltmann also asserts that the Eucharist cannot be associated with office,[37] his very presentation precludes the perception of the freedom of God as Barth has just described it.[38]

A question which naturally arises at this point, but which will not be considered until later, is whether Barth's Christology is really docetic as some have argued.[39] A further question then would be whether or not it is this factor which leads him to what Alasdair Heron labels his more "Zwinglian" view of the sacrament. Barth's Christology is not docetic since he stresses the inseparability of Jesus' divinity and humanity; his view of the sacrament is not docetic insofar as he actually emphasizes our *human* participation in grace and does not detach grace from Christ and the Spirit. He stresses our actual *human* need to pray and to rely on God's presence which cannot be controlled. Even if his view is Zwinglian, the question remains as to whether it is possible to reconceive Christ's actual presence by ascribing it in any way to the created action or elements, as in symbolic ontology.

Promise/Command

Barth avoided the predicament of the phenomenological approach by directing us to God's promise and command which meet us within the phenomenological realm but which are effective without becoming dependent on the phenomena. He argued that the possibility of the community consists in its obedience to the command of God, such as, "do this as a memorial of me" (Lk. 22:20). As the community obeys the command of God, it lives by grace, i.e., by God's promise to be with his church always.[40] The apparent lack of resolution evident in the fact that the community *cannot* control its being either before or after its encounter with God, but can only obey his command and hope in his promise, reflects an actual encounter with grace. It bears the mark of this encounter with God himself by not attempting to resolve what cannot be resolved, namely, the mystery of God's freedom to be self-sufficient, even in his communion with his church. The church must rely only upon God's promise to be faithful. It must not seek to translate this divine activity into an *idea* of sacramentality or an *experience* of morality by which it is thought that the church can guarantee its own obedience. The church has the divine promise that Christ, and therefore the Father and Spirit as well, will be always with it. But because this is a divine and not a human promise it can in no way be instituted or guaranteed by human beings.[41] This divine action is obscured whenever this is thought possible. What specifically does it mean to live by the promise in connection with the Eucharist?

For Barth one lives by God's promise by believing in Christ (Jn. 6:29–30). He is the sign which the Old Testament manna could not be. Christ himself is the bread of life. Believing in him and knowing and acting in accordance with that belief is itself the work of God required of everyone (Jn. 6:22). Following the long discourse on the necessity of eating Christ's flesh and drinking his blood in order to have eternal life, the bread and wine are decisively related to the Spirit (v. 63). "It is the Spirit that gives life, the flesh has nothing to offer. The words I have spoken to you are spirit and they are life."[42] According to John, whoever does not recognize Christ as the one sent by the Father does not have his Spirit.

The decisive point here is that as people obey the divine command and not a supposed divine command, they actually have and live the promise of eternal life. As people in the community are one with Christ as his body, they participate in God's supra-temporal eternal existence.[43] In that way the community (insofar as it is his body on earth) already has the very same eternal life which is its future hope at the end of time.[44] If we do not recognize ourselves as the body of the risen Lord, we do not recognize our actual *oneness*.[45] Clearly, the knowledge of faith which is the work of God is knowledge that leads to living the oneness of the body with its eternal head. This is the memorial (anamnesis) which remains clear of idolatry (1 Cor. 10:16ff.).[46]

Sacramental Implications of Oneness with Christ

According to Markus Barth, 1 Cor. 10–11 "does not contain a timeless doctrine on the eucharist" but instead meets certain practical problems "head-on."[47] Paul opposed people at Corinth who today would "be called high church sacramentalists." They were convinced that they had the Holy Spirit as indicated by their speaking in tongues and by their belief that, since they were full of new life, "everything" was permitted; they behaved accordingly. Some felt free to attend pagan banquets and the Lord's Supper.

It was "because of their sacramental and spiritual security" that the Corinthians showed a lack of care for the social bonds and obligations respected by Jews, Christians, and even Gentiles. This became obvious at the Lord's Supper when the richer and supposedly "better" members of the community had their full meal while the poorer members were still working. When they arrived and the Lord's Supper was celebrated, the effect was a splitting of the congregation. The sacred meal became an occasion for preventing the poorer members from "enjoying full communion with others." Barth paraphrases Paul's response:

> You believe that being drenched in the Holy Spirit and fed with spiritual food makes you immortal? Look at the people of Israel! . . . How they were nourished with manna . . . They drank from the rock—the rock that was Christ . . . But look how they displeased the Lord! . . . So much for sacramental security and conveyed immortality! Israel's history demonstrates that even a gift from heaven and trust in the Lord's presence can be useless when it leads to idolatry and scandalous conduct. Sacrament is not an alternative to ethics, but ethics is essential to it.[48]

Paul reminds the Corinthians that the first commandment is still valid and asks concerning the wine "over which we say grace—is it not communion with the blood of Christ?" and "The bread that we break—is it not communion with the body of Christ?" The bread is one and we, though many, are one body; for we partake one bread.

Paul is against the congregation being in communion with demons present in the sanctuaries of pagan worship. They should be in communion with God's altar by facts (such as election and education) that preceded the service. What they celebrated therefore was a sign "of the community that they were privileged to enjoy, not a means of attaining it." By analogy then, Israel is God's people "not because they ate and drank water miraculously provided by God in the wilderness, but by God's love, election and revelation manifested in the calling of the patriarchs and of Moses and by the liberation from Egypt." *Positively*, the Lord's Supper means "intimate existential communion between the participants in the meal and the person of Christ crucified . . . their life is in him as he is in them—he *is* their life. In the Parousia they will be with Christ." *Negatively*, koinonia does not mean

> a joining, a common essence or function of diverse *things*—be they physical or heavenly elements, forces, ideas, or symbols. The notion that the body and blood of Christ might enter a mysterious union with bread and wine, whether by changing their substances or by adding some heavenly matter, would require the use of a word other than *koinonia*.[49]

Hence when Paul speaks of the spiritual food and drink of Israel in the wilderness he does not mean to consider bread and wine "transubstantiated" or "transformed" into heavenly matter or the flesh and blood of Christ. Rather spiritual means typological: even in the wilderness what was done was typical or precedential. The rock, hidden in the earlier events, was revealed to be Christ (v. 4). According to Markus Barth, Paul is not saying that in the Lord's Supper the Corinthians "are eating and drinking, as it were, the Holy Spirit" any more than he was saying that the Israelites were eating something other than real manna and drinking something other than real water.

It is unfortunate that Moltmann's presentation tends to play off the practice of the community against belief in Christ arguing that Jesus is concerned for the poor as we must be, instead of showing that it is Christ himself here and now who, through his promise and command brings about the community through our faith and practice. By contrast Karl Barth was very clear on this point, e.g., when he spoke of Christ's prophetic office:

> It is in this superiority [of truth and light] that He exists . . . is the Lord of humanity, Head of the Church and basis, theme and content of faith, that

He speaks as the Prophet of the reconciliation accomplished by Him . . .
If he is known, it is in the superiority proper to Him as the One He is, in
His unconditional superiority.[50]

Hence for Barth this superiority is identical with Jesus' being as the Word.
Because he *alone* is this Word "To know Him is to know God . . . the One who
is incomparably free and loving."[51] His "unconditional superiority is proper
neither to the race, the Church nor faith" but is in fact unexpected and decisive
just because "it does not arise from within man but comes from without, from a
great height and distance, it reaches and strikes the real man as a call from the
Father's house . . . "[52]

Christ himself, then, is the point at which the *koinonia* between God and
creatures actually intersects and is visible. This is the prior and actual possibility
which is the *basis* of the church's activity here and now.[53] Without their basis
in Christ himself both baptism and the Lord's Supper may be regarded only as
interesting customs which may be dispensable in favor of some more profound
practice. Unless the Lord's Supper has a clear basis in the history of Christ as
described above, it can always be disregarded as an interesting ritual used by the
church for any number of reasons. But such a difficulty only arises if the Lord's
Supper has no recognizable basis in the New Testament testimony to Jesus Christ,
very God and very man.[54]

Lex Orandi/Lex Credendi

Everything depends upon the fact that *faith* (or more precisely the object of
faith) and not the practice of the church is normative here. Concerning the *lex
orandi* and the *lex credendi* Geoffrey Wainwright suggests that this topic has been
neglected by Protestant theology, perhaps because Roman Catholic theologians
have used liturgical practice to legitimate doctrines and developments which
Protestants have rejected. The question here is how does worship (practice)
influence doctrine and vice versa if they should be seen as mutually conditioning
as Wainwright thinks.[55]

We cannot discuss the many fascinating details which Wainwright presents on
this subject. Instead we must ask in what sense he can make the practice of the
church a norm for doctrine. He does not object, e.g., to Bonhoeffer's view that
"Worship becomes the starting point and criterion for the theologian's task of
christological investigation and reflection."[56] While Wainwright correctly argues
that modern attacks upon Jesus as God-man leave us with just another human
figure unworthy of worship, his own belief that the church's practice could be a
criterion for christological investigation, as we have seen, has left him actually

open to a modified adoptionism. And this is a dogmatic position which would actually have to be excluded if faith rather than practice were the constant criterion here. Wainwright also argues convincingly that participation in worship of other confessions, as far as this is possible, will "draw divided Christians and churches closer together."[57] But the question which Barth's thinking raises here is left unanswered by such an approach.

And this becomes a major problem when, in view of cultural pluralism, Wainwright suggests from within his "unifying framework" that the liturgy provides that "In so far as Jesus Christ fails to be accepted as giving meaning and setting values, it is the Christian faith as a whole which is diminished."[58] In view of disparate reductionist tendencies today, Wainwright would wish to err on the conservative side when revising the liturgy. His solution, however, does not close the door to dogmatically false solutions: "The 'theology' expressed in official worship must be acceptable to the broadest possible range in the present Christian community and must be as faithful as possible to what is sensed to be authentic in the past."[59]

Neither of these criteria, i.e., a broad consensus on the one hand and a "sense" of the authentic on the other hand, addresses the question of what particular object actually decides whether and to what extent our doctrine and worship are authentic or not. Actually this thinking leads Wainwright to suggest that we might call God Father and mother in order to overcome discrimination between men and women and to avoid a neuter view of God. None of these suggestions, however, address the real problem of whether the Bible actually intended to speak of God in an utterly unique sense as Father, which meant that merely adding feminine images to God would lead to polytheism and to gnosticism.[60]

While there is a close connection between the *lex orandi* and the *lex credendi*, both of these activities are ultimately governed by the truth of God's action in the history of Christ. Thus, Thomas Torrance holds that assertions of Christian belief had "regulative force in themselves in so far as they were rightly related to that truth."[61] The truth itself could not be confused with either the church's worship or creeds. In this connection there is a clear difference between making liturgy the foundation of systematic theology, as Wainwright does, and seeing both liturgy and systematic theology governed by the truth of God revealed in Christ and attested by the Spirit.

Barth himself held that in faith we are sure that our criterion is not a conservative or liberal custom (or tradition) which may be here today and gone tomorrow.[62] The weakness of all religion consists in its attempt to maintain liberal or conservative positions instead of faith. Faith recognizes that our norm is not the good or bad practice of the church. In faith we know that, in and with a multitude of customs, the church's eucharistic action is true and good *only* in the *fact* that it *really* attests the one Lord who is its basis and possibility. It cannot do this if it accepts another norm than the object of faith, even momentarily. This of course can only occur historically as an *event* enclosed in the mystery of God's trinitarian action *ad extra*. This important point is compromised by Wainwright's method.

Analogia entis, as rejected by Barth, cannot and will never admit this. The possibility of sacramental theology means a simple decision for faith, revelation, and grace and therefore for the one being of the triune God *ad intra* and *ad extra* as one's criterion. The limitation of sacramental theology consists in the fact that this prior, simple decision of faith excludes any other norm, criterion, or basis. As there is only one God, one Christ, one Spirit, and one baptism, there is only one criterion of truth for the church's communion with God. If *analogia entis* is normative side by side with faith or even in contradistinction to it—this particular possibility and limitation is denied *de facto*. Interestingly, this reversal of divine and human being takes place frequently in the name of faith and therefore in the name of God.[63]

The Lord's Supper involved Christ's free submission to the clear command of God.[64] His election as God's covenant partner meant he would relinquish his physical body and blood so that the grace of God could be revealed.[65] God freely chose to take upon himself the judgment which is our due for having said "no" to the covenant of grace. This is why Christ's death and *only* his death is a saving death (Heb. 10:10). Only he was electing God as he was elected man. God and humanity exist together *not* generally, but only (and therefore uniquely) in him. For that reason, he alone was faithful as we could not and cannot be. In his resurrection this was revealed to be true. But because what he did was done for us, we can participate in the fulfilled covenant as we hear and believe this particular word of salvation.[66]

But everything depends upon *not* defining Christ's deity by the *for us*. It is not because he was wholly *for us* that he was divine as Rahner, Moltmann, and Wainwright imply. Rather it is because he was divine (i.e., the eternal Logos) that he could be for us. This is why Barth insisted on distinguishing God *in se* and God *for us* in his Christology. If this is not done in Christology it will not be done here. The result is the confusion and reversal of human and divine being. Divine being is not the metaphysical entity which we know by viewing the *oikonomia* as such; it is the self sufficient and antecedent existence of the Son with the Father and Spirit. For that reason the humanity of Christ can be recognized as revealing and saving history only as the triune God is perceived acting here in faith. Direct sight means cessation both of faith and talk about God. Again, Barth's concept of analogy is decisive. He insists that John 1:14

must be normative.[67] As the discussion of the *lex orandi/lex credendi* illustrates, natural theology cannot take this limitation seriously, especially in epistemology and moral philosophy, and compromises this, its *one* and *only* criterion.

Jesus Christ alone is the fulfilled covenant; he alone is the new and everlasting covenant to which all people are called. Since this is what the Lord's Supper attests, faith makes it clear that the Lord's Supper as a human act, does not direct our attention to the ecclesial action as such or to the elements of bread and wine as such. Rather our attention is directed to Christ's saving death and resurrection and to his creation of fellowship with us in his Spirit. This is why Barth emphasized that what takes place at the "center of the Church's worship" is not a new sacrifice. This, Barth believed, was the basic misunderstanding of the Eucharist since the second century.[68] What the church confesses here is its actual reconciliation, justification, and sanctification in and by Christ himself. The church's confession of this divine action and its obedient living of this confession cannot be confused with the divine action. The creature as such can really share in this fulfilled covenant as he or she lives this knowledge of faith in obedience to the one Word of God.[69]

Sin

In understanding the Lord's Supper from the human side we cannot think away the fact that God's judgment was right.[70] Practically speaking this means admitting the need for forgiveness of sin. To be obedient to the Father includes admitting that God's gracious way of dealing with his creatures in his Son is acknowledged as the way in which he was in fact true to himself.[71] The human change which takes place in obedience to the command of God must be a total and practical alteration of one's attitude and direction. It must not simply involve one's thoughts and feelings but one's total being in relation to the triune God.[72] The change in direction which takes place in baptism is the condition for the possibility of attesting this new direction in worship and daily behavior.[73] For Barth, baptism "is related to the foundation of the Christian life . . . and the Lord's Supper is related to the renewal of the Christian life . . ."[74]

It is precisely because Christ was committed unreservedly to subordination to God that he was committed totally to solidarity with sinful humanity. He belonged to his fellow humanity in every way. Everything depends here, as in the doctrine of God, Christ, and the church, upon the fact that sinful persons are not displaced by some hero figure or an ideal person.[75] Moltmann emphasizes this point admirably and yet in his own one-sided emphasis upon Jesus as *related* to the Father and to us, he actually presents us with his own *ideal* of a man who is becoming the Son of the Father. The New Testament presents us with no such picture. Barth avoided this problem by arguing that it is from the reality of Jesus Christ, very God and very man, that we know that the humanity which the Logos assumed was a sinful humanity; a humanity which had accepted a basis, norm, and goal other than God himself and his grace. That is why he was not generally accepted by his people as the expected one of the Old Testament witness.[76]

Because Christ fully lived his election to be for God and did not pursue some abstract idealism, he did not fulfill the covenant in some arbitrary and futile manner. In his own human obedience to God's election of grace, the man Jesus was led to total and definitive commitment to his fellow humanity. The command to love God and to obey his commandments could only mean something formless and mysterious or vague when seen in abstraction from Christ himself. In him we know that to love God and to obey his command means to love one's neighbor.[77] But this does not mean that we can discern the truth of God's love by a phenomenology of neighborly love. The human act of loving is not identical with God's command to love. At all times faith in Christ himself is necessary to see the relationship between love of God and love of neighbor.[78]

The ministry which Christ began with his baptism in the Jordan was a ministry of reconciling the world to the triune God which began to take place as *his own* history. *In him* we can be part of that reconciliation with God. For that reason he alone is the possibility and limitation of knowing who one's neighbor actually is and then acting accordingly.[79] Love of neighbor is what is demanded of the person reconciled with God by God. We, however, are *not* co-reconcilers in this event because we are not divine.[80] Barth applied this possibility and limitation to ministry arguing that the ministry of witness can only serve God and humanity; it can neither carry through God's work to its goal nor can it lead us to the point of accepting it. The church violates its limit as a sign (witness) of God's act of reconciliation if it sets itself alongside or above Christ in its sacraments or its teaching capacity.[81] We participate in the reconciliation of the world with God, begun in the history of Christ, and continued by God in the history of his church by the power of his Spirit. In this limited way we participate in the mystery of God. In this limited way, by loving our neighbor, we attest the one Reconciler. This restricted participation is what we celebrate in the Lord's Supper, until he comes again and completes the reconciliation which he alone can complete. This is the meaning of such synoptic statements as "I shall not drink wine until the day I drink the new wine with you in the kingdom of my Father" (Mt. 26:28).

It is in and through his concrete human actions of obedience to the Father that Christ freely became different from sinful creatures. It was not by mixing his divinity and humanity that he was obedient; it was by humanly doing the will of the Father that Christ was the messiah. Though he was made sin for us, he was obedient. In this way God and creatures and human and divine activity were not confused in him and must not be confused in analyzing the Lord's Supper. In this connection Barth notes that the Evangelists were not satisfied with Christ's simple act of obedience in receiving John's baptism with water so they recounted the happening mythologically by speaking of the voice from heaven saying "This is my beloved Son in whom I am well pleased."[82] There is however no indication here or even in Luke 3:22 that Christ *became* God's Son at that moment.

Moltmann manifests his customary merging of the immanent and economic Trinity on this point also. While he argues that Jesus is "*essentially* God's Son" and did "not become so at some point in history," he also contends that as the messianic Son "his beginning is to be found in his birth from the Holy Spirit."[83] Moltmann merges Christ's human miraculous birth from Mary (of which Matthew and Luke speak) with his Sonship at this point because he is unwilling to abide by the fact that, as Son, Jesus was begotten before all worlds. As seen above, he identifies the Spirit's presence in Jesus as the beginning of the kingdom and obscures the eternal pre-existence of the Father, Son, and Spirit by suggesting that the Spirit's presence in Jesus enables the Father and Son to relate to each other in eternity. Although he correctly stresses that Jesus is denied the means for seizing messianic power, he also detaches Jesus' Sonship from his messiahship claiming that the divine Sonship mentioned in the temptation stories does not refer to a "metaphysical divine Sonship, but the messianic kingdom of Jesus."[84] While Barth strongly opposed this christological adoptionism, Moltmann makes it the cornerstone of his Christology. The purpose of the scriptural authors, in Barth's view, was to emphasize the divinity of Christ's mission. Though Moltmann speaks of the divinity of Christ's mission, he refers to a divinity which begins with Christ's resurrection and thus redefines even the word divinity by making Jesus, in his divinity, dependent on others to be what he actually is in himself.[85]

Rejection of Ex Opere Operato

Barth's key reason for insisting that Christ's water baptism, and by application, his action at the Last Supper be seen as *pure acts of obedience*, is to avoid *any* notion of a human disposing of grace. Because of God's gracious election of Christ in eternity to be the one who fulfilled the covenant, the man Jesus was who he was. It is not the other way around. This is God's grace.

Christ did *not* enter upon or begin his ministry as the One Mediator "in an act whose performance He *ex opere operato* became and has ever since been Lord, Owner and Worker of God's grace and revelation."[86] Christ was very God who became very man. His divinity and humanity were united but not merged, as Barth contends *ex opere operato* must in some sense assume. It is either through the pre-existent Logos and his Spirit that Christ is the revelation and grace of God or it is through something else, i.e., the work working. If this latter view is admitted, then Christ is *de facto* denied as the one and only *mediator* between God and us. This is an extremely important point, because in contrast to Moltmann's view that adoptionism and pre-existence may be complementary, Barth contends that unless Christ's pre-existence is acknowledged, one's Christology will actually be adoptionist (as Moltmann's actually is). Furthermore, while Moltmann would be against a disposing of grace theoretically, his panentheism, as we have seen, actually compromises the Reformation doctrine of grace insofar as it presents God's action as dependent on developments within history. The real problem with the *ex opere operato* is not that it is a doctrine which attempts to avoid making God's grace depend on the disposition of the minister or recipient; it is that it avoids the problem by making the *work* and not grace the objective guarantee.

From what has been presented above (chapters two and three) it would appear that all concepts of analogy which are maintained apart from the Christian *credo* actually identify God with their concept and deny Christ's role as the One Mediator. Yet Christ's obedience could not cause him to be what he already was, i.e., the eternal Logos. For Barth any concept of *ex opere operato* repudiates this christological fact. Further, this specific mystery must be the *basis* for any ecumenical discussion of how grace is to be understood in connection with the working of the sacraments.

Barth's understanding of the *communicatio idiomatum* discussed above illustrates how and why he emphasized the absolute priority of the Logos. His view of analogy, which insists that human knowledge is true only as it recognizes and allows God to precede it absolutely, bears this out. *Ex opere operato* compromises this priority, first by implying that in the human act of obedience creatures can *activate* or even obstruct God's gracious action; second, it denies the *free* grace of God to be immanent in the way which he chose, i.e., in Christ and consequently without any reversal or confusion of his divinity and humanity. Barth's negative view of *ex opere operato* issues from his positive notion of grace in relation to the three views he rejected (cf. chapter two above).

The man Jesus accepted his election of grace as his free calling by God. His baptism was his own acceptance of the will of God. Only in this way did water serve him. "For it is in no sense an instrument of grace and revelation."[87] His obedient human action took place in *response* to grace and *not* in *identity* with it.

Similarly, Christ did not *infuse* bread and wine or a particular human action of fellowship with grace and revelation. Such an idea necessarily obscures the fact that Christ did not abandon his subjectivity to an element in creation or to a model construct of society. What he gave was himself. For this reason it is only as he is recognized as the one grace of God and God's act of revelation itself *ad extra*, that this conception is perceived as false. Christ and the community remain *distinct* in their union because the community can only follow and not precede him noetically or ontically. Neither the church nor its eucharistic action are continuations of the incarnation. First, this thinking implies that a reality distinct from God is no longer distinct, to the extent that grace and revelation are thought to inhere in the elements or in the human action of fellowship which involves common eating and drinking. Second, this thinking implies that grace is not totally self-sufficient; God is free only to the extent that fellowship, communion, and bread and wine are thought to embody *directly* the sovereign God. In that way God is conditioned by an *a priori* or *a posteriori* idea or experience of fellowship which can be discovered generally by us, apart from faith, and re-applied to the inner divine *esse*.

As we saw above, Markus Barth was certainly arguing against this kind of thinking in connection with his analysis of 1 Cor. 10 and 11. There are all kinds of problems with this. To the extent that the creature becomes superior to the creator in either of these ways (because the creature can now control the being and act of God by means of ideas and experiences) God can no longer be seen as the *only* self-moved being.[88] Pannenberg, Moltmann, and Rahner all speak of God as dependent on the world and to that extent they compromise this fact; at the same time they assert God's freedom.

We cannot present a detailed discussion of how Rahner tried to overcome a magical view of the sacraments by blending the church's nature as *opus operatum* together with an individual's *opus operantis*. We simply note that his own explanation of the *ex opere operato* finally rests on the notion that, symbolically speaking, the historical act of the church (in the person of its ordained ministers) is "essentially and irrevocably a manifestation of grace, so that the manifestation necessarily renders present what is manifested." For Rahner "grace is conferred 'on account of' the sacramental sign" because "the sign is an effect of God the dispenser of grace."[89] Moreover sacramental and non-sacramental grace are "not identical" and the church is the instrumental cause of grace only in this symbolic sense. Rahner then argues that it is only in the mutual relation of the *opus operatum* and *opus operantis* that sacraments can be fully effective.[90] In this mutual relation grace externalizes itself *ex opere operato*. For Rahner then *ex opere operato* means that the Word of Christ on the lips of the church confers grace.[91] It also means that our disposition must be seen as "necessarily borne by grace which, as already pointed out, is, on the one hand, grace of Christ and of the Church, and, on the other hand, finds its outward bodily expression in the space and time of history by this activity of man."[92] While Christ is really present, irrespective of the minister's disposition or the disposition of the recipient, there might be no effect of grace for the individual without his or her faith. In this dialogue between Christ, the church, and the individual a *metanoia* takes place *ex opere operato*.[93] The important point here is that the historical church is irrevocably the sign and bearer of God's grace. This can become effective for us as we open ourselves to God in our disposition of faith. Sacramental signs manifest the basic acts of Christian existence which have become visible. The grace signified is the human radicality and divine depths of acts in which the fullness of human existence is itself achieved.[94]

Eduard Schillebeeckx also, quite properly, wishes to avoid a "magical or mechanical concept of ex-opere-operato." He correctly argues that the post Tridentine theologians have separated their sacramental doctrine too much from Christ. Yet, he does hold that a valid sacrament (which is in some sense dependent on the *intention* of the minister and the recipient) works "ex opere operato" as long as it is valid. But what makes a sacrament valid? Certainly it is neither the disposition of the minister nor the recipient. It is, however, contingent in part, Schillebeeckx believes, on the "intention" to "authentically extend Christ's work of redemption in and through the sacrament."[95] Hence a valid sacrament is only a sacrament in the full sense "when it is fruitful"; this for Schillebeeckx requires that the recipient have the proper disposition, i.e., "the recipient has but to reach out and hold on to" Christ's presence in faith. But how exactly do we know Christ is present? The answer is that a valid sacrament simply as the ritual prayer of Christ and the church, for the recipient "is therefore the presence on earth of the heavenly reality of salvation."[96]

Once this kind of thinking is admitted, implicitly or explicitly, in Barth's eyes, God is no longer absolute and Jesus cannot be seen as the *One* Mediator. He is relativized by the *a priori* or *a posteriori* idea or experience (disposition). Barth contested this point throughout the *Church Dogmatics*. On the basis of this kind of reversal of divine and human being, secondary objectivity becomes the norm for primary objectivity; creatures thus have created God in their own image.[97]

Alasdair Heron notes what Schillebeeckx himself explains,[98] i.e., that "grace is objectively *there* in the sacraments, that it is available." Here the language of cause was used. "It did not mean that the sacraments as such *create* grace; for that creativity lies in God alone . . . It meant rather that they are the *means*, the *instruments* by which God works and gives grace." Since God gave them this objective validity and works through them they "were said to be effective *ex opere operato*, through the performance of the objective rite." Regarding the doctrine of *ex opere operato* Heron concludes:

> though pointing chiefly to the objective working of God, [*ex opere operato*] carries with it the ideas of *priestly and episcopal power*: where

that power is lacking, the objective sacrament cannot be performed. In this sense, the doctrine serves not simply to point to the objective action of God, but also to anchor that action in the activity of his chosen instruments, the priests and bishops of the church. The channels of the divine grace cannot be by-passed![99]

In this analysis we can still see the problem to which Barth originally objected when considering a proper view of grace, i.e., the idea that God's objective action *ad extra* might be grounded in anyone or anything other than himself in his Word and Spirit. In the next chapter we shall see that because the basis of the church's sacramental action is objectively grounded in Christ and subjectively grounded in the Spirit, Barth avoids any immanentist view of the sacrament. The goal of the sacrament is neither the sign itself nor the faith of Christians, but the continuing action of Christ imparting himself to people after Pentecost.

Notes

1. C.D. 2, 1, p. 156.

2. Cf. C.D. 1, 1, pp. 402ff., C.D. 3, 2, pp. 54, 444–47, and chapter three above.

3. See above, Symbol and Mediated Knowledge, in chapter two.

4. Moltmann, *The Way of Jesus Christ*, p. 116. Also Moltmann, *The Church in the Power*, pp. 250ff.

5. Moltmann, *The Church in the Power*, p. 62. Cf. also Moltmann, *The Way of Jesus Christ*, p. 102 where he expresses the same idea of mutual conditioning in a different context by saying that "Jesus brings the gospel to the poor, and discovers the kingdom of God among the poor. The poor need him, and he depends on them." With Moltmann, Richard J. Bauckham, *SJT* 44 (1991): 519–531 "Moltmann's Messianic Christology," seems to think that without this specific concept of "reciprocity in relationship" Christology is bound to be docetic. Yet neither he nor Moltmann sees the importance of distinguishing Christ's humanity and divinity here. Certainly Jesus the man was dependent socially. But can we elevate this visibly social aspect of the humanity of Christ to the level of a norm for determining his "personhood"? Bauckham interprets Moltmann accurately when he writes: "Moltmann stresses Jesus' social personhood: even in the salvific acts of his ministry he is dependent on others as much as they are dependent on him," pp. 526–7. But even Bauckham seems to have doubts, such as the ones I have expressed, since he also writes: "Hopefully the chapter also stresses the priority of God's grace sufficiently to head off the

expected accusation of Pelagianism (p. 96)," p. 527.

6. See C.D. 3, 2, pp. 301ff. and C.D. 4, 2, pp. 223ff.

7. See C.D. 2, 1, pp. 302ff. It is because God is the *only* self-moved being that in Christ and the Spirit we have to do with one who is *free* in relation to the church. Compare this with C.D. 4, 1, pp. 717ff. and C.D. 4, 3, pp. 117ff.

8. See C.D. 4, 2, pp. 631–33ff. The church, as the earthly-historical form of Christ's body, is not built in relation to an anonymous God but in and through Christ in the power of the Spirit. See also C.D. 2, 2, p. 22.

9. C.D. 4, 4, p. 44. Cf. also C.D. 2, 1, pp. 218ff., 227ff.

10. C.D. 4, 2, pp. 695ff.

11. Cf. C.D. 2, 1, pp. 235ff.

12. See C.D. 1, 2, pp. 163ff. and C.D. 4, 2, p. 91. This cardinal insight is missed by Moltmann when he argues that the *only* freedom God has is freedom for others and freedom to suffer. This very thinking leads Moltmann to introduce the necessities of creation into the nature of God who is really free.

13. C.D. 4, 4, p. 45.

14. No phenomenology of meal or bread and wine will lead to the knowledge of faith. Such a position assumes the possibility of analogies of parity. See, e.g., C.D. 2, 1, pp. 190 and 224ff. In Barth's mind the Lord's Supper decisively reflects the fact that for the Christian there is one true church (see C.D. 4, 1, pp. 702ff. and C.D. 4, 3, p. 566).

15. See C.D. 2, 1, pp. 218ff., 227ff. and chapters one and two above.

16. A perfect illustration of this thinking can be seen in T.I. 16:60–78 "Faith Between Rationality and Emotion." Here Rahner explicitly describes faith and freedom without allowing the specific God of Christian revelation the freedom to determine their meaning. Hence true faith and freedom mean self-acceptance. "If a man freely accepts himself as he is . . . then it is God he is accepting," p. 67. But if this is true, then knowledge of God, revelation, and grace are conceived as part of the structure of human being. That is the point of contention here. This is a logical conclusion for the *analogia entis*. But the *analogia fidei* excludes this thinking in order to maintain God's freedom. The rest of the article describes grace and revelation as the process in which we accept ourselves in this way. This leads directly to the docetism discussed above: "The revelation history which occurs in *Jesus* and is grasped by us in faith should not in the first instance be treated as a particular occurrence," p. 69.

17. Rahner, *C.S.*, p. 38. Concerning phenomenon and underlying reality (grace) Rahner writes: "it is possible to perceive why the symbol can be really distinct from what is symbolized and yet an intrinsic factor of what is symbolized, essentially related to it," p. 38. The relation is "a case of an intrinsic and mutual causal relationship. What is manifesting itself posits its own identity and existence by manifesting itself in this manifestation which is distinct from itself . . . The sign is therefore a cause of what it signifies by being the way in which what is signified effects itself, " p. 38. And "The sacramental sign is cause of grace in as much as grace is conferred by being signified," p. 39

18. Ibid., pp. 39–40.

19. See, for e.g., C.D. 1, 2, pp. 164ff. and C.D. 4, 1, pp. 49ff.

20. T.I. 4:106. Rahner began his consideration of the incarnation denying "ourselves all consideration of the subject of the statement, the Word of God as he is in himself," p. 106. Admitting this may be very dangerous because it might leave us with a vague or misleading idea of the Word which might then lead us to misunderstand the meaning of the incarnation, he still began with the man that the Word of God was supposed to have become. And his major conclusions are that "The incarnation of God is therefore the unique, *supreme*, case of the total actualization of human reality," that "God has taken on a human nature, because it is essentially ready and adoptable," p. 110, that "Christology is the end and beginning of anthropology," p. 117, and that "Anyone . . . who accepts his existence . . . his humanity . . . says yes to Christ, even when he does not know that he does," p. 119.

21. Ibid., p. 116.

22. Ibid., p. 119.

23. Moltmann, *Creation*, p. 7 and Moltmann, *The Way of Jesus Christ*, pp. 61ff. and 301ff.

24. Moltmann, *The Way of Jesus Christ*, p. 63.

25. Ibid., p. 62. Jesus is "*the messiah on the way* and *the messiah in his becoming* . . . Jesus does not *possess* the messiahship; he grows into it . . . since he is moulded by the events of the messianic time which he experiences," p. 139. For more on this see above, chapter three.

26. Ibid., p. 68.

27. Ibid., p. 74.

28. Ibid., pp. 92–3. For more on this see Molnar, *The Thomist* (1992). Even Bauckham, *SJT*, seems to see the problem here: "Moltmann seems to see Jesus

as a human being whose relationship to the Father in the Spirit makes him the unique Son of God. Presumably it is this relationship which constitutes Jesus' identity with the eternal Son, but Moltmann offers only the merest hint of this (p. 143). At this point Moltmann's focus on pneumatological Christology evidently enables him to sidestep a classic christological issue; it is less clear that his own trinitarian theology ought to allow him to evade it," p. 527.

29. Ibid., pp. 305f.

30. Ibid., p. 319.

31. C.D. 1, 2, p. 164ff.

32. Moltmann, *The Way of Jesus Christ*, p. 50.

33. See, e.g., Karl Rahner, T.I. 4:221–252, "The Theology of the Symbol" and chapters two and three above. For a critique, see Paul D. Molnar, "Can We Know God Directly? Rahner's Solution From Experience," *TS* (1985).

34. C.D. 2, 1, pp. 55ff.

35. C.D. 4, 4, p. 49.

36. See C.D. 1, 2, pp. 125–130ff. This is basically the same as the relationship between sign and thing signified discussed variously throughout C.D. 1, 2.

37. Moltmann, *The Church in the Power*, writes: "Everyone whom he [Christ] calls and who follows his call has the authority to break the bread and dispense the wine," p. 246.

38. Ibid., p. 260.

39. Sykes, *Karl Barth*, p. 60.

40. C.D. 4, 4, p. 52.

41. This thinking opposes Rahner's view that sacraments which were not instituted by Christ are traced to the church's sacramental nature and that the church as a whole has the guarantee of infallibility.

42. See C.D. 1, 2, p. 516 re: the relationship between spirit and matter in the Bible. The differences between Moltmann and Barth on the relationship between spirit and matter are substantial and result from Moltmann's panentheist attempt to synthesize spirit and matter in light of a common future he thinks they share in their "evolution" toward future glory. See, e.g., Jürgen Moltmann, *Creation*, pp. 100ff. This also affects his view of the soul and body, heaven and earth, creation and covenant, and nature and grace.

43. C.D. 2, 1, p. 627.

44. Ibid., pp. 608ff. Barth explains the meaning and relationship between God's pre-temporal, supra-temporal, and post-temporal existence.

45. 1 Cor. 11:24ff.; see also C.D. 4, 1, pp. 668–685 et al.

46. See C.D. 3, 2, pp. 534f. for a false use of memory to overcome the problem of our existence in time which is captured by our inability to restore the past, guarantee the present, or bring about the future.

47. Markus Barth, *Rediscovering the Lord's Supper*, p. 30. See C.D. 4, 1, 664ff. for the same point.

48. Ibid., p. 32.

49. Ibid., pp. 37–8.

50. C.D. 4, 3, p. 266.

51. Ibid., p. 267.

52. Ibid., p. 271.

53. C.D. 4, 2, p. 641; C.D. 4, 4, p. 53.

54. See C.D. 4, 4, p. 54. The man Jesus requested John the Baptist's baptism in a very human way so as to submit his will to God's will for us. His election as Son of the Father to do this in order to accomplish our reconciliation is confirmed by the Holy Spirit.

55. Wainwright, *Doxology*, pp. 218–19.

56. Ibid., p. 274.

57. Ibid., p. 289.

58. Ibid., p. 342.

59. Ibid., p. 344.

60. Cf. Roland M. Frye, "Language for God and Feminist Language: Problems and Principles," *SJT* 41 (1988): 441–469 and Frye in Kimel, *Speaking the Christian God*, pp. 17–43. See also Wolfhart Pannenberg who writes that: "the fact that patriarchal relations which influence the concept of God at this point are time-bound does not justify the demand for a revision of the concept of God as Father because there have now been changes in the family structure and the social order, especially as regards the relation between the sexes," *Systematic Theology I*, p. 262. Hence Pannenberg explicitly rejects Mary Daly's approach because it "presupposes a projection theory of ideas of God after the manner of Feuerbach." Pannenberg believes "This applies esp. to the demand that we should address God as Mother as well as Father," p. 262, n. 9. By contrast Moltmann calls God "a

motherly father" in *Trinity*, p. 164. Similar views are expressed in *Creation*, p. 88. For a critical appraisal of Moltmann's position see Molnar, *TS* (1990).

61. Torrance, *The Trinitarian Faith*, p. 34.

62. See esp. C.D. 1, 2, pp. 316ff.

63. On this point see, e.g., George Kuykendall, "Thomas' Proofs as Fides Quaerens Intellectum: Towards a Trinitarian Analogia" *SJT* 31 (1978): 113–131. In C.D. 4, 3 Barth spoke of three factors in us which resist God's grace: 1) indifference, 2) the attempt to fit Christ into a world-view and 3) activity which Barth characterized formally as the Antichrist, i.e., it is the pattern of a community which formally accepts Christ in its worship, preaching, and theology, but which nevertheless basically has rendered "the Word of grace" innocuous because this has been assimilated "to the Christians and worldlings to whom it is addressed by the careful blunting of its rough edges and the suppression or softening of the strangeness of its declaration," p. 259. Barth regarded this third factor as worse than the other two.

64. C.D. 4, 4, p. 54. See Mt. 26:39. He obeyed his Father's will after asking that the cup might pass him.

65. Cf. C.D. 2, 1, pp. 363ff. re: the connection between judgment and grace.

66. See C.D. 1, 1, p. 315 and C.D. 2, 1, p. 252.

67. C.D. 2, 1, pp. 199ff., 640ff. and 461ff. and C.D. 2, 2, p. 96.

68. C.D. 4, 2, pp. 639–40.

69. Ibid., p. 681.

70. C.D. 4, 4, p. 57.

71. Cf. C.D. 2, 1, pp. 396ff.

72. C.D. 4, 4, pp. 57–60.

73. C.D. 4, 2, pp. 706 and 710.

74. Barth, *The Christian Life*, p. 287.

75. See, e.g., C.D. 1, 2, pp. 151–53 where Barth notes that any attempt to ground the incarnation in the intrinsic goodness of human nature misses this key point. By contrast, Rahner maintains that "Because it [the world] is good, it can be redeemed. But all this goodness, all this meaning, needs redemption, from the meanest atom to the highest spirit. All is to be redeemed, because as good it is capable of redemption, because apart from Christ it is all lost, as a whole, with all its goodness," T.I. 1:178–9.

76. Cf. C.D. 2, 2, p. 243.

77. See C.D. 1, 2, pp. 419ff. See also C.D. 4, 2, pp. 783ff. and C.D. 4, 3, pp. 833ff.

78. Eberhard Jüngel, *God as the Mystery of the World*, concludes that "In the event of love man is at his most mysterious . . . In the event of love, God and man share the same mystery" and that "What serves love is human . . . . But what hinders love is inhuman," p. 392. The synthesis of human and divine love under the concept of mystery leads in fact, and against Jüngel's own desire, to a docetic definition of love, i.e., a definition which is not exclusively dictated by the love of God revealed in Jesus Christ. This is what Barth sought to avoid. Karl Rahner reflected upon the unity of love of God and neighbor and concluded that "the one does not exist and cannot be understood or exercised without the other, and that two names have really to be given to the same reality," T.I. 6:232. He even went so far as to argue that "love of God and the love of neighbor are one and the same thing," p. 233 and that we ought to think in the direction of "a radical identity of the two loves," p. 236. And this thinking led Rahner to the conclusion that Barth wished to avoid, i.e., that "wherever man posits a positively moral act" then (without any knowledge of or faith in Christ) "this act is a positive supernatural salvific act," p. 239. All of this was true for Rahner because we are inescapably oriented toward God in all genuine inter-human love by virtue of our "transcendental horizon" which "is given gratuitously by God's always prevenient saving grace," p. 238. This clear confusion of nature and grace follows Rahner's method as noted above. Wolfhart Pannenberg sees this problem and criticizes Herbert Braun for his view that for Jesus "the fatherly love of God is simply an expression for obedience to Jesus' call for love of neighbor. Love of God and love of neighbor are the same thing. Now there is a core of truth in this thesis, for the two do in fact belong very closely together . . . Nevertheless, they are not identical," Pannenberg, *Systematic Theology I*, p. 263. Of course Pannenberg himself does not firmly close the door to the identity which he criticizes, because instead of appealing to Jesus, the Son of God as the basis for the command to love God and neighbor, he appeals to "Experience of the love of God" and substitutes Jesus' message for his person and work. Hence "Jesus is the Son inasmuch as it is in his message of the nearness of the royal rule of the Father . . . that this God may be known as Father," p. 264. John Thompson, *The Holy Spirit in the Theology of Karl Barth*, notes that love to God and for one's neighbor are inseparable but not identical, p. 142.

79. C.D. 1, 2, p. 373.

80. On this point see esp. C.D. 4, 3, pp. 598–99.

81. Cf. ibid., pp. 830–33 and 836.

82. C.D. 4, 4, p. 64.

83. Moltmann, *The Way of Jesus Christ*, p. 84.

84. Ibid., p. 92.

85. For more on this problem see Molnar, *The Thomist* 56 (1992): 669–693.

86. C.D. 4, 4, p. 65. See esp. C.D. 4, 1, pp. 696–99 for Barth's specific statements against *ex opere operato*. He rejects it for the same reason he rejects sacramentalism, pp. 695–96.

87. Ibid. Barth used the term *instrument* earlier in the *Church Dogmatics* to refer to the fact that people can actually point to God's action *ad extra* as they are epistemologically and ontologically obedient (see, e.g., C.D. 1, 2, p. 306 and esp. p. 227). But he never implies that the person or action as such conveys or even mediates grace. Barth rejects the term now for the same reason he would reject the term sacrament.

88. C.D. 2, 1, p. 268. See Barth's interpretation of the body of Christ in relation to 1 Cor. 10.16, C.D. 4, 1, p. 665.

89. Rahner, *C.S.*, p. 40.

90. T.I. 2:129–30.

91. T.I. 4:272.

92. T.I. 2:124–5.

93. Ibid., pp. 117 and 125.

94. T.I. 14:156.

95. Schillebeeckx, *Christ the Sacrament of the Encounter with God*, pp. 108–9.

96. Ibid., p. 100.

97. C.D. 2, 1, pp. 22–5, 40–3, 49ff., 56, and 58–79.

98. Schillebeeckx, *Christ the Sacrament of the Encounter with God*, pp. 100–109.

99. Heron, *Table and Tradition*, pp. 90–1.

VII

The Goal of the Lord's Supper as the Work of Creatures

In its human act of obedience to the divine command, what goal does the community have in view when it celebrates the Lord's Supper? For Barth, the action of the community can have only *one* basis and goal. This particular basis and goal is the *sole* distinguishing factor between the community's action as Christ's body on earth and a general and directly visible fellowship which is not his body on earth.[1] To seek the goal of the Eucharist in anyone or anything other than the one who loves in freedom points us away from the object of faith. If this happens even the eucharistic celebration of the church can become a disobedient human action. It does not *necessarily* point to God's actual presence in his Word and Spirit; it may also point away from him, its true goal.

For Barth the goal of the Lord's Supper is the human decision and action taken in obedience to the command and promise of Christ himself.[2] It is the celebration of the fellowship into which we were called in baptism. As we have seen, this is a fellowship whose origin and goal is grace and not nature. For this reason the telos of baptism and the Lord's Supper is transcendent and not immanent (more accurately, it is immanent in virtue of its transcendence). The goal of the church's human eating and drinking is the fellowship these people have with each other in virtue of having been cleansed by the Holy Spirit. They affirm this goal as they are faithful to the covenant of grace which was fulfilled *extra nos pro nobis*.[3] As the church does this, it actually lives as Christ's earthly-historical form of existence. But none of this is part of the very structure of the church just because this particular goal is identical with Jesus Christ.

Therefore the goal of the church's action does not lie in the administration of baptism or the Lord's Supper. These actions point to the action of the Holy Spirit by which the church is what it is as the provisional representation of Christ's presence on earth.[4] Barth observes that Jewish and pagan baptism always seek to be more than this—i.e., more than pointers to something beyond their action as such. Similarly, if the goal of the Lord's Supper is the human administration of the Supper as such, the church could claim for itself the power of the Holy Spirit. Then, a reversal between head and body takes place and the community no longer points to the Spirit of the transcendent God, but to its own spirit.

The goal of the Lord's Supper then is the act of reconciliation which took place in the history of Christ and is recognized here and now as effective through the Holy Spirit. The goal is *God's act* of judgment and grace in the history of Christ, and *God's act* of salvation and revelation in Christ. Our human act must acknowledge and not obscure this divine act if it is to make any sense. The Lord's Supper must attest God's action without being confused with it. In this limit lies the possibility of recognizing the church's communion with God himself, i.e., the totally other. This divine act is obscured whenever the human act seeks to be more than an act of pure obedience.[5]

Obedience, Human Freedom, and More Recent Theology

More recent theology is especially unhappy with the idea of obedience. It seems to imply an authoritarian approach to reality rather than one of mutuality, friendship, and interconnectedness. For instance Jürgen Moltmann resists Barth's conception of God's freedom just because he believes that "In God there is no one-sided relationship of superiority and subordination, command and obedience, master and servant, as Karl Barth maintained in his theological doctrine of sovereignty . . ."[6] He believes that Barth's view of analogy was dictated by this starting point and that this affected his view of the relationship between God and the world, heaven and earth, soul and body, and man and woman. Feminist theologians point out that language which stresses obedience is language drawn from a patriarchal society and expresses the male need to rule and dominate.[7] While Wolfhart Pannenberg is also unhappy with an authoritarian approach to theology,[8] he insists that we cannot simply change our concept of God as Father because it is a received tradition coming directly from Jesus and cannot be altered for some social purpose.[9]

Yet the problem which is not addressed by these theologians concerns whether and to what extent Barth's notion of obedience was dictated by grace rather than nature. By that I mean that the friendship and fellowship which we have with God is due only to his free action *ad extra* on our behalf. Hence it is a friendship and fellowship to which we have no claim (against those who argue that, in one way or another God needs us), and it is a friendship and fellowship between utterly unequal partners, i.e., between a God who is superior to us as creator, and creatures who are utterly dependent upon this God. When Barth spoke of pure obedience he attempted to preserve the priority of God's action together with the need for faith and obedience, in order to show that the God who is immanent in history is not an apotheosis, but the one who *alone* has the divine power to make us his friends as he opposes our sin (disobedience) in the power of the Spirit.

Many examples of this thinking in Barth's theology could be adduced, and we have already spoken of his notion of free human obedience above. One example here will suffice. When Barth discussed "Man as Doer of the Word" he analyzed

Jas. 1: 21–25. Merely to be a hearer of the Word and not a doer means exercising a type of sovereignty which is impossible in relation to the Word. We may act autonomously in relation to human words but not in relation to God's Word.

> Because it is the Word of the Lord, to hear the Word of God is to obey the Word of God. Not to obey the Word of God is therefore to deceive oneself . . . first by dealing with the engrafted Word, as though it were not the Word of the Lord; and then by imagining that to ignore the engrafting is to rob it of its power, as though resisted grace does not become judgment by the very same power by which it may be blessing.[10]

For Barth this Word claims us in the sense that it claims our freedom, i.e.,

> our own free and spontaneous obedience. It does not claim individual works. It claims ourselves as the doers of the work which corresponds to its content . . . It demands that we leave the sanctuary of an abstract 'inwardness,' and give ourselves to the decision not merely of obeying, but of obedience, of accepting it as the truth without reserve, of submission to the truth.[11]

As Barth explained, the positive significance of the concept of work for both James and Paul consists in the fact that it is really we who work and live the Christian life, but because this takes place through our obedient response to God's Word by the power of the Holy Spirit, it is clear that it is not our work which sanctifies us but God himself. There is thus no conflict between faith and works. Indeed faith itself can be described as "that work which confirms the divine action [of reconciliation]." This life of faith in Christ the reconciler is our life work.

> It is man who believes. This does not justify him. What justifies him is the fact that he believes in Jesus Christ. But man believes. And when he believes, his faith is not an accidental or partial, but a necessary and total, determination of his existence. It may be a weak and tiny faith, but if it is not necessary and total even in its weakness and tininess, it is not faith, and Jesus Christ is not its object.[12]

Works then are the true and necessary expression of faith in Jesus Christ. But the word obedience preserves both the freedom of God as the giver of the gift of reconciliation and of us as the active and passive recipients of God's grace.

By contrast, many theologians tend to equate human and divine action by contending that, in some sense it is the human act of symbolizing which itself actually can overcome our theological and political problems. Hence Elizabeth Johnson suggests that, because the symbol God functions, therefore, *we* must make it function inclusively by using female images for the divine. She equates the truth of the symbol with its social function and thus ignores the problem just raised. Jürgen Moltmann also equates the social functioning of symbols with his goal to establish an ecological doctrine of creation, i.e., one which no longer distinguishes between God and creatures as utterly unequal partners; and a holistic Christology, i.e., one which blends Christian practice with Christ so that Christ can be described as not yet fully the messiah without the full belief of the community. Hence he can argue that Barth's conception of sovereignty is one-sided. But his own view of God's freedom is dictated by a relational metaphysics which can seek its knowledge of creation in the knowledge of nature as "made accessible to us by evolutionary theories."[13] It is precisely by shifting the norm for theological truth away from Christ himself that these theologians compromise the fact that true freedom and true understanding come from grace alone and not from a general grasp of relationality. Moltmann actually recognizes this problem:

> If we deliberately place the starting point of this doctrine of creation in the context of the present world situation, this does not mean that we want to adapt the doctrine apologetically to that situation . . . Nor does it mean that the doctrine of creation has to be subjected to laws and limitations of the present situation.[14]

Yet his method leads him to argue that the more we grasp and accept current experiences and the "impasses of the present situation . . . the more clearly and unequivocally belief in creation can speak."[15]

In connection with Christology he writes that "talk about 'the cosmic Christ' cannot mean that Christ has to be fitted into the laws and rhythms of the cosmos as it is . . . Christ is not integrated into the era of this world, as some New Age thinkers would like to have it, following C. G. Jung." Yet, in spite of his criticism of this cosmic Christology which does not speak of a "reconciled, Christ-pervaded cosmos" as it should, Moltmann claims

> All things are created in the *vista* that stretches forward to the messiah, for the messiah will redeem all things for their own truth . . . thus completing and perfecting creation. But this means that the risen Christ is not present only in the Spirit of faith and in the Spirit that animates the community of his people. Nor is he present merely in hidden form in world history. He is also immanently efficacious 'in the heart of creation', as Teilhard de Chardin put it . . . [and] in victimized nature too.[16]

The problem with this thinking is that, on the one hand, it leads Moltmann to make Christ's resurrection a process inherent in nature, i.e., "Love is . . . the immanent power of resurrection in the flesh,"[17] and, on the other hand, it enables him to construct an image of God's kingdom from the suffering of nature and persons rather than from God's Word and Spirit. This thinking leads him to the idea that suffering is part of God's nature,[18] since he actually believes that love which does not suffer is not divine.[19] Now the problem with this reasoning is that it leads Moltmann to conclude that there is a "Liberating power inherent in vicarious *suffering*," and that the solution "in our nuclear age" to mutual threats by enemies is to love them:

> Love of our enemies . . . is *creative* love. Anyone who repays evil with good . . . [is] creating something new. Love of an enemy presupposes the sovereignty which springs from one's own liberation from enmity . . . Through love, we draw our enemies into our own sphere of responsibility . . . It is superior to the ethic of self-assertion, which we find in friend-enemy thinking . . . it is the only reasonable thing, if we are to ensure lasting peace on earth.[20]

But that is the problem. Can *we* insure lasting peace on earth? Is *our* love of enemies the kind of creative love which will enable us to become the solution? Does this not compound the difficulty, by making the peace of Christ and his salvation, factors which can be perceived directly in the cosmos by all reasonable people who then can attain salvation by their actions within history? What need is there for Christ, grace, and revelation if we can do all this? In fact, the peace Christ offers is the peace of God which passes all understanding (Phil. 4:7) and sanctifies us. It is the Lord himself who gives this peace (2 Thess. 3:16).

While Moltmann does not wish to go as far as Gerhard Lohfink and say that "without the practical witness to peace of the community of his people, Jesus cannot be the messiah," since this binds "Jesus' messiahship to the messianic works of his followers," his own "holistic perception" makes Christ's peace and saving grace identical with and dependent upon the community's actions just as his person is dependent upon the community.[21] Moltmann says that we must look at Jesus' humanity to know his divinity and that we must think of his divinity to know his humanity. But, he does not say that Jesus the man really *is* God in the flesh; this smacks of the old metaphysical (dualistic) approach to theology, which sees God as one who is apathetic and remote from us and defines nature and grace through mutual negations instead of seeing their "mutual interconnectedness." But by not starting to think from Jesus, true God and true man, Moltmann is led to define his person and action by his abstract notion of interconnectedness.

Gordon Kaufman overtly appeals to the evolutionary processes within which modern life is conceived and explicitly fits Christ into that process. He argues that the task of contemporary Christology is to appropriate "the story of Jesus in the light of a contemporary understanding of God, on the one hand, and of the most profound problems facing human existence today, on the other."[22] Since his understanding of God and of Christ is dictated by his evolutionary view of the world, God is defined pantheistically "as that ecological reality behind and in and working through all of life and history;" God is the complex web of all created organisms: "God—this whole grand cosmic evolutionary movement—is giving birth . . . to finite freedom . . ."[23] And Christ cannot be the Lord as we find him in the New Testament, i.e., the only human who, as God and man actually can save and redeem us. Rather,

> in the biological and historico-cultural terms with which we now conceive human existence, no individual person can have this sort of absolute significance and cosmic efficacy for all others, for every individual is an expression of and interdependent with the complex ecological web of life and nature which gives them all birth and sustains them all.[24]

Refusing to speak in terms of obedience Kaufman thus substitutes his reconstructed God and Christ for the real God who acts for us in the particular history of Jesus. His God is in fact indistinguishable from the cosmic process. His Christ cannot free us at all but remains only a vacant symbol for human attempts at reconciliation and reconstruction.[25] Barth's insistence that we may only speak of God in the free human act of obeying the Word has profoundly practical significance here. Kaufman's attempt at a less authoritarian theology has led to the authoritarian conclusion that it is *impossible* for an individual person (Jesus Christ) to be the absolute savior of all persons. And Kaufman's theology is reduced to anthropology and mythology. That which is impossible in Kaufman's theology is the very possibility of freedom and truth in Barth's theology. Here people are faced with a choice between reality constructed according to their own goals and viewpoints, and accepting reality as established and maintained by God alone.[26]

Why then can we not present the church's action in the Lord's Supper as itself divine speech or action in Barth's theology? Because human speech and action are united with the divine action of salvation and revelation *ONLY* in Christ.[27] This is not merely a mythological manner of speaking as Kaufman assumes. Rather it is a fact that only Christ is very God and very man. This is Barth's acknowledgment and application of the fact that Christ is unique.[28] As such he is one of a kind. There is no other like him in the sense that only he is divine and human. We are not. But even in Christ his human actions do not become divine and his divine actions do not become human. It is in distinction that they are *one*. Precisely because he is this *one*, without dissolution of either aspect, the church deceives itself and the world if it thinks that in baptism or the Lord's Supper it "accomplishes something more and better than a human answer . . . in face of God's grace and revelation."[29]

It is exactly for this reason that, in his ecclesiology, Barth insisted that the being of the community is Christ's predicate but that Christ is *not* the predicate of the being of the community.[30] It follows that Christ's Spirit does not supplant human knowing, willing, and action in claiming human obedience. This is why Barth emphasized that even in its sacraments, and therefore in the Lord's Supper, the distinction between the divine change and the human decision remains. The distinction between creator (heavenly-head) and creature (earthly-historical form—body of Christ) remains even in the Eucharist; creator is not collapsed into creation (bread and wine). This is why Barth believed that water baptism and the Lord's Supper must never be presented as instruments or channels of grace.[31] Christ's movement toward us is always his movement for which we must pray.

Interestingly, Alasdair Heron believes that the critical distinction between Christ (the sacrament) and the church deserves to be underlined as Barth himself insisted. But he believes that Barth went too far in the opposite direction and subtly redefined Christ's historical presence "in terms of our response to him, our 'ethical act' of obedient witness." Hence he rejected the medieval notion of sacraments altogether arguing that there is but one sacrament, i.e., Jesus Christ. We shall have to examine this problem in more detail below, namely, whether and to what extent Barth's rejection of the term sacrament entailed a shift away from his earlier view that, in some sense, sacramental reality referred to a sign bearing witness to revelation. For now it is important to note that Heron argues that the notions of sacrament and sacramentality which stem from the early church rather than from the New Testament can have validity today as long as Christ's centrality is not compromised. Thus, they may be seen as secondary and dependent means of his presence and action. Heron thus describes the sacramental reality of the church as Christ's body:

> Its nature and meaning lie deeper than the surface appearance; it is both visible and invisible, both an empirical entity and a divinely grounded mystery. But it is not in and by itself a sacrament apart from Christ, nor is it a sacrament of the same sort as he, for only in him is its own identity grounded, disclosed and promised. It is sacramental as a sacrament *of Christ, the sacrament*, as participant in him, as imaging him, and as witnessing to him.[32]

Hence, the Christian life is "sacramental at its core." Each person is "called and challenged and—however brokenly and fragmentarily—empowered to be a sign and channel of the everlasting mercy." Barth's objection to the language of instrument, channel, or means of grace was an objection to the idea that Christ's present action could be ascribed to these human activities and elements. Heron argues that baptism and the Eucharist "are only real, effective and valid insofar as they are not simply *our* acts and declarations but *his* in the energy of his Spirit. As such they are and repeatedly become visible and tangible forms of the Word which he himself is." But exactly how do they repeatedly become this? According to Heron they do so as "the risen Christ unites us to himself, imparts himself to us, and engages us with him" through these signs and instruments. "In this secondary sacramentality his primary sacramentality is, as it were, projected on to the plane of his relation to us and ours to him."[33] This may offer a solution to the more juridical medieval view of Christ's presence as Heron suggests. But does it capture Barth's insistence upon our constant *need* for prayer just because sacramental reality must continually receive its veracity from outside itself? For Barth, Christ's movement toward us

is always His movement, which we may expect and hope for with certainty and joy, but for which we have always to pray. It is His affair. It is His free rejoinder to the answer which we give to Him with our faith and baptism. It is not the affair of our faith and baptism.[34]

In the Lord's Supper then the community does not confess its *own act of faith* which is an immanent reality but it confesses the transcendent and divine act of grace and revelation which is the origin, theme, and content of its faith. The church's action is always distinct from God's act in Christ. In itself the church has no access to the "totally other," but in Christ it has access because he alone, of all humanity, was and is the eternal God himself. No other human being was or is God. Therefore humanity in general cannot recognize the true God by looking at what it considers important. Because the divine act of grace and revelation always remains God's action *ad extra*, it remains *distinct* and *free* in relation to the community. The church can neither anticipate nor accomplish this divine act of grace and revelation[35] because the divine *esse* is not inherent in the human and visible actions as such. The church is the body of Christ only as it attests his divine-human action in its human action. The common act of the church then can only *refer* to the *event* in which it recognizes and accepts its basis, goal, and limit; i.e., Christ himself active and present mediating God to us and us to God.[36] When the church's action of eating and drinking is celebrated in recognition of this particular basis, goal, and limit, it has the divine promise that God's work will definitively demonstrate its power in their lives. They live the promise of eternal life.[37]

As noted above the *terminus a quo* and the *terminus ad quem* of human knowledge and action is God's own action in history. Only when the actual basis and goal of human knowledge is recognized, in faith, will people be able to act obediently. As we have seen, for Barth, the actual basis of human knowledge and action is the triune God himself. Precisely because it has this divine promise, there is absolutely no need for any "bureaucratic concern for validity in the administration of the sacraments."[38] The basis and possibility of the church's thanksgiving in the Eucharist are not in us or our actions, but in God and his action. We can only obey the Lord and pray that God will make himself known again and again. When this actually happens and by the Holy Spirit the community in fact lives its election in Christ, it is a miracle, i.e., a fully human act initiated, upheld, and brought to completion by God himself.[39]

Pentecost and Human Action

But what then is the decisive difference between the community's action in the Lord's Supper and other apparently similar rituals in existence both before and after the history of Christ? For Barth, the answer can be seen by looking toward Pentecost. This is the turning point both of salvation history and of world history. Pentecost is the event in which Jesus showed himself to be different from John the Baptist as well as from Moses and the Prophets. He did this by *actually enabling* his disciples to be his witnesses.[40] He had the power to do this. Neither John nor any Old Testament figure had this same power; no other has this particular power. No one else is eternal electing God as he is elected man. In view of Pentecost several insights become possible.[41]

1. The divine kingdom became an element in world history as such. Naturally without faith, this kingdom may be associated with all kinds of panaceas and will never be associated decisively and uniquely with Christ himself who, as the eschaton, is fulfilled time itself. The fact that the divine kingdom was now an element in world history as such did not mean that it could no longer be misunderstood. It was and is still possible to see it simply as an element in history and not also as the revelation of God himself. It is only as the Holy Spirit enables us to recognize this history as saving history that we can know the truth of revelation at all. This is why Barth calls it an *event* and a *happening* and not a state. Christ really was a man like all others. This fact confronts both believers and unbelievers. Whatever they make of Christ, in his humanity he is part of world-history, and cannot be avoided. This is how God confronts humanity. He does not force himself upon people but leaves them the freedom to decide whether

they will accept this man as their Lord, reconciler, and redeemer. In light of what was said above about Christology, it is important to realize that whenever Christ's particularity is neglected, as it is in all Christologies of the ebionite and docetic type, then his Lordship and our reconciliation and redemption are called into question as well. But the important point here is that the kingdom of God which is present and presses for continuation and completion causes more tension than before Easter because the demand for attention to grace and revelation is increased.

2. After Pentecost, baptism and the Lord's Supper derive from the outpouring and impartation of the Holy Spirit. From the Holy Spirit we know that the Christ event, which is the basis and goal of the Eucharist, was not simply a past event. It continues anew each day in the lives of Christians, i.e., the body of Christ on earth. Recognition of this ongoing divine activity in history means bearing the noetic and ontic mark of that acknowledgment. It means not attempting to be more than an act of *recollection* and *expectation* of this event.

This means that the church's celebration of the Eucharist can be no more than a constant prayer—i.e., *veni creator spiritus*.[42] As the church does not control its oneness, holiness, catholicity, or apostolicity, so it does not control its being as the body of Christ. If the church could control its being in any way, then there would be no need for *eucharistia* (thanksgiving), simply because thanksgiving is due for receiving what we cannot and could not procure for ourselves. It is precisely because we cannot produce revelation, grace, or faith, and for that reason our being as the body of Christ (his special presence on earth), that we must be thankful for his freely giving himself again and again according to his promise of election. For Barth, this is what *ex opere operato* denies. Such a concept claims direct identity between its act and the working of the Holy Spirit. The result is that where the act takes place, it is thought that the other *must* also take place. This means that the action of the church in celebrating the Lord's Supper cannot be more than a petition for the Holy Spirit to open their hearts to the fellowship established by him in Christ. As water baptism cannot guarantee reception of the Holy Spirit, but can only be a prayer for him offered in confidence because of Jesus' promise, so the Lord's Supper cannot seek to be more than a prayer ventured in expectation that God will disclose himself again and again as the One who loves in freedom. After Pentecost the kingdom of God which has come and is also future is closely connected to the Holy Spirit. Before Easter, John the Baptist could only look forward to this outpouring and imparting of the Spirit. But now Christ is present in the power of the resurrection imparting the Spirit. There can be no separation of the Spirit from the Word incarnate.

3. The judgment suffered by Christ removed the sin of the world and any further compulsion toward sin.[43] After Pentecost there is a heightened emphasis

on God's judgment. "He who had come as Judge allowed Himself to be judged and executed as the One condemned and rejected in place of all the rest."[44] No other human suffering and death could or can accomplish this. It can only attest this truth. In that way human being participates in the divine action of the Father *ad extra* in his Word and Spirit. This action of Christ is the Day of Wrath. We can be hopeful because this was not the last word to us. The Day of Wrath was not the goal of the incarnation. Its goal was a word of grace by which we may know that we are in reality spared this final and ultimate suffering and humiliation. Human suffering can never be viewed as more than what took place in the history of Christ. In the power of the Spirit, the Day of Wrath was unveiled as the manner of God's revelation of his grace. It cannot be viewed as more than this. We must not think this needs to happen again to be effective. The judgment of God in Christ happened once for all. No other act of divine judgment has any autonomy. It points to the history of Christ and is enclosed therein or it is not divine judgment.[45] In light of Christ's death we have no future as sinners. As God claims us, he judges us and forgives us anew each day. In fact "Man is always on the point of coming to the divine judgment and coming from it."[46] In faith we recognize that we are directed to live by God's grace.

In the Lord's Supper then the focus is not on the common eating and drinking or the bread and wine but on the saving significance of the death of Christ.[47] The common eating and drinking and the bread and wine are important, but only insofar as they point to this, their basis and goal. For this reason the church's action in the Lord's Supper cannot be viewed as a human offering of Christ to the Father in a sacrificial sense. Atonement occurred in the history of Christ once for all. Only God could accomplish this atonement. This divine action neither can nor needs to be repeated. The church's eucharistic celebration recognizes the priority of the divine action in Christ by not attempting to recreate, noetically or ontically, a situation which no longer exists—a situation in which Christ's act of atonement may be conceived as not *fully* and *completely* effective in itself. Christ's fulfillment of the covenant needs no theoretical or practical completion. As God is self-sufficient *in se* and *ad extra*, so his action in Christ is self-sufficient.

For that reason it is effective for us, irrespective of our obedience or disobedience. The significance of Barth's distinction between the immanent and economic Trinity, the divinity and humanity of Christ, and between Christ and the church can be seen here. Because it is God himself whom we encounter in Christ and the Spirit, we cannot re-define his inner self-sufficient *esse* by assuming that humanity in itself (apart from Christ) can fulfill the covenant which was fulfilled in Christ. Unless these dogmatic distinctions are clearly made, humanity itself may be seen as the *basis* and *goal* of the Lord's Supper and not humanity as it is included by God in the fulfilled covenant. The problems with this are obvious. For instance, the problem of confusing theological truth with the social functioning of symbols as discussed above shows that without these deliberate distinctions, it is easy to equate what is supposed to be a transcendent act of God in history on our behalf, with our own anthropological or theological program. In this way the basis and goal of our action is set by our own view of ourselves and the world we inhabit. Nothing could be more enslaving than this; this perspective does not allow Jesus to be the one light of life that he actually is.

Therefore, in the Lord's Supper the church does not offer to the Father what it cannot offer. Rather, it thankfully recognizes that such an offering is no longer necessary. In Christ, the church has been represented before the Father once for all by the One Mediator.[48] The church cannot be his body in subordination to *any other mediator* because there is literally no other who is of the *essence* of the triune God. Any other concept here means admission of another mediator of reconciliation. Other concepts will be thought necessary in proportion as creation, reconciliation, and redemption are thought to be *necessities* rather than free acts of grace. The concepts of identity and necessity are pivotal both in grasping Barth's *analogia fidei* and in understanding why he insisted that creation, reconciliation, and redemption cannot be understood correctly if seen and described as necessary and not free acts of grace. Necessity presupposes that creatures are essential to God and that these gracious acts are self-evident.[49]

Forgiveness of sins is the starting point of a theology which perceives that our human relationship with God is and remains real *only* as it remains grounded in God's gracious actions *ad extra* in Christ and the Spirit. Since our relationship with God can never be self-grounded, therefore creation, reconciliation, and redemption are never necessary to God. God is in no way identical with the necessary processes of the world accessible to a phenomenology formulated outside scriptural faith. Only if this is actually recognized and carried through will it be possible to avoid collapsing theology into anthropology (as Kaufman, Rahner, and Moltmann each do in their own ways).

Eberhard Jüngel presents a particularly instructive analysis of how sacramental theology should be grounded in forgiveness of sins rather than in a conception of sacramentality which thinks of the church as "not really touched by that weakness [sin]," which weakness applies only to individuals.[50] In this connection Jüngel reconceives the notion of the church as mother so as to avoid any idea that the juridical church might be placed on the same level as God the Father. Conceiving the church as spotless mother (as did Pius XII in *Mystici Corporis*) would then imply that the juridical church stands over individuals. But Jüngel's point is that "mother church *is* Christians as they belong together through the Word of God and derive from the Word of God . . . Christians are generated by other human beings only by the proclamation of the gospel, which is the real generative power."[51] Hence if there is any opposition, it is not between individuals and mother church but between the church and the Word of God. For this reason, appealing to Luther, Jüngel rejects thinking of the church as the basic sacrament arguing that the basic sacrament is Jesus himself actively making the church of sinners holy. The church is not our source of holiness because Christ himself is the only source of holiness.

> He is the sacrament which the church receives, to which the church can only testify and which the church must hand on as a recipient. And so prayer for the forgiveness of its *own* sins is the criterion by which we decide whether, in representing itself and presenting the sacramental event, 'mother church' understands itself *secundum dicentem deum* or whether it misunderstands itself as self-representation.[52]

We will perceive the mystery of revelation, i.e., Christ himself only as we see our inclusion in the divine acts of lordship, creation, reconciliation, and redemption as *free* divine actions which can neither be anticipated nor explained. They are facts (*events*) which we may know and rely upon as we encounter the Word of God. This occurs in the human actions of recollection and expectation which bear the mark of this encounter. In this way we will actually perceive God himself in the *form* of creation, without identifying or separating the two. This occurs in the faith given us by God for the purpose of this perception. As we see our inclusion in the divine actions of lordship, creation, reconciliation, and redemption as *necessities*, however, which can be perceived directly in our unconscious drives, our collective unconscious, or some other psychological, sociological, ethnological, philosophical, or anthropological reality (e.g., the human heart as against the human mind), we will perceive only the idea of grace.[53] We will neither perceive the realities of grace, revelation, and faith nor, for that reason, God's *actual* presence. Thus, everything said of Christ's divinity and of the divinity of his real presence will not correspond to an objectively existing reality and will not be real knowledge. This, of course, means admission of another god beside the triune God and in that way demonstrates an abstraction from faith. We have seen that to be in such a position is to have ceased thinking theologically *de facto*.[54] This is why Barth strongly objected to the idea that we can speak truly of God or of his real presence apart from faith. Theological thinking is thus distinguished from philosophical thinking by its acknowledgment that true knowledge takes place *only* in ever new *events* in which people respond obediently to Christ, the object of faith. This reflects the need to begin theology with our reconciliation in Christ acknowledging our need for forgiveness.

4. After Pentecost Christian liturgical action is more urgently oriented toward the remission of sins. This means that because the promise of judgment and grace was fulfilled in Christ we can no longer view grace as overshadowed by judgment. The Gospel of Christ is good news and not bad news to us, i.e., all actually are saved in and with the history of Christ. We need not have a pessimistic viewpoint. This is not because of anything in the world as such, but because of what came *into* the world in Christ, i.e., God himself.

In the Lord's Supper Christians look first to the love and election of God and only in light of this election do they make sense of sin and suffering. Only by seeing first the salvation which we have in virtue of Christ's death can the impossibility of continuing in sin be perceived.[55] Because Christ was this one fully and completely, the church, in its sacramental action and in its ethical action, does not have to concern itself with making amends for its past, present, and future failures. It really has an advocate in the *One* Mediator. The church lives without this anxiety because it has the divine promise, fulfilled in Christ, that its sins are actually forgiven. It may truly live by this promise. The church demonstrates the fact that it does this by not attempting to justify or to sanctify its eucharistic or ethical action. Barth really means that we are relieved of anxiety just because the Lord is at hand to relieve us.

> *The Lord is at hand*. Not, some comforts of religion are at hand; these are but another sign of man's inability to comfort himself. Nor is the Church at hand with its old and new teachings and theologies or with its orders and institutions and with its traditions. The Church's existence is validated not by witness to itself, but only by witness to the Lord who is not dead, but alive, who has not passed away and is past, but comes.[56]

This means that in faith we receive forgiveness of our sins; not through the *seriousness* or *force* of our repentance or our human faith. Nor do we receive forgiveness by the seriousness, force, or frequency of our participation in the Lord's Supper. We certainly do not receive it through any power inherent in the church's action in baptism or the Lord's Supper. Rather we receive this only through Christ himself, in whom we are baptized and in whom we live and move and have our being as in the activity of the Lord's Supper.[57] In faith, repentance does not mean that I ask what I must do to receive forgiveness. Rather I ask what must I do to live the forgiveness which is real and effective apart from my apprehension of it.[58] This analysis by Barth escapes both legalism and licence.[59]

He recognized that no sacramental form, however proper, can effect what has already been effected by God and is continually revealed as effective in the power of the Spirit. This avoids emphasis on the legality of form as the condition for forgiveness. He recognized that in Christ, humanity is very seriously called to live its reconciliation by living by the divine promise. This means obedience is our only human possibility. This avoids emphasis on an abstract concept of freedom which may suggest that because God's forgiveness is not in the power of the church, we are free to do anything we want to do. This is licence. For the pilgrim church, the growth and renewal by the Spirit, involved in living by this promise, must never cease. The moment it is thought to cease, legalism and licence become the probable options.

Jürgen Moltmann also argues persuasively against legalism and licence: "A common law demands uniformity, but the gospel spreads individuality in fellowship. Legalism makes a Christian way of life (and the church's way of life too) pervasively timid and narrow-minded."[60] Hence, Moltmann can argue in connection with the Lord's Supper that "Communion with Christ in his supper is obeying Christ's own invitation, not a christological dogma. For it is the *Lord's* Supper, not something organized by a church or denomination."[61] Emphasizing Christ's pre-eminence over the church, Moltmann maintains that any "denominationally limited 'church supper'" is thus called into question. Hence the Lord's Supper is not the place to practice church discipline. If confession and absolution precede the supper then Christ's "prevenient invitation . . . is linked with legalistic injunctions and moral conditions for 'admission'."[62] Thus, Moltmann properly opposes moral and dogmatic legalism.

Yet, one may legitimately ask about the locus from which the corrective of legalism is to emerge. For Moltmann "We should therefore start from the Lord's supper as something done together and openly, and try to explain the moral questions on the basis of this action and this fellowship."[63] But that is exactly the problem. If the appeal is to the Lord's Supper and not exclusively to the Lord himself as known in faith by those who celebrate this meal, then how can one avoid making the "open" experience of those involved in the meal the criterion for avoiding of legalism? Without going into the many practical and positive suggestions which Moltmann offers, we may note that he does appeal to the "Christian life" in order to overcome legalism and licence. The freedom for which "Christ has set us free" (Gal. 5:1ff.) not only rebels against legalism but it rebels against "libertinism." This is beyond question. But at the decisive point in his argument Moltmann does not in fact appeal to Christ as the solution:

A life 'in accordance with the gospel of Christ' seeks the individual and common messianic way of life. It cannot have anything to do with either legalism or lawlessness, for it looks for forms of the liberated life in experience and for forms of life's liberation in practice. The messianic gospel liberates oppressed life. It gives it bearings and meaning. It gives its stamp to the life in the Spirit.[64]

But if the gospel really is the norm here, then one would not look for forms of a liberated life in experience, including the experience of liberation from oppression. The gospel does indeed bring liberation from oppression, but such liberation follows our obedience to Christ and not our search for liberating forms of activity, whether they be ritual activity or more mundane activities. If legalism and licence are overcome in this way, the door is opened to seeking life in the Spirit in the experience of liberation rather than in the death and resurrection of Christ as preached and known in faith by the community celebrating the Lord's Supper. In my view this leads once again to the reduction of dogmatics to the social functioning of religious concepts, i.e., to a form of self-justification.

5. Baptism and the Lord's Supper have a certain gathering character. In the Eucharist, those individuals who recognize their actual relation with the One Mediator proclaimed in baptism, realize *eo ipso* that they are members of his body and in that way are called in him.[65] As individuals they are called to live as his community. After Pentecost there can be no individualistic application of baptism or the Lord's Supper. It involves and includes the individual, but it does not involve the individual in abstraction from the community. After Pentecost Christ is manifest as Lord of his body, the church. His heavenly-historical form of existence at the right hand of the Father actually includes his earthly-historical form of existence. In him, and therefore by grace, both go together. In him transcendence and immanence can neither be separated nor played off against each other. In him transcendence and immanence have been given a *definite* and *limited* form. Hence transcendence and immanence can no longer be conceived as *formless*, boundless, or limitless. This is the error of all general phenomenologies; they do not proceed from or lead to this particular form of revelation.[66] As the Eucharist does not attest this specific transcendence and immanence it is false (disobedient) action.

Human beings actually are represented before the Father by the risen Lord of the church. They cannot know and live in accordance with this fact if they seek transcendence in some other place or according to some other form. Because Christ is very God and very man even after the resurrection, in the power of the Spirit, we know that individuals are not called to seek the techniques and mysteries of some new religious society. They are called into a "personal relation to the Lord of the Christian community as the one source and cause of all salvation."[67]

A general definition of transcendence and immanence attained apart from the *analogia fidei* will not be bound to this particular form as the human expression of communion. Since a general definition of transcendence and immanence does not necessarily begin in faith in *vere Deus vere homo* it does not have to end in faith in *vere Deus vere homo*. Hence, it cannot be knowledge which is limited on all sides by the triune God. It cannot be knowledge enclosed in the mystery of the Trinity. Thus it cannot be true and certain knowledge of transcendence or immanence. At best it can only be one opinion among so many others. Faith is essential as the starting point and conclusion of any intelligible discussion of transcendence and immanence; thus grace and revelation are the indispensable presuppositions for true knowledge in this matter. Grace, faith, and revelation must precede and determine human thinking. Otherwise all three factors may be dismissed or transformed to mean something other than the actions of the triune God who loves in freedom.[68]

Part of living as one who is called into this fellowship consists in the "breaking of bread and prayers."[69] Celebration of the Lord's Supper is a decisive response to one's baptism by the Holy Spirit and one's free entrance into the body of Christ in the act of requesting water baptism. The human action of the Lord's Supper is possible because the Spirit of Christ continually awakens the members of his body to the realization of the fellowship which he alone creates and sustains. People are not called into the body of Christ for themselves or for nothing; they are called into his body to attest the fact that God is the One who loves in freedom and thus includes them in his own knowledge and love. In that way the person who celebrates the Eucharist will accept his or her fellow-humanity as God accepted and accepts him or her. This is how Barth avoided individualism without falling into monism or collectivism.

6. After Pentecost the Lord's Supper can neither be viewed simply as a fellowship meal nor as an action which is initiated or fulfilled by people for their personal edification. It is a meal whose basis and goal is the messiah and savior of the world.[70] Thus, the community can recognize its actual inclusion in the fulfilled covenant only as it knows in faith that its particular basis and goal is in the history of Christ; any other supposed inclusion can be dismissed as an ideology. Both Jews and Gentiles are called to unity by recognizing the true basis and goal of their existence. To seek unity on any other basis and goal is to seek a false unity.[71] What was once the promise of Israel is now also a promise for the world. From the standpoint of Christ alone both Jews and Gentiles may know that there is really one Lord, one faith, one baptism, one God, and only one body of Christ and one bread. The goal of the Lord's Supper acquires unmistakable clarity and precision after Pentecost. It is no longer an unknown and future possibility. It is known clearly in faith. It is Christ, the savior of the world.[72]

As Israel and the church, in their unity, attest the one being of Christ, so the Passover meal and the Lord's Supper go together. But even in their unity, there is a distinction. Both attest the reality of revelation. Both are meaningful as they are faithful human expressions of God's election of grace.[73] The Passover meal and the Eucharist attest the twofold form of God's eternal election of Christ himself.[74] Neither the Passover nor the Eucharist have meaning in themselves. They have it only as the community recognizes its actual reconciled being in Christ. The Passover meal attests God's judgment upon human sin and his merciful decision to remain faithful to humanity in and through his community. In the Eucharist the church witnesses to God's mercy.[75] The actual form of God's *yes* to humanity was in the path from judgment (Christ's rejection and death on the cross) to mercy (Christ's resurrection and the concrete overcoming of the power of death). The eternal election of Christ is effective for us irrespective of our positive or negative attitude. This is what is attested in the Lord's Supper. Because Christ's death is remembered as a sacrifice *for us*, i.e., an eternal intercession by Christ on behalf of those (us) who are helpless, the Eucharist is a "cause for joy, hope, and gratitude."[76] The basis and goal of the Lord's Supper is the church's eternal election in Christ. Hence the community does not *control* its being, even in the Eucharist. The truth of its being consists exclusively in its faithful *following* of its living Lord. Even the slightest idea of mutual conditioning between Christ and the church is thus excluded.[77]

From the point of view of eschatology this free act and gift of God, this divine salvation and revelation was the work begun at Easter. It has continued in the various outpourings of the Holy Spirit in confirmation of this beginning. It is God's promise that this will continue until its completion in the last definitive and universal revelation of Christ.[78] Non-Christian eschatology, however, will not keep to this point.[79] A general eschatology, formulated outside the *analogia fidei*, will identify the finality of world history with all kinds of peculiar and dark events. But Christians know in faith that, as Christ is the goal of baptism and the Lord's Supper, he is the goal of redemption. Consequently because the election of grace was God's effective *yes* which included a definite *no*, only a false eschatology will try to present this *no* and *yes* as though they were symmetrical. Because the *no* is only explicable in light of the *yes* we can trust that God does not seek our final destruction but our salvation. No more than this can be said without resolving the mystery of revelation itself.

We may conclude this chapter by noting that for Barth, as Christ alone and not an idea or experience of Christ is the basis and goal of baptism and the Lord's Supper, he *alone* is the guarantee that, in both of these events, the church is living something different from *all other* rituals known and unknown, imaginable or unimaginable. In connection with baptism this means that all initiation rites or acts of dedication differ from Christian baptism at this decisive point. In connection with the Lord's Supper this means that all supposedly sacred meals or rites of fellowship which can be seen and investigated by a philosophy of religion differ from the Christian act of worship which has a very specific basis and goal. This basis and goal determines its truth character. Jesus Christ in person and he alone is the salvation history which God planned in eternity and effected in history.[80] Kingdom, judgment, grace, nature, human and divine being, transcendence and immanence refer absolutely to him. Only in light of his history will the church recognize that the living Christ himself is the possibility and limitation of the church's fellowship with God which it celebrates in the Eucharist. The limitation here is the fact that the church can only follow and never precede its living Lord. In this specific limitation the church lives the possibility, given by God, of being humanly faithful to the covenant of grace.

Because Christ is very God and very man, we know it is the triune God whom we meet in the Lord's Supper. He is the only possible basis and goal of the church's action in the Lord's Supper. After the resurrection, the Holy Spirit does not reveal someone or something else. He reveals Christ, the eternal Logos of the Father, who is one *ad intra* and *ad extra* in the act of being creator, reconciler, and redeemer. He himself—not a sign or symbol of him—in the power of his Spirit stands as the *terminus a quo* and the *terminus ad quem* of the Eucharist. Baptized Christians do not move from an *unknown* toward an *unknown* in the faith given them by the Holy Spirit or in their faithful human response to the Holy Spirit, i.e., their ethical behavior. They move from the triune God toward the triune God who pre-existed and upholds them in time as time moves toward its completion in him. Christians go forward as those who have their entire being in Christ. They have no other basis and therefore seek no other goal, noetically or ontically. In other words, Christians live their lives theoretically and practically enclosed in the mystery of the Trinity. They do not try to escape this by thinking away this mystery or by abstracting from it. This means that Christians have and can live their lives as members of Christ's body on earth only in *faith*.[81] If that is the case then the meaning of the Lord's Supper as a human action is decided by its basis and goal.

Notes

1. C.D. 4, 4, p. 69, C.D. 4, 2, p. 655.

2. Ibid.

3. See Barth's portrayal of the *terminus a quo* and *terminus ad quem* of our knowledge of God in C.D. 2, 1, pp. 185ff. This applies here.

4. See C.D. 4, 2, pp. 653ff. and C.D. 2, 1, pp. 462–90.

5. C.D. 4, 4, pp. 71–3.

6. Moltmann, *Creation*, pp. 16–17.

7. Cf., e.g., Elizabeth A. Johnson, *She Who Is: The Mystery of God in Feminist Theological Discourse* (New York: Crossroad, 1992), pp. 34ff. and 68f. See also Sallie McFague, *Models of God: Theology for an Ecological, Nuclear Age*, (Philadelphia: Fortress Press, 1987, hereafter abbreviated: *Models*). Gordon Kaufman certainly sees the situation this way, *TNA*, pp. 32–33, *TI*, pp. 274, 287, n. 5, and *An Essay On Theological Method*, p. 64. Elizabeth Johnson's argument is that "The symbol God functions," p. 38 and that it must be made to function to include women which it cannot do unless God is described in female as well as male categories. She ignores the theological problems of whether such a social purpose should dictate theological usage of language; whether naming God as male and female means introducing Arianism and Gnosticism into the Christian doctrine of God; and whether or not women's status is indeed better in societies in which people believe in gods and goddesses. For an accurate analysis of these issues see Roland Frye, *SJT*.

8. Cf. Wolfhart Pannenberg, *An Introduction to Systematic Theology*, (Grand Rapids: William B. Eerdmans Publishing Company, 1991 hereafter abbreviated: *Introduction)*, p. 15. Cf. *Systematic Theology I*, p. 242 and chapter one.

9. Pannenberg, *Systematic Theology I*, pp. 261–3.

10. C.D. 1, 2, p. 365. Barth's understanding of the election of the community and individuals in Christ and of election and rejection is a fine application of this, C.D. 2, 2, pp. 306ff.

11. Ibid., pp. 365–66. Cf. also C.D. 4, 3, pp. 380ff. Jesus Christ, as the true Witness, is the truth of our reconciled human nature acting in the world as the promise of the Spirit. This is his prophetic office. His human life was a free act of obedience because it was lived in service of God for us. God, in his care for this man, enabled him to be faithful and approved and accepted his life. Thus, "on both sides freedom is the form and character of the intercourse between true God and true man, i.e., of the intercourse which determines the existence of this man and in the fulfilment of which He declares the truth and is the true Witness. It is in this way and this way alone, in this reciprocal freedom, that this intercourse corresponds to the relationship between God and man and man and God by which the existence of this man is constituted. The offering which corresponds to God's turning to this man, His act of obedience, His rendering of service, is His free act. It is not prompted, motivated or conditioned by the thought of a reward to be received from God . . . In exactly the same way the distinction which corresponds to the address of God to this man, and with which He crowns Him, is God's free act. He bestows it without any consideration of merit. It is not a counter-achievement to the achievement required by Him and

fulfilled by this man. It is God's great reward, but it is not a payment . . . on the basis of a higher law." pp. 381-82.

12. Ibid., p. 366.

13. Moltmann, *Creation*, p. 206.

14. Ibid., p. 22.

15. Ibid.

16. Moltmann, *The Way of Jesus Christ*, p. 278f.

17. Ibid., p. 263.

18. Ibid., p. 178 and Moltmann, *Trinity*, pp. 160 and 168. Cf. also John Thompson, *Modern Trinitarian Perspectives*, pp. 50-2 and 61-3.

19. Moltmann, *Trinity*, p. 38.

20. Moltmann, *The Way of Jesus Christ*, p. 131.

21. Ibid., pp. 135ff.

22. Kaufman, *TNA*, p. 54.

23. Ibid., pp. 44-45.

24. Ibid., p. 56.

25. Ibid., p. 57.

26. Sallie McFague, *Models*, pp. 136ff., reaches similar conclusions regarding Christ while arguing against Kaufman that God should be conceived personally rather than impersonally. But her criticism of Kaufman is questionable because both she and Kaufman are led by their interpretation of Christianity to deny the basis and goal of all Christian theology, i.e., Jesus as true God and true man and as the One Mediator.

27. C.D. 4, 4, p. 73.

28. C.D. 1, 2, p. 500.

29. C.D. 4, 4, p. 73.

30. C.D. 4, 2, p. 655f.

31. C.D. 4, 4, p. 88.

32. Alasdair Heron, *Table and Tradition*, p. 157.

33. Ibid. pp. 158-59.

34. C.D. 4, 4, p. 88. Barth is right not to identify Christ's free action with our faith and obedience. But at this point in our discussion we begin to see the problem in Barth's thought identified by Heron. The church's act in the Lord's Supper is not itself (of its own power) God's speech and action. But why can it not become so in the power of the Spirit?

35. C.D. 4, 4, p. 72. Cf. also C.D. 2, 2, p. 320.

36. C.D. 4, 3, pp. 213–20.

37. C.D. 4, 4, p. 74.

38. Ibid., p. 50.

39. See C.D. 1, 2, pp. 446ff. where Barth notes that for human witness to be a sign of God's act we must recognize that we cannot give it, make it effective, or bring the help which it attests. See also C.D. 1, 2, p. 701. Barth's understanding of miracle is decisive for every aspect of his theology. It might even be said that it is his insistence that theology itself takes place as a miracle (a human act which is begun, upheld, and completed by God without compromising humanity or divinity) that sets Barth off most sharply from other contemporary theologians who believe it is no longer possible to understand God as intervening directly in human affairs. Cf. Rahner *HW*, pp. 66–7 and *Foundations*, p. 87 for how Rahner sees God operating in history. Cf. Moltmann, *Creation*, p. 211 for his view. In contrast to Barth, Moltmann and Rahner virtually rule out God coming into history from outside. For specific details in connection with Barth's understanding of miracle, see, e.g., C.D. 1, 2, pp. 60 and 63. Among contemporary commentators on Barth, George Hunsinger, *How to Read Karl Barth*, (New York: Oxford University Press, 1991) notices this important aspect of Barth's thought and takes it seriously.

40. C.D. 4, 4, p. 75.

41. Important here is the fact that the disciples' hope was not empty but fulfilled in Christ, C.D. 3, 2, pp. 493ff. The Passover meal becomes an Easter meal in the fact that the disciples actually ate with the risen Lord (Lk. 24–31–35; Jn. 21:4, 12, 15; Ac. 10:41), "'(We) did eat and drink with him after he rose from the dead'. This not only proves the reality of the resurrection (Lk. 24:41f.), but also its tremendous import and far-reaching consequence. No longer, as at the Last Supper, will they sit at meat with Him in anticipation of His sacrifice, but in retrospect of its completion; not in a re-presentation and repetition . . . but in a simple and full enjoyment of its benefits, of the eternal life won for us in Him . . ." The Lord's Supper as an Easter meal has its basis in the resurrection and yet looks forward to the parousia as the final event "consummating that of Easter," C.D. 3, 2, p. 502. For more on how the second coming relates to Easter (as the completion of the parousia) see C.D. 4, 3, pp. 274–367.

42. See C.D. 1, 1, pp. 465–6, C.D. 1, 2, pp. 221ff., C.D. 2, 2, pp. 764–781, C.D. 4, 1, pp. 668ff., 693ff., and C.D. 4, 3, pp. 274–367.

43. C.D. 4, 4, p. 79. See Barth's definition of sin as the impossible possibility, C.D. 1, 2, p. 398, C.D. 2, 1, p. 506, and C.D. 3, 2, p. 146. This is what he

means. Cf. also C.D. 4, 3, pp. 249–274.

44. C.D. 4, 4, p. 78.

45. Cf. C.D. 2, 2, pp. 318–19.

46. Ibid., 764ff.

47. C.D. 4, 4, p. 79.

48. C.D. 4, 3, p. 8. This is what we know from the Holy Spirit. The Spirit is no less valuable and helpful than the presence of Christ. The Spirit actually is the prophetic presence of Christ, C.D. 4, 3, pp. 358ff.

49. In connection with Rahner's theology of the symbol we saw that his thought followed a logical sequence: Christ is a particular instance (the highest) of symbolic mediation. Therefore "The revelation history which occurs in *Jesus* and is grasped by us in faith should not in the first instance be treated as a particular occurrence . . ." T.I. 16:69. Symbols are the necessary expression of the reality symbolized and thus sacramental signs have "an effectiveness *inherent* in the sign precisely *as* such," T.I. 14:177. It follows that "If a man freely accepts himself as he is . . . then it is God he is accepting," T.I. 16:67. These necessities compromise the freedom just discussed.

50. Eberhard Jüngel *Theological Essays*, trans. and Intro. J. B. Webster, (Edinburgh: T. & T. Clark, 1989), chapter seven, pp. 189–213, at pp. 206–212.

51. Ibid., p. 208.

52. Ibid., p. 211.

53. Cf. C.D. 1, 1, pp. 149ff. and 204ff.

54. See, e.g., C.D. 2, 1, pp. 15–26 and Barth, *Anselm*, p. 128, where the idea is expressed that a God who exists merely epistemologically "would be called God but would not be God."

55. C.D. 4, 4, pp. 80–1. Barth gave a particularly compelling presentation of this in *Credo* (New York: Scribner's, 1962), p. 43. "Jesus Christ is the background from which man's misery and despair receive their light and not vice versa. What is the significance of that? Clearly, this: there is, so to speak, an unfruitful knowledge of sin, of evil, of death and the devil, that succeeds in making it hard for man to have happy and confident faith in the Almighty Father and Creator, but without making possible for him, or even bringing nearer, faith in Jesus Christ as reconciler . . . Grace must come first, in order that sin may be manifest to us as sin, and death as death . . . " pp. 43–44.

56. Karl Barth, *Deliverance to the Captives*, (New York: Harper and Row, 1959), p. 104. This was a Christmas sermon based on Phil. 4:5–6.

57. See Ac. 10:42ff.

58. See C.D. 4, 3, pp. 670–71 and C.D. 2, 2, pp. 742–81; C.D. 4, 4, p. 82. On this distinction turns the difference between self-justification and justification in Christ. The former consists in abstraction from faith, grace, and revelation. The latter means living by faith, grace, and revelation. For an important additional analysis of this see Karl Barth, *Prayer*, pp. 76ff. and, regarding religion and revelation see C.D. 1, 2, 349ff.

59. For more on legalism and lawlessness as the alternatives to abstraction from faith, see C.D. 2, 2, pp. 486ff.

60. Moltmann, *The Church in the Power*, p. 277.

61. Ibid., p. 244.

62. Ibid., p. 245.

63. Ibid.

64. Ibid., p. 278.

65. C.D. 4, 4, pp. 82–3.

66. Sallie McFague's "ontological (or cosmological) sacramentalism," *Models*, p. 135, overcomes the problem of individualism by making the world God's body and then obliterating both individual and divine freedom. We "do not love God one by one in vertical relationships of beloved to lover, but as we love the world, God's body . . . we are in this loving of the world loving God . . . now the beloved cannot be God alone: it must also be the world that is the expression of God and that God loves," p. 129. Here individual freedom is compromised by the fact that individuals are merged into the rest of creation and cannot relate "vertically" with God. God's freedom is compromised since God is intrinsically related to the world as his bodily expression or as McFague says: "God needs it," pp. 131ff.; thus creation is necessary for God to be God and "God needs us to help save the world!" p. 135. Here it is clear that compromising God's freedom by defining God from the human experience of love, rather than from God's free action of love in Christ, has practical consequences. It leads McFague directly to the idea that we have the capacity to be our own saviors (denying our actual sinfulness and the need for forgiveness) and that Christ himself cannot be the only savior because he is only paradigmatic of God's love but not ontologically unique, pp. 136 and 144. Here, in the name of Christianity, the very center of Christianity is denied, i.e., that Christ is the only savior, because he is indeed ontologically unique. Recognizing this particular uniqueness actually safeguards our individual freedom (as well as that of the community) by acknowledging its basis and goal in God's *free* action *ad extra*. In Christ individuals (together with the community) may relate with God vertically and *for* the world on the basis of forgiveness. And in Christ we know that God neither needs the world nor is

displaced by the world as the object of our love, as he is in McFague's pantheism.

67. C.D. 4, 4, p. 83.

68. See C.D. 2, 1, p. 303 on this point.

69. Cf. Ac. 2:42ff. In *Acts* the practical connection between baptism and the Lord's Supper was explicated in the "house-and table-fellowship between the baptised and the one who administers it" (Cf. C.D. 4, 4, p. 83).

70. C.D. 4, 4, pp. 84ff.

71. See, e.g., C.D. 4, 1, pp. 665–739.

72. C.D. 4, 4, pp. 84, 87. A clear illustration of how this truth is compromised is seen in Knitter's idea of "doing before knowing" in order to understand who Jesus is. He appeals to liberation theology to argue that it is only in the practical following of Jesus that we can know him. All Christians would agree with that. But Knitter does not mean that we must actually follow Jesus; he means that we must work for the kingdom vision of liberation with the rest of humanity and then discover that Jesus cannot be the only savior and only norm for truth because Christians cannot really know who Jesus is unless other religions are consulted. Therefore, there must be other saviors since in fact other people also are working for the betterment of society and do not actually regard Jesus as the only savior. Cf. Knitter, *No Other Name?* and Molnar *The Thomist* 55 (1991): 486ff. for more on this problem. Like McFague, Knitter is led by his starting point to deny the most basic claims of the Christian faith in the name of Christianity. He denies that Christ is the only savior; that we actually need Christ to know the kingdom of God; and that we are saved by faith alone, because he affirms that we can save ourselves by working for the liberation of society.

73. See C.D. 2, 2, pp. 233–59; C.D. 4, 1, p. 672.

74. C.D. 2, 2, p. 199. See also Markus Barth, *Rediscovering the Lord's Supper*, pp. 23ff. who argues persuasively that the Lord's Supper does not signify a radical break between Israel and the church.

75. I.e., God's eternal decision for fellowship with us, C.D. 2, 2, pp. 1–25.

76. Markus Barth, *Rediscovering the Lord's Supper*, p. 22.

77. Cf. C.D. 1, 2, pp. 350ff., C.D. 2, 1, pp. 66, 141–51ff., 215–17, C.D. 4, 2, pp. 651–60.

78. C.D. 4, 4, p. 89.

79. Cf. C.D. 2, 1, p. 393.

80. C.D. 4, 4, p. 90.

81. Ibid., pp. 95ff.

VIII

The Meaning of the Lord's Supper as the Work of Creatures

We have seen that for Barth the basis and goal of the human action in the Lord's Supper is and remains God himself in the action of the Holy Spirit. This particular basis and goal is no different from the basis and goal of all human knowledge and action, including the acts of knowing connected with the church's christological and ecclesiological reflections. For Barth we know this from faith, which, as we have seen, thrives upon the *fact* of God's objective existence as attested in scripture.[1] Knowledge which takes place in faith neither attempts to *identify* the spheres of primary objectivity (God in himself) and secondary objectivity (the reality distinct from God and dependent upon him) nor does it attempt to *separate* the two spheres. But it does not ascribe this binding of the two spheres to anything or to anyone other than the *free grace* of God himself. It is only because the one who is self-sufficient *in se* and *ad extra* does not cease being self-sufficient in revealing himself in and through the sphere of secondary objectivity that true human knowledge and action are possible. Because God is really like this, true human knowledge and action can only be *events*, i.e., *actions* in which people faithfully respond to God who is known in faith. Human knowledge and action, however, do not escape the sphere of secondary objectivity in an encounter with God; they do not become more than human actions and for that very reason they do not confront God *directly*. Human thoughts and actions confront only other human thoughts and actions directly. We know and act *indirectly* in relation to God, as we apprehend God in himself (primary objectivity) in and through the objects *chosen by God* to bear witness to himself (secondary objectivity). But the sole norm for the truth of this knowledge is God and not the objects chosen by God to bear witness to himself. Hence we can do no more than recall the divine action and pray that God will continue to act.

Barth's belief that human knowledge is an *event* in which people respond obediently to the triune God applies decisively to the church's eucharistic action. The truth of Barth's analysis depends entirely upon the truth that the triune God is the same *ad intra* and *ad extra*. What is different, as we have seen, is the *ad extra* reality (creation) in and through which God encounters people. This means that everything depends upon the fact that it is with the immanent Trinity that we have to do in the economy of salvation (i.e., creation).[2] Consequently, in the man Jesus we do not have to do with a God who is *in any way* different from the one who loves in freedom *ad intra*, i.e., in the sphere of primary objectivity. We must emphasize here that it is the failure to perceive this fact that is the point of origin of all nominalistic or idealistic interpretations of the incarnation, of the church, and of the Lord's Supper. This certainly applies to those nominalistic views discussed above. On the one hand, Barth does not leave the being of God open to any arbitrary definition by creatures. On the other hand, he can ground human freedom decisively in the being of God rather than in human being conceived according to some religious or social model. To put it another way, Barth does not allow God to be defined by our experiences of salvation. Therefore, while God certainly is in relation to creation from creation to consummation, this is a relationship of grace. For that reason, relationality never becomes the subject, with God the predicate. God always remains the subject.

One example here should help. Sallie McFague asks what is to prevent her models of God as mother, lover, and friend from being arbitrary. Her answer is that they are not arbitrary "because, along with the father model, they are the deepest and most important expressions of love known to us, rather than because they are necessarily descriptive of the nature of God." In this thinking we have not moved beyond the experiences of love known to us in the sphere of creation. On the one hand, this leads to the idea that one cannot know whether these models describe God's inner being. On the other hand this leads to the idea that the only love we can know anything about and that matters is the love we experience in these basic relationships. And the problem with this nominalistic thinking is that it promotes the very dualism which McFague intends to oppose. It compels her to a "pragmatic view of truth" which reduces the reality of God to "a personal, gracious power who is on the side of life and its fulfillment, a power whom the paradigmatic figure Jesus of Nazareth expresses and illuminates."[3] But if one wished to identify that power more precisely, one would not turn to Jesus of Nazareth, but to the experiences of love which are dear to us. Thus, her thought is not governed by who Jesus was as the unique mediator (the only Son of the Father). Rather, his love only helps to illuminate the kind of love that McFague presupposes will make the world more humane. Hence

His [Jesus'] illumination of that love as inclusive of the last and the least, as embracing and valuing the outcast, is paradigmatic of God the lover but is not unique . . . Jesus is not ontologically different from other paradigmatic figures . . .[4]

Her understanding of salvation similarly departs from any knowledge of God's inner being as Father, Son, and Spirit and thus leads to the dualistic conclusion that there could be many saviors.[5] The idea that there could be many saviors is only possible in a version of Christianity which insists that God the Son did not indeed become incarnate in the history of Jesus of Nazareth. Karl Barth overcame dualism just because his knowledge was grounded in the incarnate Son of God. Thus our knowledge is governed by who God really is in his inner being and who he has shown himself to be in the history of Jesus Christ. We can really know and distinguish God from idols as our knowledge is grounded in Christ as the knowledge of faith. We can also be certain of our salvation as we believe in the only savior. By contrast, for McFague, we cannot know but may "wager" about who God is. And the certainty of salvation becomes the uncertainty with which we humans can and must work for a more humane world.

One might object to this analysis, as Sallie McFague indeed does, by saying that it is simply "Barthian" and that therefore one must say that all love should conform to the "divine pattern." But, simply dismissing the fact that the reality of God's inner being as Father, Son, and Spirit can be known (and indeed must be known if theology is to recognize its true object and its true source of freedom) does not solve the problem here. For, in the gap provided by the nominalist assumption that God's inner essence cannot be known,[6] McFague has actually introduced her own pragmatic view of the truth of Christianity in place of the truth recognized by the tradition. And the problem with this is that it not only permits no *actual* knowledge of God's inner being, but that God's inner being becomes whatever we can imagine it to be in order to create a more humane world. Hence, in this perspective, there can be many gods and many saviors just as God, in reality, is indistinguishable from *our pragmatic use* of models in order to realize various social and political objectives, such as overcoming the nuclear threat or improving the environment.

To return to Barth's view, we again emphasize that we do not relate with God *directly* because we do not exist in the sphere of primary objectivity. Thus, any assumption of direct knowledge here (including the assumption of nominalism) would be a denial of the distinct existence of both God and creatures. Still, we do have to do with God himself and not someone or something else. We have to do with him *indirectly*, in and through the sphere which is proper to creation, i.e., the sphere of secondary objectivity.

Similarly, the work of the Holy Spirit in the economy of salvation (creation) cannot be regarded as different *in any way* from the being of the one who loves in freedom *ad intra*.[7] The work of the Holy Spirit *ad extra*, through which the community is enabled by God himself to live its communion with him and its fellowship with others, cannot point to anything other than the history in which the man Jesus was disclosed as the Son of God. This history is recognizable insofar as the church is the provisional form of Christ's continued special presence in the world.[8] To obscure this divine action in any way means we fail to recognize God himself acting here. The divine action is obscured: first, if it is thought to be identical with the *oikonomia*;[9] second, if even momentarily, we try to reverse the *priority* of God's immanent and economic existence; or third, if we try to *separate* the two rather than to distinguish them (this would end in dualism); and finally, if we ground the communion between God and us in anyone or anything other than Christ himself. This is the reason why Barth insisted that an abstract concept of analogy was useless in theology. As one's analogy is not subordinate to Christ as known in faith, creatures become the criterion both of human and of divine action. This was the classical error illustrated by Feuerbach.

When, as in the case of Feuerbach, this confusion and reversal of the creator/creature relationship takes place, there can no longer be any serious talk of *either* creator *or* creatures, divine or human reality, and therefore of church or sacraments; these distinct entities would invariably be indistinguishable from one another. This is why Feuerbach thought he could define God as the "epitome of the generic human qualities distributed among men, in the self-realization of the species in the course of world history."[10] And Christ is defined as

the consciousness of the species. We are all supposed to be one in Christ. Christ is the consciousness of our unity. Therefore whoever loves man for the sake of man, whoever rises to the love of the species, to the universal love adequate to the nature of the species, is a Christian; he is Christ himself.[11]

As both God and Christ are indistinguishable from our own human act of consciousness and love in this way, the question of any real relationship between God and us is dissolved into an apotheosis. This problem arises when it is thought that there are true analogies for God and Christ *apart* from *faith* in God's *action ad extra* in his Word and Spirit. The importance of the *analogia fidei* can be seen here: in faith theologians clearly distinguish God and Christ from the rest of us in order to explicate the truth that we relate with God (as a distinct being) by grace and revelation.

Union of the *Analogia Fidei* and the Event of the Lord's Supper

Some further explanation as to why we do not know God *directly* is necessary. Because God is and remains the *same* one who exists in his triunity *ad intra* and *ad extra*, he alone, in the unity of his being and action, absolutely precedes and determines human being and action without dissolving the character of human self-determination.[12] It is because God is God in his actions of creation, reconciliation, and redemption *ad extra*, and we are human in our actions as creatures (the ones who are reconciled and redeemed) that we do not see or conceive God *directly*. Only another God could do that.[13] In this sense God in himself remains hidden from us, even in his action *ad extra*. Hiddenness is not something ascribed to God by us. It is part of the divine being itself. Consequently, it is the nature of the divine being itself which dictates the Christian's understanding of human being and action, including human being and action in the Lord's Supper. This is a key point. God has chosen to encounter humanity *indirectly* in and through creation without abandoning or dissolving his divinity (self-sufficiency), or the created realm. Unless we recognize both of these facts, we comprehend neither of them.

It is precisely because God is who he is antecedently in himself that the possibility and limitation of human being and action is not found in any positive or negative conception or experience of God or creatures. God is the one who loves in freedom and *not* by necessity. God is one who is revealed yet hidden, unveiled and yet veiled,[14] immanent yet transcendent. Thus, the possibility and limitation of human being and action is *nothing* and *no one* other than the triune God himself who is the same *ad intra* and in his action *ad extra*. Only Christ is this factual possibility and limitation for people in the church. As such, he (the grace of God) is necessary for people to know that God is the *terminus a quo* and *terminus ad quem* of the Lord's Supper.

Following a phenomenology of meal or of personal presence, the negative aspect of the divine freedom is invariably forgotten. For Barth, the negative aspect of the divine freedom (God's transcendence and divinity) can only be conceived correctly if the positive aspect (God's freedom to exist in himself) is first acknowledged. The negative side of God's freedom (his freedom from internal and external conditioning) is important. But the emphasis is on the positive and not the negative.

> We cannot possibly grasp and expound the idea of divine creation and providence, nor even the ideas of divine omnipotence, omnipresence and eternity, without constantly referring to this negative aspect of His freedom. But we shall be able to do so properly only when we do so against the background . . . that God's freedom constitutes the essential positive quality, not only of His action towards what is outside Himself, but also of His own inner being. The biblical witness to God sees His transcendence . . . not only in the distinction as such [from creation] . . . without sacrificing His distinction and freedom, but in the exercise of them, He enters into and faithfully maintains communion with this reality other than himself in His activity as Creator, Reconciler and Redeemer.[15]

Absolute Basis and Goal of the Lord's Supper

For this reason, a clear concept of the Lord's Supper typifies a clear explication of the being and activity of the triune God himself *ad intra* and *ad extra*. God himself (primary objectivity) is not identical with creation (secondary objectivity) even and especially in Christ. This has both positive and negative implications. At this point it will be useful to summarize Barth's view of the incarnation and of God's freedom in order to show how this relates to a phenomenological approach to the sacraments. The aim is to see how his *analogia fidei* connects with his view of the Lord's Supper and to be able to assess his rejection of the term sacrament later in the *C.D.* Here it is important to see exactly why the meaning of the Lord's Supper as a creaturely work must always be found in the free action of God if it is to have a theological and not just an anthropological meaning.

Incarnation

For Barth, the incarnation is the historical *event* in which we know that God has in *fact* chosen to unveil himself and in reality has done so.[16] But the locus of this particular unveiling is always the veiled reality of creation in which he reveals himself. This actuality is our human possibility and limitation. We know this with certainty from the incarnation as such, which is God's special action of unveiling that which is by nature veiled. That is why the incarnation is not and can never become a general dogmatic principle. It is an *event* which takes place in the freedom of God on the basis of which dogmatics is possible. Thus, in answer to Gogarten, Barth distinguished the two natures and the immanent and economic Trinity in order to maintain both the divinity of the unveiling and the positive point that history (creation) actually exists and has its true basis and goal in an act of the sovereign God. Moreover the secularity of history includes the fact that the veil is thick, namely, that history not only does not disclose God's unveiling but actually contradicts it—a miracle is needed for God's mystery to be unveiled without setting aside the utter secularity of creation. For Barth

> Theological thought is distinguished from philosophical thought by the fact
> that it does not regard the incarnation of the Word as the truth of a state,
> e.g., the truth of the unity of subject and object, of the man-relatedness of
> God or the God-relatedness of man, which is then an underlying principle
> of dogmatics that has to be exegeted . . . but regards it rather as the truth
> of a divine act . . . then the *terminus a quo* ('God in himself') and the
> *terminus ad quem* ('man in himself') must be differentiated and then

interrelated in the description of the act as such . . . the Word of God is
properly understood only as a word which has truth and glory in itself and
not just spoken to us.[17]

We have already seen in chapters three and four that Barth rejected both the
idea that Christ's humanity as such reveals God and the idea that there are
analogies which are true in themselves. Here it is important to stress that the
underlying reason for his position is traceable to his distinction between
philosophy and theology and ultimately to the distinction between the truth and
glory of God's Word *in se* and *ad extra*. Rejecting identity here, Barth
maintained the traditional Chalcedonian formulation of the two natures, unmixed
(and therefore not identical), distinguished but also not separated.[18] Because faith
is from God *alone*, it is not identical with any immanent human transformation
(moral or otherwise) which may take place in consequence of faith.[19] Therefore
God, the Holy Spirit, must always be distinguishable from our human response
if there is to be any true theological understanding. As discussed above, Barth's
rejection of identity in speaking of the incarnation determines both his concept of
analogy and of reality.[20] It even caused him to repudiate his own position in the
first edition of *C.D.* 1, 1, because it led people to think he embraced natural
theology. For Barth the principal point here is that there is a way from
Christology to anthropology, but there is no way from anthropology to Christology.[21] To identify the two natures or the immanent and economic Trinity
would represent another attempt by the creature to become God's master.[22] For
Barth, the error of mysticism,[23] of Schleiermacher,[24] of Hegel,[25] and in general
of nineteenth-century theology, consisted in their uncritical presumption of
identity here.[26] They failed to note God's holiness which, as we have seen,
implies the divine freedom in which God has the right to make himself known as
he so chooses, while at the same time he remains uniquely transcendent. Since the
Godhead remains transcendent, even in relation to Christ's humanity, its
immanence cannot cease to be an event in the Old Testament sense, namely,
"always a new thing, something that God actually brings into being in specific
circumstances."[27]

As we have seen, this insight led Barth to maintain that there can be no
divinization of Christ's human nature,[28] and that in becoming man Christ did not
change himself *into* a man so that his *divinity* in some sense ceased.[29] The point
here is that unless this distinction is seen in the doctrine of God and in
Christology, the human action or the elements in the Lord's Supper will be seen
as meaningful in themselves. But then a phenomenology of the action or elements
will be thought to supply what only faith, grace, and revelation can in reality
supply. Once again the creature will have been substituted (in his or her self-

understanding) for the grace of God revealed in Christ. In that way, God's real presence in his Word and Spirit would become confused with the human action, the elements, or with both of them.

We have seen that, for Barth, there is communion between God and creatures in Christ but no merging of primary objectivity into secondary objectivity. Christ is unique because in him *alone* there was restored perfect communion between God and humanity. Humanity in general does not have this communion with God. People have it only in Christ and only as Christ's fulfilled history becomes a saving history for persons at particular times and places. This must be an *event* in which the freedom of God and human freedom remain intact. It must occur again and again that God speaks and people respond. Any merging of these two spheres destroys any *real* communion between the two distinct realities of God and creatures. This is why Barth was concerned that theology speak of the reality of God and not just an idea or experience of God. In speaking of the reality of God who seeks and creates fellowship in freedom, the Lord's Supper has a transcendent, firm, and absolute basis and goal which was not discovered by us and can neither be controlled nor called into question by us.

Experience and the Knowledge of God

This insight then represented a consistent application of Barth's conviction that because human knowing did not discover God for itself, God's existence could not be called into question epistemologically.[30] Similarly, as God's existence was not discovered existentially, i.e., on the basis of human existence as such, it could not be called into question by any existential questions. A god who exists on the basis of human knowing (idea) or human existence (experience) is not God at all. Hence, to question the existence of God on epistemological or existential grounds would be to question the existence of something that in reality does not exist. This important insight shows that unless the basis and goal of the church's activity in the Lord's Supper is in God himself, and not an idea or experience of God, it can be questioned from without on epistemological or existential grounds. This would mean that, on the basis of a general epistemology or ontology (i.e., one conceived in abstraction from *faith*), a person may ask whether in the Lord's Supper he or she has to do with God himself. Abstracting from faith, people may assume that they merely have to do with a profound idea or experience which may in reality have nothing to do with the reality of God. God may then be described as our friend in the sense that God is "relational" and indeed "intrinsically relational" and is thus interrelated with other forms of life. Using human friendship as the model for defining God's relation with us then would lead to the absolutizing of relationality rather than to any genuine recognition of

God. Thus, for example, Sallie McFague writes that "the Christian insistence on relationality, expressed scripturally in a number of different ways, received dogmatic status in the doctrine of the trinity."[31] Yet, following Barth's logic, it is not the Christian insistence on relationality which received dogmatic status in the trinitarian doctrine. This would have to mean that the human experience of friendship and the consequent ideal of relationality had defined God's inner being and action as well as his action *ad extra*. Instead, the trinitarian doctrine was an attempt to speak about who God really *is* as God exists in eternity and in time as the Father, Son, and Holy Spirit. This particular being is *uniquely* relational but is certainly not defined by relationality as is the God who is seen as our co-worker and friend and whose salvation is thus dependent upon us and equated with our efforts to improve the world. It is in this context that McFague argues that sharing food is inclusive and that Jesus' table fellowship is intrinsically inclusive. In her view, the shared meal ought not to be seen as an exclusive ritual. Rather, what creates friendship, as indicated in shared meals, is "to stand with him [Jesus] and with all others united by and committed to the common vision embodied in the shared meal extended to the outsider." Friendship "invites and needs all who share the vision."[32] In this thinking God *must* be included in a relationship with the world, and creatures have the capacity for salvation and indeed exercise that capacity by uniting with Jesus in a common vision which includes both human and non-human beings in a relationship of friendship. Since this thinking never actually recognizes the reality of the trinitarian God, it equates sin with failure to unite in a common vision for the planet and for society, and salvation with the living of that common vision. In both cases neither sin nor salvation has been described, simply because God's being and action as savior are both established and defined on the basis of the experience of friendship.

As seen above, Barth held that we really have to do with God himself, but not *directly*. We meet him *indirectly*, in faith. We meet him in human thought and action which is obedient to the divine action *ad extra*. We can neither get beyond human ideas or experiences to encounter God himself, nor can we encounter God on the *basis* of human ideas or experiences, or directly in the human ideas or experiences, as though the ideas and experiences were the goals here and not God himself. We encounter God on the *basis* of his self-disclosure whose *goal* is not the dissolution of human ideas and experiences but their rightful and limited inclusion in the mystery of the Trinity. Accordingly, their inclusion can never be anything but an obedient noetic and ontic encounter with this specific self-disclosure. This priority of divine in relation to human activity is the possibility and limitation of an actual encounter with God. Real knowledge of God and real eucharistic action must take place again and again as *events* in which people actually are obedient to the *One Mediator*.

In speaking of an *idea* or an *experience* of God one is not absolutely bound to faith in the one who loves in freedom. On such a view the Lord's Supper has a weak, transitory, and relative basis and goal which, as we have just seen, can be discovered and *controlled* by us in our ideas and experiences. On this view, people can alternatively *identify* their action and being with the divine action and being or *separate* them. But they can never decisively recognize their actual communion as grounded in God alone. In this instance we cannot be sure that we have to do with God himself either in the liturgy or in our ethical action which takes its point of departure in the same object of faith which is the basis and goal of the Eucharist.

With this recapitulation of the connection between the doctrine of God and the Lord's Supper, we now come to the decisive part of this treatment of the Lord's Supper as a human act upheld by grace. We have seen that a clear and intelligible conception of God demands a clear and intelligible view of Christ and the church. Such a clear and intelligible view could neither be monistic, dualistic, nor synthetic in orientation or design. Further, a clear and intelligible conception of the Lord's Supper would not find its possibility and limitation in its doctrine of God (its concept of analogy), its Christology, or its ecclesiology. Rather, its possibility and limitation will be the object of faith, namely, the one who is loving *yet* at the same time free; the one who enters into communion with us but does so as the one he is, i.e., as the one who remains transcendent and self-sufficient. *Only* because he is and remains *divine* can we have the certainty that we are not dealing simply with another human theory or experience.

A correct view here will *not* conceive the church's action in the Lord's Supper as a *continuation* of God's action (monism).[33] Nor will it conceive Christ's action as enclosed in the elements. It will not conceive the church's human action in the Lord's Supper as one which has meaning *independently* or in *separation* from the divine action (dualism). Nor will it focus on the elements independently or in separation from this divine and human action. It will not envision the church's human action in the Lord's Supper as *identical* with the divine act (synthesis). Nor will it imagine the elements in identity with the divine being. It will certainly not try to combine any of these false perceptions into some third and supposedly higher construct. That would only blend the errors of all three positions into an amalgam in which clear thinking about God and creatures as two distinct entities encountering one another on the basis of grace is rendered hopeless. This is how the situation will be unless there is a decisive return to faith in the triune God who loves in freedom.[34]

Faith of course always bears the mark of an actual encounter with God by allowing God himself the freedom to precede and to determine the form and content of what is known. Thus, unless we learn of God's freedom *in se*, apart from all human ideas of his freedom, any statement about his freedom from conditioning *ad extra* might be indistinguishable from wishful thinking.[35] Apart from faith, the existence of created reality confronting God in its difference can only imply a difficulty in relation to the transcendent God if the concept of transcendence gains its meaning on the basis of the opposition between the two which is perceptible to people reflecting on the concept of transcendence. Any such human conception of transcendence will hover between two extremes: 1) As it is consistently affirmed, the real existence of the other, i.e., the reality of creation, is obliterated; 2) As creation is inconsistently given a degree of independent reality, the so-called absolute (transcendent) is necessarily *conditioned* by this created other, so that the subordinate reality of creation determines the semi-absolute character of what is "absolute."[36]

For Barth, the only possible solution to this dilemma is the real freedom of God which cannot be defined by its relation to creation. Such a definition will acknowledge God's inner freedom first, in both its positive and negative aspects, and only then will it perceive his independence from the world. Precisely because what makes God transcendent does not derive from his relationship *ad extra*, but from his inner being as Father, Son, and Spirit, he can enter a *real* relationship with creation.[37] In this way there can be a real world not threatened with destruction by the divine absoluteness but existing because of it.

This same analysis applies to all synthetic attempts to define God's being, i.e., all noetic constructs not determined by the fact of revelation (God's action in Christ). Thus, for example, a conception of the divine *esse* as pure reality leaves us in the same dilemma. We would have to be *consistent* and assert the existence of impure reality distinct from it or we would have to be *inconsistent* and limit the "pure" reality by the "impure." This dilemma illustrates the difference between God's being as being in freedom and the human attempt to define that being by reference to created reality rather than revelation. Here Barth rejected the idea that God can be classified or included with that which he is not (creation). There can be no synthesis here except from the point of view of pantheism. Humanity really possesses no category (e.g., being, love, freedom) with which anyone could predicate the same meaning for God and something else (e.g., creation); *parity* is thus precluded as a possible way of knowing God. Whenever God is conceived as one idea among others, rather than the one who loves in freedom, a synthesis between human concepts and the reality of God has already been attempted. Rejecting this Barth cited Thomas' statement that "Deus non est in aliquo genere (Thomas Aquinas, S. theol. I qu. 3, art. 5)" as the corrective.[38]

It is important to see that this very thinking challenges Moltmann's method which, as seen above, speaks of nature and grace in a "forward perspective" in light of the "coming glory, which will complete *both nature and grace*."[39]

Accordingly, nature and grace are not defined over against one another but in terms of their relation to a process common to both of them.[40] While part of Moltmann's analysis seems close to Barth's (i.e., nature and grace are not defined over against each other) there is an enormous difference. For Barth, grace is identical with the self-sufficient glory of God and cannot be included in the processes of nature and then understood; it must be grasped in its own light through the revelation of the glory of God in Jesus Christ. For Barth, following Aquinas, this means that there cannot be a process common to both nature and grace and freedom and necessity, which encompasses them and determines their present and future meaning.[41]

But for Moltmann this is not only possible but is necessary because his theological starting point, as seen above, is a version of panentheism which maintains that we cannot cling to any distinction between the immanent and the economic Trinity. Thus, "The economic Trinity not only reveals the immanent Trinity; it also has a retroactive effect on it."[42] Hence,

> *Christian panentheism* . . . started from the divine essence: Creation is a fruit of God's longing for 'his Other' and for that Other's free response to the divine love. That is why the idea of the world is inherent in the nature of God himself from eternity. For it is impossible to conceive of a God who is not a creative God. A non-creative God would be imperfect . . . if God's eternal being is love, then divine love is also more blessed in giving than in receiving. God cannot find bliss in eternal self-love if selflessness is part of love's very nature.[43]

Here Moltmann clearly has fallen into the second segment of the dilemma just indicated; he has compromised God's absoluteness by defining his essence as creative love rather than seeing his essence as free and creation as a free and distinct new divine action *ad extra*. Hence Moltmann's theology is governed by the principle of mutual conditioning which Barth insisted must be rejected in order to illustrate the priority of divine over human being and action. Barth thus distinguished divine and human being and action. While Moltmann insists that there must be a distinction between God and creatures, his distinction is not between two utterly different entities but between two beings which are distinct within a *common process* which will complete both of them. Hence, for Barth, grace is complete in itself and will complete the kingdom on earth when Christ returns. For Moltmann both grace *and* nature need to be completed in the kingdom of glory; thus the economic Trinity will be "raised into and transcended in the immanent Trinity."[44] Yet if God is indeed active within the economy of salvation, then the economic Trinity is already God's saving presence at work within history. It is not transcended in the immanent Trinity; the immanent Trinity is fully present within the economy and does not need future completion. Moltmann has now abandoned the conceptual framework which includes immanent and economic Trinity because he believes that such "distinctions derive from general metaphysics, not from specifically Christian theology."[45]

For Moltmann then the meaning of the Lord's Supper is at least partially dictated by the fact that shared meals indicate the kind of friendship that Jesus experienced while one earth and the kind of friendship which we ought to create now as a community. In this respect there are elements in common between Moltmann's understanding of the God-world relationship in terms of friendship and the understanding advanced by Sallie McFague and discussed above. The problem with this understanding is that it leads to the Pelagian idea that we can and must, to some extent, become our own saviors by creating friendship rather than division. Moreover, God's action for us is somehow merged with and dependent upon this human action; this view compromises the fact that our salvation is as sure and certain as is God's own action *ad extra*. These theologians are by no means alone in jeopardizing God's freedom with this thinking. We have seen above that similar difficulties accompany Rahner's symbolic view of God's revelation and freedom.

Meaning of the Lord's Supper as a Human Act

If, however, we presuppose the absolute priority of God in his being and action *ad intra* and *ad extra*, what then is the meaning of the Lord's Supper insofar as it is and remains a human act which responds to the divine act in Christ revealed and effected by his Spirit? We must now see how Barth answered this question in order to see the interrelationship between his doctrine of God and his definition of the Lord's Supper as a human action. We are now answering the question raised above as to how an action which is not holy *in se* can become holy by God's judgment. If human holiness can be shown to be based in a *sovereign* action of God in our favor, then both Pelagianism and human uncertainty with regard to salvation are ruled out by the fact that the meaning of our human actions is grounded in and explained by God's action in Christ and the Spirit.

Holiness

The meaning of the church's human action in the Lord's Supper is lost if holiness is sought in a supposedly immanent divine work. If this is attempted, either the human action of eating and drinking is overshadowed by the divine work itself, or the human act as such is equated with the divine action of the Holy Spirit. Either way, the Eucharist is treated docetically according to Barth's viewpoint and it ceases to be a truly human word and work hastening from the *basis* toward the *goal* as described above. To seek the holiness of the eucharistic celebration in an immanent divine work is to *identify* the meaning of the human action with its *basis* and *goal*. As we have seen, the basis and goal of the Eucharist is God himself, i.e., one who is defined not by his immanence (his "for us") but by his transcendence (the inner divine being which is loving and free). Because the basis and goal of the human action (which includes the elements) remains transcendent in this way, they cannot be equated with the meaning of the immanent human action. The meaning is the meaning of the *human action* as such which has a transcendent basis and goal but cannot be collapsed into either.

This must be made clearer. For Barth, the basis and goal of the human action is God himself in his action *ad extra* in his Spirit. As God himself in his action *ad intra* and *ad extra* remains *distinct* from us as our Lord, Reconciler, and Redeemer, the church's action in the Lord's Supper cannot be understood except in subordination to Christ himself, very God and very man. This *distinction* between Christ and the church disappears if and when it is thought that the meaning of the human action of the Lord's Supper as such is a divine action.[46] This means that in light of the absolute priority of the divine action in Christ and the continual attestation of this fact in the power of the Holy Spirit, the church's act *never* is or becomes Christ's act. As seen above, this is exactly what a phenomenology cannot and does not say. Here Barth's Christology applies to the Lord's Supper.[47]

For Barth it is the living Christ alone who is the One Mediator between God and creatures. If our idea of Christ or our experience of Christ were to become normative in grasping this, then this very truth would be denied in a practical way by our method. Thus, a Christology which sees Christ in abstraction from what he is and was among Israel and his disciples and the world will inevitably take on the appearance of a dramatic ontology arbitrarily contrived from scripture and tradition. Soteriology and ecclesiology, either as a doctrine of grace, justification, and sanctification which comes to us, or as a doctrine of Christian piety, will never escape the tendency to substitute itself as that which is of practical importance and existentially relevant for the person and work of Christ; Christology could become "ballast which can be jettisoned without loss." Indeed "An abstract doctrine of the work of Christ will always tend secretly in a direction where some kind of Arianism or Pelagianism lies in wait."[48]

This is why Barth clearly distinguished between God *in se* and God for us.[49] He maintained this noetic distinction because it "bears the mark" of its encounter with the free grace of God himself. Where a clear distinction between God *in se* and God for us is not maintained, the incarnation, the church, and consequently the Lord's Supper will be described as essential to God's inner *esse*. In Barth's theology this can only be done if God himself is merely our own apotheosis. But in that case, it is we in our human actions as such who are the subject not only of faith but also of grace and revelation. To that extent humanity is the subject of the divine action in the Lord's Supper as well. Faith, grace, revelation, and the divine action in the Lord's Supper can be nothing more than anthropological or ethnological predicates discovered by people to add some depth to their already moderately self-sufficient existence. This kind of thinking will *always* follow in one way or another whenever the *distinction* between God *in se* and God *for us* is not clearly maintained in a doctrine of God, Christology, ecclesiology, and in sacramental theology.[50] Naturally the fact that there really is communion between God and us on the basis of grace (i.e., God's eternal election of Christ and of all people in Christ) cannot and must not be denied. That is why it would be equally false to assume that God *in se* is somehow different (perhaps more divine) than the God we meet in the sphere of secondary objectivity, i.e., the man Jesus and in the church insofar as it is the earthly form of his transcendent existence.[51]

The Lord's Supper relates to the one divine Word and work which took place in the history of Christ. But the human action of the Lord's Supper is not itself a divine Word and work. The human action is and remains the word and work of those who have been cleansed by the power of the Holy Spirit and who have become obedient to Christ. In this sense the Lord's Supper, like water baptism, takes place in recognition of the one grace of God which justifies, sanctifies, and calls us.[52] But in no sense whatsoever is the Lord's Supper to be conceived as an instrument, bearer, or means of grace.[53] Both the human action of obedience in water baptism and the church's obedient action in the Lord's Supper take place in light of the action of the Holy Spirit described above. Because that action is both loving (i.e., it seeks and creates fellowship) and free (it remains free with respect to its object), water baptism is always water baptism.[54] Similarly the church's action of eating and drinking and the elements involved, are *always* the church's action and the created elements, respectively.

Barth maintained this same point throughout the *Church Dogmatics*. In the covenant of grace the creature is not seen as the *means* but only a witness and a sign of grace. As the only divine reality God alone is gracious. It is God himself who works in creation and is known indirectly, i.e., in and through the signs and witnesses to his divine act of grace in Christ. He is a living God and would not be a living God if there were a moment at which he were absent or inactive in creation. The mystery of grace itself consists in the fact that he can be our sovereign Lord without destroying humanity *as* humanity.[55] He does not eliminate our human free decision to be obedient to his sovereign power.

For that is how stronger creatures work on other and weaker creatures. But the work of God on the creature is far more than comparatively a stronger or superlatively the strongest work . . . there is no place for conceptions in which the divine operation is related to the creaturely in the way that an actual is to a potential, as for example, a motor to the mechanism associated with it . . . For creatures can act in this way on other creatures which are capable of action but do not act . . . there is no place for conceptions in which the operation of God produces that of the creature in the way that a first and general action gives rise to a series of actions and thus brings about a united activity, like a locomotive setting in motion the carriage immediately next to it, and by means of this carriage all the carriages and therefore the whole train . . . But of course we shall fall into the opposite error if we try to represent the divine operation in terms of the imparting of a quality or quantity of the divine essence or operation to the creature and its activity, as a kind of infusion of divine love or divine power or divine life into the essence of the creature. The difference in order between the working of God in, with and over the creature, and the working of the creature under God's lordship, cannot be envisaged as one which has been resolved or removed . . . It is the secret of grace that God does this, and the creature experiences it. But it is also the secret of grace that even when He does it He alone is God, that He alone has and retains the divine essence, that the essence of the creature is not affected or altered . . . He does not subtract anything from the creature or add anything to it, but He allows it to be just what it is in its creaturely essence . . . There is still a genuine encounter, and therefore a genuine meeting, of two beings which are quite different in type and order.[56]

Sacrament

The human action of the church in the Lord's Supper freely responds to a mystery, namely, to the "sacrament of the history of Jesus Christ, of His resurrection, of the outpouring of the Holy Spirit. It is not itself, however, a mystery or sacrament."[57] It should now be quite obvious why the term sacrament has been largely absent from this presentation of Barth's concept of the Lord's Supper so far. There was for Barth *only one* mystery of God (i.e., sacrament). Barth did not wish to describe baptism with water or the church's action in the Lord's Supper as sacraments because one might then be tempted to look at the human actions and miss the mystery of God which is their basis, goal, and norm. Or one may be tempted to define God's inner *esse* by the human actions. We have seen above that this is no small issue for contemporary theologians. On the one hand, some are led into nominalism and thus substitute their ideas of God for the Christian God. On the other hand some are led into dualism by insisting that the world is God's body. Hence God cannot have become incarnate in a single individual (Jesus of Nazareth). The problems noted in connection with the Christologies of Wainwright and Rahner in chapter three exhibit similar difficulties, even though these theologians would shrink from McFague's conclusions that Christ cannot be the unique savior.

It is quite true that throughout the *Church Dogmatics* Barth defined sacramental reality as created reality which has been determined by God to bear witness to himself.[58] He maintained that the form of revelation (i.e., what can be established historically) is part of its mystery; thus he strictly defined Christ as *the mystery* of revelation. Everyone is not Christ and therefore can only participate in the mystery of revelation by faith in him. There is and will be no other mystery of revelation. In this man the mystery of revelation consists in the fact that God, in his freedom, acted and acts in the *form* of this man. Therefore, to know revelation we are bound to his history. But because the form is not directly identical with its content, it is possible for us to apprehend the form while missing the content.[59] This is in fact what happens for the neutral observer, for one who examines the data in abstraction from faith. The historical elements of revelation, for example, the temple of Yahweh, the humanity of Christ, the empty tomb, are all open to very trivial explanations. None points unequivocally to the triune God who loves in freedom. Only the believer recognizes that this form is the form in which God acts to and for us. There really is no other *form* of revelation. God has chosen the form of the man Jesus Christ. He has chosen to disclose himself in and through human history without dissolving his deity or our humanity. Therefore while revelation is not identical with its form, it cannot be separated from it either because this is how God freely chose and chooses to act in relation to his creatures. There can be no other reason.

Event

Barth maintained that the objectivity of God is not naturally inherent in the objectivity of the creature instituted as a sacrament.[60] He applied the patristic concepts *anhypostasis* and *enhypostasis* in order to maintain both the positive and negative aspects of the divine freedom. As seen in chapter six, it is this thinking which is determinative for his insistence that the objectivity of God is not naturally inherent in the objectivity of the creaturely witness to God. Thus, for Barth, *anhypostasis* denotes the negative fact that Christ's human nature has no meaning except by, in, and through the Word;[61] and *enhypostasis* denotes the positive fact that Christ's human nature actually does acquire meaning as a result of the incarnation. Both of these conceptions must stand together in order to describe properly the unique union of divinity and humanity encountered in Christ. Thus, when seen in light of this unique union of God and humanity in Christ, sacramental reality will always acknowledge Christ's living lordship by not attempting to ascribe his effective divine working to the reality in which he meets us (history). This attempt will always confuse the presence of God seen in faith with the historical phenomenon of the church.

That is why he maintained the absolute priority of divine in relation to human activity in his Christology and ecclesiology. A reversal of divine and human being and action can only occur when faith is ignored or neglected.[62] It is precisely for this reason that Barth held that knowledge of God, namely, real apprehension of the mystery of revelation in the sphere of historical reality (in and not without its *form*) is an *event* enclosed in the mystery of the Trinity. It is the unveiling of what is by nature veiled.[63] We have already seen that for Barth this meant that we humans have no obediential potency for this knowledge; no innate capacity for fellowship with God; and that the *event* in which our views and concepts actually point to God himself does not come about *through* our work. God *alone* initiates, sustains, and completes this event. In this respect it is always a *miracle*.[64] In no way and at no time does this act of God *inhere* in historical reality as such. Historical reality is and remains distinct from God's act (revelation). That is why faith is always necessary. Accordingly, the immanent and economic Trinity could be perceived as identical (in Rahner's sense) only when faith has ceased to be normative for understanding the relation between God and history.[65]

Rejection of Term Sacrament

When Barth rejected the term sacrament did he reject his prior understanding of sacramental reality as just described? If he did, then it would seem that his whole *Church Dogmatics*, which was his attempt to avoid monism, dualism, and syncretism in explaining the relationship between God and creatures, is questionable. At this point we must be very clear in describing what Barth meant here by the term sacrament.

Barth rejected the following explanations. First, that the Lord's Supper is "a sign which was instituted by Jesus Christ Himself and which is used and guaranteed by Him (through the Church's baptism). It is filled with divine power and . . . it also symbolises and causally underlies this power." In this way the symbol, i.e., the eating and drinking and the bread and wine, insofar as they point to and participate in the history of Christ's death and resurrection, actually control and mediate the reality to which they refer. To the extent that the sacrament is thought to do this, it is conceived as a basic extension of His existence. But as such it is also the medium and instrument of His mediatorial person and work . . . In it, if it is given correctly (with the intention of doing what the Church does), and if they do not oppose the corresponding intention to receive it (if they place no *obex*), the work of the Holy Spirit is done in them, and the Spirit is imparted to them. In it . . . they also acquire an active part in the priestly offering and royal rule of Jesus Christ. In it the theological virtues of faith, love and hope are poured into them once and for all. In it they receive . . . the indelible character of men who belong to Jesus Christ, who are fashioned in the likeness of His human nature . . . All this takes place *ex opere operato*. Though faith and obedience are both demanded and established, it takes place quite independently of the faith, the personal orthodoxy, or the moral worthiness of either minister or recipient . . . (the Eucharist is the central sacrament in this system).[66]

The position which Barth rejected is the position which he rejected at the outset of this discussion, namely, the view of God's gracious action to, for, and in creatures as an "infusion of supernatural powers." This Barth maintained is the position of Roman Catholic Dogmatics.[67]

Second, Barth rejected the Lutheran view which he explained is half way between the Roman Catholic and the Reformed view. According to this view, the church's human action in the Lord's Supper becomes *more* than a visible sign proclaiming Christ. Instituted by Christ himself it becomes an objectively powerful bearer of the promise of God. It becomes "the effective means, organ or instrument of an invisible grace."[68] The Lutheran idea attempts to avoid the notion of an *ex opere operato* effect of the sacrament by noting that without faith there can be no actual use of the promise received in baptism and attested in the Lord's Supper. Faith does not make the human action or the elements of bread and wine holy. Only the Word of God does that. According to this view, holiness means that the action and the elements are thought to become more than *signs* and *pointers* to God's actual presence. "Like the Lord's Supper, and like the written and preached Word, it is, as sign, a means of grace, too."[69]

Third, Barth rejected the Reformed view as conceived by Calvin and H. Heppe,[70] but he did not reject this view entirely.[71] What is it then that Barth rejected here? It is the idea that although water baptism and the Lord's Supper cannot be seen as *causae salutis*, they can be regarded as mediating the *cognitio* and *certitudo* of salvation.[72] For Barth, the *cognitio* and *certitudo* of salvation come only from God and not from the *medium* used by God to create this knowledge and certitude. Without denying the relative importance of baptism or the Lord's Supper, Barth denied them precedence in relation to the divine action.

Barth's position then was that all three of these views agree that the church's human action in water baptism and in the Lord's Supper ought to be explained as a mystery. He opposed this view in order to maintain that the church's action is "the human action which corresponds to the divine action . . . It is the human action whose meaning is obedience to Jesus Christ and hope in him."[73] God's action in and on us is his presence and his mystery. As his work and revelation it mediates itself. It has and needs no other mediators to accomplish fellowship with us. God does not hand over his divine self-disclosure to the form in and through which he chooses to reveal himself.[74]

For that reason God's action does not supplant or suppress the human action of the church, either in its celebration of the Lord's Supper or in its ethical behavior. The divine action does not rob the human action of significance.[75] In Barth's opinion each one of the above views, to one degree or another, ascribes to the human action or to the elements a *mediatorial* role in relation to grace. For Barth, the term medium cannot be understood in this way;[76] instead, the term *medium*, as well as the terms witness, sign, and obedience have no theological meaning in themselves. They have no innate or God-given power to effect what only God himself can effect, i.e., the mediation of his grace. They may become true participants in grace in the power of the Holy Spirit as they actually point to the being and activity of the triune God himself. But their limitation is that they cannot do this if they are confused in any way with the action of God. For Barth, any concept which suggests that this mediation of divine being and action can be ascribed to anyone or anything else than God himself whom we meet and know in Christ, confuses God and creatures. This is what Barth contested here. To one degree or another each of the above views ascribes the power which is Christ's *alone*, to the human action or to the elements used in the Lord's Supper. This of course is the problem of applying a concept of symbolism to real presence without allowing the Christ of faith to precede and determine its truth content.[77]

Therefore Barth rejected any notion which does not clearly and strictly maintain the distinction between the mystery of revelation (God's action as such in Christ and in the Holy Spirit) and the action of those who believe in this divine action and respond humanly in accordance with that belief. But this interpretation can only mean that for Barth a correct explanation of the Lord's Supper must clearly demonstrate that it is knowledge of the church's being and activity which is an *event* enclosed in the mystery of the Trinity. Otherwise it has no true and certain basis and goal and therefore no definite meaning. As the knowledge and action of the church is grounded in revelation, it is incontestably true. As it is grounded in anything else it is contestable.[78] If it is not seen as an *event*, it might be seen as a *state* which could be surveyed and controlled either by an *a priori* or *a posteriori* principle. Then theology would be reduced to anthropology.

If this is true then, noetically and ontically, it is knowledge, being, and action whose possibility consists in recognition of its limitation. What is the church's limitation here? For Barth the church's *only* true and certain limitation is the prior and determinative being and action of the triune God who loves in freedom. This particular limitation is also the church's *only* possibility for true knowledge, being, and action. We know this only in faith which never questions the fact that people are truly what they are only as they follow and do not attempt to precede the One Mediator (ontically and noetically). Any other claim here denies the absolute priority of the being and activity of the triune God *in se* and *ad extra*.

Faith knows that God is not defined in his action *ad extra* by the reality distinct from him and used by him to bear witness to himself. Faith also knows that God is not defined by the communion which he freely established between himself and us in Christ, i.e., the covenant of grace. Faith knows that God is defined only by the *fact* that he is who he is as the one who loves in freedom. His divine being and action itself therefore accounts for the fact that human being and action are *not reversible* or *identical* with the action of God, i.e., his grace.[79] For Barth then, it is the being and action of the triune God himself which prohibits defining the Lord's Supper as a mystery, i.e., a sacrament. It is included in the mystery in a limited fashion—indirectly, but it is not itself the mystery. People have not invented this being and action and therefore they cannot control it. This insight proscribes any notion that in the Lord's Supper God is the one who is acting in the place of the creature. Such a view completely relativizes the human action in the Lord's Supper and in human ethical behavior generally. Still, the human action must be taken with strict seriousness. To conceive the human action in identity with the mystery of revelation obscures this positive point. In this way a "sacramental view" conjures away "the free man whom God liberates and summons to his own free and responsible action."[80]

It is clear that what Barth rejected by rejecting the term sacrament was any confusion between the mystery of the Trinity as such and our free, but limited inclusion in that mystery. He equated the term sacrament with the being of God in Christ. Thus, only the history of Christ is a *sacramental event*. Only in the history of Christ can humanity in general participate in the mystery of God. This means that the possibility and limitation of the human action in the Lord's Supper consists in *recollection* that God was faithful to himself in Christ and for that reason did not exclude us, and *expectation* of this continued faithfulness. People can trust the fact that God will be their God in the future because they recognize, in and through the risen Christ, that their humanity stands before God in justification.

Rejection of Monism, Dualism, Synthesis

The mystery of God is denied if it is thought that the human action can be more than an act of faithfulness corresponding to God's faithfulness.[81] Barth's rejection of the term sacrament is a rejection of any identity between creator and creature, even in Christ. This is the same point he maintained in his doctrine of God by rejecting the identity of the immanent and economic Trinity. It is the same point Barth maintained in his Christology by rejecting the identity of the humanity and divinity of Christ and the mutually conditioning view of the *communicatio idiomatum*. It is the same point he maintained in his ecclesiology by rejecting identity of the head with the body. In this sense Barth rejected the term sacrament but retained his prior understanding of the relationship between God and creatures explicated above.

Barth's rejection of the term sacrament is also a rejection of dualism, i.e., the idea that there is an unbridgeable gap between God and creatures. A dualism of this kind is possible *only* in *abstraction* from the history of Christ in which God and creatures are one. On a general view (one formulated outside the *analogia fidei*) dualism is plausible because it is a fact that God did not become one with humanity *generally*. It is true that we do not control God and cannot attempt to reverse divine and human being either noetically or ontically. But this does not mean that God has *not* in *fact* established his covenant of grace in the particular history of Christ. Dualism would deny God's freedom to be reconciler and redeemer as well as Lord of the covenant. On this view the human action of the church in the Lord's Supper could be defined as something other than pure obedience to the command of God; it could be defined as our action in accordance with our deepest religious motives and drives for fellowship with other human beings. But on such a dualistic view, the question of a human response to an objectively existing transcendent reality is evaded completely. This is the same point Barth affirmed in his doctrine of God by rejecting separation of the immanent and economic Trinity.[82] In his Christology Barth maintained this point by rejecting the separation of the humanity and divinity of Christ. In his ecclesiology Barth maintained this point by rejecting separation of the head and the body of Christ on earth. On a dualistic view, the church could be defined as something other than the "special presence of Christ on earth;"[83] and creatures could be seen as the subjects and objects of their own activity.

This was in fact Feuerbach's conclusion, when, for example, he defined the Holy Spirit as "the sighing creature, the longing of the creature for God . . . Man is the beginning, the middle, and the end of religion."[84] In an introductory essay to Feuerbach's *The Essence of Christianity*, Barth noted that when revelation, religion, and our relation with God can be defined as human predicates, this kind of apotheosis is what takes place.[85] Indeed this very method of attempting to define God, Christ, Spirit, and church from subjective experience is the key weakness of all theology which does not begin decisively with the biblical revelation and begins instead from experience. That is why Barth also rejected Schleiermacher's understanding of the church.

> The Church has to be believed. No one really needs to believe the Christianity defined and described by Schleiermacher: in its own way it is a historical phenomenon like all others, and as such it can at bottom be perceived generally. What Christianity really is, the being of the community as 'the living community of the living Lord Jesus Christ,' calls for the perception of faith, and is accessible only to this perception and not to any other.[86]

Barth's presupposition here is his *analogia fidei*. There are true analogies. We may truly know God in his revelation. But no general concept can disclose what God alone discloses in his special action in Christ and the Spirit. Thus, unless one's concept allows God's special action in his Word and Spirit to precede it normatively, one will inevitably ground knowledge of God in humanity itself idealistically, romantically, pietistically, or existentially. When that happens, faith has been bracketed, and so also has the possibility of true knowledge of God's real presence in history. Certainly God's presence does not cease to be real. Rather, people confuse it with their own image and thus substitute themselves for the object of faith.[87]

Finally, Barth rejected any pantheistic or panentheistic notion of creator and creature by rejecting the term sacrament. For Barth God enters *freely* into fellowship (communion) with men and women who remain different from him. He does not enter into a synthesis with us or with bread and wine. This is why, as we shall see, any concept of local presence is out of the question. So also is any question of reposition or exposition of the bread used in the Lord's Supper. If God can be identified with bread and wine, then he is no longer *free* to be the divine object actively present; this view is an exact parallel to Barth's grasp of scriptural inspiration.[88] Such a conception would deny the actual union of God with men and women in favor of a general idea of oneness. Insofar as the term sacrament connotes a union of this kind between creator and creature it confuses and denies the real union willed by God in his Word and Spirit.

This is just the same point that Barth maintained in his doctrine of God by insisting that God is indissolubly one in his three distinct modes of existence. It is the same point which Barth maintained in stressing the real union of the immanent and economic Trinity. Similarly Barth held, in his Christology, that

there is a real *union* of God and man in Christ.   Finally Barth maintained the
same fact in his ecclesiology by emphasizing that between Christ and his church
there is a real *union* realized and maintained on the basis of *grace*.

We shall not give a detailed analysis of Barth's etymological treatment of the
term *mysterion* in the New Testament here.[89]   In summary Barth held that the
New Testament use of the term *mysterion* referred to God's work and revelation
in history and not to the corresponding human reactions.   This concept of mystery
faded early in church history in favor of the Greek conception that the
corresponding human reactions were cultic rites partly presupposing one's relationship with God and partly conveying it: "Baptism and the Lord's Supper . . .
began to be regarded as cultic *re-presentations* of the act and revelation of God
in the history of Jesus Christ, and consequently as the granting of a share in His
grace.   They thus began to be described and treated as mysteries."[90]

The term sacrament was taken from Roman law and originally referred to a
military oath of loyalty which was "accompanied by an act of religious devotion."
This was the term which was used to translate *mysterion*.   In that way, according
to Barth, it came to mean "re-presentation of the cultic deity = means of
grace."[91]   This is why Barth rejected the term; he defined this kind of thinking
as "sacramentalism."[92]   The sacramental act is thus thought to be the cause and
guarantee of the presence of the Spirit.   Barth also insisted that the term
sacrament was not used in the New Testament.   But that cannot be the focus here
since he word Trinity does not appear in the New Testament either; but it can be
a correct interpretation of the revelation encountered in the biblical witness.   The
focus here is on the *meaning* of the terms and not the terms as such.

Assessment of Barth's View of Sacrament

In connection with the rest of the *Church Dogmatics* then, Barth's "radically
new" view of sacrament is not entirely new since it expresses the logic of his
presuppositions previously explicated in his doctrine of the Word of God and his
doctrine of God.   We have just summarized those presuppositions and their conclusions.[93]   This is the positive aspect of his work which we have tried to present.
But there is an ambiguity in Barth's thought on this point.   It is primarily with
reference to the term sacrament and not to his understanding of the relationship
between signs and things signified.   But it also concerns the relationship between
Christ and Christians.   Earlier he used the word sacrament to speak of the church
as a sign bearing witness to revelation and of Christ's humanity as sacramental.

Revelation means the giving of signs.   We can say quite simply that
revelation   means   sacrament,   i.e.,   the   self-witness   of   God,   the

representation of His truth, and therefore of the truth in which He knows Himself, in the form of creaturely objectivity and therefore in a form which is adapted to our creaturely knowledge.[94]

Christ's human nature is the "sacramental reality of His revelation."[95] Sacrament refers to "the outward creaturely sign of word and elements." Thus unity with God means that

> man's speech, that water, bread and wine are real not only through God, but as inseparably bound to God, and similarly . . . that believing man may live not only through God but inseparably bound to God. But unity with God cannot mean in the former case that man's speech, that water, bread and wine, or in the latter case that believing man, is identical with God.[96]

Accordingly, there is no identity or separation of sign and thing signified because of the grace of God. When he eventually rejected the term sacrament he intended to express this same idea. But there were problems. He made his distinction between Christ acting and our human acting so sharp that instead of arguing, as he had previously done, that in the event of preaching about God we actually hear God's Word in faith, he later argued that what God promises and can alone bring about in the sacrament "does not take place in and with the event as such."[97] It is always a promise to be grasped in hope. Indeed, it is this, but, if the church is the historical form of Christ's presence on earth, then God is also free to act in this particular sign so that his real presence can actually be celebrated at particular times and places.

Earlier he spoke of sacraments as the indispensable means of grace and as instruments used by God to speak objectively (in sign) within world history.[98] In this sense there could be no new sign of revelation since revelation was objectively given "once and for all at the inauguration of the apostolate."[99] As long as grace is emphasized (and not the means of grace) Barth even said "on its objective side the church is sacramental;"[100] this church form of revelation was God's objective presence in the world. Indeed our justification and sanctification

> which is the meaning of all divine sign-giving, does not rest upon an idea but upon reality, upon an event . . . the event of the entry of this Creator into our history . . . ὁ λόγος σάρξ ἐγένετο (Jn. 1:14)—preaching, too, can and must say this. But in a way which preaching can never do, the sacrament underlines the words σάρξ ἐγένετο . . . [In this sense we may see] the divine sign-giving as the objective side of the Church . . . It may well be that a theology allows itself to learn from the very simple fact that

in the Church baptism must always be administered and the Lord's Supper celebrated. By this fact it is reminded that, since it is the reality of revelation, the subjective reality of revelation necessarily has an objective side. It is from this objective side that our thinking must invariably derive . . . what is involved in the water of baptism and in the bread and wine of the Lord's Supper is the establishment and recognition of the sign of the concrete, living, creatively active lordship of God.[101]

In other words where it is a *fact* that the community baptizes and celebrates the Lord's Supper, there we have the life of Christians regulated by the prophetic and apostolic word taking new form. We participate in objective revelation (Jesus Christ) through the Holy Spirit. This is the subjective reality of revelation and if we wish to understand the Holy Spirit and his work we must look "at the place from which He comes and at what He brings . . . we must look to the objective possibility of our communion with Christ . . . we must look at Christ Himself." Do we have the Spirit? This is only decided by Christ since it is only from him that we have this. Thus, "The Church and Holy Scripture and preaching and the sacrament are . . . the only possible criteria in any practical investigation." True and proper proclamation will not point to anyone's "seizure" but "in pointing to the divine seizing" it will point "to Christ Himself."

True preaching will direct [a Christian] rather 'rigidly' to something written, or to his baptism or to the Lord's Supper, instead of pointing him in the very slightest to his own or the preacher's or other peoples' experience. It will confront him with no other faith than faith in Christ, who died for him and rose again. But if we claim even for a moment that experiences are valid and can be passed on, we find that they are marshy ground upon which neither the preacher nor the hearer can stand or walk. Therefore they are not the object of Christian proclamation . . . proclamation does not lead the listener to experiences . . . It leads them right back through all experiences to the source of all true and proper experience, i.e., to Jesus Christ.[102]

Later he rejected the term sacrament in order to distinguish God and creatures, sign, and thing signified. Barth insisted that the human decision and action in baptism and the Lord's Supper were not channels, instruments, or means of grace because Christ alone is this means.[103] Still, he also insisted that in baptism

The reference is absolutely to Him when the kingdom of God, the judgment of God, and the sin-forgiving grace of God are proclaimed. The reference is to the life of the body of which He is the Head when God's people is gathered, edified and sent out.[104]

So he continued to refer to the *factual* history of the church as the sphere of revelation in history. From this situation I think it is fair to decide that while one may and must distinguish creator and creatures (and sign and thing signified), one need not reject the term sacrament in order to accomplish this. Barth's own *Dogmatics* proves this point. But the fact is that Barth has called attention to what has now become a widespread method of contemporary theology, namely, a method which moves from below to above. As seen throughout this work, such a method invariably *confuses* primary and secondary objectivity and so makes God dependent upon creation in some way or another. This compromises the sovereignty of grace with the effect that our own knowledge of salvation becomes doubtful. Here Barth's rejection of the term sacrament was almost prophetic.[105]

In connection with the rest of church history, Barth's view of sacrament is undeniably "radically new." But it is radically new in Barth's eyes because, from the very earliest days of church history, the *limited* (and therefore real) nature of the community's participation in the mystery of the Trinity was not consistently and clearly explicated.[106] In one way or another this happened by assuming that the human actions of eating and drinking and the created elements of bread and wine were somehow included in a *direct* rather than an *indirect* relationship with God. This is not different from the position taken by Barth in the doctrine of God in connection with the divine perfections. As we have seen, Barth contended that traditional theology falls immediately into partial or total nominalism in considering the divine attributes;[107] this, because the criterion is not the antecedent being of God but its general idea of God derived from analysis of creation as such.[108] The key to Barth's rejection of nominalism is the key to his understanding of the truth of the Lord's Supper. He rejected nominalism because it represented a creaturely attempt to interpret the being of God *in se* by human being. Historically this was done in terms of psychology, religio-genetics, and historico-intuitively.[109] All three errors reverse the being of God *in se* and *ad extra* because their criterion is not the being of God *in se* but an abstract view of God's being *ad extra*. This fails to note that God is fully revealed and yet fully concealed in his self-disclosure.[110]

Throughout this work we have seen that this problem is alive and well in contemporary theology. Those theologians who uncritically accept Rahner's axiom of identity regrading the immanent and economic Trinity eventually are led to deny either or both of these points. Either they collapse the immanent Trinity into God's actions of creation, reconciliation, and redemption; or they adopt analogies for God's existence *in se* arbitrarily because they assume that God *in se*, who is transcendent, can thus never actually be known. Such a viewpoint proceeds inevitably to the idea that we ourselves, in our liturgical actions, have been entrusted with the divine mysteries. To that extent, the mystery of revelation must be portrayed as under human control. It is exactly this thinking that Barth consistently and rightly rejected throughout the *Church Dogmatics*; he denied it emphatically in connection with the church's sacramental practice.[111]

Nonetheless we must underline the fact that where Barth abandoned his earlier emphasis on the objective facts of revelation for us (church, scripture, preaching, and sacrament) there is an ambiguity in his presentation. If the church's sacramental actions are only ethical responses to Christ's command and promise then Barth has removed from the visible historical sphere one of the signs to which he previously believed we could refer in an attempt to find assurance that we are living in the Spirit. To be sure, even before, this could only be an assurance achieved in faith and thus on the way from the basis and toward the goal which is the Triune God. But it is such an assurance. It is here that Barth's sacramental theology opens itself to the charge of a subtle ethical redefinition of Christ's real presence (Alasdair Heron) and of Gnostic dualism (Thomas Torrance) despite his explicit rejection of both. Barth was so intent on rejecting subjectivism by pointing us to Christ that, at times he could, as we shall see, call upon the Holy Spirit while ignoring the work accomplished by the Spirit in the visible sphere.

But in fact, even later on, Barth did insist that our fully human action in the sacrament is necessitated by God. By participating in the sacraments a person confirms his or her justification. By refusing them a person rejects the will of God.[112] In both cases it is our relation with God that is the decisive issue and not any ideology, doctrine, or custom. Barth did not here deny the activity of grace. Conversion is

> a distinctly human action. That it is God's grace and gift to be awakened, summoned and empowered to do this, that man cannot start to justify God except in the freedom which is given him by God—that is one thing. What he does, however, when he starts to do this, the movement which he executes in conversion, is not superhuman or supernatural . . . It is not divine. It is a human action which simply responds to divine action.[113]

All but one thing is well stated here. Previously Barth argued that faith has its origin in a mode of being of God (the Holy Spirit) even as it is a fully human act. He thus had recourse to this miraculous action of the Holy Spirit and could speak more of our life as enclosed in the mystery of the Trinity rather than as simply a response to God's grace and revelation. The proper emphasis here could overcome any appearance of ecclesiastical docetism which Barth opposed in a number of ways and particularly by refusing to define the church as purely invisible.[114]

We have established the fact that Barth's rejection of the term sacrament did not constitute a substantial change in his *theological* position to the extent that he never ceased rejecting identity, separation, and synthesis. While there is an ambiguity which we began to note in chapter six, his theological position could also support using the *term* with the proper safeguards. Our human responses to God in worship are and remain fully human *but* God can use them objectively to unite us to him through faith, grace, and revelation. The problem which accompanied Barth's rejection of the term sacrament was the tendency to separate the church's actions in baptism and the Lord's Supper from the Holy Spirit. But as we have seen throughout this work, he never really made any radical separation, since he constantly returned to Christ and the Holy Spirit to see the factual unity which obtains between Christ and Christians in baptism and the Lord's Supper as human actions which become holy in the power of God. When he rejected the term, this represented a consistent rejection of any idea that God's action could be grounded in anything other than his free decision to be who and what he is in himself and in his action *ad extra* and the need for faith. This is important for understanding the significance of the Lord's Supper as a human action which is enclosed in the act of God. To this we now turn.

Notes

1. See C.D. 2, 1, pp. 13–25ff. and pp. 188f.

2. See C.D. 1, 1, p. 479f. It is exactly this point which is basic to Barth's understanding of the *Filioque*.

3. Sallie McFague, *Models*, p. 192.

4. Ibid., p. 136.

5. Ibid., p. 150.

6. Ibid., p. 192. She writes: "I do not *know* who God is, but I find some models better than others for constructing an image of God commensurate with my trust in a God as on the side of life." But if we can't know who God is, what is the point of constructing an image of God at all? Why not admit that the image is merely our human way of trusting in "reality" and of getting others to have the same trust?

7. See C.D. 1, 1, pp. 370ff. Barth developed the important patristic concept of *perichoresis* in his trinitarian theology and never ceased applying it together with two other presuppositions: a) *opera trinitatis ad extra sunt indivisa* and b)

appropriation. *Perichoresis*, for Barth, means that neither Father, Son, nor Holy Spirit may be known as God without knowing the other two. There is complete participation of each mode of being in and with the other, though the distinctions remain. This position at once implies that if we are not bound to the reconciler (Christ) and the creator (Father) in our knowledge of the Holy Spirit, we have already substituted the human spirit for the action of God. Various Spirit Christologies proposed by contemporary theologians frequently confuse the human spirit with the Holy Spirit.

8. C.D. 4, 1, pp. 662–63; C.D. 4, 3, p. 793.

9. Rahner's axiom of identity leads logically to the idea that God cannot exist *in se* but that creation, reconciliation, and redemption all take place as part of a single being of God. Ted Peters, e.g., *God as Trinity,* has imposed the logic of Rahner's axiom onto Barth's theology and thus compromises the freedom of God he intends to uphold. Moreover, by beginning his trinitarian theology from our experience rather than from faith in God's action *ad extra*, Peters mistakenly defines God's being by the nature of personal relationality which applies to human interpersonal relationships. The result is that God *cannot* exist without being related to the world (p. 125) and that God's being is constituted by the relations *ad intra* and *ad extra*, p. 126. Thus God *depends* upon the world in order to attain his oneness. This reasoning, which is intrinsic to Peters' argument, represents a failure to recognize that the God who relates with us in Christ really is *free*, i.e., he could exist without us but chose not to; he is not constituted by his relations *ad intra* or *ad extra* but exists freely in those relations; and God does not depend upon the world (or time) to attain his oneness but relates with the world through time *as* God just because he is one prior to the history of creation through consummation. It must be stressed that the logic of Rahner's axiom leads directly to the incorporation of creation and history into the inner being of God which is typical of all pantheism. Peters thus believes that "God's way of being in relationship with us is God's personhood," p. 126. Such a pantheistic viewpoint achieves the opposite effect from the one intended by Peters. He intends to use trinitarian theology to make Christianity more relevant. But if we cannot distinguish God's free existence from our own personal experiences described in trinitarian terms (as we cannot according to Peters' statements), then Christianity is rendered completely irrelevant in my view.

10. Feuerbach, *The Essence of Christianity*, p. xvi.

11. Ibid., p. xviii.

12. See C.D. 2, 1, pp. 16ff. re: primary and secondary objectivity. Barth's treatment of God's hiddenness (C.D. 2, 1, pp. 179–203) worked out the implications of his distinction between primary and secondary objectivity. In his

Christology, Barth maintained the absolute primacy of the Logos for the same reason by noting that the formula *vere Deus vere Homo* is irreversible, C.D. 1, 2, p. 136. Barth's consistent rejection of any notion of mutual conditioning between creator and creature also reflected this insight (cf. C.D. 2, 1, p. 128).

13. C.D. 2, 1, pp. 59-60.

14. See esp. C.D. 1, 1, pp. 40ff. and C.D. 1, 2, p. 513 re: the nature of a sign and the necessity of the working of the Holy Spirit.

15. C.D. 2, 1, pp. 302-3. As noted in chapter two this is exactly the point that is missed by a phenomenology of symbolic or personal presence. This is where *analogia entis* as rejected by Barth and *analogia fidei* as he understood it begin with different assumptions and lead to very different explanations of God's presence in creation; this also affects how one views Christ's real presence in connection with the Lord's Supper.

16. Cf. ibid., p. 215.

17. C.D. 1, 1, p. 171; also pp. 168-9, C.D. 3, 1, pp. 69ff., and C. D. 1, 2, pp. 302ff.

18. Cf. C.D. 4, 2, pp. 62-5.

19. C.D. 2, 1, p. 158.

20. Ibid., pp. 224ff.

21. C.D. 1, 1, pp. 127-31.

22. Ibid., p. 323 and above, chapter four.

23. C.D. 2, 1, p. 409; also Barth, *Protestant Theology*, pp. 468 and 471ff.

24. Barth, *Protestant Theology*, pp. 468 and 471ff.

25. Ibid., pp. 412ff., esp. 418-20.

26. See also C.D. 2, 1, pp. 291ff.

27. C.D. 1, 1, pp. 322-3; also C.D. 2, 1, pp. 360ff.

28. C.D. 4, 1, p. 132.

29. C.D. 4, 2, pp. 40ff.

30. Cf. C.D. 2, 1, pp. 7ff., p. 44, and C.D. 3, 2, pp. 302ff.

31. McFague, *Models*, p. 166.

32. Ibid., p. 175.

33. See C.D. 4, 3, p. 729 and C.D. 1, 2, p. 215 for Barth's rejection of this idea. As seen above, it is intrinsic to the nature of symbols that they "continue" or "prolong" God's immanent being and action *ad extra*. Those theologians who follow Rahner inevitably speak of the church's human action in the Lord's Supper as a continuation or prolongation of the incarnation as Rahner himself does.

34. On this point see C.D. 2, 1, chapter six.

35. Ibid., p. 308.

36. See, e.g., ibid., pp. 448ff. on this.

37. Ibid., p. 309. This thinking opposes contemporary attempts to think about the Trinity in terms of field theories of modern physics or in terms of personal relationships as understood through social psychology. In both of these cases God surrenders his deity because his freedom to pre-exist creation in reality, and his freedom to exist within creation only in his Word and Spirit, are denied *de facto* and *de jure*. His freedom is denied methodologically because God is defined by his relation with us rather than by who he actually is *in se* and *ad extra*. While most contemporary theologians see the need to overcome the dualist idea that God cannot have real relations with creatures, they follow Rahner's axiom and overcome this by redefining God's Word and Spirit in terms of the mutual conditioning associated with all human experiences within creation.

38. Ibid., p. 187.

39. Moltmann, *Creation*, p. 8, emphasis mine; and above chapter five.

40. Ibid.

41. It is frequently asserted that the idea that God is *a se* is indebted to a substantialist philosophy. It is further stated that, for this reason, God cannot interact with the world. Undoubtedly, philosophy has conceived God as *a se* and has concluded that God cannot be involved in the world (Aristotle's God for instance). But Barth's view that God is *a se* is explicitly grounded in revelation and not in philosophy. If he is right, and I think he is, then we can say that God is free to relate with us without surrendering his freedom because that is the way we know God as he has *acted* in the history of Jesus Christ. Moltmann and others surrender that freedom because they do not consistently ground their theology in revelation.

42. Moltmann, *Trinity*, p. 160.

43. Ibid., p. 106.

44. Ibid., p. 161.

45. Jürgen Moltmann, *The Spirit of Life A Universal Affirmation*, trans. Margaret Kohl (Minneapolis: Fortress Press, 1993), pp. 343 and 290. Moltmann now prefers to speak of the concepts of the *Monarchical, Historical, Eucharistic Trinity*, and *Trinitarian Doxology*. His basic position described above is unchanged. He misunderstands Barth's theology because he believes Barth identified the immanent and economic Trinity and thus left us with no real immanent Trinity. And he grounds his understanding of the immanent Trinity in experience (an experience of identity and of differentiation, p. 300 and finally an

experience of ecstasy, pp. 303-4) which, as we have seen, Barth consistently refused to do. He thus incorporates history, experience, and suffering into God and finally argues that the immanent Trinity, as conceived in the trinitarian Doxology, completes the other three concepts of the Trinity. Moltmann finally appeals to an immanent Trinity which is nothing more than a description of our doxological experience of an eternal moment of ecstasy (p. 304). While he speaks of a distinction between God and creatures, pantheism seems to have the upper hand: "The person who worships and adores becomes in his self-forgetfulness part of the worshipped and adored counterpart [God]," p. 305. John Thompson, *Modern Trinitarian Perspectives*, pp. 33f. also thinks that Moltmann confuses the immanent and economic Trinity.

46. See C.D. 4, 4, pp. 100-102.

47. See C.D. 2, 2, pp. 26ff. and 100ff.; C.D. 4, 1, pp. 124 and 128.

48. C.D. 4, 1, pp. 124 and 128. It is important to note that the conspicuous Arian views of Gordon Kaufman and Sallie McFague (no individual human can be the savior and Jesus is paradigmatic of God's love but not unique) lead logically to their conspicuous Pelagian views that it is we creatures who are responsible for the salvation of the world. In a less radical sense similar connections can be seen in the theologies of Wainwright, Rahner, and Moltmann.

49. See C.D. 1, 1, pp. 171ff., 139, 321, 354, 426f. and C.D. 1, 2, p. 135f.

50. One practical example may help. Justin J. Kelly, *Faithful Witness Foundations of Theology for Today's Church*, ed. by Leo J. O'Donovan and T. Howland Sanks (New York: Crossroad, 1989) in chapter five, describes revelation as symbolic in the Rahnerian sense. Among other things, he concludes that Moses brought to his encounter with Yahweh "the essence of the revelation he receives . . . Thus the call Moses hears as emanating from the bush also has a basis in himself,"(p. 70). This necessity seems inherent in a symbolic view of revelation because such a view cannot distinguish God *in se* from God *for us*; the one depends upon the other. "Real symbols thus involve a paradoxical presence-in-absence, an identity and a difference," (p. 68). By contrast Barth correctly argued with respect to Ex. 33:11-23 that biblical faith excludes any idea of our faith in ourselves or religious self-sufficiency just because it thrives upon God's objectivity. Faith is grounded in God *alone* and not at all in Moses, Paul, or any other human being (including the man Jesus). Kelly finally argues that Jesus' faith "enables him to perfect or complete the faith of others . . . Jesus appeals to a faith knowledge of God latent in the hearts of his hearers to ground the truth of his observation," (p. 77). Since Jesus reveals only insofar as he empowers his hearers to be in touch with what they already know, he receives revelation by discovering this himself, and gives revelation "insofar as he makes this

connection explicit for his hearers," p. 78. Hence "The revelation or message . . . does not preexist the symbol that conveys it . . ." p. 78. Here the complete confusion of Jesus' human faith with revelation traces Jesus' revealing power to a process which makes perfect sense to anyone with a prior knowledge of God. There is no need to believe in Jesus, the Word, since the source of revelation is partially found in our prior knowledge of God and in his and our human experience of faith. Here the sovereignty of grace has been obliterated.

51. See C.D. 1, 1, pp. 139ff., 428 and C.D. 3, 2, pp. 218ff.

52. See, e.g., C.D. 4, 1, pp. 693ff., C.D. 4, 3, pp. 357ff. For Barth, Jesus himself, in the power of the Spirit is the *One* active Mediator here and as such the *one* grace of God. The positive point which can be affirmed on this foundation is that this one grace of God is not transformed into something within the creaturely realm. It is thus the unshakable basis of faith, knowledge, and hope. If that basis were in the world as such then we could only place our faith, knowledge, and hope in ourselves and we would be lost once again in our attempt to save ourselves (the impossible possibility).

53. This obscures our actual justification and sanctification by God alone to the extent that it claims this power for something other than God in His action *ad extra*, i.e., the bread and wine or the human eating and drinking. Once this is seen, Barth's rejection of the three views of grace (i.e., the popular Roman Catholic view, the Neo-Protestant view, and the Lutheran orthodox view as discussed in chapter two above) can be seen more clearly as his attempt to assert both our *need* for Christ and Christ's *uniqueness* as God's own action *ad extra* on our behalf.

54. C.D. 4, 4, p. 102.

55. See C.D. 3, 3, pp. 64, 133 and 135–6.

56. Ibid., pp. 135–37. This positive description of the divine/human relationship, which respects divine and human freedom, is possible only if it is distinguished in the manner discussed in chapter two above. This is crucial because many contemporary theologies define God *by* his relation with the world just because it is thought that God's action in creation can be understood in light of personal relationships existing in time. This obliterates the fact that there is a genuine encounter of two *different* beings.

57. C.D. 4, 4, p. 102. This statement by Barth was made in connection with water baptism, but it applies just as definitely to the church's action in the Lord's Supper. Barth expresses the same idea in relation to the connection between creation and covenant. Cf., e.g., C.D. 3, 1, p. 232.

58. See, e.g., C.D. 2, 1, p. 55 and C.D. 1, 2, pp. 228ff. Cf. C.D. 2, 1, p. 188 for how this thinking relates to God's hiddenness.

59. C.D. 1, 1, p. 325. It is crucial that the difference between Rahner and Barth be seen here. As Rahner believed that Christ's humanity as such revealed his divinity, he directly equated divinity and humanity in various ways as discussed above. We can therefore experience Christ and know him without ever hearing the gospel. Christ's humanity as such can be described as God's eternal love for us. As Barth believed that Christ's humanity receives its power from the *Word alone*, he avoided any such docetic interpretation of history and revelation. He made no such equation, but insisted that, by grace, God has become man in Christ, without surrendering his deity. This is a critical point which is compromised by those theologians who follow Rahner in identifying the immanent and economic Trinity without any qualification. Invariably they make God dependent upon the outcome of history and define God's nature by the nature of human personal and relational love.

60. See C.D. 2, 1, pp. 50–55ff. and pp. 179ff.

61. C.D. 1, 2, pp. 163ff. Cf. also C.D. 1, 1, pp. 163ff. for an application of this insight to knowledge of the Word as mystery.

62. See C.D. 2, 1, pp. 78ff., 180ff.

63. Ibid., pp. 204ff. and C.D. 1, 1, p. 166.

64. C.D. 1, 1, p. 407; C.D. 1, 2, p. 60; p. 467 et al.

65. Ibid., pp. 172, 210ff., and 481. Barth distinguishes the immanent and economic Trinity and our experience and God's Word in a way that Rahner does not.

66. C.D. 4, 4, p. 103.

67. See ibid., p. 102; also above chapter two. With reference to baptism, Barth's notion of *character indelibilis*, C.D. 1, 2, p. 423, is formulated against the Stoic notion that it becomes a human quality. The believer has this character as he or she lives in faith. Therefore, as one who is obedient to the covenant of grace, the believer has the indelible character of a witness to revelation.

68. Ibid., p. 103.

69. Ibid., p. 104.

70. Ibid., pp. 104f.

71. Ibid., pp. 159–61. Barth held that if sacrament means *no more* than a human yes to God's yes in Christ's history, it is acceptable. It bears witness to the divine action in Christ and as such participates in the economy of salvation.

72. Ibid., p. 105. To this tradition Barth ascribes his previous conception of Baptism as treated in 1943.

73. Ibid.

74. See C.D. 4, 1, p. 694. This is why Barth insists that Christ "Himself is fully present and active. He does not really need any representatives, any anointed or unanointed, great or small, sacramentally or existentially endowed vicars," C.D. 4, 3, p. 350.

75. C.D. 4, 4, pp. 105-6. Like the form of revelation (historical words and works of creatures) the divine action gives the human action its proper place and perspective. This cannot be seen if the human act is thought to be identical or reversible with the divine action.

76. See, e.g., C.D. 2, 1, chapter five, esp. pp. 10ff. and 29ff.

77. This is the difficulty faced by Rahner, Wainwright, Moltmann, and Pannenberg to the extent that each theologian sees God as dependent upon history. For Barth, the very idea that God is dependent upon history means that his eternal being and nature has already been collapsed into history and redefined by experience.

78. Cf., e.g., C.D. 2, 1, p. 205.

79. See C.D. 1, 1, pp. 414–89 re: the antecedent being of God as Father, Son, and Spirit. Everything depends upon recognizing that it is God's *antecedent* existence which is the foundation for the events of creation, reconciliation, and redemption. To the extent that Moltmann defines God's inner being by the experience of suffering love, he is led to obliterate God's antecedent existence; he makes it purely eschatological and sees the relation between God and history as a mutually conditioning relationship. To the extent that Rahner believes his symbolic theology (drawn from our experience of the nameless which we call God) can explain God's antecedent being and action he is led to think that God's expression of himself *ad intra* simultaneously results in the exteriorization of the Logos. Thus Jesus in his humanity as such is God's revelation. The symbol is full of that which is symbolized. And the symbol (the humanity) has the power to reveal. It effects what it signifies. God's antecedent existence is not only conditioned by creation but it has no reality independent of creation, despite Rahner's intention to preserve God's freedom. To the extent that Pannenberg defines God's inner being by the idea of the infinite, drawn from our supposed unthematic knowledge of God, he is led to argue that Jesus *becomes* the eternal Son of God and that it is history itself which conditions God from creation through consummation. Jüngel still believes the distinction between the immanent and economic Trinity is important and sees the question of whether Jesus'

humanity as such reveals God as crucial. But, to the extent that he relies on a phenomenological analysis of human love before understanding God's love for us, he compromises his own important insight. In each of these ways these theologians have departed from Barth's most basic theological insight and have thus compromised God's freedom *in se* and *ad extra*. Cf. also Paul D. Molnar, *Toward a Contemporary Doctrine of the Immanent Trinity*, forthcoming in *SJT*.

80. C.D. 4, 4, p. 106. Barth distinguished his view from Gnosticism and the Separatists arguing that they invested "experiences, inspirations, illuminations, exaltations or raptures" with the power which they denied to the sacraments. Instead of a free creature liberated to respond to "that which 'eye hath not seen, nor ear heard . . .' to that which may be known only by God's revelation and through the Holy Spirit . . . [creaturely freedom] is fundamentally eliminated again by exclusive interest in a divine factor which is to be grasped in the human," p. 106. Any depreciation of water baptism or the human actions of eating and drinking then show that people have thwarted the grace of God because these human actions cannot be avoided if it is the Holy Spirit at work. This would be arbitrary human action.

81. Ibid., p. 107.

82. See, e.g., C.D. 2, 1, p. 21. This appears to be the point that T. F. Torrance wishes to emphasize when he compares Barth's view of the Trinity with Rahner's.

83. See C.D., 4, 1, pp. 661ff.

84. Feuerbach, *The Essence of Christianity*, pp. xviii, xix, and 68.

85. Ibid., p. xx.

86. C.D. 4, 1, p. 656.

87. As one concrete example of this problem cf. Sallie McFague, *Models*, pp. 169ff. She argues that the church chose the model of the Spirit to indicate God's sustaining action and contends that, despite certain assets, it is preferable to imagine God as our friend or companion. Implied in this thinking is the idea that the church could have chosen among several different metaphors to imagine God's action. Yet this is far from the case. In truth, the church was constrained by the Holy Spirit of Jesus Christ to acknowledge the Word of the Father and thus to know God and to relate with God. The church recognized God on the basis of God's choice and sanctification and not on the basis of its choice which would have been arbitrary apart from the action of the Holy Spirit. By contrast McFague argues that our ecological, nuclear age (not God) requires, among other things, that we identify God and the world. Spirit language she argues will not help in this. We have repeatedly seen that a theology which is not arbitrary

makes a clear and sharp distinction between God and the world in order to recognize God's Spirit as the Lord and Giver of life.

88. C.D. 1, 2, pp. 516–27ff.

89. For a full treatment of this concept by Barth see C.D. 4, 4, pp. 108–27.

90. Ibid., p. 109. Emphasis mine.

91. Ibid.

92. Cf. C.D. 4, 1, p. 695f. See above chapter one.

93. See esp. C.D. 1, 2, pp. 179–80. In connection with the virgin birth and the empty tomb Barth explains the proper relationship between sign and thing signified. Regarding the "empty grave" he writes: "No one will dream of claiming that this external fact in itself and as such had the power to unveil for the disciples the veiled fact that 'God was in Christ.' But was it revealed to them otherwise than by the sign of this external fact?" (p. 179). For Barth one could not arbitrarily ignore or change the external sign without ignoring the content of revelation. While sign and thing signified are strictly distinguished in the Bible they cannot be separated in such a way that one might have the content without the form. This led him to criticize Schleiermacher and Althaus for describing Christmas in such a way as to obviate the need for the Virgin birth as a sign of this particular miracle. Christmas cannot really be seen as a miracle at all if it is equated with the general concept of the supernatural and its fulfillment in Christ. Signs are significant as they are set up in the world by God's choice and cannot arbitrarily be changed or ignored. But signs have no innate power to reveal.

94. C.D. 2, 1, p. 52.

95. Ibid., p. 53.

96. C.D. 1, 2, p. 162.

97. C.D. 4, 4, p. 134.

98. C.D. 1, 2, pp. 223–4, 227, 229, and 232.

99. Ibid., p. 228.

100. Ibid., p. 232.

101. Ibid., pp. 230–31.

102. Ibid., p. 249.

103. C.D. 4, 4, p. 88.

104. Ibid., p. 90.

105. In chapter six we saw that Eberhard Jüngel follows Barth in rejecting the term sacrament. And in Part One we saw that Markus Barth also rejected the term. According to Karl Barth it was Markus who influenced him in rejecting the

term in connection with baptism (cf. C.D. 4, 4, p. x).

106. See esp. C.D. 1, 2, pp. 333ff. There Barth outlined three historical stages during which the church, he believed, succumbed to the temptation not to live by grace.

107. C.D. 2, 1, p. 332.

108. Ibid., p. 336. As we have seen in this book, this matter is complicated by the fact that numerous theologians today appeal to the Trinity in order to validate a generally defined concept of relationality. In this way, and contrary to their own intentions, they fall into partial or total nominalism.

109. Ibid., pp. 338-9.

110. Ibid., pp. 341-2.

111. See esp. C.D. 1, 2, pp. 211ff. This is important in connection with the power of the "keys." Cf. C.D. 2, 2, pp. 437ff., 441-2, C.D. 4, 1, p. 719, and C.D. 1, 2, 680ff. and 487ff.

112. C.D. 4, 4, p. 141.

113. Ibid., p. 143.

114. Thus he contested Brunner's view of the church because it did not give sufficient emphasis to the external law of the church, C.D. 4, 2, pp. 684ff. Cf. also C.D. 1, 2, pp. 214-279. Barth could even say "The activity of the sign is, directly, the activity of God Himself . . . God has bound us, but not Himself, to the signs of His revelation," p. 224.

IX

The Significance of the Lord's Supper as the Work of Creatures

Now we must explain more precisely the nature of the meaning of the church's eucharistic action. Three preliminary remarks are in order. First, the *form* of the Lord's Supper cannot be chosen arbitrarily. It is not a capricious act initiated or commanded by people and must be an eating and drinking of bread and wine; its basis and goal, as we have seen, are in the history of Christ, very God and very man. God alone determines the *form* in which he meets us.[1] This must be recognized and acknowledged or else an arbitrary change in form will lead to a completely different content.

Second, it must have a *communal* and *social character*.[2] When baptized Christians gather in the name of their heavenly Lord, the body of Christ, which is the earthly historical *form* of his existence at the right hand of the Father in his glorified humanity, actually appears and engages in witness to the world in a new form, in and through new witness in different places and ages.[3]

Third, those who come together do so *freely*. If this coming together and attesting Christ's living presence in its act of being his body is not a free human decision, it is *not* obedience to God.[4] For Barth, obedience is not a human choice between two possibilities as with Hercules at the crossroads. It is a free human decision to confirm God's prior decision concerning humanity. God does not force us to be obedient in this way. Nor does he give us the possibility of making one choice as against another. If we freely confirm the divine decision concerning us, we are obedient and free for God. If we deny the divine decision concerning us, we are disobedient. Because God wills our free decision in this matter, he has not made disobedience physically impossible.[5] God does not protect us from nothingness by force, but by commanding our free obedience to himself. To stand between two choices here is to misuse our real freedom which is to be faithful to God.

We must freely recognize the fact that "God has affirmed and therefore denied, that He has chosen and therefore rejected, that He has willed one thing and therefore not willed another."[6] We are not coerced by God to recognize his real presence. We must recognize it with our free decision.[7] This free decision is in fact denied when Christians are viewed as *instruments* or vehicles of grace; actions conceived in this way cannot have the character of free human decisions corresponding to a divine decision.[8] The command of God is an *event* which involves the divine claim which is self-grounded, as well as the human decision and judgment. The fact that people are not physically restrained from embracing the sphere of negation, i.e., that which God has not willed for them, reflects the fact that human obedience can only be a free decision.

As to the material meaning of the Lord's Supper, we must admit theoretically and practically, that it is solely the affair of God before whose countenance the Lord's Supper is performed to bring about that which is promised and which is thus to be expected. This is entirely consistent with Barth's view that because the church does not control its *esse*, it can only be a praying church. It can only fall back entirely upon God's promise to be faithful to his covenant of grace. Only by recognizing this fact will the church abstain from attempting to establish a *direct* encounter with God rather than an *indirect* encounter, i.e., in faith.[9]

This is denied theoretically if this divine promise is ascribed to right administration of the sacrament; this evades the *real* action of the Holy Spirit.[10] This is denied practically if the words or actions seek to establish or guarantee the divine presence. This is and remains *God's act alone*. The eucharistic words and actions must bear the mark of their encounter with God by not attempting to do more than follow the preceding sovereign act of God.[11] Of course this is exactly what *analogia entis* as rejected by Barth cannot admit.[12] A general phenomenology of "media" will never admit this limitation but, as seen above, will assume that what is mediated and the medium are mixed and mutually conditioned. Rather than deriving from Christ's humanity, the Logos is the *irreversible* prerequisite of Christ's human possibility. Similarly, God does not derive his divine power from human action in the church. Rather it is because the Word of God is at work in Christ and in the church that we can live in knowledge of the truth and in a real unity and peace which reflect God's real presence.[13]

Valid Sacrament

The crux of the meaning of the church's action in the Lord's Supper therefore lies in the strict *correlation* and *distinction* between human action as such and the divine action from which it comes, on whose basis it is possible, and towards which it moves.[14] We cannot enter a detailed discussion of the meaning of valid but unfruitful sacraments here. But it is worth noting that, while Karl Rahner stresses the fact that the church is the measure of a person's faith because the Holy Spirit is united with the church,[15] and while he insists that the visible form of the church remains essentially distinct from God's sovereign grace, he also equates the church with its visible and juridically verifiable existence to the extent that he believes that the church's historical and visible form as such "actually causes the grace which it renders present."[16] In so doing he is compelled to think of the church as a "valid sign" of grace both with grace and without it: "in other words Church as parallel notion to Sacrament, understood as sign *and* grace, taken as the valid sacramental sign, even as far as this can be thought of, and indeed can exist, without an effect of grace."[17] Hence the church as a whole can be a valid sign of grace with no effect of grace for the individual.[18] Even if the church is the church of the sinner "its external juridical verifiability" remains a "sacramental sign of the sanctification of the individual." Rahner wished to maintain the freedom of God together with the notion that God has given the church in its historical and visible dimension permanent validity through the ontological change effected in the incarnation. He did this by asserting on the one hand that in principle there must be "merely valid Sacraments which really are Sacraments and yet are empty of grace."[19] On the other hand, he asserted that if we try to comprehend "the sacramental rite separately from its effect of grace, then the Sacrament would lose all its meaning and significance."[20] In a way similar to the way he conceives "pure nature" he believes that the idea of a sign without grace is in reality non-existent. But the concept is necessary to maintain God's freedom. The visible church is a "continuation of the historically tangible reality of Christ" and thus "signifies and effects that we have this freedom [of the *pneuma*] of God."[21] Hence the church is always a valid sign, even though, in its administration of the sacraments, grace might not be there for an individual and we may not be sure of our salvation.[22] Following Barth, however, the problem here is that the correlation and distinction of our free human actions and God's grace cannot be accomplished in this way. First, the church is not identical with grace as a continuation of the tangible reality of Christ and thus has no validity simply as a sign. It might not serve revelation. If it does serve revelation it is only by God's grace, which cannot be seen and described juridically. Second, Christians do not look to the church as the guarantee of their salvation, but to Christ alone. Thus, on the one hand they have an absolutely certain faith. And on the other hand, they recognize that sacraments have no inherent meaning apart from God's grace and revelation.

*Divine/Human Action—*Analogia Fidei

We shall try to explain more specifically divine and human action. For Barth the divine act takes place in the form of the divine command and promise.[23] The human action is always ambiguous but becomes eternally important in relation to this divine act.[24] Just as the church is one, holy, catholic, and apostolic *only* as it recognizes its *true* basis and goal in the act of God in Christ and his Spirit, so the church can only be what it is humanly (i.e., the body of Christ on earth), as it obeys its basis (God) and has hope in its goal (God). As the church points beyond itself to the living God in its midst, it is obedient in this way. As such it is the human, historical, and visible form of his real presence on earth which actually is chosen and sustained by God. This is the mystery of grace itself.[25]

As it points beyond itself the church is not confused with God and it lives its election as Christ's body on earth; it lives by grace, faith, and revelation. This is the *meaning* of the Lord's Supper. The individuals who constitute the community are called away from self-will (sin) to God himself.[26] The church's material commitment to the God revealed in the history of Christ in the power of the resurrection is this common eating and drinking. In this way the church actually attests its oneness, holiness, and catholicity *in* Christ. The church is and has *none* of this as it abstracts from the *reality* of Christ. It is important here to remember that this abstraction takes place whenever Christ's meaning is dictated by the content of an *idea* or *experience*; this necessarily leads to the christomonism and anthropomonism discussed above. The criterion here must be the living Christ, recognized in the power of the Holy Spirit, and no one and nothing else.

Resurrection and Knowledge of Christ

The problem here is enormous and is frequently ignored, misconceived, or denied. While it is certainly true that we cannot know the church's oneness, holiness, and catholicity without an experience of God's Word, such an experience can in no way be equated with special revelation. This would mean that God's sovereign action in Christ and the Spirit *for us* would be controlled by the church in its liberal or conservative doctrines. Sallie McFague, e.g., speaks of the power of the resurrection as follows: "The resurrection is a way of speaking about an awareness that the presence of God in Jesus is a permanent presence in our present."[27] For her the "power of the resurrection" is obviously not dictated by the fact that the crucified Jesus is alive and acting in the power of his Holy Spirit. It is instead an expression referring to the "awareness" (which is no more than a subjective experience) of what is supposed to be Christ's continued presence and to our subsequent attempts to create a better society on earth. Here both the meaning of the resurrection and of Christianity are falsified since in the New Testament, resurrection language described an *event* in the life of Jesus which was eternally significant for all people, including us. And the power of the resurrection refers to Christ himself acting now in the power of the Spirit bringing people to a knowledge of the truth which frees them from the anxious need to look to any other savior.

Gordon Kaufman sees the power of the resurrection as the symbolic expression of human triumphalism, imperialism, and self-interest.[28] Therefore, in his supposedly less authoritarian view of theology, *only* the traditional view is no longer acceptable. Christ's resurrection cannot refer to what the New Testament writers thought they were describing (an actual Easter history in which Jesus appeared to his disciples); it must now be seen as an inadequate mythology which has ruined the basic story of Jesus by distorting the real myth of the cross. For Kaufman (and McFague), Jesus can no longer be the only savior because salvation means ecological and social harmony and many saviors are needed to accomplish this.

Paul F. Knitter uses the expression "resurrection from the dead" to describe the disciples' "conversion" or "faith" experiences after Christ's death on the cross. Since any religious person can have such experiences, Knitter concludes that there may be many saviors and that Jesus cannot be the only one.

> Is not such a conversion or faith experience essentially what countless men and women have felt in their experience of other archetypal religious leaders after the deaths of these leaders? . . . What happened, therefore, to the early Christians and to Jesus after his death might possibly have happened to other believers and their saviors. The resurrection of Jesus . . . does not necessarily imply 'one and only.'[29]

Here the disciples' conversion experiences and Jesus' becoming the savior on the basis of these experiences are substituted for Jesus' Easter history and a new mythology is created: any religious figure could be a savior equal to Jesus, since the reality behind the Easter stories is not in fact limited to an experience of Jesus.

Karl Rahner does not deny Christ's uniqueness or the teaching of the church that there is only one savior and that Jesus is that savior. But his explanation of the resurrection and of Christ's uniqueness leaves him with difficulties similar to the ones just discussed. He actually (though unintentionally) makes Jesus' historical resurrection pointless by grounding it in an experience which makes perfect sense without ever explicitly believing that Jesus is actually risen and alive. Thus, as seen above, he believes that our very experience of hope is an experience of Jesus' resurrection even without reference to the name of Jesus.[30] Following this reasoning, one could conceivably argue that Rahner means that a person may experience the power of the Spirit without actually adverting to this at any given moment. But Rahner actually grounds the meaning of Christ's resurrection in our transcendental experience and thus explains Jesus' historical resurrection (which he believes is indispensable) as a factor in the faith of

Christians. In this way he goes far beyond this limited understanding: "we might now formulate the proposition that the knowledge of man's resurrection given with his transcendentally necessary hope is a statement of philosophical anthropology even before any real revelation in the Word;"[31] even though Rahner acknowledges that this hope was initially expressed historically as hope of resurrection through revelation in the Old and New Testaments, he allows this transcendentally necessary hope to ground our belief in the resurrection.

Certainly, Rahner also ascribes this hope to grace. But by grounding this particular hope in our experience of hope (which can be known quite apart from any experience of or knowledge of the Word in faith), he actually makes grace identical with our own hope for life after death. In this way he, in contrast to the others just mentioned, unintentionally obviates the need to ground that hope in the history of Jesus as the basis for our understanding. While Rahner insists that "*because* Jesus is risen, I believe in and hope for my own resurrection," his thinking is shaped by the experience of hope and not by the fact that Jesus is risen and alive. Thus, on the one hand, he can say that "the 'facts' of Jesus' resurrection must simply be determined in the light of what we have to understand by our own 'resurrection'."[32] On the other hand, he can say that "*faith* in his [Jesus'] resurrection is an inner aspect of that resurrection itself. It does not simply mean registering a certain fact . . . " Rahner even thinks it is appropriate to say that "Jesus is raised 'into' the faith of his disciples" and that "this faith into which Jesus is raised is not really and directly faith in this resurrection; it is the faith which is experienced as liberty from all the forces of finitude, guilt and death."[33] Rahner insists that Jesus' resurrection is the enabling condition of all of this and that Jesus' resurrection cannot be replaced by any other content. But his very method has already replaced Jesus and the "fact" of his resurrection with our experiences of faith, and liberty from guilt, and death. In this respect he has factually made Jesus' historical resurrection pointless exactly by making this event indistinguishable from the experiences of faith and hope.

These examples show that when Christology begins with our religious experience (rather than with faith in Jesus Christ himself as the Word made flesh), it invariably ends with a docetic interpretation of who he is and who we are as those who depend on him. More importantly, such Christology always compromises the certainty of our salvation in him by suggesting that there may be other saviors or that salvation itself may and must become our own concern and work. In each of these examples, and in different ways, the being and nature of the church is compromised by being defined on the basis of experience. Since the significance of the church and of the Lord's Supper is grounded in Christ and in the power of his resurrection, it is crucial that theology begin with Jesus' history as the unique history of revelation and salvation and thus with Jesus' Easter history.[34] To the extent that Jesus' unique history is compromised, so also will the church's celebration of the Eucharist be jeopardized by becoming docetic. Instead of moving from the certainty of its salvation and coming redemption in Christ through the Holy Spirit, the church might seek its certainty in its experiences of faith, hope, or liberation; it will thus compromise its true foundation and ultimate certainty by seeking these in new mythologies, whether overtly Christian or not; it will thus proceed toward some form of sacramentalism or moralism. It may even think it necessary to change the nature of its liturgy in accordance with these new mythologies instead of being faithful to the ongoing acitivity of the Holy Spirit in and through the biblical word.

Real Presence

The church must be especially clear and certain regarding the real divine action and the real human action which take place in the Lord's Supper. Here, in its worship, the church most clearly confesses and lives its actual relationship with God himself.[35] If the church's self-understanding is clear and true here, it can be clear and true in its every day behavior in relation to this same God. But if the church confuses itself with God's actual presence and action here, it will inevitably do the same in its every day behavior: its theology, preaching, ethics, and other activities will also be confused. If the church encounters only a symbol, idea, or experience of God in its worship, then how can it suppose that it meets the reality of God outside its worship? Renouncing what he called "indirect Christian Cartesianism," Barth rejected the idea that the Word of God, as the criterion of theology, could be sought and found in our "own personal experience of faith as such."

> The presence of truth in the Church or its absence from it might depend on whether the Church goes the one way or the other at this point. Jesus Christ can and will confess in some way—and that a salutary and victorious way—even a Church with a bad dogmatics and a bad proclamation due to a wrong decision at this point. This can and should be said by way of comfort. But we neither can nor should be content with that.[36]

The church's action in the Lord's Supper is for Barth not just a general sign of reciprocal union and obligation between creator and creatures. It is the concrete and specific ratification of the church's knowledge of the purifying and renewing work of God himself.[37] In this specific human form the church actually lives its conversion to God himself. In the Lord's Supper Christians confirm their baptism by the Holy Spirit in free responsibility. The meaning of the Lord's Supper then is our *human living* of our *knowledge of faith*. This would not be knowledge of God's act and a corresponding faithful act of the creature if it remained theoretical or idle. Herein lies the connection between word and sign and word and action which Barth stressed throughout the *Church Dogmatics*.[38] As seen above, to confess God with our lips and not with our action is incomplete and false knowledge of God; Barth related theory and practice by comparing this to faith and works.[39] It would not be real knowledge then if this action did not follow at once and self-evidently.[40] But the human action of the Lord's Supper "is neither a causative nor a cognitive *medium salutis*."[41] It is simply the obedience called for by the divine command. The meaning of the Lord's Supper is the church's recognition of its actual transition from self-will to obedience.

The church recognizes that this knowledge and its action are grounded in the very Word and work of God. Consequently, as the Christian is not converted by the Holy Spirit to an idea of the divine or an experience of the holy, but to God himself in his action *ad extra*, the meaning of the Lord's Supper is completely missed if it is thought to be comprehensible apart from faith. In eating the bread and drinking the wine, the church does not enact its idea or experience of oneness, holiness, catholicity, or apostolicity. Rather the church obediently recognizes and attests its oneness, holiness, catholicity, and apostolicity as already effected and established *in* Christ himself. Because God himself (in his act in Christ and his Spirit) is the basis, origin, and norm here, God's presence cannot be equated with any ideology or any human decision taken with respect to an ideology.[42] That is why God himself cannot be perceived *directly* by looking at bread and wine or by considering general ideas of fellowship meals or oneness, holiness, apostolicity, or catholicity. No generally demonstrable concept or experience binds anyone *necessarily* to the triune God revealed in the history of Christ and his Spirit; this especially includes the ideas of relationality and temporality.

The Lord's Supper for Barth is a completely human response to a distinctively divine command (action). The divine action in the history of Christ is the origin, basis, and goal of the human response in the Lord's Supper and cannot be confused with it. The church attests God's actual presence and action as it lives by the divine command and promise.[43]

In recognizing God's actual presence, the church realizes at once that the divine presence to which it responds in the Lord's Supper is not something different or more profound than the divine presence encountered in scripture, preaching, or in its ethical behavior. God is not more present in the Eucharist than in baptism or in scripture. Everything depends upon the fact that the object of faith which is the basis, origin, and goal of the eucharistic action is the God who is the same *ad intra* and *ad extra*. He is not a quantity which can be apportioned to this or that action of the church or to this or that element in creation.[44] Interestingly, while Rahner also insisted that God is not a quantity which can be calculated, he still insisted that God is more present in the Eucharist than in other sacraments and in other places and events.[45]

Doctrine of God (Analogia Fidei)/ *Eucharistic Event*

Barth's criterion for understanding God's "real presence" in Christ is the being of God as the one who loves in freedom. Faith seeking understanding does not reverse its general understanding with the object of faith, i.e., the antecedent existence of God himself. Therefore, a correct concept of real presence literally cannot be attained apart from faith, namely, apart from the preceding and determinative knowledge of the antecedent being and action of God himself.[46] In Barth's theology, the divine perfections belong essentially to God.[47] His essence and act are indissolubly one, though distinct. He *is* God in his *act* of being Father, Son, and Spirit. We do not know God apart from his action. Any attempt to know God apart from his special action as Lord, creator, Reconciler, or Redeemer means abstraction from faith and false theological knowledge. Theological knowledge and true liturgical action are *events* enclosed in the mystery of the Trinity. At every moment they are dependent upon God's free action *ad extra*. Thus, prayer is always crucial for right knowledge and action.

Consequently, if by real presence we mean in any sense at all what can be demonstrated apart from faith in the Father, Son, and Spirit *ad intra* whom we know in his action *ad extra*, we do not refer to the presence which is the basis, goal, and norm for the meaning of the Lord's Supper. All concepts of *local presence* or *symbolic presence* fall under this category.[48] Here, as seen above, there is an irreconcilable conflict between Rahner's symbolic view and Barth's view. Rahner's theology leads logically to the idea of local presence (conceived, of course, in a non-materialistic way). Barth's view leads logically to his rejection of this.

Both the idea of local presence and the concept of symbolic presence suppose that God, in his action *ad extra*, can be perceived *directly* by simply viewing bread and wine or the human action in which the church celebrates the Lord's Supper. We have seen, however, that a god who can be seen directly—i.e.—by looking at the created elements and human action *cannot* be God at all because both God's veiling and his unveiling can be seen indirectly, and only in faith. In addition, without revelation, it might be supposed that people in the church had been given the power to render God present by human consecratory words and actions. If the *analogia fidei* is the norm, however, this in *no sense* can be admitted; because if only God can reveal God, then only God can make himself present to his creatures. God did not give his divine power over to creatures so that they now might control God either locally or symbolically (theoretically or practically). Rather we creatures must live entirely by the promise that God will reveal himself again and again in the power of the Holy Spirit.

This is an *event* in which God precedes and we may follow. If we could render God present, we would, in some way be superior to God and our sacramental action could no longer be defined as pure obedience. Human action would then effect what it signifies. In that way divine and human action would be confused and reversed. The only hope in such an instance is a return to faith.[49] The ideas of local and symbolic presence variously may mix and separate divine and created being and action first by assuming that the sacrament celebrates something that is going on in the world and then by assuming that it is full of the reality symbolized. Yet neither idea can maintain clearly and consistently the *correlation* and *distinction* between divine and created being and action as known from the being and activity of the triune God. This clear correlation and distinction is a must for the knowledge of faith.

As discussed above, this is precisely Barth's point in defining the possibility of analogy *only* as a possibility of faith. To speak of similarity between God and creatures on the basis of any other possibility is an attempt to speak of God without God. It will end where it begins, either in parity (monism), disparity (dualism), or a combination of the two (synthesis). But it will never begin and end by making a clear distinction between God and creatures. For that reason it will never end by speaking of a definite *relationship* between *two different* beings.

This does not mean that for Barth God is present in some vague way. Barth clearly would follow Calvin by arguing that the Holy Spirit actually unites Christians with Christ; "our life before God flows from the flesh and blood of Jesus Christ."[50] The objective bond here, however, is the Holy Spirit. Therefore, Christ's presence in the Supper does not affix, enclose, or circumscribe him by the bread. His presence must "be such as neither divests him of his just dimensions, nor dissevers him by differences of place, nor assigns to him a body of boundless dimensions, diffused through heaven and earth."[51] God is fully and completely present in the sphere of secondary objectivity. This indicates that we cannot recognize him by ignoring the fact that in his presence he is veiled. Nor can we deny that he is unveiled. He is really and fully present by the power of his Spirit, but we can only perceive this indirectly as our views, concepts, and actions point beyond themselves to the object of faith. In other words, the Lord's Supper, like the act of knowing God, is an *event* enclosed in the mystery of the Trinity. It cannot be understood except as an *analogia fidei*. This is what Barth meant when in the *C.D.* 2,1, he spoke of symbolical, sacramental, and spiritual presence. In the sphere of creation his real, full, actual, and complete presence can be known indirectly as he gives himself to be known. This cannot be anticipated or guaranteed by the church in the Eucharist, but can be recognized and appreciated.[52]

Necessity of Faith

It is precisely in connection with God's actual presence to humanity that the affinity between Barth's doctrine of God and his concept of sacrament is most apparent. Barth's contention that we cannot know God without God is decisive here. This connotes that we cannot know God in his inner *esse* unless the views and concepts which are generally comprehensible to us are clarified first and *normatively* by his particular *antecedent* being and action. Faith alone knows that God *in se* determines the definition of the God we meet *ad extra*. Without faith there is nothing to prohibit a reversal here. Without faith we may think that the human action of Christ, the human action of the church in general, and the human action of eating and drinking *define*, and to that extent determine, God's inner *esse*. Without faith, then, we are left wholly exposed to Feuerbach's critique.[53]

The irreversibility of analogous concepts is pivotal to everything Barth has to say about the relationship between faith and understanding. His insistence on the unity of God's being and action in *C.D.* 2, 1, is the determining presupposition here. This is not an arbitrary insight, but stems from Barth's trinitarian insight that God is the one true God in his threefold action *ad intra* and *ad extra*. For that reason we meet God in Christ and in the proclamation of his witnesses. But if any of this can be reversed, then true knowledge is lost. If we can think or say that we know God's holiness or mercy, his love or his freedom simply by knowing the human actions of mercy, love, freedom, or holiness, we have already confused revelation with ourselves and reversed the relationship of grace between God and creatures established and maintained by God alone. Barth's extensive and revealing treatment of the divine perfections (attributes) is a brilliant attempt to work out this insight.[54] But the pivotal point to be noted here is that the whole positive weight of Barth's sacramental and dogmatic thinking is formulated against any kind of theoretical or practical *reversal* of the predicates of divine and human being.

This was Feuerbach's fatal mistake and as Barth was fond of noting, Feuerbach was not alone in reading Christology, atonement, and other theological doctrines in light of "the personal experience of the human subject." De Wette, Tholuck, Hegel, and his disciples had all sought God's revelation in some aspect of human being, action, or feeling. Thus, "The question arises whether Feuerbach does not represent the point of intersection where all these lines converge."[55] But, of course, this is not the essential point here. Here the crucial point is the idea, apparently derived from Luther, that as the predicates of

Christ's humanity and divinity could be reversed, so the positions of God and creatures could be reversed. The fatal mistake involved in this reversal is that one's attention is now directed to the humanity of Jesus and to the "sacred elements of Holy Communion . . . as such and *in abstracto.*" Thus,

> In principle this clearly meant that the higher and lower positions, those of God and man, could be reversed. And what the theologians of old had seen as being right for the person of Christ was now, to more modern and even less restrained speculating minds, capable of seeming proper for man in general. German theology had for centuries guarded itself perhaps all too rigidly against the Calvinist corrective, so that it was bound to become uncertain now whether the relationship with God had really in principle to be thought of as irreversible.[56]

For Barth the truth of every aspect of theological knowledge was determined by this irreversibility. Reversibility means *identity* between God *in se* and creatures; a complete dissolution of the truth of theology itself; and confusion of nature and grace. Hence, Barth maintained that this irreversibility was decisive in countering confusion of God's presence with human self-presence in his lecture on Feuerbach in 1926 at Münster,[57] and regularly in the *Church Dogmatics.*

As it concerns the sacrament, in such a reversal, God *in se* can really be nothing more or less than the being which we discover for ourselves by directly and phenomenologically examining the man Jesus, the visible church, and the church's action of eating and drinking, or the elements themselves. On this view creatures are really lords not only of themselves but of God *in se*. This is why Barth continually maintained the *distinction* between God *in se* and God for us.[58] This led him to maintain the distinction between the humanity and divinity of Christ in his Christology and between Christ as transcendent head and his earthly historical form of existence, the church, in his ecclesiology. This is why Barth maintained the distinction between the God, present in the power of the resurrection and by the Holy Spirit, and the Christian who participates in that same power as one whose whole being is in God. All of these factors are correlated *not* because it has pleased us to discover this for ourselves but because it has pleased God to be known *in this particular way*. It is because we cannot know God apart from the place and manner in which he chooses to be known that we actually are bound to his revelation. We shall now apply Barth's concept of real presence as derived from the antecedent existence of God to the Lord's Supper. This is controversial in the modern context because, as we have seen, many post-Barthians and Rahnerians rather overtly define God's antecedence *by* his action for us in the economy of salvation.

Omnipresence/Real Presence

In himself God is omnipresent. This means that in his inner *esse* God is remoteness and proximity itself. Because he is this way apart from creation, self-sufficiently, creation is possible.[59] Omnipresence is a determination of the freedom of God and denotes the sovereignty on the basis of which everything that exists cannot exist without him.[60] Because God exists in this way *in se* we cannot attempt to define his divine presence either as non-spatial or as timeless. God's remoteness and proximity *in se* as Father, Son, and Spirit is the condition of the possibility of created space. God's eternity, i.e., the simultaneity of past, present, and future, is the condition of the possibility of time. In both instances God's inner *esse* cannot be understood if the criterion is a general concept of infinity. Such views are comprehensible only in relation to what is spatial or finite. But they cannot explain God's inner being which exists beyond the dialectics observable in creation. God's inner *esse* is not defined in *relation* to anything or anyone outside itself. In a Christian concept of God, his eternity does not prevent him from becoming time as one who is at the same time eternal, i.e., in Christ. In a Christian concept of God we know that he is not absolute non-spatiality. Non-spatiality means existence without distance, which means identity. But his triune existence is not presence in identity. It is togetherness at a distance.[61] God possesses space as Father, Son, and Spirit. This means that divine spatiality is his being, and therefore *different* from every other being. He is spatial only as the one who loves in freedom and in no other way. Finally there is no place that he is less present than in all others. He is everywhere and always the "One" who he is.[62]

Because God is spatial in his *unique* way of being Father, Son, and Spirit *in se* and *ad extra*, he is present to himself and to everything outside himself as Lord. That is why he cannot be defined in his inner *esse* by creation. His inner space transcends and as such includes created space. Created space makes sense only as included in God's divine space and not vice versa.[63] In his doctrine of creation Moltmann saw this problem and tried to improve upon Barth's view of God's freedom by grounding divine spatiality in the Jewish-mystic view of creation. But in this way Moltmann's own view of creation actually does not respect the fact that God's spatiality is different from every other form of space.

In Barth's theology then there is no absence of God in relation to his creation. The fact that he is present to himself and to creation is an expression of his love. It denotes his freedom as Lord but at the same time expresses his desire for fellowship with a reality distinct from himself. God is present to the world in general. But this general presence is determined and guaranteed by his special presence, namely, his presence in his Word. Therefore the way from God's self-presence (*ad intra*) to his presence to the world is not direct but indirect (through his eternal Word). God's omnipresence therefore is bound up with the special nature of his presence in his revealing and reconciling action ontologically and not merely epistemologically.

There is of course a contrast between the special places determined by God in the Old Testament and in the New Testament. Barth notes that in Deut. 12:1-14 the gods of the heathen are characterized by the arbitrary and accidental way in which the places of their dwelling and worship are fixed. The God of Israel is described as one who dwells in a definite place chosen by him alone. The place itself is not regarded as holy as though the Lord could be enclosed possessively. He is not imprisoned in this place but can destroy it. But he always will dwell with Israel and he possesses a definite place.[64] Christians can no longer seek holy places like a holy land or a holy mountain because the distinctive dwelling place of God on earth, of the God of Ex. 29:45, Lev. 26:1ff. and of Rev. 21:3 is not a dwelling place made by human hands. It is none other than Jesus Christ himself.[65] Jesus Christ, very God and very man is the center of the Old and New Testaments. He is the special presence through which all else *must* be seen. It is only through him that humanity in general can encounter the triune God. He is the only element in creation that is of the same essence of God *ad intra*.[66] Only in this particular form can God's presence in the world in general be recognizable.

Because the triune God is really like this *in se*, self-sufficiently, we can have confidence that God himself is actually present as the basis and goal of the church's thanksgiving. But we actually know of no other divine presence than what became a reality in Jesus Christ.[67] Thus, in the Lord's Supper and in creation generally, we do not speak of the real *event* of God's presence except *in* Christ. This means that if our understanding of his real eucharistic presence is merely psychological or sociological, then "The Holy Spirit has vanished in thin air."[68]

Christ and Church

Here we must recall that the *unio* in Christ is unique. Only he is very God and very man, unconfused and unmixed; yet also unseparated and undivided. *No other creature can say this.* That is why this *unio* is the basis of everything that is included within it on the basis of grace.[69] Christ is the revelation and the reality of the divine space by which all other spaces are created, preserved, and surrounded; because of him there can be no docetic explanation of real presence. God's actual presence on earth is *not* non-spatial. Because Christ is like this and we, by nature are not, we can recognize and participate in God's real presence only in him, both noetically and ontically. It is precisely this God who dwells properly in Christ and in creation in general *indirectly*.[70] For that reason he can be known only in faith.

This is why Barth defines the church as the earthly historical *form* of Christ's presence on earth. The church is the "sacramental" presence of its heavenly Lord only as it is epistemologically and ontologically obedient to the God encountered in Christ. In this way the church actually is the earthly form of the transcendent existence chosen by God here and now. Only as the Lord's Supper truly attests this transcendent presence does it attest Christ's real presence in creation. It cannot do this by confusing its words and actions with those of its Lord. It can only do it by following and not attempting to precede the divine command and the divine promise. This is the *distinction* which is real and which remains between Christ and his church. He is really our brother but he is not only that. He is not primarily that. He is primarily one who is self-sufficient and for that reason capable of becoming our brother without ceasing to be fully divine and therefore fully free. The actual *event* of Christ's presence must be respected as the divine present; therefore it is because of a free act of God, if it takes place that in our recollection and expectation, it actually happens that God reveals himself.[71]

"At the Right Hand of the Father"

Barth's solution to the problem of how to interpret the ubiquity of Christ's human nature after the resurrection rests on the priority of God's antecedent existence both before, during, and after creation.[72] For Barth, as we have just seen, Christ is God's proper presence in the world. This historical fact is the fulfillment of the Old Testament expectation and the source of New Testament recollection. There really is *no other access* to the immanent Trinity for Barth. Of course, after the resurrection we recognize this only by the Holy Spirit.

We have already seen that Barth would reject Karl Rahner's *identifying* the immanent and economic Trinity because it leads to the docetic view that a person can be a Christian anonymously. In connection with the resurrection it leads to the idea that our transcendental experiences of hope can explain the fact of Christ's own resurrection as we have just seen. For Barth, Rahner's anonymous Christian would be one who either had not yet or no longer recognized Jesus as the mystery of revelation. For Barth, there is no access to the immanent Trinity if we bypass the historical Jesus in order to define revelation. Because of this, the corporeality of the historical and exalted Christ who sits at the right hand of the Father, must have a definiteness and distinctness from all other spaces.[73] It is this distinct presence which the Eucharist attests but does not bring about or guarantee. The church cannot confuse its history with Christ's unique history which the Spirit opens to humanity.[74] It is the presence of the triune God that is attested in the form of its human action. That is why it cannot be conceived by directly associating it with bread or by calling it a symbolic presence. He himself is *directly* present and active in his Spirit. But because the mode of that presence is the realm of secondary objectivity (i.e., the church in its obedient action) he is not directly disclosed, even in the Eucharist. He remains veiled even in his real presence. His actual presence therefore is not symbolic. It is directly the prophetic work of the One Mediator.[75] But the church's *apprehension* of it is symbolic; in its human words and actions the church attests the actual divine action.

Only in the very restricted sense of pure obedience then can the meaning of the church's act be described as symbolic, sacramental, and spiritual. The reason for the distinction is that a phenomenology which mixes the medium with the object mediated also mixes the church's action with the divine action of the One Mediator. Both are quite impossible in Barth's theology. The community is to proclaim his presence in this way until his presence, now visible only in faith, already experienced here and now with this eating and drinking, is revealed.[76] Herein lies the eschatological importance of the Lord's Supper. In this regard Rahner's theology of the symbol goes too far by claiming that the symbol is related essentially to what is symbolized and thus can render it present because it is full of what is symbolized, contains it, and thus causes what it signifies.[77] This thinking logically dissolves the immanent Trinity into the economy of salvation. Assuming all reality has received this infinite depth of symbolic reality[78] Rahner logically concludes that all theology is anthropology and that "Anyone who accepts his own humanity in full . . . has accepted the Son of Man, because God has accepted man in him . . . he who loves his neighbour has fulfilled the law . . . because God himself has become this neighbour."[79] Here everything is reversed. Instead of having to believe in the Son of Man in order to know one's neighbor (who is not identical with God or with Jesus) Rahner substitutes the neighbor for God and equates acceptance of Christ with self-acceptance.[80] Though Rahner intends to make Christ more relevant than past mythological views of the incarnation, this very view of Christ could not in fact make him more irrelevant. And the problem stems from the idea that Christ's presence in history can be explained symbolically.

In light of this study we can say that these views result from reversing the christological predicates in the *communicatio idiomatum*. This thinking compromises God's freedom to precede and determine the meaning of sacramental reality. Those many theologians who uncritically follow Rahner's trinitarian axiom are invariably led, in one way or another, to insist that God has, in some sense made himself dependent upon the world. This is the point at which faith and the logic of symbolic ontology really do lead to different views of reality. What symbolic logic cannot perceive is that, although God *freely* creates fellowship, as symbolized by the Lord's Supper, he never abandons his divine power (the power of the Spirit) to the human action or to the elements. In other words, if the sign is indeed effective, it is not because of any intrinsic capacity, but solely because God makes use of it. Thus, God's real presence can only be seen and explained in faith, i.e., through the object of faith, Jesus Christ. But it can so be seen and explained. And when faith is normative, the relation between the sign (human action/elements) and the thing signified (the action of the Spirit) is never described as *intrinsically* and *essentially* related in this way.

It must be remembered also that Christ was not just omnipresent in his divinity. His divine act included a human and corporal presence. The corporal or real presence of Christ cannot simply be equated with the divine action which is its basis, sustenance, and goal. Yet on the basis of grace, the corporal presence of Christ cannot and must not be denied in any way at all.[81] For this reason the presence of the whole Christ must not be denied or restricted to his divinity, his Spirit, or his grace. All of this is true and actual as an *act* of God which *freely* includes us in fellowship. It is precisely in virtue of the fact that it is his Spirit and grace that are actually present as the church is obedient to the divine command and lives by the divine promise, that he himself is wholly present.[82]

It is the *same whole Christ* who exists at the right hand of the Father in one way, and in Israel (in terms of expectation), and the church (in terms of recollection), and in the world in another. He is at the right hand of the Father properly and originally (i.e., in primary objectivity) and he is present to Israel, the church, and the world "symbolically, sacramentally, and spiritually."[83] He is here no less than there. The whole Christ is present in both places. That is why the human action of obedience to the promise can neither be denied nor underestimated in an encounter with the reality of Christ, very God and very man. We have been given a definite share in God's loving. But we have been given this *indirectly*, i.e., through Christ and the Spirit as attested in scripture and in church history. Because the logic of symbolic ontology does not determine what Barth has to say here, he does not ascribe an infinite depth to humanity and claim that self-acceptance amounts to acceptance of Christ. Here Barth can distinguish and unite nature and grace rather than mixing and confusing them just because his norm is the unique man Jesus and not some idea of sacramentality or symbolism as generally defined. Barth treated this problem thoroughly in his doctrine of creation where he applied once more his notion of real presence as *event*. He insisted that the man Jesus is really but transcendentally present here and now, as the church is obedient noetically and ontically. In him, salvation is fully and completely realized. We can grasp this in faith through his Spirit.

His past history, His yesterday, cannot be understood or portrayed as a thing of the past, a thing of yesterday. The yesterday of Jesus is also to-day. The fact that He lives at the right hand of God means that even now He is absolutely present temporally . . . These men do not make or feel or know themselves the contemporaries of Jesus. It is not they who become or are this. It is Jesus who becomes and is their Contemporary. As a result of this, His past life, death and resurrection can and must and actually do have at all times the significance and force of an event which has taken place in time but is decisive for their present existence . . . if there is anything doubtful for Christians here, it is not His *presence* but their own. And if there is anything axiomatically certain, it is not their presence but His. There is obviously no baptism or Lord's Supper without His *real presence* as very God and very Man, both body and soul. But this presence cannot be regarded as restricted to what were later called 'sacraments.' For these are only a symbolical expression of the fact that in its worship the community is gathered directly around Jesus Christ Himself, and lives by and with him, but that through faith He rules over the hearts and lives of all even apart from worship . . . the historical distance, the past, in which Jesus confronts them is not abrogated by His presence. His yesterday is not cancelled by His to-day . . . even the presence of Jesus in the Spirit, for all its fulness, can only be a pledge or first instalment of what awaits the community as well as the whole universe, His return in glory. But it must never be forgotten that He who comes again in glory, this future Jesus, is identical with the One proclaimed by the history of yesterday and really present to His own to-day . . . The fact that the man Jesus will be includes the fact that He is; but the fact that He is does not exclude that he is 'not yet.'[84]

Eschatology

What this means is that the church actually exists as the earthly historical form of God's special presence in the world after the resurrection. Therefore the church must live in recollection of the fact that Jesus is not merely a past or present being. He is also a being in the future.[85] The living Christ will be missed if his coming is stressed more than his past and present. The real presence of Christ is no less in expectation than in recollection.[86] If this insight was taken seriously today, then, instead of arguing that all life comes from the future, one would have to argue that our life in the future is established by who God is before creation, within creation (in the history of Christ and in the history of the church) and in the new creation as the Spirit brings to completion our redemption.

In light of this, it is clear that Moltmann's eschatology ignores God's pre-temporality because he explicitly denies that God could have freely existed without the world. And he transforms God's supra-temporality by making Christ dependent on the faith of others to become what faith acknowledges he always was, is, and will be. He also transforms his post-temporality into a principle which is dictated by and produced from our experience; thus he believes that God needs the world just because he believes that "From eternity God has desired not only himself but the world too . . . That is why the idea of the world is already inherent in the Father's love for the Son . . . "[87] God's freedom therefore does not mean that he is free to decide to act or not; his freedom is reduced to the essence of love as selflessness. Moltmann thus reduces God's essential nature to his creative love and argues that "Love is a self-evident, unquestionable 'overflowing of goodness' which is therefore never open to choice at any time."[88] But the very idea that God is not free to choose to love before created time, within it, and after it has ceased is a denial of his deity.

That is why Barth wrote to Moltmann in 1964 about his concern that he had subsumed "all theology in eschatology":

> To put it pointedly, does your theology of hope really differ at all from the baptized *principle* of hope of Mr. Bloch? What disturbs me is that for you theology becomes so much a matter of principle (an eschatological principle). You know that I too was once on the edge of moving in this direction, but I refrained from doing so and have thus come under the fire of your criticism in my later development. Would it not be wise to accept the doctrine of the immanent trinity of God? You may thereby achieve the freedom of three-dimensional thinking in which the eschata have and retain their whole weight while the same (and not just a provisional) honor can still be shown to the kingdoms of nature and grace . . . If you will pardon me, your God seems to me to be rather a pauper . . .[89]

Moltmann's response to Barth seems not to have really appreciated the depth of the difficulty toward which Barth was pointing:

> The nub of your criticism caused me the most cogitation, namely, that in place of eschatology—to escape its dominating onesidedness—the doctrine of the immanent Trinity should function as an expository canon for the proclamation of the lordship of Jesus Christ. I must admit that in studying *C.D.* at these point I always lost my breath. I suspect that you are right but I cannot as yet or so quickly enter into this right . . . I thought I could so expound the economic Trinity that in the foreground, and then again in

the background, it would be open to an immanent Trinity. That is, for me the Holy Spirit is first the Spirit of the raising of the dead and then as such the third person of the Trinity.[90]

The problem here is that the Holy Spirit which Barth had in mind is Holy because he is the Spirit of the Father and Son in eternity (before all worlds) and only as such the Spirit who enables us to participate in the power of Christ's resurrection. By abandoning the traditional distinction between the immanent and economic Trinity[91] Moltmann concludes that the economic Trinity "has a retroactive effect" on the immanent Trinity. And the problem with this is that history defines the nature of God's love and freedom; nature defines the meaning of grace and sovereignty; and ultimately suffering and nothingness define not only the essence of the Godhead but the nature of revelation and salvation. Indeed, the Holy Spirit cannot finally be distinguished from the cosmic Spirit or the Spirit of evolution in Moltmann's thought because he believes the Spirit is first the Spirit of the raising of the dead and only then the third person of the Trinity. Thus he writes

> The Spirit whose efficacy forms body, soul and their living Gestalt is not merely the creative Spirit: he is at the same time the cosmic Spirit . . . this Spirit must be called the Spirit of God and the presence of God in the creature he has made. But according to biblical usage, this is not the Holy Spirit. The Holy Spirit is the name given to the Spirit of redemption and sanctification . . . 'The Holy Spirit' does not supersede the Spirit of creation but transforms it.[92]

It is interesting to note that Moltmann directly addresses Barth's concern about the doctrine of the immanent Trinity in his recent book on the Trinity. What Moltmann seems to object to most is the fact that for Barth "everything has its hidden beginning in the mystery of the immanent Trinity."[93] In fact there is nothing wrong with this. Indeed, if everything does not have its beginning in this mystery (election), one would be compelled (as Moltmann is) to seek that ground in creation, thus obliterating the distinction between God and the world.[94]

If it is the presence of Christ which dictates our knowledge of God's future then God's freedom cannot be compromised as Moltmann does because, in Christ we know that God's future includes his free existence before time and within time as the Lord and Savior. By not distinguishing the immanent and economic Trinity in the traditional sense, Moltmann's views are grounded in a social doctrine of the Trinity which does not overcome tritheism and modalism as he thinks.[95]

Keeping to Barth's insight that neither Christ's pre-existence, nor his existence in history in Palestine, nor his future existence can be played off against each other, we may say that the community which celebrates the real presence of Christ himself does not have in view some utopian goal, perhaps in the form of an ideal community or an ideal "new creation." For the apostles there was no hint of growth toward a better future either here or hereafter. The future of the New Testament is the wholly new order which exists quite independently of all Christian growth and development. This new future is not an ideal state but the coming of the Lord.[96] It is the definitive and general revelation and therefore the justification and redemption of individuals in judgment. The resurrection was the revelation of the kingdom of God in glory. This is God's grace of revelation and thus it cannot mean what Moltmann thinks it means, i.e., that the coming glory "will complete both nature and grace."[97] Christian hope consists in the fact that the goal of that hope is the same as its basis, namely, the one who will come. He is the same one who was yesterday and who is now.[98] For us, the resurrection and second coming are two separate events; for God they are one. The resurrection is the anticipation of his parousia as his parousia is the completion and the fulfillment of his resurrection. Because Christ alone is the object of church's recollection and expectation and as such the one who is present as the presupposition and *telos* of the Eucharist, the church's hope is already fulfilled in him. It is just because this realized eschatology plays no decisive role in Moltmann's thought, that he believes that Christ's Lordship will be complete only when he hands the kingdom to the Father and that "God and the world are . . . involved in a common redemptive process . . . we need God's compassion and God needs ours . . . God himself will only be free when our souls are free."[99] Because the church's hope is already fulfilled in the history of Christ, it is not an empty hope.[100] The church must continue to wait because what was fulfilled in Christ can be known only in faith in his having become a real man and hope in his glorious return. This is the meaning of the Eucharist as an Easter meal. It is the celebration of the already of the resurrection in view of the not yet of Christ's return.[101]

These two very different eschatological views of Christ's real presence illustrate that a faulty trinitarian theology will obscure the church's eucharistic celebration. For Barth, the real presence celebrated in the Eucharist is grounded pre-temporally, supra-temporally, and post-temporally in specific acts of the Triune God in whom we believe and hope. These are the *events* which the Eucharist celebrates as the real presence of the Lord. It is truly the supper of the Lord who assures those who share in it the fullness of hope which is and can be theirs as an action of God. For Moltmann, this specificity is compromised by his grounding real presence so fully in the future to the exclusion of the past and the present, and by detaching Christ's presence from Christ himself, and locating it in a principle of hope.

We have now presented Barth's view of Christ's real presence showing how the Jesus who lived and now lives at the right hand of the Father can be truly present through the power of the Holy Spirit. We have seen how none of this is grounded in experience because Christ actively makes himself present and can be recognized in faith. Concepts of local presence and symbolic presence compromise this need for faith in the invisible action of the Holy Spirit. We have seen that Christ's presence propels the community forward in hope toward his coming again. Therefore the future Jesus is identical with the one who came and the one who acts now.

Notes

1. C.D. 2, 1, p. 479.

2. C.D. 4, 4, pp. 131ff. re: baptism. The parallels with the Lord's Supper are obvious.

3. See the basis and meaning of the church's oneness, holiness, catholicity, and apostolicity in C.D. 4, 1, § 62, esp., pp. 650–725.

4. C.D. 4, 4, p. 132; C.D. 1, 2, pp. 661ff. and p. 670. See also C.D. 2, 2, pp. 444ff. and 487ff. and C.D. 3, 1, p. 264.

5. C.D. 3, 1, p. 266.

6. Ibid., p. 260.

7. See also C.D. 2, 2, pp. 177–81, 767, and 778ff.

8. Ibid., pp. 463ff.

9. Cf. C.D. 4, 1, pp. 672–73. This counters S. W. Sykes, ed., *Karl Barth: Centenary Essays*, chapter 4, "Authority and Openness in the Church," p. 77 who believes that Barth has given no *"concrete* limit to the power of ministry" by appealing to prayer in order to say that office is tied to Christ but that Christ is not tied to office. This is exactly the *limit* which is visible only to faith. Sykes thinks Barth has not diagnosed the differences between Reformed and Roman Catholic dogmatics here. Yet, since we have shown throughout this work that the basic problem is one of mutual conditioning (which follows identification of nature and grace), I think we have also illustrated that Barth had correctly diagnosed the problem by rejecting any such mutually conditioned relationship between the church and Christ. This did not mean there was no relationship. It meant that the relationship had an *absolutely* firm foundation in grace; it escaped both epistemological and ontological questioning from without and attempts to verify the church's oneness and holiness etc. by pointing directly to elements of the church's existence. This relates to the *opus operatum*. Barth opposed this because God's presence can neither be confused with nor guaranteed by the

visible church. The church is what it is as it lives by faith, grace, and revelation. Since there are no analogies which are true in themselves, even the visible church has no truth in itself. Its truth is only visible in its "third dimension" (C.D. 4, 1, p. 661). *Opus operatum* seeks a verification of *grace* which detaches grace from Christ acting *ad extra*. Therefore I would say that Barth's theology of ministry *concretely* acknowledges Christ's sovereignty in this way. Just because his Christology is neither ebionite nor docetic (chapter three above) Barth is able to show that Christ alone can act in the power of his Spirit to preserve the church in truth. But only faith can acknowledge this and then understand. This is how I believe Barth's theology answers Sykes' objection as to whether "Barth's theology of the ministry . . . . *concretely* acknowledges the sovereignty of Christ," p. 76. Sykes seems to recognize this in connection with Barth's eschatological view of dogma (pp. 81ff.). Problems arise when he concludes that the "innovatory Word of God [needs] to be 'managed' in everyday, sociological reality," p. 83. Sykes readily acknowledges that Christian unity could not develop from the "co-operative activity" of institutions but "by their common participation in the dynamics of the Word and of the Spirit," but the very idea that the Word needs to be managed actually negates the insight.

10. Cf. ibid., pp. 695ff.

11. Cf. C.D. 2, 1, pp. 38ff.

12. Thus I do not agree with Sykes, that Barth misrepresented the Catholic view of the *analogia entis*, p. 73.

13. Thomas F. Torrance, *Karl Barth*, notes that if we take seriously Jesus' consubstantiality as Word and Son, then scripture cannot be understood in a "dualistic" symbolical or metaphorical way (following Augustinian or Thomist thought) which divides sensible and intelligible to know God. Scripture must be seen "as the miraculous act of God speaking to us personally, creatively calling from us the hearing of faith," p. 173.

14. See Barth's understanding of the *terminus a quo* and *terminus ad quem* of human knowledge of God above, chapter one and C.D. 2, 1, pp. 179–254. The exact same understanding applies here. Barth also applies this insight to his entire treatment of the being and activity of God throughout C.D. 2, 1.

15. T.I. 7:107ff.

16. T.I. 2:5–6, 47, and, 73. This, however, does not mean that Rahner believes there is no room for pluralism: The Roman Catholic church "in no way subscribes to the notion that the one Church consists solely of juridically and liturgically homogeneous segments," *The Unity of the Churches An Actual Possibility*, Heinrich Fries and Karl Rahner, trans. Ruth C. L. Gritsch and Eric

W. Gritsch, (New York: Paulist Press, 1985), p. 44. Insofar as the church is an *opus operatum* it escapes juridical definition: "This concept [of the church as sacrament] cannot be defined simply by saying, in formal juridical terms of a decretal theology, that such a process is efficacious of itself . . . the *opus operatum* is to be taken as the supreme degree of the Church's actuality, as the act of its self-*realization* . . . such an act participates in the nature of the Church, as described when we said that it was the final, unvoidable [*sic*] and instrinsically [*sic*] definitive sign of God's absolute self-bestowal . . ." T.I. 4:274. Thus, Rahner can say that sacraments have been instituted by Christ "because and to the extent that the Church as such derives from him," T.I. 14:146. But because the church is a real symbol of Christ's grace "It is possible to point to a visible, historically manifest fact, located in space and time, and say, Because that is there, God is reconciled to the world . . . There is the spatio-temporal sign that effects what it points to," *C.S.*, p. 15 and T.I. 12:9. Because the Spirit is united with the church, i.e., the Roman Catholic church "with the bishop of Rome at its head" (T.I. 2:5), Rahner believes this juridical order constitutes the church and brings about grace and the Holy Spirit, T.I. 7:189. Thus the juridical church as a whole is a guarantee against an individual seeking this tangibility for himself, T.I. 7:190f.

17. T.I. 2:74.

18. *C.S.*, p. 32.

19. T.I. 2:76.

20. Ibid., pp. 71f.

21. Ibid., p. 96.

22. Ibid., pp. 58 and 76.

23. See C.D. 1, 2, pp. 409ff. and 847–48; C.D. 2, 2, pp. 509–781; C.D. 3, 1, pp. 259–76; C.D. 4, 1, pp. 156–57; C.D. 4, 2, pp. 190ff. This, as we have seen, is the basis of the church's celebration of the Eucharist and of its fellowship with God and creatures.

24. C.D. 4, 4, p. 135. This is Barth's application of his insight that no analogy is true in itself. It becomes true only in faith.

25. Cf. C.D. 4, 1, pp. 650ff. and pp. 717ff.

26. C.D. 4, 4, p. 137.

27. McFague, *Models*, p. 59.

28. Kaufman, *TNA*, pp. 49–50.

29. Knitter, *No Other Name?*, p. 200. Cf. Ibid., pp. 197–202.

30. See above chapter three and Rahner/Weger, *Our Christian Faith*, p. 113.

31. Rahner, T.I. 17:18.

32. Ibid., p. 20.

33. Ibid., p. 22.

34. Regarding the importance of the resurrection in Barth's theology see Thomas F. Torrance, *Karl Barth*, pp. 22-3, 100, 164ff., and 207f.

35. C.D. 4, 2, pp. 706ff.

36. C.D. 1, 1, p. 215.

37. C.D. 4, 4 p. 138.

38. Cf., e.g., C.D. 1, 1, and C.D. 1, 2, pp. 500ff. For more on Barth's view of the relationship between faith and works see above, chapter seven.

39. See C.D. 1, 2, p. 737.

40. Cf. Ibid., pp. 362ff. The human action (sign) seals the knowledge of faith as a special witness to the *event* of fellowship effected between God and us by God alone. Sacraments "can only bear witness. They cannot as on the Roman Catholic view effect it as a means of grace" (C.D. 1, 2, p. 762).

41. C.D. 4, 4, p. 156.

42. Ibid., p. 140.

43. Ibid., pp. 143, 147.

44. C.D. 2, 1, pp. 234ff.

45. T.I. 10:80. Also Cf. T.I. 4:281-86.

46. C.D. 2, 1, pp. 340-50. See also C.D. 1, 1, pp. 375-489.

47. Ibid., pp. 340f.

48. On this point see esp. C.D. 4, 2, p. 657 and Lk. 17:20ff. Barth notes that we cannot establish the presence of the kingdom directly indicating it with a here/there. Yet it is in our midst.

49. See C.D. 2, 1, pp. 12-31ff.; C.D. 2, 2, pp. 766-774 and C.D. 3, 3, pp. 250ff. where Barth describes faith as a summoning of the whole person. See also C.D. 4, 2, pp. 657-60. It should also be noted that the relationship between the words and actions of those involved in celebrating the Lord's Supper is the same as it is between the noetic and ontic encounter with God which Barth describes in the doctrine of God. The words are necessary because they express the knowledge of faith. Without specific reference to the object of faith we might have in mind someone or something else when celebrating the Lord's Supper. The actions of eating and drinking are important since they confirm what is known in faith. They are called for by the God who is known on the basis of faith, grace, and revelation.

50. Calvin quoted in Alasdair Heron, *Table and Tradition*, p. 141. Cf. C.D. 1, 2, pp. 355-6. Forgiveness "denotes a definite event . . . it denotes the unification of the eternal divine Word with the nature of man, and therefore with the rectification of that human nature . . . This rectification . . . is the work of Jesus Christ from birth to death, and it is revealed to be such in His resurrection from the dead . . . if [Christians] live by the grace of God, if they participate in the human nature of His eternal Son, if they are nourished by His body and His blood as earthly members of His earthly body in communion with Him as their heavenly Head: then for the sake of this fellowship their sins are forgiven . . . " In C.D. 4, 4, *The Christian Life*, Barth insists that true calling upon God is certain since "It is participation in *his* [Jesus'] calling upon *his* Father. 'We pray as it were by His mouth' (Calvin . . .)," p. 105.

51. Ibid., p. 142.

52. See also C.D. 1, 2, pp. 210ff., 303, 765-66, and 768.

53. While Pannenberg believes he has overcome Feuerbach's critique by appealing to anthropology and religion, he actually does not escape the sphere of subjectivism because he grounds his view of reality in our subjective experience of anticipation. Cf., e.g., *Systematic Theology I*, p. 332 and Paul D. Molnar, "Reflections on Pannenberg's Systematic Theology" in *The Thomist*, 58 (1994): 501-12 and "Some Problems with Pannenberg's Solution to Barth's 'Faith Subjectivism'" *SJT* (1995).

54. C.D. 2, 1, pp. 322-677.

55. Barth, *Protestant Theology*, p. 537.

56. Ibid., p. 538.

57. Cf. on this point Barth's Introductory essay to Feuerbach's *The Essence of Christianity* where he writes: "Feuerbach has become a thorn in the flesh of modern theology, and perhaps will continue to be so: so long as the relation to God is not unconditionally inconvertible for us, and does not remain so under all circumstances, we shall have no rest in this matter," p. xxiv.

58. In C.D. 1, 1, this distinction was the key to his doctrine of the Trinity. In C.D. 1, 2, it was the key to his treatment of the incarnation as the action of the one triune God. In C.D. 2, 2, it was important for his treatment of the doctrine of election; it was critical for his presentation of the doctrines of creation in C.D. 3 and reconciliation in C.D. 4. Cf. e.g., C.D. 1, 1, p. 321, 3, 2, pp. 49ff. and 4, 1, pp. 123ff.

59. C.D. 2, 1, pp. 462-63. Cf. also C.D. 3, 1, pp. 3-41. God's omnipresence includes the fact that he loves. He does love the world. But he does not have to relate with the world to be this loving God. In connection with

his omnipotence then: "Absolutely everythings [*sic*] depends on whether we know God as the One who is omnipotent in Himself, and . . . recognise His omnipotence, of course in His omnicausality in creation, reconciliation and redemption . . . Absolutely everythings [*sic*] depends on whether we distinguish His omnipotence from His omnicausality," C.D. 2, 1, p. 528. If God's power to be present or to exist in himself only comes into existence with creation or if it is in any way dependent on creation, reconciliation, or redemption, then creation has defined God. Then God's Triunity merely describes his actions *ad extra* and to that extent no longer the trinitarian God who is omnipotent in himself before acting *ad extra*. Everything we have said depends upon the fact that God is subject of his works. He is not an unconscious being (thing) but "He has awareness. He establishes and grasps His own being, and with it all being, in an act of knowing," Ibid., p. 566. God is neither imprisoned by his own being nor by the being of creation.

60. C.D. 2, 1, p. 461.

61. Ibid., pp. 467–68.

62. Ibid., p. 470. For a full treatment of this subject see C.D. 2, 1, pp. 470–77.

63. Colin Gunton, *The Promise of Trinitarian Theology* (Edinburgh: T & T Clark, 1991), argues correctly that speculation about the inner being of God is no mere speculation: "the distinction between economic and immanent Trinity achieves more than a concept of God's freedom. It is . . . a matter of human freedom as well," p. 138. He thus indicates that God's eternal space and time are the pre-conditions for our space and time which are not God's but need God to exist. This is the case, even though it is not always clear that Gunton avoids defining the immanent Trinity by the economic Trinity as when he seeks to understand God in terms of the field relations of modern physics, pp. 156ff. By arguing that the persons of the Trinity are mutually constituted, the danger of defining the Son and Spirit by their actions *ad extra* is heightened. An example is Gunton's criticisms of Augustine. Gunton argues that Augustine gives little weight to a concept of love derived from the incarnation. "There, the essence of the love of God is its outgoingness: its dynamic seeking of the other," p. 51. There is no clear distinction between God's self-sufficient seeking of his other and his free seeking of another distinct from him in this reasoning. How can the essence of God's love be its outgoingness? God can and does go out of himself, but if his essence is his outgoingness then the incarnation is no longer a free act but a necessary expression of his love.

64. C.D. 2, 1, pp. 478–80.

65. Ibid., p. 482. Barth notes that if Christianity tries to proclaim special places again in the Old Testament sense, it will lapse into Judaism.

66. Ibid., p. 484.

67. Ibid., p. 485.

68. C.D. 3, 2, p. 493.

69. See C.D. 2, 1, pp. 150ff.

70. Ibid., p. 486.

71. C.D. 1, 2, pp. 503ff.

72. For a historical analysis of this problem see C.D. 2, 1, pp. 487–90. See also C.D. 3, 2, pp. 509–11; C.D. 3, 3, pp. 285 and 264. For Barth, the guidance of the Holy Spirit means obedience to the Word of God and not one's own heart or other's hearts. See also C.D. 4, 2, p. 652. The power in which the Holy Spirit works is not a remote operation of Christ. It is as the Lord seated at the right hand of the Father that Christ is superior to the earthly community which exists in Him. See also C.D. 4, 1, pp. 662–68.

73. C.D. 2, 1, p. 489; C.D. 4, 1, pp. 661–62; C.D. 4, 2, pp. 351ff. and 652.

74. C.D. 4, 2, pp. 653, 727ff. and C.D. 4, 1, pp. 663ff.

75. C.D. 4, 3, pp. 348–59. See also C.D. 1, 1, pp. 169–71 and C.D. 3, 3, pp. 131ff.

76. C.D. 3, 2, p. 214f. Cf. C.D. 1, 2, p. 516.

77. Karl Rahner, T.I. 4:221–252, pp. 237–242. See also *C.S.*, pp. 37–39.

78. Ibid., p. 239.

79. Ibid., p. 119. Cf. also T.I. 13:195–200 where Rahner does not deduce the meaning of the Christian faith from Jesus through revelation, but from our *relationship* to Jesus which can be explained by *our* experiences of neighbor, death, and the future.

80. See above, chapter three for more on this matter and for Ratzinger's criticism of Rahner's theology on this point.

81. See, e.g., C.D. 1, 2, pp. 140, 147ff. and C.D. 4, 1, pp. 663ff.

82. C.D. 2, 1, p. 490.

83. Ibid.

84. C.D. 3, 2, pp. 467–68. Emphasis mine.

85. Ibid., p. 485.

86. Ibid. Cf. also 2, 1, p. 631 where Barth properly insists that there can be "no basic rivalry with regard to the three forms of eternity [i.e., God's pre-temporal, supra-temporal, and post-temporal existence]."

87. Moltmann, *Trinity*, p. 108.

88. Ibid., p. 55.

89. Karl Barth, *Letters*, pp. 175–6.

90. Ibid., p. 348.

91. Moltmann, *Trinity*, p. 160.

92. Moltmann, *Creation*, 263.

93. Jürgen Moltmann, *History and the Triune God: Contributions to Trinitarian Theology*, trans. John Bowden (New York: Crossroad, 1992, hereafter abbreviated: *History and the Triune God*), part two, chapter three, esp., p. 130.

94. Moltmann does call attention to an ambiguity in Barth's thought in C.D. 4, 1, pp. 200ff. Since Barth spoke about the immanent relations of Son and Father in terms of obedience, Moltmann accuses him of projecting human images into God "along the lines of Feuerbach's critique of religion . . . " Moltmann, *History and the Triune God*, p. 130. The view that there is subordination within the Godhead is actually contradicted by Barth's previous view expressed in C.D. 1, 1, p. 393.

95. See Molnar, *TS*, 1990.

96. C.D. 3, 2, pp. 486–87; 1 Cor. 16:22.

97. Moltmann, *Creation*, p. 8.; Molnar, *TS*, 1990.

98. C.D. 3, 2, p. 489.

99. Moltmann, *Trinity*, p. 39.

100. C.D. 3, 2, p. 493.

101. Ibid., pp. 502ff.

X

Transubstantiation: Occasion for Unity and/or Dialogue?

Finally, a discussion of the doctrine of transubstantiation will show the chasm that exists between Reformed and Roman Catholic theology,[1] and will summarize many of the essential arguments in this book. On the basis of Barth's doctrine of God, Christology, ecclesiology and sacramental theology there can be no notion of transubstantiation. Based on Rahner's doctrine of God, Christology, ecclesiology and sacramental theology, the idea of transubstantiation can make logical sense. But for Barth, such a concept ignores: 1) the actual *correlation* and *distinction* between God and creatures which exists in the church's action of the Lord's Supper, and 2) the fact that "in the Lord's Supper it is distinctively a question of outward and inward, visible and invisible, physical and spiritual nourishment at one and the same time."[2] Since the event of God's action is totally different from any other knowable event, divine events cannot be differentiated from non-divine events by distinguishing nature and spirit, soul and body, inner and outer, and visible and invisible reality. If they could, we would end in the dualism which is so regularly rejected by Thomas Torrance and others.

Barth maintained that in scripture the event of revelation has a natural, bodily, outward, and visible component, i.e., creation, Israel's existence in Palestine, the birth of Christ, miracles, the death of Christ, and the physical resurrection. Just because of this, a description of God as absolute spirit, as a type of chemical purity as against "nature," may confuse the reality of God with the reality of the spiritual world created by God, and just as dependent upon him as the world of nature. For Barth, "The divine being must be allowed to transcend both spirit and nature, yet also to overlap and comprehend both, as attested in His revelation." If God has no nature, as is supposed by any purely spiritual understanding of the divine being, he would be unable to do anything. This conception is controverted by revelation which, as God's action, occurs only in the unity of spirit and nature without compromising God's divinity (freedom). Any denial of this fact is a denial of the reality, truth, and real history of God's activity *ad extra* and for that reason of God's life *ad intra* as well.[3]

For Barth, transubstantiation implies either that the created elements of bread and wine or the human actions of eating and drinking become essentially transformed *into* something else; it makes no difference whether it is conceived primarily as a *spiritual* change or not. A spiritual change which blurs the distinction between creator and creature (and creation) can have nothing to do with the Holy Spirit of the triune God. An abstract spiritualism is as mistaken as an abstract naturalism.[4] Unless the free grace of God is respected at the outset it will inevitably be identified with an element in creation, whether spiritual or natural. In that way faith would be evaded. At this point we may say that transubstantiation is a doctrine which typifies the discussion of God's freedom *in se* and *ad extra*.

Faith is evaded when scriptural inspiration is seen as a natural element in the human word as such. Detached in this way from the free working of the Holy Spirit, scripture could at best be seen (as it was during the Enlightenment) as a highly relevant historical record. When the church wanted tangible certainty instead of the certainty of faith and sought it in the natural sphere as such, the outcome was either the Enlightenment position or the equally preposterous opinion that the scriptural writers were "mere flutes in the mouth of the Holy Spirit."[5] Whenever scripture is perceived as self-grounded, and understood apart from the mystery of Christ and the Holy Spirit, it will invariably be spiritualized and naturalized. Similarly, when the Lord's Supper is seen as self-grounded, it too will be spiritualized and naturalized. But the proper *correlation* and *distinction* between spirit and nature will never be seen. From this vantage the result of a conception of transubstantiation is that we only have left the appearances of bread and wine and of the human actions of the participants.[6]

If we try to escape this problem by focusing once more on the elements, we shall escape docetism by falling into the waiting arms of ebionitism. Then God's acts will be identified once more with a reality distinct from him.[7] To put this in historical terms, we refer to Barth's assessment of the historical attempt to deduce the meaning of Jesus' uniqueness from history or psychology on the part of theologians confronted with this same dilemma: "The situation was such that in running away from Feuerbach they ran straight into the arms of Strauss."[8] In other words, they left the sphere of faith in an attempt to deduce Jesus' divinity from history. For Barth we do not have to sacrifice the *realities* of bread or the human action this way, since neither is *identical* with God's real presence.

Barth maintained that this notion confuses human and divine being and action. In terms of the doctrine of God (*analogia fidei*) it presumes identity between the immanent and economic Trinity by suggesting that God *in se*, who is the basis and goal of the eucharistic celebration, becomes indistinguishable from the sphere in which he meets us, i.e., the oikonomia—the bread and wine and the human actions. We have seen the problem with this above.[9] Such a view may identify, separate, or synthesize the spheres of primary objectivity (the immanent Trinity) and secondary objectivity (the economic Trinity). And when this happens real knowledge of God is dissolved into creation or denied altogether. Because Barth wished to ground knowledge of God's real presence in God alone but did not wish to deny humanity a real place in this knowledge, he maintained that we could know God analogously in faith. This, however, would mean recognizing that analogies of parity (monism), disparity (dualism), or synthesis (pantheism) are excluded as possible ways of apprehending the mystery of God's presence in history by the real presence of God himself. In addition, a view which makes God indistinguishable from creation, denies God's hiddenness.[10] In fact God can be seen only in faith, by the power of the Holy Spirit. This does not imply a purely spiritual presence because God's spiritual presence *includes* nature without compromising God's transcendence.

In terms of Christology, it confuses the humanity and divinity of Christ by implying that his deity was merged essentially into his humanity. On such an assumption, however, both his divinity and our humanity lose their character as two distinct entities. Either his humanity is only an appearance of his divinity or his divinity is an appearance of his humanity. The problem here is that the historical Jesus is not respected in his actual uniqueness since we might just as easily know the truth which he brought without ever knowing him. Thus, the determining element of the truth in this context becomes once again our human idea of truth and not God in his unique action in Christ and the Spirit.[11] Both ebionite and docetic Christology miss the truth of God's revelation because they seek to ground the uniqueness of Christ in human experience or reflection. The result of reversing faith and understanding in this way is an apotheosis. Barth's analysis and rejection of christomonism and anthropomonism in describing the sacraments finds its basis in his rejection of ebionite and docetic Christology. We may know the truth of God's real presence only in faith and not directly in our experience or any ideology. This crucial insight is frequently ignored by current theology with the result that the very mystery of revelation is, to that extent, dissolved into the sphere of anthropology.

In terms of ecclesiology, it confuses the heavenly head with the earthly-historical form in which he continues to relate with us. In this way the church becomes indistinguishable from God in his special presence on earth in his Word and Spirit. This misses the fact that the church can be this special presence only in obedience to Christ and his Spirit and not in its actions as such.[12]

In terms of the sacrament of the Lord's Supper such a view confuses the elements of bread and wine and the human eating and drinking with the divine action which is their basis, origin, norm, and goal. In this way the elements and the human actions become indistinguishable from the sovereign and divine action of one who is *Lord*, and only as such, brother as well. The mystery of God's presence to, for, and in us is exactly that. It is his real spiritual presence[13] which cannot be resolved by dissolving the created substance. The two exist in free relation and full distinction in an encounter with the Holy Spirit.[14]   The Holy Spirit opening people to revelation from within "is not identical and cannot become identical with ourselves;" thus God remains Lord within us and does not become part of our essence.[15]   This is the most important practical consequence of distinguishing the immanent and economic Trinity.   Rahner, Moltmann, and Pannenberg each, in the different ways discussed above, actually merge the Holy Spirit into our creaturely essence.   And the seriousness of this problem is indicated by the fact that although each theologian speaks of God, Christ, and the Spirit in emphatic terms, each has, to a greater or lesser extent, shown how really unnecessary it is to *believe* in the historical Jesus as the Word *in order* to understand divine and human reality.

Whenever Barth directly rejected transubstantiation in the *Church Dogmatics* his reason was christological.   This is both a warning and a sign of hope.   It is a warning because no genuine discussion of Reformed and Roman Catholic sacramental theology can take place without a detailed conversation about Christology.   It is a sign of hope because both Reformed and Roman Catholic theologians accept the major scriptural and conciliar definitions regarding Jesus Christ; and they are willing to insist together that God's self-revelation ought to be the point of departure for future discussions.[16]   This is their common ground and it must not be underestimated.   Another sign of hope is that when Barth insisted that anthropology cannot make sense if Christology is only one instance of what we creatures can discover generally, he opposed both Catholics *and* Protestants who failed to respect Christ's sovereignty.   Thus, a genuine rapprochement between Catholics and Protestants need not mean "taking sides" against each other.   Both sides could recognize and assert the uniqueness of Christ and their own unique inclusion into fellowship with the Trinity by the grace of God and then expound upon the nature of and meaning of the sacraments.   But in order to do this, the arbitrary method of theological inquiry, which begins from anthropology in order to explain Christology and is "one of natural knowledge," would have to be abandoned.   For Barth such a method leads inescapably

into an impasse . . . That Jesus, who is true man, is also true God, and real man only in this unity (the unity of the Son with the Father), does not destroy the difference between divinity and humanity even in him . . . There is a divinity of the man Jesus. It consists in the fact that God exists immediately and directly in and with him, this creature . . . that He is the divine Saviour in person, that the glory of God triumphs in him, that He alone and exclusively is man as the living Word of God, that He is in the activity of the grace of God . . . that he is man for God. But there is a humanity of the man Jesus as well as a divinity. That He is one with God,

Himself God, does not mean that Godhead has taken the place of His manhood, that His manhood is . . . swallowed up or extinguished by Godhead, that His human form is a *mere appearance, as the Roman Catholic doctrine of transubstantiation maintains of the host supposedly changed into the body of Christ.* That he is true God and also in full differentiation true man is the mystery of Jesus Christ.[17]

Barth recognized clearly the distinction he wished to maintain:

The decisive principle in the Roman Catholic doctrine of change is that through priestly consecration there takes place a *conversio totius substantiae panis in substantiam corporis Christi Domini nostri et totius substantiae vini in substantiam sanguinis eius (Trid. sess. XIII, Decr. de ss. Euch. cap.,* 4) and this in such a way that only the *accidentia* of bread and wine remain *sine subjecto (ib. can.* 2 and *Conc. Constantiense* 1415 *Errores Joannis Wicleff* 2, Denz., No. 582).[18]

In Barth's view, however, "Bread remains bread and wine wine, to put it in eucharistic terms. The realism of sacramental consecration does not imply destruction of the signs' own existence."[19]   As Alasdair Heron had done in connection with *ex opere operato*, Barth associated transubstantiation with the question of ecclesiastical power and its relation to Christ, the mediator.[20]   In Heron's view, the problem is not that the doctrine does not intend to speak objectively about God's action. Insofar as it does, Heron thinks it ought not to be surrendered.[21]   The problem is that God's action is objectively located in priests and bishops who cannot be bypassed as the channels of grace.

For Barth, the unity of the sign with the thing signified does not imply a change in the sign *qua* sign.[22] The two go together only because of grace. Thus, speaking of the miracle of the virgin birth as a sign of the mystery of God's incarnation, and of the empty tomb as a sign of the revelation of this mystery Barth wrote: "If we cannot separate the sign from the thing signified, as, with so many others, even Brunner unfortunately wishes to do the *sign* is *still* not *the thing signified.*"[23]   Signs do not explain what is signified but bring to light its character as mystery by clearly denoting it. It is precisely in the limited fact that human words and actions as such are used by God to point to himself in his presence that they may become true. They could only become more than signs if sign and thing signified are mixed as in a general phenomenology.

Here we see the major disagreement between Barth and Rahner. It is methodological and christological. It is methodological because Barth will not begin thinking about God or sacraments apart from explicit faith in Jesus himself.

It is christological because if Jesus' uniqueness is respected, then he literally cannot be understood phenomenologically or symbolically (in the sense of Rahner's Real Symbol). Understood symbolically, Christ will be seen as the highest instance of revelation or the supreme actualization of humanity. In this way his uniqueness cannot be respected. Rahner is led to maintain that the hypostatic union arises from history in the sense that if human nature is assumed as God's own reality

> then it has reached the very point towards which it is always moving by virtue of its essence . . . the very thing which necessarily takes place in man in an initial way [orientation toward God—obediential potency for the hypostatic union] . . . this takes place in an unsurpassable way . . . when this nature of man as so understood so gives itself to the mystery of fullness and so empties itself that it becomes the nature of God himself.[24]

Christ's uniqueness cannot be respected because theology must either acknowledge this man's uniqueness as the eternal Son of God or think of him as the highest symbolic expression of a revelation which it can know apart from faith in him. There really is no third way here. Consequently, for Barth, there is no change in the sign or human action as such just as there is no fusion of deity and humanity in the incarnation. The sign never becomes more than a sign. For Rahner, as we have seen, the only way he can make sense of our relationship with God is by referring to an alteration in the structure of our human consciousness, i.e., to the supernatural existential. For Barth, the sign and action can never be more than a pointer to the mystery of revelation in which it really is involved. It is in that indirect involvement in the mystery of the Trinity that human being and action actually change without becoming semi-divine or semi-human. They change in their relationship to God and for that reason and to that extent they themselves have a different being and action than they would otherwise have had.

It is only on the basis of a general phenomenology that Rahner can say that "the dispenser of the sacraments takes the place of Christ himself in the dimension of the sign that effects what it signifies."[25] Rahner carefully indicates that the dispenser of the sacraments does not bring about the grace in any proper sense because that is reserved for Christ (the *res sacramenti*). Thus the human dispenser "does not take the place of an absent Christ, but rather represents Christ as present in the dimension of the 'effective' sign, even though it is Christ himself who, of his own power, brings about the grace in his *pneuma*."[26] But the problem is that his conception of Christ's presence in the dimension of the sign is such that the *res* necessarily expresses itself and the sign effects what is signified by being the way in which grace becomes incarnate. In other words, according to Rahner's theology of the symbol, there is a mutual causal relationship between sign and thing signified.[27] This includes the ideas that the church "contains" the reality signified and that "The grace of God no longer comes (when it does come) . . . from a God absolutely transcending the world . . . it is permanently in the world in tangible historical form, established in the flesh of Christ as part of the world, of humanity and of its very history."[28] Hence while Rahner intends to distinguish the "dispenser" of the sacraments from Christ, he actually makes them mutually dependent:

> sacraments after all cause the graces they signify as visible signs . . . the union of the many grains of wheat in the one bread and the communal eating . . . are signs of the unity . . . of the table companions of Christ among each other . . . Hence the Holy Eucharist must also increasingly cause such a unity . . . Holy Communion causes the fullness of the Spirit to increase in everyone . . .[29]

Additionally, while Rahner correctly rejects any materialistic understanding of transubstantiation and prefers a personalistic view, he does believe that the bread, as an anthropological reality, changes[30] and that Christ's full presence is somehow dependent on the intention of the priest and the disposition of the individual.

Barth maintained that Christ alone is and remains his own mediator. Only as human words point to this *fact* without becoming confused with it can they have the character of truth. This is exactly what cannot be maintained by saying that the dispenser of the sacraments takes the place of Christ on the level of the sign. It is the other way around. Christ mediates himself. Insofar as this real divine mediation is perceived and explicated, human language is enclosed in the mystery of the Trinity. For that reason a consistently clear distinction between Christ and humanity must be maintained. Because Rahner's thinking is dictated by his theology of the symbol, he makes no such consistent distinction and even argues, as seen above, that grace is implanted in the world so that a person's self-acceptance means accepting Christ; and grace is part of the consciousness of a person who lives life bravely.[31] Even more importantly, Rahner concludes that because Christ's human nature is "the constitutive, real symbol of the Logos himself"[32]:

> It is possible to point to a visible, historically manifest fact, located in space and time, and say, *Because that is there*, God is reconciled to the world . . . There is the spatio-temporal sign that effects what it points to.[33]

Necessity of Faith

The entire theme of Barth's theology is that ideas such as transubstantiation cannot be recognized as problematic except in faith. Transignification is equally problematic because it claims that the church, in its obedient act of proclaiming Christ's actual presence until he comes, is *more than a sign* and pointer to the mystery of revelation, which is its basis and goal. Barth would reject this for the same reason he rejected the Lutheran view of sacrament discussed above.[34] Here it might appear that Barth is offering a Zwinglian separation of sign and thing signified. But as noted above he is actually insisting that the sign remains subordinate to grace and revelation and only thus participates in the life of the Trinity. But it really participates. Faith perceives the actual interrelationship between what is believed and known in the doctrine of God, Christology, ecclesiology, and consequently in sacramental theology.

The norm for each dogmatic consideration is the same. It is God himself in his action in Christ and the Spirit, i.e., the one who is hidden and revealed, loving and free. If the correlation between God *in se* and God acting *ad extra* is clear and decisive, then the same clarity will be maintained between the humanity and divinity of Christ, the head and body, and between the human eating and drinking and the divine action which is its presupposition and goal. This is what we have sought to point out in deriving Barth's theology of the Lord's Supper from his view of baptism and correspondingly from his notion of *analogia fidei* as developed in his doctrine of God. As we have seen, this very thinking structures Barth's Christology and ecclesiology.

As the celebration of the Eucharist actually recognizes, in its words and actions, the living Lord of the church in his divinity and humanity, it is a joyful and saving action, even though it is a fallible work of creatures. This is the case simply because it actively and prayerfully recognizes and honors the Savior in his grace and freedom.[35] In other words it recognizes the positive and negative aspects of the divine freedom. In this sense the human action may be described as a visible sign of invisible grace.[36] But the emphasis is never on the elements. They are important only as used by people in their act of *eucharistia*. Everything depends upon "revelation speaking and being apprehended through this sign."[37] Ideas of transubstantiation and transignification, as well as related theories such as transfinalization, all mistakenly think that creator and creature and the human action or the elements are in some way transformed *into* something. While Barth opposes this, that does not mean that God remains in heaven and nothing happens here on earth.

What is transformed is the *relationship* between creator and creature. It becomes one of faithfulness instead of one of faithlessness. Because it is the living Christ who is attested in this action of the community, it transpires that the community actually is the living *form* of Christ's special presence on earth. In and through the human acts of faith and obedience (not in admixture but together with them) the Holy Spirit actually sets apart these men and women as a sign and witness of the triune God himself. These persons constitute the historical form of God's continued self-attestation. It is in this respect that the church's celebration of the Lord's Supper in itself and as such is *epiclesis*. Like baptism with water, the human action of the church in the Lord's Supper is an action in which the community is gathered around its living Lord.[38] As such it is a saving and protecting action in which Christians are kept from other forms of activity which, in reality, may have nothing to do with worshiping God himself. In this very human way, divine and human action correspond and are distinguished on the basis of grace, faith, and revelation.[39]

It must be remembered that the church is not set aside by God in this way for itself; it is chosen for witness to the world of God's election of all people in Christ.[40] Where God's actual word and work in Christ are perceived, believed and confessed in *active obedience* there, as a sign, signal, and witness of God's purpose for all, the form of his *direct* and continued self-attestation takes shape.

> Where God is truly served, there—with no removal of the human element
> . . . the willing and doing of God is not just present as a first or second co-
> operating factor; it is present as the first and decisive thing . . . Without
> depriving the human element of its freedom . . . its humanity . . . or
> making its activity a purely mechanical event, God is the subject from
> whom human action must receive its new and true name . . . where it is
> true according to His judgment . . . where . . . its character as an event
> that can be seen and heard on earth is not set aside.[41]

It took place in the Old Testament in the form of those who were humanly obedient to the divine command.[42] It takes place now as the community proclaims the saving action of God in Christ as that which is its basis, norm, and goal until he comes again. The church does not control what takes place in its eucharistic celebration. It can only pray that this human action of faith and obedience will become an *event* in the freedom of God. In light of the divine promise, the church can be confident that its action is both justified and sanctified by God himself. This is how a human action can become holy as it is enclosed in the mystery of the Trinity. It can only be seen and understood in *recollection* and *expectation* of the mystery which must always act to make this human action part of the *event* of his real presence.[43] More than this cannot be stated without trying to explain the *how* of the mystery of revelation[44] and therefore without dissolving the mystery itself.

The significant contribution then of Barth's analysis to the modern attempt to express Christ's real presence more accurately resides in linking a clear understanding of the matter both to the doctrine of God and to Christology. Christian theologians no longer have to argue "Reformed," "Lutheran," or "Roman Catholic" terminology to re-express traditional controversies sometimes based upon mutual misunderstanding. The Christian theologian can now ask whether the meaning of the language used actually clarifies the *distinction* and *correlation* between creator and creature recognized in the *analogia fidei* which all Christians accept. In this context, the focus of debate is not on whether or not we accept or reject terms such as transubstantiation, transignification, or transfinalization. This would amount to a repetition of the Denzinger theology which Rahner properly rejected. Instead, the focus is on how Christians can best express to themselves and to the world the mystery of Christ's real presence. Seen in connection with the doctrine of God (and particularly in light of the action of the Holy Spirit) it will be necessary not to confuse God's transcendence (positive and negative freedom) with the historical realities of bread, wine, and human action either conceptually or really. In this way God's real direct presence in history will be seen without depriving the historical church of its reality and true sacramental validity. Otherwise the church and sacraments may be misunderstood as mere "appearances" absorbed into the mystery of God. Or they may be seen as interesting antiquated customs which may be dispensable in favor of new customs which express a reality which is generally accessible to all persons apart from faith in the triune God.

Eucharistia

We may thus conclude this exposition of Barth's view of transubstantiation by noting that at the heart of both its worship and its every day life, the church can be no more and no less than thankful. In this way the church knows that it has actually encountered God himself and not a human apotheosis.[45]

True thanksgiving means that we do not grasp at the command and promise given by God alone in the history of Christ and in the provisional history of his church until he comes again. True thanksgiving recognizes the prior and determinative action of God in Christ there and then (i.e., in the history of the man Jesus). It recognizes that men and women, here and now, have no real history except in that completed history in which the eschaton entered the sphere of secondary objectivity. This is the gift of grace which is proclaimed in the Lord's Supper. Because of Christ's history, true thanksgiving never attempts to precede the Lord that it meets in and through the sphere of immanence in which it lives. The church bears the mark of this meeting in and by the fact that in its sacramental action there is no reversal of this knowledge of faith with its own human action or with the created elements. In other words, the church, in its liturgy, never attempts to be more than human in relation to the One Mediator. In this particular and limited way the church is enabled by God himself, in virtue of the divine command and promise, to be truly thankful. The church cannot offer its *eucharistia* in and of itself. It can do it only as it is *in* Christ himself, who lives as the transcendent head of his earthly body in the power of his Spirit. The church can only be obedient. This is its new possibility in Christ.

The church which is truly thankful in the Lord's Supper will continually ask itself whether and to what extent it really conforms to its heavenly head. It will continually ask whether and to what extent it secretly wishes to exist as a *continuation* of God's completed act in Christ; whether and to what extent it wishes to exist in identity or separation from the Word heard and believed.[46] In this sense the church is truly a pilgrim church. By proclaiming the death of Christ as the completion of the Old Testament and the beginning of the New Testament it will recognize that its noetic and ontic possibility and limitation is and remains God *alone*, present in the power of his Spirit. It is and remains God who did *not in fact* will to exist self-sufficiently without being creator, Lord, reconciler, and redeemer. As one who did not cease to exist self-sufficiently, God willed to have fellowship with another and in fact did so, in Christ.[47] In and through this particular form of grace he continues to seek and create fellowship until his revelation is disclosed generally. When Christ comes again in glory, his body will see its head face to face. This is the basis and norm of Christian thanksgiving. This is the true source of Christian unity, i.e., the object of faith present in history as one who is both loving and free. In his doctrine of God, Barth defined and applied his view of thanksgiving as the substance of creaturely participation in divine grace.[48] If we recognize Christ as the event in which we are awakened and called to participate in the being of God we will be kept from pantheism. The simple fact that God does not will to be God without us, is a grace that we can only thank and serve. Barth also noted that even when we see God "face to face" and "Tears and suffering and crying and death will be no more," even then "we shall not be gods, let alone God himself. There can certainly be no question of our being or becoming this now." "There will be no more Christs. No second or third person will be able to come with the promise and claim: 'I am he!' According to Mk. 13:5 and Mt. 24:5, only 'deceivers' will be able to say this of themselves."[49] Unless we recognize the real divine promise and claim in our thinking and action we may be deceived. This is why the knowledge of faith is so important.

Prospects for Rapprochement

Can there be a rapprochement between Roman Catholic and Reformed theology in the persons of Karl Rahner and Karl Barth? Some theologians such as Thomas Torrance think so.[50] Barth himself was hopeful. Commenting on Rahner's "Notes on the Reformation" Barth wrote to Karl Rahner in 1967:

> . . . it is wonderful that today we can discuss such problematical things [the pope and Mary] without biting and devouring one another . . . I was very pleased at what you wrote . . . about our future fellowship in the Lord's Supper, which is so very different from what we Reformed still hear today from the Lutherans, at least in principle. Think of it: A year ago I was in Rome . . . at a Catholic service, and was seriously tempted to go with my Catholic doctor to the communion rail, refraining only so as not to embarrass the officiating priest who had previously greeted me, and not to cause offense later among the Roman Waldensians. Conversely I do not think there are many Evangelical pastors (apart from some obstinate Lutherans) who would forbid a known Catholic to partake of our Lord's Supper.[51]

But I would say that any potential dialogue between Barth's Reformed view and the Lutheran and Roman Catholic views of real presence would have to take into account the questions raised by the *analogia fidei*. Barth's question was not *whether* God is really present in the church's action at the Lord's Supper; but whether we can truly recognize it as God's presence if our thinking represents this presence in ways that compromise his freedom for and his freedom from internal and external conditioning. Obviously, for Barth, God's freedom to be present in his Word and Spirit (as the enabling condition of the church's obedient action) is compromised if its reality is ascribed to or thought to be guaranteed by the faith of the individual or of the community. God alone is the guarantee in this matter. Consequently that guarantee can never be the response of the community, the action of the priest, or even the words of consecration together with the bread and wine. This does not mean these human actions are insignificant. As the former is seen as true in faith, the latter (ecclesial action) *may* be a sign and historical pointer to God's self-sufficient action of love here and now. This is why the existence of the church can only be seen by Barth as an *event* or a happening in which specific individuals respond faithfully to God as his community at specific times and places. To see its true actuality as a phenomenologically observable state compromises God's freedom.

Rahner certainly sees the validity of this thinking. He thus suggests that "Catholic theologians have something to learn from the '*in usu*' doctrine of

Protestant Christians, without denying the teaching of Trent."[52] But again the problem with Rahner's conception of the Protestant view is in evidence. He believes that the doctrine of Christ's presence held by Zwingli or Calvin is best characterized by saying that "Christ is present only in faith, indeed only through faith;" thus, "God's in his heaven; but nothing happens where the bread is."[53] Yet given what was said above, that is not the issue at all. According to Barth, Christ is really and personally present in the community as the community eats the bread and drinks the cup in remembrance of Christ's promise to be with his community. This presence is his own personal presence. Therefore it cannot be that of an *opus operatum* and cannot be dependent upon any *opus operantis* or anyone's faith. And his presence did not mean that he was transformed into the substance of bread. The focus then is not *on* the bread, but as Rahner himself suggests, upon the union with Christ in faith, grace, and love.[54] Perhaps if we see the significance of the Lord's Supper in the context of Barth's view of analogy, some prospect for reconciliation may be envisioned. Viewed in the context of the analogy of faith one would not ignore the form of the eucharistic celebration which includes Word and elements and cannot be arbitrarily changed. On this point there is no disagreement among theologians.

But because Rahner's Christology has both the ebionite and docetic proclivities built into it from the start, he and Barth are divided first, because union with Christ for Rahner means either an individual's decision with respect to himself/herself or an individual's decision in relation to the church in its sacramentally valid juridical structure. And second, Rahner actually believes that transubstantiation is to be predicated of the bread and wine. And this is connected with his notion of the church, as an *opus operatum,* and with priestly power.

> Christ acts on man through the Church by giving his grace the form of a constitutive sign, it is *he* who renders his grace inwardly efficacious in man, and not his servant nor the recipient of the sacrament. This is the meaning of the term '*opus operatum,*' . . . The gestures of Christ which he performs through the Church . . . are gestures meant in earnest; he on his part really effects by them what he expresses by them, simply because he performs them. If these gestures of the Church are understood from the outset (as they must be) as Christ's gestures . . . then it will be quite easy to understand that there is no sense in asking oneself whether and how they 'act on' the divine (and divine-human) Agent of grace . . .[55]

The point is that sacraments, like Christ and the church are symbolic and thus necessarily express themselves to realize themselves and are constituted by the reality symbolized. Therefore the causality Rahner has in mind is a quasi-formal causality which would give the priest "an essentially higher function" than others and would make him indispensable for the sacrament. While all the baptized faithful offer the sacrifice, the priest is the indispensable guarantee of "its saving validity." Thus, "only the priest does what determines the sacramental validity of the liturgical oblation . . ."[56] Regarding the bread,

> If . . . what our *experience* knows apart from our faith in the word of Christ is the same as before: then this two-fold premise, if it is not to be voided in one direction or the other, can be expressed by saying that what is given is really and truly the body of Christ, under the experimental reality (but only this!) of bread. If . . . I call the proper, definitive and true reality of a concrete 'substance' the species (appearance, look, understood as an objective but partial and particularly prominent reality); and if I see the species as the way the reality presents itself to a particular standpoint, but . . . not as . . . disclosed in its relativity from . . . the word of God; then it can be said that what is given is not the substance of bread, but the substance of the body of Christ under the species of bread.[57]

Christ's real presence is not restricted to this for Rahner, but there is no doubt that his focus is on a change in the elements analogous to his idea that human nature is entitatively modified by virtue of the incarnation.

Here then are the differences. For Barth, union with Christ means a faith decision to accept him and thus to accept our actual reconciliation accomplished in his history. This excludes *any* idea of reducing our union with Christ to a decision for or against ourselves. For Barth the church is not a *sacrament* as it is for Rahner. Hence the church does not have the juridical or spiritual power to stand between individuals and their salvation. The church witnesses to and participates in the fact that Christ actually mediates himself without becoming identical with and dependent upon preaching and administering the sacraments.

Regarding the question of transubstantiation, both Rahner and Barth believe that scripture should be foundational. But if we follow Markus Barth's exegesis of the scriptural texts as discussed above, then despite Rahner's insistence on the humanity of Christ and sacramental realism, he is forced into an awkward position. He cannot say that bread remains bread and wine remains wine because symbols are "full of the thing symbolized," and indeed they are the very reality of that which is symbolized (just as Christ's humanity as such reveals). Yet this, for Barth, is a docetic view of the Lord's Supper because it presents as an appearance something which really is what it is, namely, bread and wine. Christ's real presence is not in his humanity as such or in the bread and wine as such or in the church as a sacramental sign or in the priest as mediator. It is his presence in his Word and Spirit. Thus it really includes human words, actions, bread, and wine in a real relationship which can be seen and grasped only in faith. But God's Word and Spirit are and remain free; our freedom with respect to sacramentalism, moralism, and even ecclesiastical power depends on this fact.

Critical Discussions

Rahner, Barth, and Unity

There is a hopeful and positive tone of new ecumenical openness in *Unity of the Churches: An Actual Possibility* written by Heinrich Fries and Karl Rahner. Similarly there is a conciliatory and hopeful, but realistic tone in Alasdair I. C. Heron's book *Table and Tradition*. Rahner and Fries rejected the idea of "using simple confessional methods of comparison whereby one's own historically actualized confessional viewpoint was made the decisive criterion for judging the other."[58] But it must be asked whether they see the depth of the difficulties here. I will only give two examples: Rahner's view of the sacrament and Fries' view of justification.

Regarding Roman Catholic church unity with Reformation churches, Rahner believes that "With regard to the ultimate essence of the sacraments, there should be no difficulties, if Thesis II is taken into account."[59] According to this thesis "The church itself is the guarantor, through its formal teaching authority, of the truth of the individual doctrines it presents;" though this doctrine itself is not the "first or most fundamental truth of the Christian faith . . ."[60] Rahner further believes that separated mainline churches could be united with the Roman Catholic church "if no church declares that a proposition considered by another church to be absolutely binding on itself is positively and absolutely irreconcilable with its own religious understanding."[61] If such a situation existed, then there could be no unity of faith. But Rahner believes that no such discrepancies as these exist today. The only requirement for union then is that "other churches not reject out of hand an explicit doctrine of the Catholic Church . . ."[62] The fundamental norm for unity then is that prospective partners "not reject any definitive dogma of the Roman church as contrary to the faith."[63] However, that is precisely the problem. As Rahner explains Thesis II, he means that he will accept a formal ideal unity in which member churches do not explicitly reject Roman Catholic dogmas. They may acceptably ignore some since many Catholics now do the same and there is a hierarchy of truths.[64]

But such a unity is vaporous because according to Barth's theology, the truth of doctrine is finally guaranteed by the Holy Spirit and not by the church. Doctrines are important just as church law is important. And insofar as doctrines are correct, the Christian could no more ignore the propositions than he or she could ignore the truth of faith itself. Thus, to acquiesce in the minimalist view of the church which Rahner suggests, namely "that their members exist in a human, juridical, and liturgical unity as baptized and active members" would be out of the question for Barth, at least on *these* terms. This, because the *true* church can only be believed. It is visible and invisible: "Because He is, it is; it is because He is. That is its secret, its being in the third dimension, which is visible only to faith."[65] But its unity cannot be explained juridically in the way Rahner suggests without denying faith.

There is a practical consequence here. Rahner says "All the large churches of the Reformation have an understanding of this manifest Word of grace derived from Christ (which is identical with what the Catholic church calls *opus operatum*)."[66] But given what we have established in this study, we can certainly say that this is mistaken. Barth's *analogia fidei* challenges the notion of an *opus operatum* at root because he refuses to define the church as a sacrament in that sense. The challenge comes from the very fact that Barth's view of analogy is patterned on the fact that *Christ alone* is the unique union of divine and human being. We have our union with God only in him; he is the only mediator and does not need any sacramentally endowed vicars. Rahner mistakenly thinks that there is agreement here. And he thus thinks that the number of sacraments can, in accord with Thesis II, be acknowledged and observed in principle, although they need not be practiced as the Roman Catholic church does.

Rahner solves the problem of the number of sacraments by arguing that baptism can no longer be thought of as being simply "instituted" by Jesus as it was during the Reformation.

> Instead, baptism may be thought of as coming from Jesus (in the manner of: 'established') which is really how one should think of it everywhere today (namely as stemming from the power of the gospel's Word and from the *essence* of the Church . . .) any insistence on any literal, tangible words of institution from Jesus with respect to sacraments would really be obsolete.[67]

In other words if we view the church as a sacrament then it is easy to say that there are sacraments other than baptism and the Lord's Supper. Certainly. But that is exactly the point which Barth's entire theology contests. The power of the Gospel's word does not stem from the church as a sacrament. This very idea transfers the power of God directly the church and *thus* undercuts the need for Jesus' active historical mediation.[68] For Barth, this epitomized the primary misunderstanding of revelation as partially grounded in the church. Many issues such as *sola scriptura* and *sola gratia* are related to this problem.[69]

Given the fact that Rahner's view has not taken account of this difficulty, perhaps theologians on both sides might frankly admit that living by grace means that we do not *need* to create a *formal* ideal unity as Rahner proposes.[70] We are really one in that we all acknowledge Jesus as the Lord and Savior by acknowledging the Trinity. Rahner already believes this, but because he also believes that *grace* is part of the structure of Christian consciousness, he also thinks *we* can bring about a universally acceptable unity. But the cost is to ignore the unity which is real and can be seen only in faith. We are already reconciled in Christ. The next step is to admit that we live in Christ now by the power of the Holy Spirit. Hence a sacramental understanding of the church which ascribes to the church's teaching office the power to be the guarantee of doctrine, or which ascribes to the church the power to effect grace for individuals, amounts to what Barth described as sacramentalism. It amounts to a form of self-justification. We do not need to do it and if we do, Christ has, to that extent, been absorbed into the official church.

This leads to the second problem, i.e., the doctrine of justification by faith. H. Fries calls attention to Luther's statement that he would accept the pope and his office if the pope accepted "'his' gospel regarding the justification of human beings . . ." What if this doctrine has "lost the quality of being church-dividing?" Fries believes that most Protestant and Catholic theologians believe it has and that "the time of interconfessional polemics is gone. So is the time of controversies focused solely on substantive differences."[71]

Based on this study we have seen that Barth's view of analogy is shaped by his view of justification by faith.[72] Barth's rejection of sacramentalism, moralism, christomonism, and anthropomonism all follow from the fact that people in the church can only live by faith, grace, and revelation. Those outside the church are *called* to live the same way. Based on his view of justification therefore, one cannot begin to explain church unity except by actually beginning with Christ himself and not an ideal form of unity. But this means that the meaning of the sacraments must be traced to a specific command of Christ, but not of course in any legalistic sense. This may seem to be a small point. But it is not. The historical Jesus who was the Son of God cannot be replaced or crowded out by the sacramental reality of the church. Here Rahner and Barth stand far apart.

In view of Barth's doctrine of justification, he rejected the idea that we can move from a general knowledge of God to the particular knowledge of revelation. He rejected innate knowledge of God, an obediential potency, and any idea of a supernatural existential because no analogy is true in itself. He rejected the ideas that Christ's humanity as such reveals and that the church has the sacramental power to effect grace. In each of these ways the doctrine of justification divides Rahner and Barth and thus Reformation and Roman Catholic theology. We have demonstrated these differences in some detail above. So it is still a church dividing issue. While I agree with Fries that the time of interconfessional polemics and controversy based solely on substantive differences should be behind us, I do not see how unity could proceed without addressing those differences.

What do we do about it? Our purpose is not to reinforce divisions and begin old antagonisms. That would be pointless. Our purpose is to say that if the majority of Catholic and Protestant theologians think the doctrine no longer divides them, then they ought to at least ask whether they have come to too easy an agreement. Have they not perhaps reached a formal unity while ignoring the scandal of the gospel? Have they ignored the substance from which unity can and will proceed by substituting another form of unity? In many respects this problem is illustrated by the fact that many Protestants follow Rahner's axiom of identity (with its vice versa) and even move beyond this today. Yet this axiom, as Rahner formulated it and applied it (even though it can have the non-controversial meaning that God is the same *ad intra* and *ad extra*) actually led him to incorporate the necessities of creation into the Godhead in ways illustrated above. We are confronted here by the problem of the *analogia entis* as Barth rejected it; for Barth the unity of the distinct communities can be infallibly guaranteed

> by the fact that each community is individually founded by the one Lord of all the communities, and that, founded in Him in obedience to His Spirit, it is continually ruled by Him. All human mediation of this unity . . . can only be a free human service. It cannot supply, let alone create, the guarantee of unity, the mutual recognition of the individual communities.[73]

This does not mean that there might not be "a particular organ of mediation" which maintains this unity. But this is not "an integral constituent of the essence of the Church."[74] The difference between Rahner and Barth seems clear. Rahner would argue that the teaching office is the *guarantor* of the Church's doctrine and unity. Barth would argue that even if there were episcopal organs to guarantee the unity of the early community (which he doubts) "no one ascribed to them either infallible authority or unconditional efficacy."[75] Rather, Jesus Christ and his Spirit create and guarantee the unity of the church. Here Thesis II simply cannot work.

Docetic Concerns

Colin Gunton brilliantly explains how Barth maintains divine and human freedom by grounding his understanding of humanity in the triune God.[76] Human freedom is based on Election which is neither shapeless nor arbitrary; God elects himself and us in Christ. Therefore creatures can only be free by obeying God's command which sets them free. Unfree in ourselves, we must find our freedom in reconciliation.[77] Still Colin Gunton is not uncritical of Barth. He believes that certain ways of thinking about God are alienating and that the historical root of the problem is found in "Augustine's one-sided emphasis on the unity of God."[78] This "tendency to modalism" gives God's threeness no primary status.

Gunton thinks Barth shifted theology to a more "relational conception of the Trinity" but repeats "Augustine's weakness" by emphasizing God's unity. Thus,

> It is as one that God is personal, rather than being one only in what the three persons give to one another. As Pannenberg has written, the weakness of Barth's theology of the Trinity is that God's unity is seen as the *ground* of his threeness, rather than the *result*.[79]

Gunton sees two options here. First, God is personal only in what the three persons give one another. Yet, for Barth, God is not one in such a way that he needs a second and a third.[80] Rather, "the point from the very first and self-evidently is both the oneness of God and also the threeness of God, because our real concern is with revelation, in which the two are one."[81] Second, God's unity should be seen as the result of his threeness rather than its ground. Yet Barth was not grounding God's threeness in a previously existing oneness of God which he brought to scripture as Pannenberg and Gunton assume. He was saying that God's essence which is one, is so precisely insofar as God is Father, Son, and Spirit.[82] Therefore God's threeness and oneness cannot be played off against each other as though one were the ground of the other. It is of the very essence of God to be Father, Son, and Spirit.

If Barth is correct, and I think he is, then Pannenberg's assessment of Barth is wrong. God's unity is neither the ground nor the result of his threeness. Pannenberg's abstract idea of relationality, which accords priority to the threeness, actually stems from the limitations associated with human relations which then define God. That is why Pannenberg sees the Father as dependent on the Son and on history;[83] why he falls into adoptionism; and why he cannot see Christ as being the only Son of God until after the resurrection.

Therefore I cannot agree with Gunton's critique of Barth on this point, even though he is quite right in calling attention to certain problems in Augustine's thought. He says that Barth's lack of attention to details of our creaturely being and freedom stem "from a fundamental flaw in his doctrine of God . . . because he [Barth] is weaker in handling the detail of that humanity, his theology can take on a docetic air."[84] This is an important critique. If Barth's doctrine of God really does take on a docetic air, my attempt to ground a proper view of the sacrament of the Lord's Supper in his trinitarian theology in the end would fail because it too would take on a docetic air. What specific detail does Gunton have in mind? Following Friedrich Wilhelm Graf he believes that Barth's Christology leads to "an abstractness in the concept of God, and a consequent loss of ability adequately to find room for the particular . . . all particularity is rolled up to force it into line with the abstract subjectivity of God."[85]   And this is characteristic of modalist views. What evidence does Gunton give for this?

According to Gunton, Barth's Christology does not give adequate weight to the Spirit and thus to Christ's humanity. By contrast Gunton argues that Jesus is the gift of the Spirit as much as the giver. Indeed "The Spirit . . . is the source of Jesus' authentic humanity . . ."[86]   But I fail to see how this analysis solves anything. Where is the Word in his action here? Certainly Jesus was guided by the Spirit in his human life. But his human life in itself and as such was not the focus of the gospels. He was not a revelation to all who met him. What exactly *is* Barth's problem with Christ's particularity then? According to Gunton, Barth sees reconciliation and election as universal for christological reasons while Edward Irving correctly limited that universality to redemption for pneumatological reasons: "Election has to do . . . with the mysterious activity of the Spirit, communicating the benefits of redemption to particular people at particular times."[87]   Certainly. But what happened to Christ who cannot be detached from the benefits? His speaking his Word here and now is the action of his Spirit in Barth's theology. At this point the Word is left out of Gunton's account. The same problem seems to be present in Irving's Christology.[88]

Gunton's argument depends on the idea that Augustine and Barth do not give adequate weight to the human story of Jesus. Gunton does not object to Augustine's treating Christ dogmatically, but to the fact that his dogmatics did not give due weight to Christ's humanity; and gives several examples. We must restrict ourselves only to Jesus' baptism in the Jordan. According to Gunton, Augustine cannot handle the story because Augustine said:

> It would be utterly absurd for us to believe that he received the Holy Spirit when he was already thirty years old . . . but (we should) believe that he came to that baptism both entirely sinless and not without the Holy Spirit (XV.46).[89]

Against this Gunton says that at his baptism Jesus "entered a new form of relationship with the Spirit, a relationship which then took shape in his enduring and conquest of temptation."[90]   Augustine is accused of treating the Spirit substantially as one who preprogrammed Jesus' life and not personally and relationally as "the means by which his humanity was realised in relationship to the Father."[91] But aside from the fact that there is no mention of Jesus' *being* the

Word incarnate at this point in Gunton's work, I do not find the evidence in Augustine to support this charge. Augustine's statement appears at the end of a discussion which includes several references to the Holy Spirit and the man Jesus. Augustine speaks about the fact that Christ who gave the Holy Spirit after his resurrection had to be God. No mere man could give the Holy Spirit. Thus the apostles did not give the Holy Spirit, but they prayed that the Holy Spirit would come upon those upon whom they laid their hands. Then Augustine says

> That is why the Lord Jesus himself not only gave the Holy Spirit as God but also received the Holy Spirit as man, and for that reason he was called *full of grace* (Jn. 1:14) . . . Nor . . . was Christ only anointed with the Holy Spirit when the dove came down upon him at his baptism . . . he was anointed with this mystical and invisible anointing when the Word of God became flesh, that is when a human nature without any antecedent merits of good works was coupled to the Word of God in the virgin's womb so as to become one person with him. This is why we confess that he was born of the Holy Spirit and the virgin Mary. (*Trinity*, XV.46)

After this analysis follows the quote cited by Gunton. It will be noticed that what is distinctly present in Augustine is noticeably absent from Gunton, i.e., any mention of the Word. At least in this instance Gunton has unintentionally displaced the Word in his treatment of the baptism, and Augustine has not. Moreover Augustine is far from docetic since he says that Jesus humanly received the Spirit in the Jordan. But he has effectively ruled out adoptionism by insisting that Jesus was God (and sinless), even when he was baptized, because what he did, he did *for us*, not for himself and it was done by the Word made flesh in Mary's womb! Certainly we can say that Jesus entered a new form of relationship with the Spirit, as Gunton suggests, as long as his union with the Word is not ignored.

If Barth was a modalist and his Christology did not give due weight to the Spirit and to Christ's humanity, then his view of analogy and of the sacrament is similarly suspect. But if he is not a modalist (I have shown why he is not) then in his Christology the problem is not that he did not give enough weight to the Holy Spirit or to Christ's humanity. But Barth refused to allow an abstract concept of relationality to define God's being as Father, Son, and Spirit. Thus, in this respect, his view of analogy and of the sacrament actually is not docetic but takes seriously our humanity in distinction from and dependence upon Christ. We are united and reconciled in him and look forward to the revelation of that reconciliation in the Spirit as we look forward to his second coming.[92]

Zwinglianism

Alasdair Heron has criticized Barth for being too Zwinglian, i.e., for emphasizing the fact that the sacrament is not more than a sign, and for redefining Christ's presence in terms of our ethical response. Barth noted that Zwingli also departed from the Roman Catholic, Lutheran, and Calvinistic ideas of baptism as a sacrament. Water baptism neither saves nor gives "assurance or confirmation to faith" as Calvin taught. "Only the direct work of God, Christ and the Holy Spirit can do these things. This alone is the basis of faith in the elect."[93] In accepting this notion and in seeking a non-sacramental meaning of the "ceremony" Barth followed Zwingli, but he believed that he was more careful than Zwingli, whose argument rested more on the philosophical idea that an external material thing cannot accomplish an internal spiritual work. Zwingli retained an "ex opere operato" view and never really explained the meaning of the human act as a "genuine human action which responds to the divine act and word." Hence Reformed theology could not accept Zwingli's "sterile baptismal teaching" and moved to "Calvin's cognitive sacramentalism." Still, Barth believed Zwingli was basically right and did not object if his view was labeled "Neo-Zwinglian, even though its development does not in fact owe anything to Zwingli's influence."[94]

Heron properly notes that Augustine's understanding of the sacraments as visible signs of invisible reality is the unquestioned starting point for reflection on the sacraments today. But he believes that such a starting point risks drawing too much of a distinction between sign and reality. It seems that the visible and invisible may "fall apart" or be related in an arbitrary way.[95] What is lost to sight is that visible and invisible are held together in Christ and not "a 'sacramental universe.'" Heron firmly insists that it is only in Christ that any sacramental view of the Eucharist "must be grounded if it is not to be both arbitrary and precarious."[96] This raises two important questions. First, should we link the visible and invisible via the notion of symbol as Rahner or Tillich have understood this term? Second, should we correct Barth's understanding which is too Zwinglian with such a view?

Analyzing the connection between the Last Supper and the Passover, Heron discusses Jesus' blessing of the bread. The relation of the bread to Jesus (This is my body) is "not simply between the bread and Jesus himself: it is between bread received and shared and Jesus given up by God for many."[97] Those who ate together were bound by that sharing. According to Heron, Paul's statement that "Because there is one bread, we, who are many are one body; for we all share in the one bread" (1 Cor. 10.17) meant that "The meal itself established a bond between those who shared in it: it did not merely symbolise the bond, but actually *constituted* it."[98]   Ordinary Jews could not regard Passover bread as ordinary unleavened bread because it "represented the entire meal, bound the group into fellowship and linked the present with the past deliverance."[99] This, Heron suggests, gives some idea about what Jesus intended when he re-named the bread and the cup. He was neither making them signs nor giving them a "purely symbolic meaning." Therefore, he suggests that if we use these words they must have a stronger meaning such as the meaning Tillich attached to symbols: "a symbol 'participates in' the reality which it signifies."[100]   This is the understanding which he believes should be preserved in order to avoid two errors. First, it avoids the idea that there is a magical or miraculous alteration in the bread. Second, it avoids the idea that there is so radical a distinction "between the material bread and its meaning that the connexion between the two is lost or becomes more than a little tenuous."[101]

Here we see the main lines of our discussion. On the one hand the main focus is not on the bread *per se*. This would lead to some idea that the bread is altered in the Eucharist. On the other hand there can be no radical disjunction between bread and its meaning. It is in this context that Heron criticizes Barth.

> Either we may conclude, as Karl Barth does, that there is *no* 'sacrament' apart from or other than Jesus Christ himself, and that the Reformers were mistaken in not rejecting the medieval notion of the 'sacraments' altogether; or we may see in this christological foundation [The uniting of God with us, the coming of God to us, and the raising of us to God which takes place in Christ] the basis for a reinterpretation of the sacraments, and indeed of the church itself as 'sacramental' . . . as does Eduard Schillebeeckx.[102]

Here the problems we have discussed above come into focus: if the church is the original and universal sacrament alongside Jesus, the sacrament, the question arises as to whether the distinction between Christ and Christians is being overlooked. Here, according to Heron, Barth's distinction must be heeded. But "Barth himself seems to go much too far in the opposite direction . . ." While he acknowledges that the church is the earthly form of Christ's presence between his resurrection and second coming "that presence undergoes a subtle redefinition in terms of our response to him, our 'ethical act' of obedient witness."[103]

Based upon what was said above I do not think Barth rejected the term sacrament *only* because he redefined Christ's presence "in terms of our response." Our response is necessary and important (otherwise faith would not be faith).[104] "To justify God is the new way which is visibly entered upon in baptism."[105] But it does not have any *inherent* validity. Its validity must constantly become an event. It was Barth's insistence upon a clear distinction between Christ and Christians which led him to reject the term. He believed that sacramental ideas tended to make Christ's *free* action for us here and now dependent upon and indistinguishable *from* our actions. We have seen that such dependence is intrinsic to Rahner's symbolic theology. Barth's notion of obedience shows that Christ alone is the basis, goal, meaning, and significance of the church's fully human action. Such action is unholy in itself but becomes holy as Christ enables believers to live as witnesses of his reconciliation and coming redemption.[106] Obedience actually preserves grace as grace and the human act as a fully human act, and as an act changed by grace, because it lives from the command and promise of God in Christ.

I agree with Heron that we should not reject the term sacrament. We have already seen that Barth actually demonstrated by his prior use of the term that it can have a perfectly proper meaning. God meets us in the form of our historical reality but can neither be identified with, separated from, nor synthesized with that form. What about our participation in Christ? Based upon what was said above we saw that symbols necessarily express themselves; also that which is expressed is intrinsically and mutually related. Hence they are full of what is symbolized (contain it) and, as such, they render present what they signify.

Here I think Barth's theology provides an important corrective. When we speak of the sacraments as symbols we cannot allow their symbolic nature to be dictated *by* any ontology of symbolic reality which can be discerned apart from faith in Christ. Its meaning must come from Christ the sacrament as Heron quite properly insists. The theologian must be clear that while Christ acts through the church and the sacrament, and while we participate in the grace of revelation, our human actions do not *constitute* our fellowship with God or with each other. Here Heron has perhaps unintentionally incorporated some of the logic of symbolic ontology into his view. For he says that the meal itself *constituted* the bond of those who shared in it. Similarly he says that sacraments are key moments in the life of the church and individuals and "actually serve to *constitute* it [their sacramental character]."[107] Following Barth's conception of God's positive and negative freedom, I think it is necessary to say that the meal itself indicates (and thus shares in) the bond which Christ himself creates among those who share the meal. The meal does not create or constitute this. Such a view would fall into a phenomenological depiction of the Lord's Supper which avoids the constant need for faith to discern the meaning of the meal.

Conversely, Heron makes an important point which is also present in Barth's theology. He believes that we cannot make such a radical distinction between Christ's sacrifice and ours that he stands over against us so that we become those who offer ourselves (alone) in response to him. He believes that Calvin certainly indicated such participation in his theology. But when it came to the notion of sacrifice he was so intent on making a sharp distinction between Christ and us that our offering "becomes simply a response — response *to* him rather than sharing *with* him in his offering, not only *of himself for us,* but *of us with himself.*" Heron insists that it is not merely the contrast between his sacrifice and ours that must emerge; there was a vicarious sacrifice. But that sacrifice *includes us* by incorporating us into his life of praising the Father. His sacrifice of expiation and propitiation was at the same time "the sanctifying and offering of our sinful human nature to God." In both cases Christ stands alone in order to act for us "so that we may be included with him; and it is to that inclusion that the Eucharist witnesses."[108]

As seen in chapter seven Heron insists that baptism and the Eucharist "are only real, effective and valid insofar as they are not simply *our* acts . . . but *his* in the energy of his Spirit."[109] They must become visible forms of Jesus, the Word. Yet if this is so, then we must admit with Barth, that the meaning of the sacrament cannot be found in our actions as such. Hence our actions do not constitute the reality signified but are constituted *by* the reality signified. And given what was said above about the fact that God's revelation makes our knowledge true without us, against us, and yet as our own knowledge and to that extent through us (chapter two) and that God can be in our words in all his glory, it seems clear that Barth affirmed our participation in revelation, but not by our own power. Just because our participation in Christ is limited in this way does not mean that it is unimportant or unreal. It is fully real, and humanly so, because it moves in Christ and thus *from* our reconciliation *toward* our redemption.

When Heron contends that the Christian life is "essentially sacramental at its core" it could be asked whether or not he takes his own insistence on Christ's distinction from us seriously enough. For Heron, the Christian life is not a matter of perfectionism or pietistic escapism; rather it has to do with "the essential orientation and direction of our human life . . . Precisely because it is sacramental, it involves from beginning to end the victory of grace . . ."[110] While he does say the Christian must be "seized by grace" and that our actions are not simply ours but his through the Spirit, it is not exactly clear how Christ's action is supposed to emerge as a free action when our "secondary sacramentality" is seen as the plane onto which Jesus' primary sacramentality is projected. Has not the sphere of secondary objectivity here been given a life of its own, independent of Christ acting here and now? This is certainly the case with Tillich's idea of symbols participating in the realities signified. His very notion depended upon the *analogia entis.*[111] To this extent it conflicts with Barth's conception of revelation as a free personal act of God. Based upon what we have seen in this study it would be more than a little tenuous to adopt this understanding of symbols simply because Christian symbols do not have an intrinsic connection with grace but receive that connection in the miraculous events of faith, grace, and revelation. When they receive it, they certainly do participate in God's life since they are events enclosed in the mystery of the Trinity; but that participation is not traceable to the human events *per se*. The human acts are free responses to the divine act which governs them.

Water Baptism—Baptism in the Spirit: Gnostic Dualism?

Thomas Torrance criticized Barth, claiming that his sharp distinction between Baptism with the Spirit and baptism with water "(already rejected by Irenaeus in the second century as a form of Gnostic dualism)" led him "back into a mode of thought which he himself had sharply rejected in earlier volumes." According to Torrance, Barth's response was to ask him to rewrite the offending portions of *C.D.* 4 to make them consistent with the rest of his theology. Torrance spent a whole day discussing Barth's book on Baptism with Karl and his son Markus. "Karl Barth himself remained silent throughout, but at the end of the day he turned to his son and said simply, '*Nicht so schlecht, Markus*'!"[112] Torrance believes "There is certainly a deep and persistent problem in Barth's thought which cannot be glossed over, one that has its roots in an *Augustinian and Lutheran dualism*;" in part this dualism lay behind his attempt to combat the Augustinian-Thomist synthesis "between the divine and human" which was advocated by Erich Przywara "in the notion that all being is *intrinsically analogical.*"[113] According to Torrance, Barth became more aware of the subtle dangers of Augustinian thought (with its inherent dualism) and its tendency to equate grace with participation in a Neoplatonic sense. It was this latter sense of grace which allowed Przywara to corrupt Thomas Aquinas' concept of analogy and led to Barth's criticisms. According to Torrance then, dualism persisted in Barth's thought for some time, particularly in his grasp of the sacraments.

At this point we face several questions. First, was Barth's distinction between water baptism and Baptism with the Spirit so sharp as to be characterized as Gnostic dualism? Second, was this inconsistent with the rest of the *Church Dogmatics* (where he sharply rejected dualism)? Third, in my attempt to show how Barth would have written about the Lord's Supper, have I made his later work consistent with his earlier work and thus arbitrarily harmonized an irreconcilable conflict of thought?

With respect to the first question I do not see a Gnostic dualism insofar as Barth actually contended and indeed demonstrated that our human work becomes holy as it is an event enclosed in the mystery of the Trinity. It is fully and completely our work. But it participates in God's action *ad extra*, not by its own power, but by the power of grace, faith, and revelation. The Holy Spirit unites what is here united: our human act and Christ's saving act. Barth avoided sacramentalism and moralism by ascribing the basis, goal, meaning, and significance of our action to God who is transcendent *and* immanent in the history of Jesus Christ. Barth certainly saw us included humanly (*simul justus et peccator*) in reconciliation and redemption in Christ alone as true God and true man (cf. chapter six). This seems to me to be a corrective to Gnostic dualism. The answer to this question turns on why Barth rejected both the three views of grace and the three views of sacrament discussed above. And in each case Barth argued that it was in Christ that God's address to us and our response must be seen *together*. When we see where the logic of symbolic participation leads, I think Barth's warning that there is no special symbolic force attached to water in the New Testament is important (above chapter six). The method of natural theology, not that of faith, starts with that insight and moves from this symbolism to an understanding of what the community does in faith. As no idea of God's Lordship will lead to his actual Lordship, so no idea of symbolic participation will lead to our *actual* participation in reconciliation and redemption in Christ through faith. Ultimately the question is how consistent Barth was in distinguishing and uniting the church's actions in a way analogous to the unity and distinction of the immanent and economic Trinity. This was discussed at length above.

With respect to the second possibility, is this position which was presented above, consistent with the rest of the *Church Dogmatics*? I have indicated why I think it is both consistent and inconsistent. Barth is inconsistent by rejecting the term sacrament. But Barth is consistent in the reasons he gives for rejecting the term: they are essentially the reasons which led to his view of analogy which we presented in chapter one. These views affected his Christology, ecclesiology, his view of nature and grace, and his view of the sacrament. He objected to any idea that *we* might have the possibility of reaching God by our own means, either sacramentally or morally. Barth did not intend to obliterate our actual relationship with God, but to emphasize that the relationship was real in Christ and through the Spirit. Here I see Barth stressing the fact that our baptism with water and our human acts of eating and drinking in the Lord's Supper can neither be equated with God's act for us in Christ (parity) nor separated (disparity) from that act. And they cannot be blended together into some sacramental or existential reality combining divinity and humanity (synthesis). Barth's rejection of both the three views of grace discussed above and the three views of sacrament followed logically his view of analogy and did not end in dualism to the extent that he never held that there was no relation between nature and grace in the sacrament. And he was not arbitrary because he insisted on the *need* for baptism and the Lord's Supper. So the really crucial question is whether his doctrine of analogy is correct or not. I have shown why it is correct and how this is connected with his view of the sacrament.

Nevertheless, as noted in chapter eight, there was an ambiguity in Barth's thought connected with his rejection of the term sacrament. Barth was so intent on proving that there is no Roman Catholic, Lutheran, or Calvinist notion of sacrament (applicable to baptism and the Lord's Supper) in the New Testament that, while he actually maintained God's freedom and the full humanity of the Christian actions and elements, he was at times led into a docetic view which he continually countered with the logic of his own theology (the *analogia fidei*). This seems strange since he insisted upon the fully human actions of the church in baptism and the Lord's Supper. But at certain decisive points he did seem to detach the Holy Spirit from Christ and then spoke of the Holy Spirit mediating our knowledge of and participation in Christ. His emphasis on Christ and the Spirit remained impressively forceful. But, as the Holy Spirit is the Spirit of the Word incarnate, Barth could have pointed to baptism and the Lord's Supper as he did in *C.D.* 1, 2 as the *form* of Christ's earthly presence whose ultimate meaning is a miracle enclosed in the mystery of the Trinity. This important notion of miracle is not as noticeable in his later work on the sacrament. In this sense the form cannot be separated from the content and its how cannot be explained because it is a fact grounded in and moving in God. It is, as Barth was fond of saying, hidden with Christ in God. He does say this, even in his explicit treatment of the sacrament later on, but he is not always so clear in including the *form* (church as the body of Christ) in the grace of the Holy Spirit acting *ad extra*. Thus, when Barth rejected understanding water baptism as a sacrament he said: "According to the New Testament, man's cleansing and renewal take place in the history of Jesus Christ which culminates in his death, and they are mediated through the work of the Holy Spirit."[114] Certainly. But the continuing work of the Spirit takes place in the form of Christ's continued presence in history, i.e., the church, scripture, preaching, and the sacraments. This does not mean that Christ cannot work outside or apart from this specific form. But these sacraments are fully human actions which are begun, upheld, and completed by the Holy Spirit. As such, they are the events through which God has objectively chosen to mediate our renewal in the history of Christ. In that sense God is freely bound to this form but not by it. At times Barth made it seem that the Holy Spirit could not come mediately through the sacraments:

Christians are people to whom the irrevocable and irreversible thing that decides their whole existence has happened, namely, that the crucifixion of Jesus Christ has become a present event for them, not as they are taught about it and persuaded of its significance, not by any sacramental act, that is baptism or the celebration of the Lord's Supper, but by the Holy Spirit in the power of his living Word.[115]

But in fact the power of his living Word can also reach us through our being taught and through baptism and the celebration of the Lord's Supper as the events in and through which God includes us in his own knowledge and love. Barth could previously think of the "earthly-historical life of the Church . . . as an annexe to the human nature of Jesus Christ,"[116] and of the Christian religion as "the sacramental area created by the Holy Spirit, in which the God whose Word became flesh continues to speak through the sign of His revelation."[117] This emphasis was shifted later on and led to the ambiguities noted by Torrance and Heron.

As to the third question. Have I rewritten Barth's sacramental theology in terms of his previous theology which was not in fact dualist and docetic? I think not because I did not deduce the three views of grace which Barth rejected at the beginning of his theology of Baptism from his previous writing. And I did not deduce the three views of the sacrament which he rejected. I found his position there, developed it with regard to the Lord's Supper, and then showed how it made sense in connection with the rest of his writing. Similarly, as noted in chapter three I found there Barth's refusal to begin his sacramental theology with what one might term a transcendental method, i.e., a method which depicts the possibility of the Christian life in terms of a direct and general relation with the deity. I also found Barth's definition of the change in humanity through Jesus' unique history as the Son who reconciled us, and his definition of a Christian as one who sees that his own history took place in Christ's history. Examples could be multiplied. What the reader will find is that I have strongly grounded this discussion in the doctrine of God and Christology. I have made this more explicit and more detailed than it is in Barth's theology of baptism *per se* but I believe I have shown how his view of analogy was at work throughout, determining his conception of the divine-human relations.

Notes

1. For an important historical and theological analysis of transubstantiation see Alasdair I. C. Heron, *Table and Tradition*, chapters five and six. Also important is Karl Rahner, T.I., vol. 4, "The Presence of Christ in the Sacrament of the Lord's Supper," and "On the Duration of the Presence of Christ After Communion," pp. 287–320. It is beyond the scope of this work to present and to assess the Medieval developments which led to the doctrine. Much can be learned from such a study. Our purpose here is to show what Barth would have

said about this doctrine, how his views were grounded in his theology of God, and how this relates to contemporary theology as it has been shaped by Rahner's axiom concerning the identity of the immanent and economic Trinity.

2. C.D. 4, 2, p. 708.

3. C.D. 2, 1, pp. 264–67.

4. Ibid., pp. 265–69; C.D. 1, 1, p. 134. Also C.D. 1, 2, p. 523.

5. C.D. 1, 2, p. 523.

6. Interestingly Barth presents his own view of the Word of God revealed, written, and proclaimed by contrasting it with the Roman Catholic view of transubstantiation and the Protestant Modernist view. Cf. C.D. 1, 1, pp. 88ff.

7. See C.D. 1, 2, p. 526.

8. Barth, *Protestant Theology*, p. 562.

9. See also C.D. 2, 1, pp. 16ff. and 29ff.

10. Ibid., pp. 179–203.

11. See, e.g., C.D. 1, 1, pp. 402–406 on this point. As discussed above this is a persistent problem in Rahner's theology just because he begins his reflections with our self-transcending experiences before allowing the Christian faith its say. It is this very thinking which is dualistic because its human idea of God's presence separates us from God's actual presence in history.

12. Cf. C.D. 4, 1, pp. 652ff., 674ff. and C.D. 4, 2, pp. 616ff.

13. See C.D. 4, 1, pp. 712ff. See also C. D. 1, 1, pp. 104, 134 et al. Because it is the presence of God's Spirit it includes an earthly form and actually does not occur without it.

14. See C.D. 1, 1, pp. 451–54. In connection with baptism, Barth wrote: "They [Christians] obey the command which is written on their own hearts by the Holy Spirit of the history of Jesus Christ . . . The man who does it [baptism with water] as it should be done avoids both all legalism and all licence . . . He obeys the Holy Spirit of the history of Jesus Christ and no one else," C.D. 4, 4, p. 154. Barth thus argued that "Baptism arises in the obedience of faith" but that materially and temporally "the obedience of faith as such is . . . prior to baptism," p. 156. God is present as the enabling condition of water baptism but "Baptism does not bring about this crisis [of God's no and yes to us]. God Himself does that. Baptism, however, acknowledges and proclaims it. Though it does not establish, it bears witness to the boundary line which God has drawn between a passing age and a coming age . . . Controlled by God's own renunciation and pledge, it receives and has in all its humanity the character of a valid and effective renunciation and pledge," Ibid., p. 159.

15. Ibid., p. 454. See also pp. 465-70.

16. See Heinrich Fries and Karl Rahner, *Unity of the Churches*, Thesis I, pp. 13-23. See also T. F. Torrance, "Ecumenism and Rome," *SJT* 37 (1984): 59-64.

17. C.D. 3, 2, pp. 207f. Emphasis mine.

18. C.D. 1, 1, p. 94.

19. Ibid., p. 95.

20. Ibid. For a full treatment of this see pp. 95ff.

21. Commenting on Paul VI's 1965 encyclical *Mysterium Fidei*, Heron writes: "The position of Trent is restated . . . The Roman Catholic Church is right to speak of 'transubstantiation', for it points as other terms do not to the objective change in virtue of which a new 'ontological reality' is present 'beneath the appearances' of bread and wine," *Table and Tradition*, p. 166. Heron is not without his criticism of the doctrine, but he concludes that since Vatican II, the Roman Catholic church has moved away from excess veneration of the elements and away from dividing the priest from the community, p. 167.

22. See C.D. 1, 2, pp. 500f.

23. Ibid., p. 183, emphasis mine. Barth uses a similar argument against Brunner's claim that there is a point of contact for revelation in human nature despite the Fall, cf. C.D. 1, 1, pp. 238f.

24. Rahner, *Foundations*, p. 218.

25. T.I. 10:79.

26. Ibid.

27. See above, chapter two and *C.S.*, pp. 37-8. See also T.I. 2:124-5.

28. *C.S.*, p. 15. Cf. also T.I. 4:240. Rahner believes: "a symbol is not something separate from the symbolized (or different, but really or mentally united with the symbolized by a mere process of addition), which indicates the object but does not *contain it*. On the contrary, the symbol *is* the reality, constituted by the thing symbolized as an inner moment of moment itself, [*sic*] which reveals and proclaims the thing symbolized, and is itself full of the thing symbolized . . ." T.I. 4:251.

29. T.I. 3:168.

30. Karl Rahner describes the elements and the human action as "appearances" in an attempt to show how the bread can be both the body of Christ and bread. Cf. T.I. 4:287-320 and 298-99.

31. See above chapters two and seven and T.I. 14:166ff.

32. Rahner, *Trinity*, p. 33.

33. *C.S.*, p. 15. See also T.I. 12:9.

34. See above chapter six and C.D. 1, 2, pp. 184–89 and 224ff.

35. C.D. 4, 4, p. 210. See also C.D. 3, 2, pp. 213–14.

36. See C.D. 1, 2, pp. 226ff.

37. Ibid., p. 184.

38. C.D. 4, 4, p. 212 and C.D. 4, 3, p. 901.

39. See C.D. 1, 2, p. 647. This is how the church in fact survives. See also C.D. 2, 2, pp. 570–71. Christ's command to follow him exists independently of what is done or not done by the person who hears it. We do not have the innate teleological power to follow him. Hence Christ is always necessary both theoretically and practically. The problem with Rahner's transcendental method is that he ascribes to us this teleological power in the form of an obediential potency and a supernatural existential.

40. C.D. 4, 3, p. 830. It is critical that God's choice is and remains the basis, goal, meaning, and significance of the Lord's Supper. Markus Barth grounds this in election: "Being in communion with God's altar meant communion with God by divine election, by birth into a chosen tribe, also by education and consecration, in short, because of the facts and events that preceded the service at the altar. The share in the sacrificial meat . . . was a sign of the community . . . not a means of attaining it . . . the Israel to whom Paul refers in 1 Corinthians 10:1–13 is God's people, not because they ate and drank bread and water miraculously provided by God in the wilderness, but by God's love, election, and revelation, manifested in the call of the patriarchs and of Moses and by the liberation from Egypt," Barth, *Rediscovering the Lord's Supper*, pp. 36–7.

41. C.D. 1, 1, pp. 94–95.

42. Cf. C.D. 4, 4, p. 212 re: Noah.

43. C.D. 1, 2, p. 525.

44. See for e.g. C.D. 1, 1, pp. 476–77 and C.D. 1, 2, pp. 125–26.

45. See C.D. 4, 2, pp. 709ff. See esp. C.D. 3, 2, pp. 166–75ff. For Barth, gratitude is the human acceptance of grace as grace which cannot be recognized without grace itself. We respond to God with trust, faith, love, and obedience.

46. This is its sole responsibility—cf. C.D. 3, 2, pp. 176ff.; also 4, 3, p. 729.

47. C.D. 2, 2, pp. 557–8.

48. See C.D. 2, 1, pp. 670ff.

49. C.D. 2, 2, p. 578. Cf. also pp. 579ff.

50. Referring to the doctrine of the Trinity, Thomas F. Torrance, "Toward an Ecumenical Consensus on the Trinity," believes Rahner may have introduced a

"necessary movement of thought (a logical necessity)" into the immanent Trinity but that his basic axiom of identity is acceptable, p. 338. Clearing away this problem, he believes, may lead to a "rapprochement between Roman Catholic theology and Evangelical theology, especially as represented by the teaching of Karl Barth," pp. 337 and 339. As seen above (chapter five) Torrance sees Rahner's axiom as a way of avoiding any separation of the immanent and economic Trinity. If that were the only issue, it might be acceptable. But the question raised in this book has been whether there can be a "rapprochement" between Barth's method and Rahner's without introducing the necessities of creation into the Godhead. That is to say Barth's very method precludes Rahner's starting point for theology (our experiences of self-transcendence) and leads to very different conclusions (that the relationship between the immanent and economic Trinity is an irreversible one in which the economy does not define who God is *in se* but is instead the theater of his glory). Torrance certainly sees this relationship, but Rahner's method actually leads to the reversibility Barth insisted was so problematic. We have also seen above that Pannenberg, Moltmann, and Jüngel actually compromise God's sovereignty to the extent that they adopt the vice versa of Rahner's axiom. My conclusion is that one must therefore be wary of any rapprochement which misses the essential issue.

51. Barth, *Letters*, pp. 279–80. For an interesting discussion of possible pulpit and altar fellowship see Fries and Rahner, Thesis VIII, pp. 123–137.

52. T.I. 4:309.

53. Ibid., p. 306.

54. Ibid., p. 310.

55. T.I. 2:124.

56. Rahner, *CE*, pp. 57ff.

57. T.I. 4:298–99.

58. Fries and Rahner, *Unity of the Churches*, p. 67. Heron's book is clearly marked by this same attitude.

59. Ibid., p. 55.

60. Ibid., pp. 32–33.

61. Ibid., p. 36.

62. Ibid., p. 39.

63. Ibid., p. 41.

64. Ibid., pp. 32ff.

65. C.D. 4, 1, p. 661.

66. Fries and Rahner, *Unity of the Churches*, p. 55.

67. Ibid. Emphasis mine.

68. See, e.g., how Barth grounds baptism in Jesus' baptism in the Jordan and then connects this with the post Easter command to baptize given in Matt. 28:19, C.D. 4, 4, pp. 52ff. et al.

69. Cf. C.D. 1, 2, pp. 552-3 and C.D. 4, 2, p. 706.

70. Fries and Rahner, *Unity of the Churches*, p. 38.

71. Ibid., pp. 66-7.

72. See chapter four above where T. F. Torrance makes this point. See also T. F. Torrance, *Karl Barth*, pp. 174-6.

73. C.D. 4, 1, p. 672.

74. Ibid., p. 673.

75. Ibid., p. 674.

76. Sykes, *Karl Barth*, p. 50.

77. Ibid., pp. 51-54.

78. Ibid., p. 59.

79. Ibid., p. 60.

80. Cf. Molnar, *SJT*, p. 380 and C.D. 1, 1, p. 354.

81. C.D. 1, 1, p. 352.

82. Cf. ibid., pp. 354-61. John Thompson, *Modern Trinitarian Perspectives*, emphasizes this on pp. 118, 130, 133, and 142ff.

83. Cf. Pannenberg, *Systematic Theology I*, pp. 311f. and above Part One.

84. Sykes, *Karl Barth*, p. 60.

85. Ibid., p. 61.

86. Ibid., p. 63.

87. Ibid., p. 64.

88. Cf. Colin Gunton, "Two dogmas Revisited: Edward Irving's Christology," in *SJT* 41 (1988): 359-76. This article makes many important and valuable points. But on this particular point it is noticeable that Edward Irving displaces any activity of the Word by the activity of the Spirit suggesting that Jesus' free choice is grounded "pneumatologically rather than christologically," p. 369. I do not think we have an either-or choice here.

89. Cf. Colin Gunton, *The Promise of Trinitarian Theology*, p. 37.

90. Ibid.

91. Ibid. and *SJT* 41 (1988), p. 370f.

92. Cf. C.D. 4, 4, pp. 50–68. Interestingly Barth gives a very detailed treatment of Jesus' baptism in the Jordan as a human act which inaugurated his messianic mission and showed him in solidarity with and in distinction from John the Baptist. Barth explicitly argued that "He [Jesus] does not . . . need to receive Him [the Spirit]. He came into being as He became the One who receives and bears and brings Him. And He was this and continued to be and still is . . . He has the Spirit at first hand and from the very first. The Word became flesh . . . He . . . lived also from the very first by the Spirit, Himself creating and giving life by the Spirit," C.D. 4, 2, p. 324.

93. C.D. 4, 4, p. 129.

94. Ibid., p. 130.

95. A.I.C. Heron, *Table and Tradition*, p. 73. Heron regards Luther's "literalism" and Zwingli's "subjectivism" as "equally eccentric," p. 119.

96. Ibid., p. 74.

97. Ibid., p. 25.

98. Ibid., emphasis mine.

99. Ibid., p. 26.

100. Ibid.

101. Ibid.

102. Ibid., p. 156.

103. Ibid., p. 157.

104. See the important discussion of how the obedience of faith as such is prior to baptism and how a person would not be a true Christian if he/she did not want to be baptized. There is no freedom from obedience in this sense. But there may be cases where this external action is impracticable. In that case Luther was right in saying that "where the Gospel is, where it is known and acknowledged, there is everything that a Christian needs," C.D. 4, 4, p. 157. His reference was to baptism with the Holy Spirit. But does this render water baptism superfluous? No, because these situations are abnormal and cannot dictate the rule which is: "the obedience of faith and baptism belong together," p. 157. This does not mean "that one can be just as good a Christian without baptism as with it, or that one may be baptised or not at will," p. 157.

105. C.D. 4, 4, p. 141. Baptism and the Lord's Supper therefore are not supernatural actions but fully human acts of reliance on God rather than on doctrine or ideology. But these actions are necessary because without them we visibly demonstrate that we either do not yet or no longer rely on the true God revealed in Christ. The human action is pre-eminent because it is full of promise.

It is "to be actually performed as a human confirmation of human conversion to God," p. 144. In relation to God it is not valid because performed but "one must say that as conversion it is certainly not valid for Him or pleasing to Him if a man arbitrarily fails or even refuses to give it visible expression in the human sphere . . . " p. 141. "In the life of both candidate and community it [baptism] denotes, though it does not create, the distinction between an old way . . . and a new way which has been entered upon . . . which has been drawn once and for all by the work and word of God and which each time, again and again, becomes effective and visible . . . this fact [a person's baptism] which cannot be reversed and which speaks once and for all in a way which cannot be mistaken even though it is so very human . . . baptism was the public and binding fulfilment of their conversion to God. Their conversion to God was the meaning of their baptism," p. 145.

106. Cf. Ibid., pp. 158ff.

107. Heron, *Table and Tradition*, p. 158, emphasis mine.

108. Ibid., p. 169. In chapter eight we saw that an ambiguity did enter Barth's thought with the rejection of the term sacrament. To that extent Heron's criticism seems justified because it is this participation which was threatened. Still, we have seen that the logic of Barth's view of analogy led almost to what he had previously said.

109. Ibid., p. 158.

110. Ibid. Also, cf. above, chapter seven.

111. Cf. Tillich, *Systematic Theology Vol. I*, (Chicago: University of Chicago Press, 1951), pp. 238ff., esp. p. 242, "The *analogia entis* gives us our only justification of speaking at all about God," p. 240. If symbols participate in the reality of God this way how can theologians avoid emanationism and pantheism? In his doctrine of creation Tillich does not, since he believes that "divine life is essentially creative," p. 252. For an excellent critique of Tillich's pantheistic view of creation see Moltmann, *Creation*, pp. 80ff. Tillich explains how and why the category symbol overcomes the problems of thinking about God as first cause and as underlying substance of creation, p. 238. For Barth these problems were overcome by God's act of speaking his Word and reconciling the world to himself and in the disclosure of our coming redemption in the power of the Spirit.

112. T. F. Torrance, *Karl Barth*, pp. 134–35.

113. Ibid., p. 138.

114. C.D. 4, 4, p. 128.

115. C.D. 4, 4, *The Christian Life*, p. 145.

116. C.D. 1, 2, p. 348.

117. Ibid., p. 359.

SELECTED BIBLIOGRAPHY

Augustine. *The Trinity.* Translated by Edmund Hill, O.P. Edited by John Rotelle, O.S.A. Brooklyn: New City Press, 1991.

Balthasar, Hans Urs von. *The Theology of Karl Barth.* Translated by John Drury. Garden City: Doubleday & Company, Inc., 1972.

Barth, Karl. *Ad limina apostolorum, An Appraisal of Vatican II.* Translated by Keith R. Crim. Richmond, VA.: John Knox Press, 1968.

_____. *Anselm: Fides quaerens intellectum. Anselm's Proof of the Existence of God in the Context of His Theological Scheme.* Translated by Ian W. Robertson. Richmond, VA.: John Knox Press, 1960.

_____. *Church Dogmatics.* 4 vols. in 13 pts.

Vol. 1, pt. 1: *The Doctrine of the Word of God.* Edited by G. W. Bromiley and T. F. Torrance. Translated by G. W. Bromiley. Edinburgh: T. & T. Clark, 1975.

Vol. 1, pt. 2: *The Doctrine of the Word of God.* Edited by G. W. Bromiley and T. F. Torrance. Translated by G. T. Thomson and Harold Knight. Edinburgh: T. & T. Clark, 1970.

Vol. 2, pt. 1: *The Doctrine of God.* Edited by G. W. Bromiley and T. F. Torrance. Translated by T. H. L. Parker, W. B. Johnston, H. Knight, J. L. M. Harie. Edinburgh: T. & T. Clark, 1964.

Vol. 2, pt. 2: *The Doctrine of God.* Edited by G. W. Bromiley and T. F. Torrance. Translated by G. W. Bromiley, J. C. Campbell, Iain Wilson, J. Strathearn McNab, Harold Knight, and R. A. Stewart. Edinbugh: T. & T. Clark, 1967.

Vol. 3, pt. 1: *The Doctrine of Creation.* Edited by G. W. Bromiley and T. F. Torrance. Translated by J. W. Edwards, O. Bussey, Harold Knight. Edinburgh: T. & T. Clark, 1970.

Vol. 3, pt. 2: *The Doctrine of Creation.* Edited by G. W. Bromiley and T. F. Torrance. Translated by Harold Knight, G. W. Bromiley, J. K. S. Reid, R. H. Fuller. Edinburgh: T. & T. Clark, 1968.

Vol. 3, pt. 3: *The Doctrine of Creation.* Edited by G. W. Bromiley and T. F. Torrance. Translated by G. W. Bromiley and R. J. Ehrlich. Edinburgh: T. & T. Clark, 1976.

Vol. 3, pt. 4: *The Doctrine of Creation.* Edited by G. W. Bromiley and T. F. Torrance. Translated by A. T. MacKay, T. H. L. Parker, Harold Knight, Henry A. Kennedy, and John Marks. Edinburgh: T. & T. Clark, 1969.

Vol. 4, pt. 1: *The Doctrine of Reconciliation.* Edited by G. W. Bromiley and T. F. Torrance. Translated by G. W. Bromiley. Edinburgh: T. & T. Clark, 1974.

Vol. 4, pt. 2: *The Doctrine of Reconciliation.* Edited by G. W. Bromiley and T. F. Torrance. Translated by G. W. Bromiley. Edinburgh: T. & T. Clark, 1967.

Vol. 4, pt. 3: *The Doctrine of Reconciliation.* First Half. Edited by G. W. Bromiley and T. F. Torrance. Translated by G. W. Bromiley. Edinburgh: T. & T. Clark, 1976.

Vol. 4, pt. 3: *The Doctrine of Reconciliation.* Second Half. Edited by G. W. Bromiley and T. F. Torrance. Translated by G. W. Bromiley. Edinburgh: T. & T. Clark, 1969.

Vol. 4, pt. 4: *The Doctrine of Reconciliation.* Fragment. *Baptism as the Foundation of the Christian Life.* Edited by G. W. Bromiley and T. F. Torrance. Translated by G. W. Bromiley. Edinburgh: T. & T. Clark, 1969.

Vol. 4, pt. 4: *The Christian Life.* Lecture Fragments. Translated by Geoffrey W. Bromiley. Grand Rapids, MI: William B. Eerdmans, 1981.

_____. *Credo.* Translated by Robert McAfee Brown. New York: Charles Scribner's Sons, 1962.

_____. *Deliverance to the Captives.* Translated by Marguerite Wieser. New York: Harper and Row, 1959.

_____. *Ethics.* Edited by Dietrich Braun. Translated by Geoffrey W. Bromiley. New York: Seabury Press, 1981.

_____. *Evangelical Theology: An Introduction.* Translated by Grover Foley. New York: Holt, Rinehart and Winston, 1963.

_____. *The Humanity of God.* Translated by Thomas Wieser and John Newton Thomas. Richmond, VA: John Knox Press, 1968.

_____. *Letters 1961–1968.* Edited by Jürgen Fangemeier and Hinrich Stoevesandt. Translated and Edited by Geoffrey W. Bromiley. Grand

Rapids, MI: William B. Eerdmans, 1981.

_____. *Prayer.* Edited by Don E. Saliers. Translated by Sara F. Terrien. Philadelphia: The Westminster Press, 1985.

_____. *Protestant Theology in the Nineteenth Century: Its Background and History.* Valley Forge: Judson Press, 1973.

_____. *The Teaching of the Church Regarding Baptism.* Translated by Ernest A. Payne. London: SCM Press, 1963.

_____. *Theology and Church (Shorter Writings 1920–1928).* Translated by Louise Pettibone Smith. With an Introduction (1962) by T. F. Torrance. London: SCM Press Ltd., 1962.

Barth, Markus. *Rediscovering the Lord's Supper Communion with Israel, with Christ, and Among the Guests.* Atlanta: John Knox Press, 1988.

Bauckham, Richard J. "Moltmann's Messianic Christology." *Scottish Journal of Theology* 44 (1991): 519–531.

Biggar, Nigel. Editor. *Reckoning With Barth: Essays in Commemoration of the Centenary of Karl Barth's Birth.* London: Mowbray, 1988.

Bromiley, Geoffrey William. *Sacramental Teaching and Practice in the Reformation Churches.* Grand Rapids, MI: Wm. B. Eerdmans, 1957.

Busch, Eberhard. *Karl Barth: His Life from Letters and Autobiographical Facts.* Translated by John Bowden. Philadelphia: Fortress Press, 1976.

Carpenter, James. *Nature and Grace: Toward An Integral Perspective.* New York: Crossroad, 1988.

Carr, Anne. *Transforming Grace.* San Francisco: Harper and Row, 1988.

Chadwick, Henry. *The Early Church.* New York: Penguin, 1967.

Feuerbach, Ludwig. *The Essence of Christianity.* Translated by George Eliot. Introduction by Karl Barth. Foreword by H. Richard Niebuhr. New York: Harper Torchbooks, 1957.

Foley, Grover. "The Catholic Critics of Karl Barth in Outline and Analysis." *Scottish Journal of Theology* 14 (1961): 136–51.

Fortmann, Edmund J. *The Triune God: An Historical Study of the Doctrine of the Trinity*. Philadelphia: The Westminster Press, 1972.

Freud, Sigmund. *The Future of an Illusion*. Translated by W. D. Robson-Scott. Revised and Edited by James Strachey. New York: Doubleday, Anchor Books, 1964.

Fries, Heinrich and Karl Rahner. *The Unity of the Churches An Actual Possibility*. Translated by Ruth C. L. Gritsch and Eric W. Gritsch. New York: Paulist Press, 1985.

Frye, Roland M. "Language for God and Feminist Language: Problems and Principles." *Scottish Journal of Theology* 41 (1988): 441–469.

Grenz, Stanley J. and Roger E. Olson. *20th Century Theology: God & the World in a Transitional Age*. Carlisle: The Paternoster Press, 1992.

Gunton, Colin. *Becoming and Being: The Doctrine of God in Charles Hartshorne and Karl Barth*. London: Oxford University Press, 1978.

————. *The Promise of Trinitarian Theology*. Edinburgh: T. & T. Clark, 1991.

————. "Two Dogmas Revisited: Edward Irving's Christology." *Scottish Journal of Theology* 41 (1988): 359–76.

Harnack, Adolf von. *History of Dogma*. Vol. 1. Translated by Neil Buchanan. New York: Dover, 1961.

Haught, John. *What Is God? How To Think About the Divine*. New York: Paulist Press, 1986.

Heron, Alasdair I. C. *Table and Tradition: Toward an Ecumenical Understanding of the Eucharist*. Philadelphia: The Westminster Press, 1983.

Hunsinger, George. *How To Read Karl Barth: The Shape of His Theology*. New York: Oxford University Press, 1991.

Johnson, Elizabeth A. *She Who Is: The Mystery of God in Feminist Theological Discourse*. New York: Crossroad, 1992.

Jüngel, Eberhard. *God as the Mystery of the World: On the Foundation of the Theology of the Crucified One in the Dispute between Theism and Atheism*. Translated by Darrell L. Guder. Grand Rapids, MI: Eerdmans, 1983.

————. *Theological Essays.* Translated and Edited by J. B. Webster. Edinburgh: T. & T. Clark, 1989.

Jungmann, Josef Andrea. *The Mass: An Historical, Theological, and Pastoral Survey.* Translated by Julian Fernandes. Edited by Mary Evans. Collegeville, MN: Liturgical Press, 1976.

Kaufman, Gordon D. *An Essay on Theological Method.* Atlanta: Scholars Press, 1990.

————. *God The Problem.* Cambridge: Harvard University Press, 1972.

————. *The Theological Imagination: Constructing the Concept of God.* Philadelphia: The Westminster Press, 1981.

————. *Theology for a Nuclear Age.* Phila.: The Westminster Press, 1985.

Kelly, J. N. D. *Early Christian Doctrines.* New York: Harper & Row, 1978.

Kimel, Alvin F., Jr. Editor. *Speaking the Christian God: The Holy Trinity and the Challenge of Feminism.* Grand Rapids, MI: Wm. B. Eerdmans, 1992.

Knasas, J.F.X. "Esse as the Target of Judgment in Rahner and Aquinas." *The Thomist* 51 (1987): 222–245.

Knitter, Paul F. *No Other Name? A Critical Survey of Christian Attitudes Toward the World Religions.* New York: Orbis, 1985.

Knox, John. *The Humanity and Divinity of Christ: A Study of Pattern in Christology.* New York: Cambridge University Press, 1967.

Krasevac, Edward. "Christology from Above and Below" *The Thomist* 51 (1987): 299–306.

Küng, Hans. *On Being a Christian.* Translated by Edward Quinn. New York: Doubleday, 1976.

Kuykendall, George. "Thomas' Proofs as *Fides quaerens intellectum*: Towards a Trinitarian Analogia." *Scottish Journal of Theology* 31 (1978): 113–31.

Lane, Dermot. *The Reality of Jesus.* New York: Paulist Press, 1975.

Leavey, Thomas. *Christ's Presence in Word and Eucharist: Illustrated by Karl Barth's Doctrine of the Word of God and Contemporary Sacramental*

Theologians' Doctrine of Christ's Activity in the Eucharist. Ph.D. Dissertation. Princeton University, 1968.

Leonard, Ellen. "Experience as a Source for Theology." *Proceedings of the Forty-Third Annual Convention of the Catholic Theological Society of America*. Toronto, 43 (1988): 44–61.

Marxsen, Willi. *The Lord's Supper as a Christological Problem*. Translated by Lorenz Nieting. Philadelphia: Fortress Press, 1970.

McCool, Gerald A., Editor. *A Rahner Reader*. New York: Seabury, 1975.

McCormack, Bruce L. "Divine Revelation and Human Imagination: Must We Choose Between the Two?" *Scottish Journal of Theology* 37 (1984): 432–55.

McDonnell, Kilian. *John Calvin, the Church and the Eucharist*. Princeton: Princeton University Press, 1967.

McFague, Sallie. *Models of God: Theology for an Ecological, Nuclear Age*. Philadelphia: Fortress Press, 1987.

————, et al. *Liberating Life: Contemporary Approaches To Ecological Theology*. New York: Orbis, 1990.

McKenna, John H. *Eucharist and Holy Spirit: The Eucharistic Epiclesis in 20th Century Theology*. Great Britain: Mayhew-McCrimmon Ltd., 1975.

Molnar, Paul D. "Can Theology Be Contemporary and True? A Review Discussion of Ratzinger's Principles of Catholic Theology." *The Thomist* 52 (1988): 513–37.

————. "Can We Know God Directly? Rahner's Solution From Experience." *Theological Studies* 46 (1985): 228–61.

————. "The Function of the Immanent Trinity in the Theology of Karl Barth: Implications for Today." *Scottish Journal of Theology* 42 (1989): 367–99.

————. "The Function of the Trinity in Moltmann's Ecological Doctrine of Creation." *Theological Studies* 51 (1990): 673–97.

————. "Is God Essentially Different From His Creatures? Rahner's Explanation From Revelation." *The Thomist* 51 (1987): 575–631.

————. "Moltmann's Post-Modern Messianic Christology: A Review Discussion." *The Thomist* 56 (1992): 669–93.

————. "Reflections on Pannenberg's Systematic Theology." *The Thomist* 58 (1994): 501–12.

————. "Some Dogmatic Consequences of Paul F. Knitter's Unitarian Theocentrism." *The Thomist* 55 (1991): 449–95.

————. "Some Problems With Pannenberg's Solution to Barth's 'Faith Subjectivism'." *Scottish Journal of Theology* 48 (1995): 315–39.

Moltmann, Jürgen. *The Church in the Power of the Spirit: A Contribution to Messianic Ecclesiology.* Translated by Margaret Kohl. New York: Harper & Row, 1975.

————. *God in Creation: A New Theology of Creation and the Spirit of God.* Translated by Margaret Kohl. New York: Harper and Row, 1985.

————. *History and the Triune God: Contributions to Trinitarian Theology.* Translated by John Bowden. New York: Crossroad, 1992.

————. *The Spirit of Life A Universal Affirmation.* Translated by Margaret Kohl. Minneapolis: Fortress Press, 1993.

————. *The Trinity and the Kingdom, The Doctrine of God.* Translated by Margaret Kohl. New York: Harper & Row, 1981.

————. *The Way of Jesus Christ: Christology in Messianic Dimensions.* Translated by Margaret Kohl. San Francisco: HarperCollins, 1989.

Olson, Roger. "Wolfhart Pannenberg's Doctrine of the Trinity." *Scottish Journal of Theology* 43 (1990): 175–206.

O'Donovan, Leo J., Editor. *A World of Grace: An Introduction to the Themes and Foundations of Karl Rahner's Theology.* New York: Crossroad, 1981.

————, and T. Howland Sanks. Editors. *Faithful Witness Foundations of Theology for Today's Church.* New York: Crossroad, 1989.

Pannenberg, Wolfhart. *Faith and Reality.* Translated by John Maxwell. Philadelphia: The Westminster Press, 1977.

————. *An Introduction to Systematic Theology.* Grand Rapids, MI: William

B. Eerdmans, 1991.

_____. *Jesus—God and Man.* Second Edition. Translated by Lewis L. Wilkins and Duane A. Priebe. Philadelphia: The Westminster Press, 1977.

_____. *Systematic Theology, Volume I.* Translated by Geoffrey W. Bromiley. Grand Rapids, MI: William B. Eerdmans, 1991.

_____. *Systematic Theology, Volume II.* Translated by Geoffrey W. Bromiley. Grand Rapids, MI: William B. Eerdmans, 1994.

Peters, Ted. *God as Trinity: Relationality and Temporality in Divine Life.* Louisville: Westminster/John Knox Press, 1993.

Powers, Joseph. *Eucharistic Theology.* New York: Herder and Herder, 1967.

Rahner, Karl. *The Church and the Sacraments.* Quaestiones disputatae, 9. Translated by W. J. O'Hara. New York: Herder and Herder, 1968.

_____. *Foundations of Christian Faith: An Introduction to the Idea of Christianity.* Translated by William V. Dych. New York: Seabury Press, 1978.

_____. *Hearers of the Word.* Translated by Michael Richards. New York: Herder and Herder, 1969.

_____. *Theological Investigations.* 23 vols.

Vol. 1: *God, Christ, Mary and Grace.* Translated by Cornelius Ernst, O.P. Baltimore: Helicon Press, 1961.

Vol. 2: *Man in the Church.* Translated by Karl-H. Kruger. Baltimore: Helicon Press, 1966.

Vol. 3: *Theology of the Spiritual Life.* Translated by Karl-H. and Boniface Kruger. Baltimore: Helicon Press, 1967.

Vol. 4: *More Recent Writings.* Translated by Kevin Smyth. Baltimore: Helicon Press, 1966.

Vol. 5: *Later Writings.* Translated by Karl-H. Kruger. Baltimore: Helicon Press, 1966.

Vol. 6: *Concerning Vatican Council II.* Translated by Karl-H. and Boniface Kruger. Baltimore: Helicon Press, 1969.

Vol. 7: *Further Theology of the Spiritual Life 1.* Translated by David Bourke. New York: Herder and Herder, 1971.

Vol. 8: *Further Theology of the Spiritual Life 2.* Translated by David Bourke. New York: Herder and Herder, 1971.

Vol. 9: *Writings of 1965–1967 1.* Translated by Graham Harrison. New York: Herder and Herder, 1972.

Vol. 10: *Writings of 1965–1967 2.* Translated by David Bourke. New York: Herder and Herder, 1973.

Vol. 11: *Confrontations 1.* Translated by David Bourke. New York: Seabury Press, 1974.

Vol. 12: *Confrontations 2.* Translated by David Bourke. New York: Seabury Press, 1974.

Vol. 13: *Theology, Anthropology, Christology.* Translated by David Bourke. London: Darton, Longman & Todd, 1975.

Vol. 14: *Ecclesiology, Questions of the Church, The Church in the World.* Translated by David Bourke. New York: Seabury Press, 1976.

Vol. 15: *Penance in the Early Church.* Translated by David Bourke. New York: Seabury Press, 1976.

Vol. 16: *Experience of the Spirit: Source of Theology.* Translated by David Morland. New York: Seabury Press, 1976.

Vol. 17: *Jesus, Man, and the Church.* Translated by Margaret Kohl. New York: Crossroad, 1981.

Vol. 18: *God and Revelation.* Translated by Edward Quinn. New York: Crossroad, 1983.

Vol. 19: *Faith and Ministry.* Translated by Edward Quinn. New York: Crossroad, 1983.

Vol. 20: *Concern for the Church.* Translated by Edward Quinn. New York: Crossroad, 1986.

Vol. 21: *Science and Christian Faith.* Translated by Hugh M. Riley. New York: Crossroad, 1988.

Vol. 22: *Humane Society and the Church of Tomorrow.* Translated by Joseph Donceel, S.J. New York: Crossroad, 1991.

Vol. 23. *Final Writings.* Translated by Joseph Donceel, S.J. and Hugh M. Riley. New York: Crossroad, 1992.

_____. *The Trinity.* Translated by Joseph Donceel. New York: Herder and Herder, 1970.

_____, and Angelus Häussling. *The Celebration of the Eucharist.* Translated by W. J. O'Hara. New York: Herder and Herder, 1968.

_____, and Joseph Ratzinger. *Revelation and Tradition.* Quaestiones disputatae, 17. Translated by W. J. O'Hara. New York: Herder and Herder, 1966.

_____, and Karl-Heinz Weger. *Our Christian Faith Answers for the Future.* Translated by Francis McDonagh. New York: Crossroad, 1981.

Ratzinger, Joseph. *Principles of Catholic Theology: Building Stones For A Fundamental Theology.* Translated by Sr. Mary Frances McCarthy, S.N.D. San Francisco: Ignatius Press, 1987.

Robinson, John. *Honest To God.* Philadelphia: The Westminster Press, 1963.

Schillebeeckx, Eduard. *Christ the Sacrament of the Encounter with God.* Translated by Paul Barrett. English text revised by Mark Schoof and Laurence Bright. New York: Sheed and Ward, 1963.

_____. *The Eucharist.* Stagbook edition. Translated by N. D. Smith. London, 1968.

Sykes, S.W., Editor. *Karl Barth: Centenary Essays.* New York: Cambridge University Press, 1989.

Taylor, Michael J., S.J., Editor. *The Sacraments: Readings in Contemporary Sacramental Theology.* New York: Alba House, 1981.

Thompson, John. *The Holy Spirit in the Theology of Karl Barth.* Allison Park: Pickwick Publications, 1991.

_____. *Modern Trinitarian Perspectives.* New York: Oxford University Press, 1994.

Tillich, Paul. *The Shaking of the Foundations.* New York: Scribner's Sons,

1948.

————. *Systematic Theology Volume I.* Chicago: University of Chicago Press, 1951.

Torrance, Thomas F. *The Ground and Grammar of Theology.* Charlottesville: University Press of Virginia, 1980.

————. *Karl Barth, Biblical and Evangelical Theologian.* Edinburgh: T. & T. Clark, 1990.

————. *Reality and Evangelical Theology.* Philadelphia: The Westminster Press, 1982.

————. *Theology in Reconciliation.* London: Geoffrey Chapman, 1975.

————. *Theology in Reconstruction.* London: SCM, 1965.

————. *The Trinitarian Faith.* Edinburgh: T. & T. Clark, 1988.

————. *Trinitarian Perspectives: Toward Doctrinal Agreement.* Edinburgh: T. & T. Clark, 1994.

————. "Ecumenism and Rome." *Scottish Journal of Theology* 37 (1984): 59–64.

————. "Karl Barth and the Latin Heresy." *Scottish Journal of Theology* 39 (1986): 461–482.

————. "Toward An Ecumenical Consensus on the Trinity." *Theologische Zeitschrift* (Basel) 31 (1975): 337–50.

Wainwright, Geoffrey. *Doxology: The Praise of God in Worship, Doctrine and Life, A Systematic Theology.* New York: Oxford University Press, 1984.

White, James. *Sacraments as God's Self Giving: Sacramental Practice and Faith.* Nashville: Abingdon Press, 1983.

Winter, Ernst F. Translator and Editor. *Erasmus – Luther Discourse on Free Will.* New York: Continuum, 1990.

Zahrnt, Heinz. *The Question of God: Protestant Theology in the Twentieth Century.* Translated by R. A. Wilson. New York: Harcourt Brace Jovanovich, Inc. 1966.

Index of Subjects

adoptionism, 33, 51, 56, 61, 104, 133, 162, 169, 173, 174, 296, 298

analogia entis, 35, 109, 114, 136, 170, 250, 295, 302

analogia fidei, 3, 5-7, 12, 25, 36, 58, 74, 114, 115, 129, 136, 142, 146, 159, 160, 163, 196, 200, 202, 213, 215, 231, 232, 257 258, 279, 285, 287, 289, 293, 305

analogia relationis, 105

analogy, 3, 5-7, 13, 23, 24, 27, 54, 59, 74, 93, 105, 106, 109, 114, 118, 129, 135-137, 141, 142, 155, 157, 158, 164, 167, 170, 174, 186, 213, 216, 219, 258, 290, 293, 294, 298, 303-306

anhypostasis, 158, 163, 226

anonymous Christianity, 60, 157

anthropology, 22, 28, 29, 32, 54, 56, 63, 72, 73, 96, 113, 155, 161, 162, 190, 196, 216, 229, 254, 264, 280, 281

anthropomonism, 71, 252, 280, 294

apotheosis, 103, 186, 213, 224, 232, 280, 287

appropriation, 100, 114, 133

Arianism, 223

atonement, 195, 259

Baptism, 4, 13, 29, 89, 92, 94, 129, 135-140, 142, 143, 146, 158, 168, 170-174, 185, 191, 192, 194, 198, 200-202, 224, 225, 227-229, 233, 235, 238, 255, 256, 266, 285, 286, 293, 297-300, 302-306

Baptism with the Holy Spirit, 143

Baptism with Water, 136, 142, 173, 225, 286, 303, 304

Catholic, ix, x, 6, 20, 89, 109, 112, 134, 160, 168, 228, 251, 278, 281, 282, 287, 289, 292-295, 299, 305

Christ, 4-8, 10-12, 21, 22, 24, 25, 27-32, 34-36, 52-62, 64-78, 87-95, 97-118, 129-132, 134-146, 155-177, 185-203, 212-217, 219-235, 237, 238, 249-252, 254-270, 278-288, 290, 291, 293-302, 304-306

Christology, ix, 6, 8, 10, 12, 13, 27-35, 40, 52-55, 58, 61, 63, 64, 67, 69, 71-74, 77, 88, 96, 97, 100-102, 104, 108, 117, 130-133, 141, 156, 158, 160-165, 170, 173, 174, 188, 190, 194, 216, 219, 223, 224, 227, 231, 232, 254, 259, 260, 278, 280, 281, 285, 287, 290, 297, 298, 304, 306

Christology from above, 31, 32

Christology from below, 30, 31, 96, 101, 132

christomonism, 71, 72, 252, 280, 294

church, xi, 3-8, 21, 11-13, 27-31, 34, 55, 57, 58, 61, 62, 70, 72, 75, 77, 89, 92, 93, 97, 99, 101-105, 110, 116-118, 129, 131, 135-144, 146, 156-160, 164-169, 171, 172, 175-177, 185, 191, 192, 194-203, 211-214, 219, 223-229, 231-238, 250-257, 259, 260, 262-266, 269, 279, 280, 284-295, 300, 301, 305, 306

command, 57, 87, 88, 102, 103, 109, 130, 139, 140, 144, 157, 164-167, 170-172, 185, 186, 231, 237, 250, 251, 256, 263, 265, 287, 288, 294, 296, 301

communicatio idiomatum, 160, 174

communio sanctorum, 4, 5, 141
communion, 7-10, 13, 57, 67, 69,
  90, 103, 109, 112, 129, 130,
  136, 137, 139, 140, 155,
  165-167, 170, 175, 186, 199,
  201, 212-214, 217, 219, 224,
  230, 232, 235, 260, 284, 289
community, 3, 4, 24, 29, 57, 58,
  74, 77, 94, 110, 117, 136,
  138, 139, 141-144, 146, 157,
  164-167, 170, 175, 185, 188,
  189, 191-193, 200-202, 212,
  222, 232, 235, 252, 264, 266,
  269, 270, 286, 289, 290, 295,
  304
cosmic Christology, 64, 188
cosmology, 32
creatio ex nihilo, 8, 34, 132, 145
creation, 7, 12, 23, 35, 37, 55-57,
  64, 65, 69, 70, 94-96, 101,
  104, 105, 109, 110, 112, 117,
  132, 133, 136, 145, 156-158,
  160, 171, 174, 188, 191, 196,
  197, 210-215, 220, 221, 224,
  230, 236, 257, 258, 261-263,
  265, 266, 268, 269, 278-280,
  295
creator, 5, 7-10, 12, 34, 35, 64,
  77, 88, 106, 108, 112, 114,
  135, 136, 141, 143, 155, 160,
  175, 186, 191, 194, 203, 213,
  214, 231, 232, 234, 236, 255,
  257, 279, 285, 287, 288
creature, x, 5, 7, 8, 10, 20, 24,
  27, 35, 37-39, 52, 59, 62, 64,
  65, 71-74, 105-109, 112, 113,
  129, 136, 140, 160, 161, 171,
  175, 191, 213, 216, 224-226,
  230-232, 256, 262, 268, 279,
  281, 285, 287
Day of Wrath, 195
disparity, 6-8, 13, 55, 56, 159,
  258, 280, 304
divine perfections, 9, 21, 236,

257, 259
docetic Christology, 53, 55, 58,
  61, 69, 280
doctrine of God, ix, x, 3, 6-8, 10,
  12, 13, 21, 22, 59, 63, 78,
  88, 102, 109, 117, 129, 131,
  137, 141, 156, 158, 163, 171,
  216, 219, 222, 224, 231-233,
  236, 257, 259, 278, 279, 285,
  287, 288, 296, 306
dualism, 9, 10, 23, 134, 211-213,
  219, 226, 227, 231, 237, 258,
  278, 280, 303, 304
Easter, 33, 95, 96, 98, 99, 101,
  104, 139, 194, 202, 253, 254,
  269
ebionite Christology, 53, 54, 73,
  156
ecclesiology, ix, 3, 6, 8, 10-13,
  57, 131, 137, 156, 191, 219,
  223, 224, 227, 231, 233, 260,
  278, 280, 285, 304
economic Trinity, 8, 10, 12, 22,
  33, 55, 65, 100, 101, 119,
  129-135, 139, 141, 156, 173,
  195, 215, 216, 221, 222, 227,
  230-232, 236, 263, 267, 268,
  279, 281, 304
epiclesis, 137, 286
enhypostasis, 158, 226
Enlightenment, 74, 117, 279
epistemology, 171, 217
eschatology, 94, 105, 134, 202,
  266, 267, 269
esse, 10, 11, 105, 175, 192, 195,
  220, 224, 225, 250, 259, 261
Eucharist, ix, x, 27, 29, 30, 68,
  92, 94, 110, 115, 135, 137,
  139, 142, 158, 164-166, 171,
  185, 191-194, 200-203, 219,
  223, 228, 255-257, 259, 263,
  264, 269, 284, 285, 299, 300,
  302
event, 6, 7, 24, 33, 53, 59-61, 65,

70, 71, 73, 75-78, 87, 88, 90,
91, 93, 94, 96-104, 106, 108,
109, 116, 118, 129, 134, 142,
146, 155, 163, 164, 170, 172,
192-194, 197, 210, 213,
215-217, 226, 227, 229, 230,
234, 250, 252, 254, 257, 258,
262, 263, 265, 266, 278, 286,
288, 289, 301, 303, 305
ex opere operantis, ix
ex opere operato, ix, 4, 173-176,
194, 228, 282, 299
expectation, 24, 25, 57, 77, 94,
96, 97, 157, 194, 197, 230,
263, 265, 266, 269, 286
experience, 4, 5, 8, 9, 11-13, 21,
24, 30, 32, 34-36, 51, 54-56,
58, 60, 61, 63, 64, 69-71, 74,
76, 88, 95, 96, 98-104, 107,
108, 112, 114, 116-118, 131,
134, 135, 138, 141, 143, 156,
157, 161, 162, 164, 165, 175,
176, 199, 200, 202, 211, 214,
217-219, 223, 232, 235,
252-256, 259, 267, 270, 280,
291
extra nos pro nobis, 76, 106, 185
faith, ix, x, 3, 5-8, 10-13, 22, 24,
25, 29, 31-39, 53, 54, 57,
59-63, 65, 66, 68, 69, 73, 74,
76, 77, 88, 92-94, 96-101,
106-110, 114, 115, 117, 118,
129, 134-136, 140-142, 146,
155-160, 164, 166-172,
175-177, 185-188, 192-203,
210, 212, 213, 216-220, 224,
226-230, 232, 234, 235, 237,
238, 250-259, 263-267, 269,
270, 279-283, 285-294,
299-301, 303, 304
freedom, ix, x, 3, 9, 13, 20, 24,
28, 35-40, 51, 54-58, 61, 74,
78, 88, 90-94, 98, 100, 106,
108-110, 118, 129, 134, 135,

140, 143, 145, 146, 155,
158-160, 164, 165, 175,
185-188, 190, 193, 194, 199,
201, 211, 212, 214-217,
219-222, 226, 230, 231, 237,
249, 251, 257, 259, 261, 264,
267, 268, 279, 285-287, 289,
292, 295, 296, 301, 305
Gnosticism, 169
grace, ix, x, 3, 5, 7, 8, 10, 12, 20,
21, 23-30, 35, 36, 51, 53-55,
58, 61-66, 69-74, 76, 77,
88-90, 93, 95, 96, 98, 101,
102, 106-115, 118, 132, 133,
135-142, 155-157, 159-161,
165, 166, 170, 172-177,
185-189, 191, 192, 194-198,
200-203, 210, 211, 213, 214,
216, 217, 219-221, 223-225,
228-231, 233-238, 249-252,
254, 259, 260, 262, 265,
267-269, 279, 281-288, 290,
293, 294, 298, 301-306
grace of the world, 62, 70
gratitude, 74, 140, 202
Holy Spirit, x, 1, 3-5, 20, 53, 57,
59, 61, 63, 77, 97, 100, 106,
111-115, 117-119, 129, 131,
135-138, 140, 142-146, 155,
157, 158, 166, 167, 173,
185-187, 193, 194, 201-203,
210, 212, 216, 218, 223-225,
228, 229, 231, 235, 237, 238,
250, 252, 255, 256, 258, 260,
262, 263, 268, 270, 279-281,
286, 287, 292, 294, 297-299,
304-306
hypostatic union, 31, 283
idolatry, 166
immanence, 51, 68, 69, 101, 106,
109, 110, 112, 114, 200, 201,
203, 216, 223, 287
immanent Trinity, 11, 21, 110,
111, 114, 129-135, 146, 210,

221, 222, 230, 236, 261, 263,
   264, 267, 268, 279
Israel, 57, 90, 166, 167, 201, 223,
   262, 265, 278, 286
judgment, 20, 27, 75, 109, 170,
   171, 186, 187,194, 195, 198,
   202, 203, 222, 235, 250, 269,
   286
justification by faith, 66, 92, 294
kenosis, 65
koinonia, 57, 139, 167, 168
legalism, 198-200
lex credendi, 168, 169, 171
lex orandi, 168, 169, 171
liberation, 64, 77, 90, 94, 117,
   144, 167, 189, 199, 200, 202,
   255
local presence, 91, 92, 232, 257,
   270
Lord's Supper, ix, x, 1, 3, 5-8,
   11-13, 20, 53, 58, 71, 72,
   90-94, 101, 105, 106, 109,
   118, 119, 129, 135-139,
   142-144, 146, 153, 155-159,
   164, 166-168, 170-173, 185,
   186, 190-196, 198-203, 210,
   211, 213-217, 219, 222-225,
   227-233, 235, 236, 238, 249,
   250, 252, 254-258, 260,
   262-266, 278-280, 285-291,
   293, 296, 301, 303-306
love, 60, 65, 67-69, 71, 73, 90,
   95, 103, 116, 132, 134, 138,
   141-143, 145, 156, 161, 167,
   172, 189, 198, 201, 211-213,
   220, 221, 225, 228, 259, 261,
   267, 268, 289, 290, 306
luminous, 114
mediated knowledge, 24, 27
mediation, 35, 96, 118, 229, 284,
   293, 295
messiah, 32, 57, 92, 104, 172,
   188, 189, 201
miracle, 3, 71, 95, 137, 193, 215,

227, 282, 305
modalism, 9, 132, 133, 268
monism, 8, 23, 201, 219, 227,
   231, 258, 280
moralism, 3-5, 8, 13, 67, 76, 156,
   255, 292, 294, 304
mutual conditioning, 30, 33, 34,
   54, 57, 92, 93, 132, 136, 140,
   160, 164, 202, 220, 221
mystery, 4-6, 13, 21, 25, 28,
   30-34, 52, 54, 56, 59, 62, 64,
   71-74, 76, 78, 93, 105, 110,
   117, 118, 134, 137, 142,
   156-159, 161, 165, 170, 172,
   174, 191, 197, 201, 203, 215,
   218, 224-227, 229-231, 233,
   236, 237, 252, 257, 258, 263,
   268, 279-287, 303, 305
nature, 3, 6-10, 12, 21, 24-26, 28,
   35, 37, 38, 54, 62, 64, 65,
   69, 74, 75, 88, 89, 91, 92,
   95, 99, 101, 102, 106, 107,
   112-116, 132, 133, 140, 141,
   144, 157, 158, 160-163, 172,
   175, 185-191, 203, 211,
   213-216, 220, 221, 226-228,
   234, 236, 249, 251, 254, 255,
   260, 262, 263, 265, 267-269,
   278-284, 291, 298, 301, 302,
   304, 306
Neo-Protestantism, 20
noetic, 20, 194, 195, 218, 220,
   223, 288
nominalism, 9, 21, 55, 212, 226,
   236
nothingness, 66, 145, 249, 268
nuda essentia, 9, 55
obedience, 65, 66, 73, 77, 101,
   102, 117, 130, 140, 157, 165,
   171-174, 185-187, 190, 191,
   195, 199, 200, 224, 228, 229,
   231, 249, 250, 256, 258, 264,
   265, 280, 286, 295, 301
obediential potency, 20, 89, 112,

114, 118, 159, 227, 294

oikonomia, 10, 130, 131, 135, 170, 213

One Mediator, 25, 58, 100, 103, 106, 136, 173, 174, 176, 196, 198, 200, 218, 223, 230, 264, 288

ontic, 20, 194, 218, 288

ontology, 7, 8, 11, 21, 32, 34, 35, 55, 88, 93, 108, 137, 159, 160, 165, 217, 223, 265, 301

opera trinitatis ad extra sunt indivisa, 100

opus operantis, 5, 89, 90, 159, 175, 290

opus operatum, 5, 89, 90, 136, 159, 175, 290, 293

panentheism, 11, 12, 55, 56, 134, 174, 221

pantheism, 12, 56, 62, 64, 95, 132, 134, 135, 145, 220, 280, 288

parity, 6-8, 11, 13, 35, 54, 56, 102, 138, 141, 159, 220, 258, 280, 304

Parousia, 90, 93, 139, 163, 167, 269

Pelagianism, 20, 222, 223

Pentecost, 177, 193, 194, 198, 200, 201

perichoresis, 100

personalist view, 91

phenomenology, 6, 24, 27, 30, 35, 74, 88, 93, 117, 158, 159, 164, 172, 196, 214, 216, 223, 250, 264, 282, 283

pledge and promise, 103, 105, 106, 108, 135

prayer, 52, 100, 130, 144, 157, 176, 192, 194, 197, 257

pre-existence, 33, 56, 162, 173, 174, 268

promise/command, 165

Protestant Modernism, 20

real presence, ix, 5, 13, 30, 57, 92, 137, 139, 158, 197, 217, 229, 232, 234, 237, 249, 250, 252, 255, 257, 260-266, 269, 270, 279, 280, 286, 287, 289, 291

recollection, 24, 77, 96-98, 157, 158, 194, 197, 230, 263, 265, 266, 269, 286

recollection and expectation, 24, 77, 96, 97, 194, 197, 263, 269, 286

reconciliation, 3, 10, 55, 66, 71, 98, 117, 137, 142, 157, 162, 168, 171, 172, 185, 187, 190, 194, 196, 197, 199, 213, 236, 290, 291, 296, 297, 298, 301, 302, 304

redemption, 10, 12, 65, 98, 104, 131, 145, 176, 194, 196, 197, 202, 213, 236, 255, 266, 268, 269, 297, 301, 304

Reformed, ix, x, 6, 228, 278, 281, 287, 289, 299

resurrection, 33, 53, 56, 60, 87, 90, 91, 93-105, 109, 110, 116-118, 131, 133, 134, 144, 146, 157, 162, 163, 170, 171, 173, 189, 194, 200, 202, 203, 225, 227, 252-254, 260, 263, 266, 268, 269, 278, 296, 298, 300

revelation, ix, x, 5-13, 21-29, 32-36, 40, 54-56, 58-60, 67, 71-77, 88, 90, 96-101, 105-110, 113-115, 117, 118, 130, 132-136, 140, 141, 155-157, 159, 161, 162, 164, 167, 170, 173-175, 186, 189-198, 200-202, 213, 216, 220-222, 224, 226, 227, 229-238, 250-252, 254, 257, 259, 260, 262, 263, 268, 269, 278, 280-283, 285, 286, 288, 293,

294, 296-298, 301-304, 306
ritual, 71, 137, 164, 168, 176, 200, 218
sacralization, 58, 59, 63, 64
sacrament, ix, x, 3-8, 11-13, 20, 23, 27, 28, 30, 31, 35, 40, 59, 62, 88-92, 108, 115, 129, 131, 141, 156, 160, 163-166, 176, 177, 191, 197, 215, 225-228, 230-238, 250, 251, 258-260, 278, 280, 285, 290-293, 296, 298-302, 304-306
sacramentalism, 3-5, 8, 13, 156, 233, 255, 292, 294, 299, 304
sanctification, 25, 26, 61, 137, 163, 171, 223, 234, 251, 268
secularization, 58, 59, 63, 64
sin, 26, 95, 113, 163, 171, 172, 186, 194, 198, 202, 218, 235, 252
Son, 22, 35, 53, 56, 60-63, 66-68, 76, 100, 102, 104, 117, 133, 134, 137, 144, 155, 156, 162, 163, 170-173, 211, 212, 218, 220, 257, 261, 264, 267, 281, 283, 294, 296, 298, 306
soteriology, 72, 73, 223
subordinationism, 132, 133, 135
supernatural existential, 20, 89, 90, 106, 112, 114, 118, 143, 159, 283, 294
symbol, 21, 27, 28, 30, 32, 34, 35, 40, 54, 70, 89, 91, 93, 118, 135, 139, 159, 188, 190, 203, 227, 255, 264, 283, 284, 299, 300
synthesis, 6, 7, 11-13, 56, 159, 162, 219, 220, 231, 232, 238, 258, 280, 303, 304
terminus a quo, 114, 129, 135, 193, 203, 214, 215
terminus ad quem, 114, 129, 135, 193, 203, 214, 215

theology, ix, x, 4-10, 12, 13, 20-25, 27-30, 32, 34, 35, 60, 62, 63, 66, 67, 68, 73-75, 87, 91, 93, 102, 110-115, 117, 118, 130, 132-136, 140, 142-144, 155-164, 168-171, 186, 189, 190, 196, 197, 213, 216, 217, 221, 222, 224, 229, 232, 234, 236, 237, 253, 255, 257, 260, 261, 264, 267, 269, 278, 280, 281, 283-285, 287, 292-294, 296, 297, 299, 301-306
transfinalization, 285
transignification, 285, 287
transcendental method, 40, 51, 112, 135, 306
transcendental revelation, 34, 76, 106-108
transcendental Thomism, 52
transubstantiation, ix, 59, 90, 143, 278, 279, 281, 282, 284, 285, 287, 290, 291
Trinity, 6, 8-13, 21-23, 33, 55, 56, 64, 65, 74, 77, 87, 94, 100, 101, 110, 111, 114, 117, 118, 119, 129-135, 139, 141, 146, 156, 158, 173, 189, 195, 201, 203, 210, 215, 216, 218, 221, 222, 227, 229-233, 236, 237, 257, 258, 263, 264, 267, 268, 279, 281, 283-286, 294, 296, 298, 303-305
unio, 55, 137, 163, 262
unveiling, 59, 60, 66, 215, 227, 257
veiling, 59, 60, 66, 257
visio beatifica, 106
Vorgriff, 114
Waldensians, 289
Word, 3, 5, 7, 10, 12, 22-27, 31-33, 35, 36, 39, 53, 58, 59, 63, 64, 66, 67, 70, 71, 73, 76, 88, 93, 96-100, 102-106,

136, 137, 140, 141, 143, 144,
157, 159-161, 163, 164, 168,
171, 175, 177, 185, 186, 187,
189, 190, 192, 194-197, 213,
215-217, 224, 226, 228, 232-234,
250, 252, 254-256, 261, 262,
280, 281, 288-293, 297, 298, 302,
305, 306
zimzum, 145

Index of Names

Anselm, 59, 115
Aquinas, Thomas, 9, 220, 221, 303
Arius, 10
Athanasius, St., 67, 134
Augustine, St., 296, 297, 298, 299
Balthasar, Hans Urs von, 6, 109, 141, 142
Baptist, John the, 193, 194
Barth, Karl, ix, x, 3-13, 20-29, 32-39, 51-53, 55-57, 59, 60, 64-68, 71-78, 87-89, 92-97, 99-115, 117, 118, 129-137, 140-142, 144-146, 155, 157-161, 163-177, 185-187, 190-198, 201, 202, 210-218, 220-238, 249-251, 255-263, 265, 267-270, 278, 279, 280-285, 287-306
Barth, Markus, 57, 90, 91, 138, 139, 166, 167, 175, 291, 303
Biedermann, A. E., 75
Biel, Gabriel, 9, 55
Brunner, Emil, 282
Bultmann, Rudolf, 68-71, 95, 99
Calvin, John, 9, 75, 228, 258, 290, 299, 301
Denzinger, 287
Eunomius, 9, 55
Feuerbach, Ludwig, 73, 213, 231, 259, 260, 279
Fichte, J. G., 38-40
Foley, Grover, 109
Fries, Heinrich, 292, 294
Gunton, Colin, 6, 295-298
Hegel, G. W., 216, 259
Heppe, H., 228
Heron, Alasdair I. C., 164, 176, 191, 192, 237, 282, 292, 299-302, 306
Hick, John, 60, 67
Irenaeus, 303
Irving, Edward, 297
James, St., 187

Jaspers, Karl, 36, 40
Johnson, Elizabeth, 188
Jung, Carl, 64, 110, 188
Jüngel, Eberhard, 6, 104, 134, 142, 196, 197
Kähler, Martin, 32
Kant, Immanuel, 162
Kaufman, Gordon, 21, 64, 190, 196, 253
Kelly, J. N. D., 32
Knitter, Paul F., 11, 253
Krasevac, Edward, 31, 32
Küng, Hans, 97, 101
Lane, Dermot, 99
Leibniz, G., 8
Lipsius, R. A., 75
Lohfink, G., 189
Lüdemann, H., 75
Luther, Martin, 75, 197, 259, 294
Martelet, G., 59
Mary, 173, 289, 298
McFague, Sallie, 211, 212, 218, 222, 226, 252, 253
McKenna, John H., 30, 91-93
Melanchthon, Philip, 21-23
Moltmann, Jürgen, 6, 12, 21, 36, 55-57, 64, 65, 92-96, 100-105, 108, 111, 112, 114, 115, 117, 131, 132, 139-141, 144, 145, 156, 161-164, 167, 170-171, 173-175, 186, 188, 189, 196, 199, 220-223, 261, 267-269, 281
Moses, 90, 167, 193
Nitzsch, K. I., 9
Occam, William of, 9, 55
Olson, Roger, 133
Otto, Rudolf, 110
Panikkar, Raimundo, 60
Pannenberg, Wolfhart, 6, 32-34, 36, 95-97, 100, 101, 103, 104, 132, 133, 141, 175, 186, 281, 296
Paul, St., 57, 66, 90, 102, 139,

166, 167, 187, 299
Paul of Samosata, 73
Pius XII, 196
Rahner, 20, 27-30, 33-36, 38, 40,
      54, 55, 60-66, 70, 71, 75, 76,
      88-91, 93, 98-101, 103,
      106-108, 112-115, 116, 118,
      131, 132-134, 139, 141, 143,
      156, 157, 159-162, 164, 170,
      175, 196, 222, 226, 227, 236,
      250, 251, 253, 254, 257,
      263-264, 278, 281-284, 287,
      289-295, 299, 301
Ritschl, A. 5, 75, 76
Schillebeeckx, Eduard, 176, 300
Schleiermacher, Friedrich, 5, 9,
      11, 21, 73, 75, 87, 112, 161,
      162, 216, 232
Strauss, D. F., 279
Teilhard de Chardin, Pierre, 64,
      188
Tholuck, F. A., 259
Thompson, John, 132, 134
Tillich, Paul, 11, 40, 63, 64, 299,
      300, 302
Torrance, Thomas F., 9, 10, 110,
      134, 169, 237, 278, 289, 303,
      306
Troeltsch, Ernst, 29, 95
Wainwright, Geoffrey, 58, 60, 61,
      67-74, 108, 112, 116, 139,
      156, 157, 168-170, 226
Wicleff, John, 282
Wiles, Maurice, 67
Zwingli, Ulrich, 290, 299

✠ ISSUES IN SYSTEMATIC THEOLOGY

This series emphasizes issues in contemporary systematic theology but is open to theological issues from the past. Works in this series seek to explore such issues as the relation of reason and revelation, experience and doctrine, the meaning of revelation, method in theology, Trinitarian Theology, the doctrine of God, Christology, sacraments and the Church. Of course other issues such as ecumenical relations or specific doctrinal studies on topics such as predestination or studies evaluating particular influential theologians may be considered.

Authors whose work is critical, constructive, and ecumenical are encouraged to consider this series. One of the aims of this series is to illustrate that Christian systematic theologians from different denominations may seek and find Christian unity through dialogue on those central issues that unite them in their quest for truth.

Paul D. Molnar, the General Editor of the series, is Professor of Systematic Theology at St. John's University. In addition to *Karl Barth and the Theology of the Lord's Supper: A Systematic Investigation* (Lang, 1996), he has published numerous articles in professional journals relating to the theology of Barth, Moltmann, Pannenberg, Rahner, and others dealing with issues in method in theology, Trinitarian Theology, and revelation.

Authors wishing to have works considered for this series should contact the series editor:

Paul D. Molnar, Ph.D.
Division of Humanities
St. John's University
8000 Utopia Parkway
Jamaica, New York 11439